Facts and Fairy Tales about Female Labor, Family and Fertility

Hettie A. Pott-Buter

Facts and Fairy Tales about Female Labor, Family and Fertility

A SEVEN-COUNTRY COMPARISON, 1850-1990

AMSTERDAM UNIVERSITY PRESS

CIP-GEGEVENS KONINKLIJKE BIBLIOTHEEK, DEN HAAG

Pott-Buter, Hettie A.

Facts and fairy tales about female labor, family and fertility: a seven-country comparison, 1850–1990 / Hettie A. Pott-Buter. - Amsterdam: Amsterdam University Press. - Ill., fig., tab.
Also publ. as Thesis Universiteit van Amsterdam, 1993 - With bibliogr., index.
ISBN 90-5356-045-9 bound
ISBN 90-5356-044-0 pbk.
NUGI 661/666
Subject headings: female labor ; history ; 1850–1990 / family ; history ; 1850–1990.

Omslagontwerp: **Harry N. Sierman**, Amsterdam

Omslagillustratie: **Hendrik Jan Wolter** (1873–1952):
The Clothing Factory (*Confectieatelier in de Sint Willibrordusstraat te Amsterdam*), 1913.
Amsterdams Historisch Museum
Herman J.C. Heyenbrock (1871-1948):
Loading the kiln, Regout pottery factory Maastricht (*Het inzetten, Regout fabriek Maastricht*),
Amsterdams Historisch Museum

ISBN 90-5356-045-9 (bound)
ISBN 90-5356-044-0 (pbk.)

To Gerard, for over thirty years of love and encouragement

PREFACE

Many researchers explain their choice of topic by pointing to personal experience or inspiration by others. I can point to both. My grandmother entered the labor market when she was only 10 years, and left it at the age of 71. My mother became a live-in servant at 13 and worked for almost 50 years. Given sustained good health and favorable social and economic circumstances, my own career in the labor market will by contrast span no more than 25 years, and of the 12.5 years to date only 2.5 have been in full-time paid employment. Yet current opinion among both economists and the public at large seems to be that women today are participating more in the labor market than ever before; even though Dutch women still do so less than their counterparts in surrounding European countries. So what is the truth of the matter?

This book represents a quest for knowledge which found its main intellectual inspiration in Victor Fuch's book, *How We Live* (1983). This was once presented to me by Jos de Beus with the challenging suggestion that I should write a similar book about the Netherlands. Under the influence of the work of two other economists, Gary Becker and Jacob Mincer, and of my own doubts about historical participation facts my quest eventually took its own course and in the end has produced something rather different.

Too many others have contributed directly or indirectly to the final version of this book for me to be able to name them all individually. I must, however, make personal mention of Marga Bruyn-Hundt, Jacques Siegers, Hans van den Doel, Monika Triest and Miek de Langen, who all gave early encouragement to write a thesis, of Klazien Laansma for her contribution to chapter 3, and of Wim Groot, who co-authored many articles with me at times when progress on this book was very slow.

My direct intellectual debt is, however, primarily to my supervisor Joop Hartog. Without his support and innumerable comments this thesis would never have been completed. I also want to thank him for his suggestion to invite Siv Gustafsson to come to the Netherlands, and for the vigorous support he lent to her appointment as a professor in our faculty at the University of Amsterdam. Siv Gustafsson (now my second supervisor) has succeeded in easing the relative isolation of the few women engaged in research relating to the economic position of women and has created an environment in which ideas on the subject can be discussed and developed.

In this environment, Siv Gustafsson and my past and present colleagues Marga Bruyn-Hundt, Ben Dankmeyer, José Houweling, Edith Kuiper, Thea van der Linden, Henriëtte Maassen van den Brink, Jolande Sap, Marieke Sloep, Kea Tijdens and Cécile Wetzels have criticized parts of my work with a keenness that has substantially improved the quality of these parts. Previous drafts of the first few chapters benefited from stimulating and helpful comments by Jan Luyten van Zanden, Leo Noordegraaf and Richard Perlman. Bas Bos provided me with Belgian figures for chapter 8, while Anne Reitsma assisted me with the bibliographical search for chapter 9, a chapter greatly inspired by discussions with Hieke Snijders-Borst. I am grateful to Agnes Koerts for her careful criticism of the original outline of the Dutch summary and her suggestions to improve it.

I wish also to express my gratitude to the women's movement as a whole, within which I have learned and shared so much. In 1988 Hedy d'Ancona emphasized the importance of having a place of one's own in which to study and write, and it was the realization of this truth that led to the first real impetus in the writing of this book.

I am grateful for secretarial assistance provided down the years by Joep Don, Philomeen Visser-van Dielen, Milada Gadourek, Tine Sybesma, Loes Lotze, Han de Vrijer, Aziza Elmahdioui and Froukje Arwert-Mebius.

Many librarians in a host of libraries have displayed enormous patience in helping me search for censuses and labor force participation figures. Among them, the librarians at the *Centraal Bureau voor de Statistiek* in Voorburg suffered most from my enquiries. On behalf of Ingrid de Boone (librarian at my Faculty of Economics), Bob Harmeijer (librarian with the *Stichting Economisch Onderzoek*) and Ina Schmidt (at the library of the *Sociale Verzekeringsraad*), I wish to thank all those anonymous librarians at the *Internationaal Informatiecentrum en Archief voor de Vrouwenbeweging* (IIAV), the *Internationaal Instituut voor Sociale Geschiedenis* (IISG), *Universiteits Bibliotheek*, *ILO* and *Europa Instituut* in Amsterdam for their assistance.

Encouragement in the final stages was provided by Peter van Roosmalen of the Amsterdam University Press. Harry Sierman applied his usual skill to designing the cover. It was a delight to accompany him to the *Amsterdams Historisch Museum* to select the paintings. Marianne Jonker of the museum helped us do so and Charlotte van Beurden and Rob Jager ensured swift delivery of the illustrations we needed. I received the same smooth and pleasant cooperation from Elly Smit (*Frans Halsmuseum*), Mw. E. Valeton (*Rijksmuseum*), Gerrie Visser (*PTT Museum*), Mw. M. van Bohemen (*Mauritshuis*), Ed Tielemans (*Limburgs Volkskundig Centrum*) and Emmy Ferbeek (*Gemeentearchief Amsterdam*).

However, the cover and illustrations merely serve to illustrate a readable text and the contents of the book are what really matter. For that reason, I wish - last but obviously not least - to thank Janey Tucker, who not only refashioned my dull and simple English into a readable, lively and elegant language but also pointed out many errors and inconsistencies. It was a pleasure to adopt her suggestions. Remaining deficiencies or errors of typing or language have undoubtedly crept in after she saw the text.

Finally, I wish to express my gratitude to my husband Gerard and our children, Mello, Erik and Christine, on whose ready support I can always rely. My personal experience in this respect has undoubtedly done much to influence my optimistic view of the future of the family and its enduring importance as the major institution shaping individual lives.

Zuiderwoude, July 1993.

CONTENTS

CHAPTER 1

INTRODUCTION

> *"The fact that women were seen to play at least two roles - the biological and the economic - rendered them less valuable as workers, less well paid and hence more depending on family support. Family relationships responded to the asymmetry of the labor market and, at the same time, reproduced the arrangements upon which the asymmetry was based. Women, work and family were thus inseparable categories, defining one another and creating relationships of interdependence." (Tilly and Scott, 1987:3)*

1.1 The low rate of Dutch female labor force participation

Dutch women intrigue scholars in a number of disciplines. Their low rates of labor force participation, far below those of surrounding and economically comparable countries, have particularly puzzled many labor market economists. Conversation between such economists at international meetings invariably comes round to the question 'why': Why are Dutch female activity rates so low? Is the phenomenon rooted in history? Is it a matter of preferences, incentives, constraints, laws or institutions? This book hopes to advance the debate by presenting data related to the issues and by considering the usefulness of some theoretical models. The choice of this approach is deliberate, if unconventional. Compared with fields more traditionally the preoccupation of economists, the area of women's work is one where the facts are not immediately and indisputable to hand. It seemed important to establish these as firmly as possible before seeking to apply the possibly relevant theories.

When this study was started the latest figures available were those for 1985. In that year the average rate of Dutch female labor force participation (as a percentage of the total female population) was only 27%. This was respectively 22, 22, 21 and 16 percentage points lower than rates in the Nordic countries: Sweden, Finland (both 49%), Denmark (48%) and Norway (43%). Furthermore, the Dutch rate was also much lower than those in other nearby countries: Germany (36%), Belgium (33%), the United Kingdom (39%), France (35%), Switzerland (38%) and Austria (33%). In fact, remarkably enough, Dutch female activity rates were comparable only with those in some of the southern European countries - Italy (28%) and Greece (27%) - although again not with those of Spain (21%) and Portugal (37%) (OECD, 1992).

The quest for an answer to this conundrum will take many directions, including the comparison of conditions in different European countries and changes in them over time, and encompassing analyses by type of work, marital status and age. The different national or historical perspectives will sometimes be combined, but obviously this is not always possible: in many cases, data could not be compiled within a reasonable period of time or are simply not available. Nevertheless, international and historical comparisons will be made wherever it is possible to do so.

The countries selected for comparison are: Belgium, Denmark, France, Germany, Sweden and the United Kingdom. The Netherlands is bounded by Belgium to the south (and Belgium in its turn by France, with the total distance between Paris and Amsterdam no more than 600 km) and by Germany to the east. It is a short sea crossing to the United Kingdom in the west or to Denmark in the north-east, and a rather longer one to Sweden in the north. Except for Sweden, all six countries belong to the European Community (EC). Sweden is included because of its high rates of female labor force participation, and because institutional arrangements may be different there from those in the EC countries.

The basic issue of the low rate of female labor force participation in the Netherlands will be divided in this book into seven separate issues.

1 Since when has the rate been low, compared to those in the other six countries?
2 Is it low because the occupational structure differs or because the female share by industrial sector varies from country to country?
3 Is it low because of differences in status?
4 Is it low because of differences in the rate of female labor participation within different age groups?
5 Is it low because there are deviant patterns in demographic trends or household composition?
6 Is it low because of particularly Dutch values attaching to the family, marriage behavior and fertility?
7 Is it low because of (dis)incentives or (un)favorable institutional and legal conditions?

These questions will each in turn be considered in separate chapters and then set against labor market and related theories. The economist's explanation for any given level of participation in the labor market is that it is the outcome of supply and demand. In reality, supply and demand are interrelated, though for analytical purposes the distinction is useful. With the simple theoretical framework in mind, question 2 (chapter 4) can be thought of as focusing more closely on the demand side of the labor market, while questions 4, 5 and 6 (chapters 6-8) refer more to the supply side.

1.2 Outline of the book

Chapter 2 presents a broad outline of participation behavior by both men and women in the selected countries. The historical evolution dates back to about 1850 and ends in 1990. National labor force participation statistics in the seven countries go back no further than the (mid-)nineteenth century, except in Denmark where the first censuses were held as early as 1769 and 1787. The chapter starts by defining of the concepts of housework, market work and labor force participation. It also provides a discussion of the connection and interrelation between these concepts and the corresponding problems created with regard to the available data.

Chapter 3 tackles the question of whether the Dutch situation already differed from that in the other countries prior to this century. The chapter outlines the history of women's work from the Middle Ages up to the time when national statistics became available. Special attention is paid to the development of towns and guilds, the Dutch Golden Age (the seventeenth century) and the Industrialialization.

Chapter 4 focuses on the demand side of the labor market, e.g. the sectoral composition of the labor market in terms of activities. In the area of market work, women have usually performed types of labor entirely abandoned to them by men. This division was regarded as fairly self-evident and generally accepted and respected, despite the male domination it implied. The sexual division of labor was and is very similar in the seven countries compared. But will the sectoral division by industry prove to be different?

The measurement of participation in the labor force is complicated by the existence of unpaid family labor and by the combination of paid and unpaid work in the home and on the farm. The figures for employed women may be expected to be more reliable than those for women assisting husbands, fathers or brothers, especially on an unpaid basis. To what extent can differences in labor force participation rates between the seven countries be attributed to differences in classification by work status? This is the main question to be answered in chapter 5.

Chapter 6 offers an introduction to supply side factors, in particular the breakdown of female labor force participation by age group. The following five age groups are distinguished, corresponding to different stages in the life cycle: *childhood* (younger than 15 years), *adolescence and youth* (ages 15-19 and 20-24), *adulthood* (age 25-49), *middle age* (age 50-64 or 50-70) and *old age* (over 65 or 70 years). Each age group has its own peculiarities and its own set of explanatory variables.

It is obvious that during adulthood women's work and employment are heavily influenced by the demands of child-bearing and by women's primary responsibility for the care of children. Fertility and labor supply interact in an important way, and this is investigated further in two separate chapters.

Chapter 7 examines other supply trends. There are remarkable differences in demographic trends in the seven countries. Is this because of varying trends in family and household size? Chapter 7 also gives the long-term trends in marriage patterns and fertility. A high proportion of women within a given population means that many of them will remain unmarried, whereas a high proportion of married women increases the potential for high birth rates and for more women to act as full-time home-makers. On the other hand, changes are not only important as between proportions by marital status, but also within marital status. The decline in family size and in duration of marriage may produce increased scope and motivation for labor market commitment on the part of women while, conversely, fertility and marriage patterns adjust to fit in with greater labor force commitments.

Chapter 8 delves deeper into the analysis of the behavior of married women in the labor force and into the long-term trends in labor force participation rates of married women in all seven countries.

Chapter 9 investigates the norms, values and constraints operating with respect to women's position in society. It describes legislation and government policies in the seven countries and again stresses the international differences. Is there a link between changes in patterns of female labor force participation and differing legal arrangements?

Chapter 10 gathers together the threads of the previous chapters and sets the assembled information against the standard theoretical models. To what extent can these findings be integrated into neoclassical microeconomic theory? Will they enable us to sift out valid from invalid explanations and to assess the value of the available theoretical models?

This chapter is the core of the monograph, as it integrates the *facts* of the empirical work and sets them against *theoretical models*: how do they explain international differences? Which explanations turn out to be *fairy tales*? This broad confrontation of theory and experience is supplemented by a small number of analyses along formalized econometric lines, intended to indicate how further analyses may proceed. After all, grand designs are made up of the minor stitchery of careful, detailed analyses, and this book aims to contribute to both.

CHAPTER 2

WOMEN, MEN AND WORK

> *"The popular impression seems to be that women today are taking a larger share of the world's work than they have done before... As a matter of fact the share taken by women in the work of the world has not altered in amount, only in character."*
>
> *Ada Heather-Bigg, 1894:53*

Historical international comparison of labor force participation is largely unexplored territory. This chapter contributes to this territory by comparing long-term trends in labor force participation of men and women in seven European countries. The main questions to be answered in this chapter are: what is the definition of labor force participation? Are Dutch female labor force participation rates low, and if so, since when have they been low, compared with the other six countries: Belgium, Denmark, France, Germany, Sweden and the United Kingdom? Do male labor force participation rates show less variation?

The picture presented here seeks to emphasize the differences in developments between the Netherlands and the six countries mentioned, especially since the separation from present-day Belgium in 1830.

To start with, section 2.1 defines the concepts *housework, market work, labor force* and *labor force participation rates*. Section 2.2 discusses the connection and interrelation between these concepts and the problems these create in the available data. Section 2.3 presents the labor force participation figures in the Netherlands. These figures, available since 1849, are compared with those in the other countries mentioned in section 2.4. A seven-country comparison of women's share in the labor force is presented in section 2.5.

2.1 Housework, Market Work, Labor Force and Labor Force Participation Rates

2.1.1 Definitions

For most people nowadays the concept of *work* is associated with pecuniary gain. Work is seen as essential to secure the income necessary to buy the goods and services that support their standard of living (definition according to Elliot, 1991:3).

In this study, however, *work*, or its synonym *labor*, is defined as any productive activity, i.e. all activity aimed at creating a good or service that has value and can therefore be sold or exchanged in the market or public sector, or used in the household sector for consumption.

Most women in nearly all societies have to work hard all their lives. That is as true now as it has always been. Throughout history, the major part of this work has been housework. The union of the two words 'house' and 'work' seems to imply that the term housework signifies activities which are conducted within the home, but this is not always the case. With the exception of food preparation, housework does not consist of a fixed body of activities common to all peoples at all times. Its scope varies from culture to culture and time to time. Common to all housework, however, is that it is and has always been *unpaid non-market* work (Davidson, 1986:1). Therefore, *housework* is unpaid non-market work. *Housework*[1] includes every activity required to maintain a home and meet the needs of the members of the household. As such, it also includes child care. Housework should be distinguished from market work performed at home for pay, such as work by domestic servants, labor in cottage industries, homecrafts and piece work.

Market work, however, is not always paid work. The term is also used to denote income-generating activities undertaken by persons who are *self-employed*, working on their own account or running a business, and by family members assisting the self-employed family head by providing *unpaid family labor*. That means that people performing market work are involved in productive activities which result in goods or services to be sold in the market. It is perhaps obvious that women performing tasks to assist the head, or another member, of the household will sometimes be credited with doing market work, but also sometimes not. If a labor contract exists, the distinction is clear; otherwise it is not (see also subsection 2.2.1).

Most countries distinguish between *wage earners* and *salaried employees*, with the term, *wage earners* signifying chiefly manual workers, whilst *salaried employees* include office and other non-manual workers and workers in positions of responsibility. This distinction will not be made in this study. Here, the term *employment* is used to signify salary or wage earning activities and the term *employees* for persons in *employment*[2]. (So, *employment* and *economically active* are not used as synonyms here). As mentioned above, *work* or *labor*, unless explicitly excepted, is used to denote all paid or unpaid activities or tasks. Figure 2.1 represents the differences in diagrammatic form.

---

1 Homework is also sometimes used, but the definitions given in dictionaries, e.g. Webster's, suggest that homework is either study or market work done in the home.

2 Demarcation difficulties can also arise in labor law (see chapter 9) in defining whether a person is an employee, an independent contractor, a partner, an agent or a member of some other legal category. The legal term *employee* is not necessarily a constant referent in each and every legal context. (Drake, 1981:5,6).

Figure 2.1 *Diagram showing different types of work*

WORK			
non-market	market work		
housework	*work in own or family business*		*work in someone else's business or household*
unpaid	self-employed profits	assisting family members unpaid wages	employed wages

Webster's Dictionary defines *labor* as "1: human activity that provides the goods and services in an economy 2: the services performed by workers for wages as distinguished from those rendered by entrepreneurs for profits" (Webster's, 1973:642). Definition 1 corresponds to *work*, defined as: "1b: the labor, task, or duty that affords one his accustomed means of livelihood" (Webster's, 1973:1350) and definition 2 to *employment* only.

The demarcation between housework and market work is not always clear, particularly for women. Generally, one of the differences between market work and housework is that in housework each woman performs small amounts of a great many kinds of work, whereas in market work she performs an appreciable share of one particular kind of work.

The labor force, also called *the total labor force*, usually (see below for more details) refers to the (total) number of persons performing market work. This is also the meaning of the term in this study. *Total* means men and women together. *The (total) labor force participation rate,* also called *crude activity rate*, is the percentage of the total population performing market work. *The female (or male) labor force participation rate* is defined as the percentage of the female (or male) population performing market work.

2.1.2 Labor Force Statistics

In the available statistical information, there is no clear demarcation between market work and housework, nor within market work between self-employment, unpaid family labor and employment. The demarcations are subject to ideas which vary over time and between countries. It is especially difficult to quantify changes in female labor force participation. What is quantified is published in the national labor force participation statistics. In six of the seven countries considered in this study (Belgium, France, Germany, the Netherlands, Sweden and the United Kingdom) these statistics date back only to the nineteenth century; the exception is

Denmark, where the first census was held in 1769. In earlier centuries, most economic data were derived from the activities of rulers and governments: taxation, expenditure and regulation. This generally meant that attention was focused on production and products and not on the laborers who produced the products. Industrialization, however, brought an increase in individual labor performed for wages and a corresponding interest in labor force statistics.

Because in all countries the definition of labor force participation centres on market work, productive activities associated with consumption and child care within the household are commonly excluded from the definition of 'productive' labor in the standard measurement of the national product, and the labor involved is excluded from the labor participation statistics. However, other (market) work performed at home (for example, in cottage industries or on the farm) is usually included.

What we would like to know is the work effort of women and men, measured in hours, distinguished by type of work: schooling, housework, various types of market work etc., preferably with details of the associated payment or income. This has not been measured, at least not until recent decades. A shift between household and market activities would at this moment influence the statistical figures immediately, although in practice hardly any change need have taken place. An ideal definition of labor force participation would distinguish between the various types of work, so as to identify each person's participation in paid employment outside the home, in the family business, in the household etc. Such a definition would acknowledge household and market activities such as those found in rural households, in cottage industries where paid work is done in the home, in shopkeeping and in lodging houses (see also Mincer, 1985:S4). The total workload would be visible and the amount of time spent on certain activities, now regarded as market activities but not previously seen as such, could be dealt with, or could have been taken into account. This is closely connected with the question of the minimum number of hours a person has to spend on market activities in order to be counted as being in the labor force. One way of dealing with this problem might be to count part-timers in terms of their working hours proportional to the normal full-time working week; the same could also be done with regard to persons working more than full-time. The statistics on labor force participation currently available do not make such distinctions.

In the labor force statistics available, there have been frequent changes in the definition and scope of market work (see also section 2.2). Before World War II, in all seven countries, persons were counted as being in the labor force if they were *gainfully occupied*, defined as those individuals who claimed to have had an occupation during the reference period, often the year prior to the census (and so usually including the short-term unemployed). In the censuses reference was made to the *normal activity* or *main activity*. Often *normal activity* was not further defined, while *main activity* was defined either in terms of source of livelihood or in terms of time spent (ILO, 1991:XIII). This meant that the only people counted were those performing *normal* (or usual) or *main* income-generating activities. The main activity of married women, certainly in the Netherlands, was nearly always 'housework', even if the woman also earned a wage. By contrast, single women or students were nearly always counted as being in the labor force if they were earning a wage (for statistical problems see section 2.2 and for some details and differences between countries the footnotes and comments on tables 2.1 and 2.2 in sections 2.3 and 2.4).

After World War II, most countries followed the ILO resolution of 1954 which recommended the use of a short reference period. This approach was used by a majority of countries in their last censuses. The criterion was also introduced in the sample surveys, in which individuals were counted as being in the labor force if they worked for pay or profit during the survey week. This criterion was often combined with the requirement of working a minimum number of hours a week, or being available to perform market work.

Since the mid-1960s, in most of the seven countries, to be a labor force participant, or in other words to be classified as *economically active*, a person has had to "furnish the supply of labour for the production of goods and services during the time-reference period chosen for the investigation..." (ILO, 1976:32). Nowadays this time reference is no longer than one week, but it used to reflect the "usual activity" over a much longer period. To be classified as *economically active* today, a person may also be either *employed* or *unemployed* (ILO, 1991), instead of only being *gainfully occupied*. For this reason, more recent statistics often use the term *activity rates* instead of its synonym *labor force participation rates*.

2.1.3 Crude and Refined Activity Rates

It may be obvious that activity rates, or labor force participation rates, will be influenced by changes in the age structure of the population, especially in the proportion of the population classified as *economically inactive*: the young and the old. A growth in the proportion of relatively elderly and economically inactive men and women will reduce the participation rates, disguising changes in the behavior of what is nowadays considered the *working age population*.

Therefore, in contrast to the *total labor force participation rate* as defined above - also called the *crude activity rate* - recent statistics increasingly use the *refined activity rate*, defined as the number of females/-males/total persons in the labor force divided by the female/male/total *working age population*, multiplied by one hundred. This *working age population* is generally considered to be the population between the ages of 15 and 65 years. *Refined activity rates* are higher than *crude activity rates*, since they exclude large portions of the economically inactive population, the segments of the population with low labor force participation rates. These refined activity rates are considered to offer better comparisons between countries, since they control for variations in the size of the economically inactive population, such as children and retired people.

In section 2.4, the long-term trends from about 1850-1990 display the *crude activity rates*, i.e. the labor force participation rates as a percentage of the total population, while the recent trends for the period 1960-1990 present the *refined activity rates*.

Before turning to the statistics for nineteenth and twentieth-century changes in female labor force participation in the Netherlands as compared with those in the surrounding countries (Belgium, Denmark, France, Germany, Sweden and the United Kingdom), the next section provides a brief background sketch of the problems connected with women's participation in labor over the preceding one and a half centuries.

2.2 Statistical problems

2.2.1 Inaccuracies in the available data

International comparisons must be regarded as no more than approximate. The trends indicated below must therefore be approached with caution. Appreciable differences existed and still exist between countries as regards general concepts, classification and methods used to obtain data on labor force participation, although since the 1970s comparability has gradually improved.

Besides the issue of comparability, there has been a (rather difficult) problem in gathering the figures presented in this study. Two different sources hardly ever present the same figures. Even when provided by the same agency (for example, national statistical offices, the ILO or the OECD), the figures presented in one publication hardly ever coincide with those in another. Where time series have been published, I have generally preferred these to the data concerning a single year. However, they seldom date back to before World War II or cover all census years. The older figures presented in the tables, certainly the ones before World War II, have all been compared to the original census figures published by the statistical offices of the countries considered. Differences of more than 2 or 3 per cent are mentioned in footnotes. Where (recent) time series have been published sequentially by the same agency (e.g. the Dutch CBS, the ILO or the OECD) and the statistics differed (which they often did from one year to the next), I have always taken the most recent figures, assuming that the corrections made were improvements, although it was often unclear why the data were changed or why they changed for some countries in nearly every publication (e.g. OECD, for Germany), while those for other countries (e.g. Sweden) remained the same. Again major differences are mentioned in footnotes.

Definitions of labor force participation are subject to continual change. Even within a single country, this hinders comparison over time, especially over a long period, and it makes international comparisons almost impossible. Besides this, early comparisons are very difficult between different countries in northern and western Europe, because these statistics are based on population censuses which do not always refer to the same periods of time, are based on different administrative structures, and depend on access to population registers and the obligation to tabulate results for regional subdivisions (OEEC, 1954:71). Some statistics give information on the hours worked, others do not; some include employers, others not; some mention unpaid family workers, others ignore them; and so on.

In 1948, the need for more complete, accurate and comparable statistics was evident when the Manpower Committee of the Organization for European Economic Co-operation (OEEC, now OECD) started its work on planning the manpower for the European Recovery Programme. A committee of statistical experts was appointed and in 1951 this committee made a number of proposals concerning the classification of the population covered by labor force sample surveys and the tabulation of results. Agreement on the outlines was reached in 1952 (OEEC, 1954). This resulted in recommendations to replace the censuses by sample surveys.

For the Netherlands it was concluded that the available statistics did not constitute a basis for international comparison (OEEC, 1954:76) and "to remedy these deficiencies, preparations (were) made to introduce labor force sample surveys" (OEEC, 1954:76). However, sample surveys were not actually introduced in the Netherlands until 1973 (as compared with Sweden, for example, where they were conducted as early as in 1960). Sample surveys usually produce slightly (one to three per cent) higher participation rates.

Outcomes are influenced not only by the method of counting and the definitions employed, but also by the drafting of questions: "The wording of the questionnaire is no less important than the choice of the concepts. Experience has shown that quite ordinary changes in the wording of the items, or even in their order, may result in very considerable variations, even when the definitions remain unaltered." (OEEC, 1954:21.)

In the 1990s, international comparisons are still imperfect because, even where the new 1981 guidelines of the International Labor Organization (ILO) are applied, various interpretations of the same concept still emerge[3]. (In the Netherlands, for example, this produces five different unemployment rates for 1989, ranging from 5.7 to 9.5 per cent, see SoZaWe, 1990:15-21.)

---

3 For relations between the present OECD and ILO concepts see also subsection 2.4.4.

2.2.2 Under-counting of women

Many of the existing inaccuracies in the available data may have resulted in under-counting of women's economic activities. It used to be quite common in domestic service, at least up to the twentieth century, for several different members of one family to work for the same employer. If the father or husband was employed, he tended to be credited with the labor of his wife or daughters as well as his own labor, and only his name was registered in the household accounts (Heather-Bigg, 1894:5). The same happened in other sectors, such as brick-works, where different members of a family worked together. In these cases, market work by women was obviously not officially registered and the individual contribution to the labor income of the family was hard to measure.

Self-employment is generally included in the official definitions and statistics. Women working in cottage industries, or women working together with their husbands or families on farms or in family businesses, are sometimes included, sometimes not, depending on the questions asked in the surveys. For example, in the Dutch censuses of 1889 and 1899 women assisting their husbands on the farm were not counted as being in the labor force unless they had a job different from their husbands'. In 1909 the rules were less strict if it was obvious that the woman had her own tasks. In 1920 and 1930 the rules were relatively strict again. By contrast, in France in 1921 and Germany in 1925 farmers' wives were nearly always counted as being in the labor force (see also chapter 4).

In many cases, however, the work of wives and daughters as agricultural laborers, artisans, petty merchants, small retailers and shop assistants was neither counted nor individually remunerated. "Women workers are underestimated in official statistics, largely because their work tends to be confined to sectors that escape registration, such as in the informal labour sector, agriculture and trade." (ILO, 1989:15).

One common international criticism of the economic activity concept is that the work many women do is of as much value as economic activity in the more conventional sense (ILO, 1989:16). "The current debate on the measurement of unpaid "economic activity" of women is basically centered around three issues: (a) the extent to which unpaid household work should be considered as "economic activity"; (b) how this "economic activity" should be identified and measured in surveys and censuses; and (c) what monetary value should be attached to the measurement of economic activity for statistical and other assessments" (Mehran, 1983, quoted in ILO, 1989:16). This problem has not yet been solved, although more and more standardization is being applied.

Changes in the questions asked in the censuses and surveys can produce dramatic reductions as well as dramatic increases in the classification of women as economically active (ILO, 1989:18). Increases in many countries may be the result of improved techniques of data collection and an increased awareness of women's work as economic activity, particularly in the case of unpaid family workers who used to consider housework to be their principal activity. The quality and quantity of the data are influenced by the attitudes and values of both the interviewers and the respondents (ILO, 1989:17).

Recent research highlights the importance of collecting information about the activities of each member of the household from each member of the household (ILO, 1989:16). Inaccuracies can be caused by the fact that it is often only the head of the household who is questioned.

Besides this, the limitations of the data may also be attributed to the time of year at which data is collected. Most data collection used to occur when seasonal participation was low, since respondents were then more likely to be available and willing to take the time to answer the questions. As a result, labor force participation of women is often under-estimated. ILO estimates based on national censuses for 82 countries highlight the importance of seasonal work for women, particularly in agriculture. A comparison of the ILO estimates with results of FAO surveys conducted during peak seasons resulted in an increase of female activity: for all 82 countries combined, the proportion of women in the agricultural labor force increases from 30 to 42 per cent (Dixon, 1982, in ILO, 1989:18).

Variations in the minimum number of hours of work necessary for classification as economically active are another important factor. Part-time employees who combine domestic activities with paid employment are sometimes counted, sometimes not, depending on the demarcation line in terms of hours worked per week. Prior to the 1981 international change in definition, unpaid family workers had to work one third of the time-reference period, usually a week, in order to be classified as economically active. The classification of unpaid family workers, however, still varies enormously (ILO, 1989:19).

It is certain that there has been under-counting of female labor force participation in the Netherlands (until very recently, see also section 2.3 and chapter 4 especially for agriculture). The question is whether the problem has been more serious in the Netherlands than in the surrounding countries. I have found no evidence that this was the case. There are clear indications of under-counting in all the countries considered. In some countries, efforts have been made to re-estimate female labor force participation (Goldin, 1990 and Silenstam, 1970), but this has not changed the underlying trends or led to any new conclusions.

2.2.3 The presented data

All the data used and presented here embody to a certain extent all the limitations mentioned above. All the data measure only a portion of the work women do. However, major changes in definition leading to different labor force supply data are easily detected. Any previous under-estimation will be revealed by a sudden, unexpected increase after adjustment of the definitions to match international standards, as will be shown in the next section in the case of the Dutch revisions of 1981 and 1987. It is important, therefore, to know whether different concepts of labor force participation were being employed in the Netherlands as compared with other countries and, if so, when these were adjusted.

The data may be under-estimates but they tend to be fairly consistent from one census to the next. This consistency per country can be used to assess past trends. The focus of the analysis is on the direction and magnitude of change since about 1850. We do not have to construct any highly accurate figures if the trends are major ones. For this reason and also because of the inaccuracy of the available data, no decimals are given in the figures presented.

2.3 Long-term trends in the labor force and labor force participation rates in the Netherlands

National female labor force participation rates in the Netherlands became available for the first time in the National Census of Population of 1849 (CBS, Volkstelling, 1849) and were published regularly thereafter until the last National Census of Population in 1971. The Labor Force Survey (A-rbeidskrachtentelling), conducted every two years from 1973 until 1985, is the second source of national labor force participation figures, while more recent rates are available in the Employment Survey (Enquête Beroepsbevolking) now published on an annual basis. All are supplied by the Central Bureau of Statistics.

2.3.1 Long term trends, 1849 - 1990

Although it is valuable as the first national record of women performing market labor, the census of 1849 paid little attention to female employment. The figures, like those of 1859, are generally considered inaccurate, due mainly to illiteracy (CBS, Volkstelling, 1899). Even at the time, the occupational counts were considered a failure because the relevant questions were poorly phrased and the answers could not be checked afterwards (Vereeniging voor de Statistiek, 1888:232, quoted in Verhage, 1989:20).

Figure 2.2 shows the Dutch *female and male labor force*, in absolute figures in thousands, for each year in which the census was held (up until 1971) and estimates based on sample surveys (for years since 1973). The corresponding total/female/male *labor force participation rates* are given in figure 2.3. The numerical data corresponding to the two figures are given in table 2.1.

Figure 2.2 *Female and male labor forces in the Netherlands, 1849-1990*

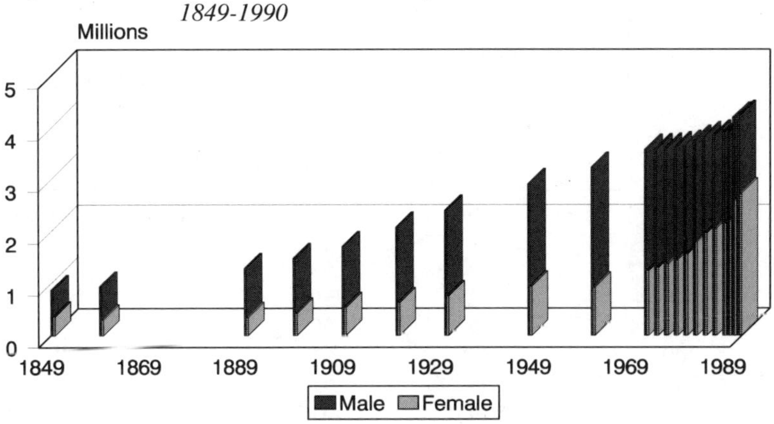

Figure 2.3 *Female, male and total labor force participation rates in the Netherlands, 1849-1990*

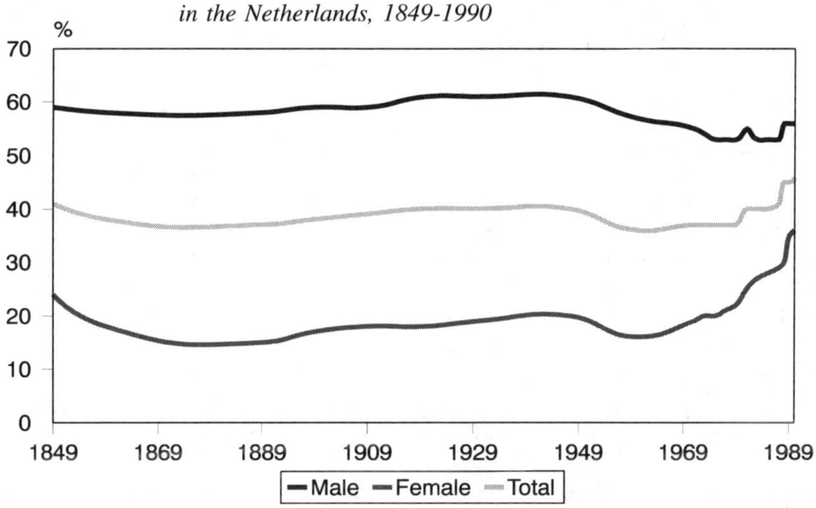

The figures and table 2.1 show that there was hardly any change in the (crude) labor force participation rates for over a century. They also reveal a steady increase in the number of women in the labor force after 1973 and a very rapid increase in both female and male participion between 1979 and 1981 and between 1985 and 1987. These two rapid increases are, however, mainly due to changes in the definition (see subsection 2.3.1). The sharp decline between 1849 and 1859 may have been due to some changes in registration, closely connected with ideas about women's work and opinions about what was considered productive market work. Chapter 4 will analyse the sectors (for example, agricultural, industrial, services) to which the differences can be attributed.

To show the effect of definition changes, two rates are given for 1987 and 1988, one according to the old definition and one according to the new (see subsection 2.3.1). The direction of these changes is usually clear even if the magnitude is not. The refined activity rates will be presented in subsection 2.4.4, together with the international comparisons.

Table 2.1 *Female, male and total labor forces and female, male and total labor force participation rates in the Netherlands, 1849 – 1990*

date	absolute figures in 1000		rates as a percentage of population		
	male	female	male	female	total
1849	881	369	59	24[1]	41
1859	943	308	58	18	38
1889	1298	349	58	15	37
1899	1489	432	59	17	38
1909	1720	539	59	18	39
1920	2090	630	61	18	40
1930	2415	764	61	19	40
1947	2923	944	61	20	40
1960	3241	928	57	16	36
1971	3590	1245	55	19	37
1973	3598	1308	54	20	37
1975	3608	1383	53	20	37
1977	3635	1455	53	21	37
1979	3662	1571	53	22	37
1981	3761	1813	55[2]	25	40
1983	3831	1979	53	27	40
1985	3859	2066	53	28	40
1987	3917/4117	2172/2476	53/56	29/33	41/44
1988	3930/4169	2226/2587	53/56	30/35	45
1989	4211	2622	56	35	45
1990	4249	2743	56	36	46

1 The percentage given by the Central Bureau of Statistics (CBS) itself is 31. However, dividing the female labor force by the female population produces the percentage of 24 given here. The percentages for male and total are correct.

2 The percentages since 1981 are also my own calculations. The CBS published higher figures, but without mentioning that these higher figures are based on the population above 15 years of age, instead of on the total population as in the previous years.

Sources: CBS, 13e Algemene Volkstelling 31-05-1960, Dl 9, 10; CBS, Arbeidskrachtentellingen, 1973-1985;
CBS, Enquête Beroepsbevolking, 1987-1990;
CBS, Vijfentachtig jaren statistiek in tijdreeksen:77;
CBS, Negentig jaren statistiek in tijdreeksen:76,77,78;

2.3.2 Definition changes in the Netherlands

Censuses 1849 - 1971

During the first century of census data collection in the Netherlands, the *gainful worker* concept was dominant in determining whether an individual belonged to the labor force or not. The question asked was: "Is he (she) working in any part of trade or manufacturing, art or science, engaged in any occupation or any craft or handiwork". Where a person was working in more than one occupation, only the most important one was to be considered (see 7th and 8th Volkstelling). So it was the fact of having an occupation and/or working for pay at the moment of the census that decided whether or not a person was in the labor force.

Some censuses are more detailed than others. The occupational counts of 1849 and 1859 and the census counts between 1889 and 1930 give information about the total labor force, but without distinguishing between those truly economically active and those unemployed (Verhage, 1989:21).

In 1869 no questions were asked about occupation, and in 1879 only to verify other questions (Schilstra, 1976:31): the information obtained about occupations served only to check the answer concerning the place of residence (Verhage, 1989:20). In the census of 1899, an assisting wife was registered only if she had her own occupation or specific task, such as making butter and cheese and selling these products on the market. In 1909 for the first time a spouse was counted individually if she answered that her main task was assisting in her husband's business or farm. In the censuses of 1899, 1909, 1920 and 1930, daughters and sons regularly assisting in the parental business or farm were counted as workers (CBS, Volkstelling 1899, 2:VI; CBS, Volkstelling 1930:VIII:64). In 1947 they were counted as a separate category.

During the period from 1899 to 1960, the unemployed are usually included in the figures if belonging to a known sector of economic activity. In all the censuses, only those reporting an occupation as their main activity were counted. Women, especially married women, may have been reluctant to admit that housekeeping was not their main activity and they could easily avoid doing so if they worked part-time, intermittently through the year or doing piece work at home or as family labor. Reluctance to confess having to work for a living may have been extensive in the older surveys, because of the disgrace attached to female labor. Well-to-do and decent women were not supposed to be in the labor market. How afraid women often were to confess that they were trying to earn some extra money becomes clear if we study the history of two organizations which from their inception in the nineteenth century advocated decent jobs for women: "Arbeid Adelt" and "Tesselschade". For example, families tried to hide needlework when visitors came, or explained their daughters' absence by saying that they were "visiting dear relatives, who did not want to do without them" (Brok-ten Broek, 1968:65). Paid female work was lower class work at the turn of the century (CBS, Volkstelling 1899:168).

Women may also have answered that they did not perform paid work if they considered their work as non-professional; this may have been the case with farmers' daughters and wives and with women who regularly did domestic jobs such as laundry for other households (CBS, Volkstelling, 1899:185). Even in 1983, more than 83 thousand of the 408 thousand wives assisting their husbands for less than 20 hours a week in the family business or farm answered that housekeeping was their main occupation (CBS, Walschots, 1984:9).

Until 1947 the censuses took place in December. Seasonal and other temporary work during the rest of the year was not counted. Examples of this under-estimation are not difficult to find (see Leydesdorff, 1977:19). In just one Dutch province in 1903-1904, the Labor Inspectorate counted 1062 women working in the brick-works, but the census of 1899 counted only 656 women for the whole country. Another example: the census of 1909 registered 20 women smoking fish, but the Labor Inspectorate counted as many as 252 in just three small fishing villages. The more recent censuses since 1947 and the sample surveys between 1975 and 1987 were held in spring and early summer, with a larger probability of counting seasonal work.

In 1947 and 1960, all persons older than 14 years were counted (excluding those living on boats and in institutions), and persons employed for more than 15 hours a week. So part-time wage earners and family members working in the business of the husband or father were still not counted if they worked less than 15 hours a week. This probably caused an under-estimation of about 25 000 persons in 1960, as compared with the situation if the definition of 1971 had been applied. In 1971, the labor force concept included all individuals in paid employment, unemployed and looking for work or performing unpaid family labor for over 15 hours a week. However, they first had to state what their main occupation was, a question misunderstood by many wives assisting their husbands. In 1971, about 15 000 part-time wage earners were working less than 15 hours a week (Berends and Boelmans, 1979:13). In 1960 full-time work meant 30 hours a week; in 1971, 25 hours.

Labor Force Sample Surveys 1973 - 1985

The Labor Force Sample Survey (Arbeidskrachtentelling) was held every two years from 1973 until 1985. The main difference from the censuses is, of course, the coverage of the population: only a sample was taken. Up until 1981 this was 3 per cent. In 1981, because the census originally planned was not held, the percentage was for once enlarged to 5. In the first sample surveys, considerable efforts were made to make the results comparable to the census of 1971 (see also Mol et al, 1988:64). In 1971, however, in contrast to the Labor Force Sample Surveys, "temporarily unemployed" were also included. In 1971 this concerned 1.25 per cent of the labor force population (for comparisons between the censuses and Labor Force Surveys see CBS, Arbeidskrachtentelling, 1975:59-63. In 1981, the minimum hours requirement of the 1973-1979 sample surveys was relaxed.

Labor Force Sample Surveys since 1987

Ever since 1987, two per cent Labor Force Sample Surveys (Enquête Beroepsbevolking), have been held yearly. These are no longer held in the spring but spread over the year.

In table 2.1, two rates are given for 1987 and 1988, one according to the old definition and one according to the new. The new 1987 definition includes every person in the labor force performing market work for at least one hour a week (or looking for a job). The old definition under-estimated female labor force participation as a percentage of the total population by 4 to 5 per cent as compared to the 1981-1985 definition, and the female economic activity rate between 15 and 65 years by approximately 6 per cent.

Both definitions may still be inadequate by international standards (CBS, 1991) but the inclusion of very small jobs since 1987 has probably been more complete than elsewhere (CBS, 1991), and has resulted in a large increase in apparent labor force participation due to persons with small jobs. About 470 thousand women participating in the labor market in 1990 - or nearly 20 per cent of the total female labor force - worked less than 12 hours a week (CBS, 1991).

2.4 A seven-country comparison of long-term trends in labor force participation rates

This section distinguishes two long-term trends in labor force participation in Belgium, Denmark, France, Germany, the Netherlands, Sweden and the United Kingdom (or sometimes England or Great Britain only): one extending from the second half of the nineteenth century until 1990 - as a percentage of the total population - and the other one dating from 1960 to 1990 - as a percentage of the population aged between 15 and 65 years.

2.4.1 Female labor force participation rates, 1850 - 1990

The developments in the female labor force participation rate in the seven countries since the middle of the nineteenth century are shown in figure 2.4. The figure corresponds to the numerical data presented in table 2.2.

It is clear that from 1849 until 1990 Dutch female labor force participation rates were lower than those in the other countries, only in 1947, 1987 and 1988 the rates were about equal to those in Belgium. This country was overtaken in 1990, the same year that the Dutch activity level was equal to that in France.

The trends are rather different in the seven countries. The only correspondence between them is that in each case the labor force participation rate reaches a relative low point somewhere between 1940 and 1960, and that all seven countries' activity rates show a persistent increase after 1970. For almost a century, from about 1870 onward, Denmark, Germany, Sweden and the United Kingdom display fairly similar participation trends, quite distinct from those in Belgium and France.

Until 1970, the Netherlands demonstrated a remarkable stability in female activity rates: the difference between the highest and lowest rate was only 5 per cent, whereas the difference in Belgium was 19 per cent and in France 18 per cent. The Dutch rate of labor force participation by women in 1849 was high compared to the rate 10 years later but, as already stated in the previous section, the reliability of these figures is in some doubt. However, this rate is comparable to those in France and Denmark (see also table 2.2).

So the figures may not be so far wrong after all. Moreover, the Belgian and British rates also declined between about 1850 and 1880. This may have had something to do with certain stages of industrialization (this will be analysed in chapter 4). That the early stages of indu-strialization are sometimes marked by a decline in female labor force participation is a fact currently being confirmed in countries like Greece and Turkey, and until relatively recently also in Ireland (OECD, 1980:26). This effect is especially clear in countries with a certain amount of cottage industry.

The Belgian census of 1846 shows the highest female labor force participation rate, at 38 per cent. Belgium shows a fairly dramatic decline between 1846 and 1947 followed by a steady increase since then, although the rate in 1990 is still lower than those of 1846-1866. Denmark's female activity rates increase fairly steadily between 1851 and 1941 from 25 to 34 per cent. In 1950 and 1960 the rates are relatively low at 30 per cent, but the rate increases rapidly over the next decade to 38 per cent and over the next two decades to over 51 per cent. The French trend is remarkable: a rapid increase at the beginning of this cen-tury, reaching a relatively high level of 42 per cent in 1921, then de-cli-ning rapidly over the next 5 years to 38 per cent in 1926 and 37 per cent in 1931, and further still to match the average 30 per cent of the majority of the other countries by about 1950 and to reach a low 28 per cent in 1960. Since 1960 the rate has increased again, but even in 1990 the 36 per cent activity rate had not yet attained the high 42 per cent of 1921.

Germany showed a similar, although much less dramatic, trend to that in France, with an increase until 1925 (it may have been higher between 1907 and 1925 but no censuses were held during that period), a stabilization after that and a relatively low participation level in 1971 at 31 per cent. It was not until 1983 that the same participation rate was again reached as in 1925: 35 per cent.

As illustrated in the previous section, the Dutch female labor force participation rate showed little movement until the 1970s, but then increased very rapidly in the 1980s. Sweden, like Denmark, is a country with a more or less continuous increase, except that 1940 was the year in which Sweden reached its lowest level. Sweden is the only country which has shown an secular increase since as early as 1940. In Great Britain there seems also to have been no trend at all before World War II; until then female participation rates remained fairly stable, but have since increased from 30 per cent in 1940 to 43 per cent in 1990. (For a comparison between France and Great Britain see also Tilly and Scott, 1987).

Table 2.2 and figure 2.4 *Female labor force participation rates: female labor force as a percentage of the total female population, a seven-country comparison, 1850 – 1990*

	[1]Belgium	[2]Denmark	[3]France	[4]Germany	[5]Netherlands	[6]Sweden	[7]U.K.
1850	[1846]38	[1855]25	–	–	[1849]24	–	[1851]30
1860	[1856]36	25	[1856]25	–	[1859]18	29	[1861]28
1870	[1866]36	25	[1866]24	–	–	29	[1871]28
1880	34	24	[1876]30	[1882]24	–	28	[1881]25
1890	29	26	[1896]33	[1895]25	[1889]15	28	[1891]27
1900	29	[1901]30	[1901]35		[1899]17	28	[1901]25
1910	25	[1911]30	[1906]39	[1907]30	[1909]18	28	[1911]26
1920	21	[1921]34	[1921]42	[1925]35	18	30	[1921]26
1930	24	34	[1931]37	[1933]34	19	29	[1931]27
1940	–	34	38	[1939]34	–	25	–
1950	[1947]19	30	30	31	[1947]20	29	[1951]30
1960	[1961]20	30	[1967]28	33	16	33	[1961]32
1971	25	37	30	31	19	39	31
1973	26	39	31	31	20	40	33
1975	27	40	32	32	20	43	34
1977	28	41	33	32	21	44	35
1979	30	44	33	33	22	46	36
1981	31	46	34	34	25	47	36
1983	32	48	35	35	27	48	36
1985	33	48	35	36	28	49	39
1987	33	50	36	37	33	50	40
1988	34	51	36	37	34	50	41
1989	34	51	36	37	34	51	41
1990	34	51	36	38	36	51	41

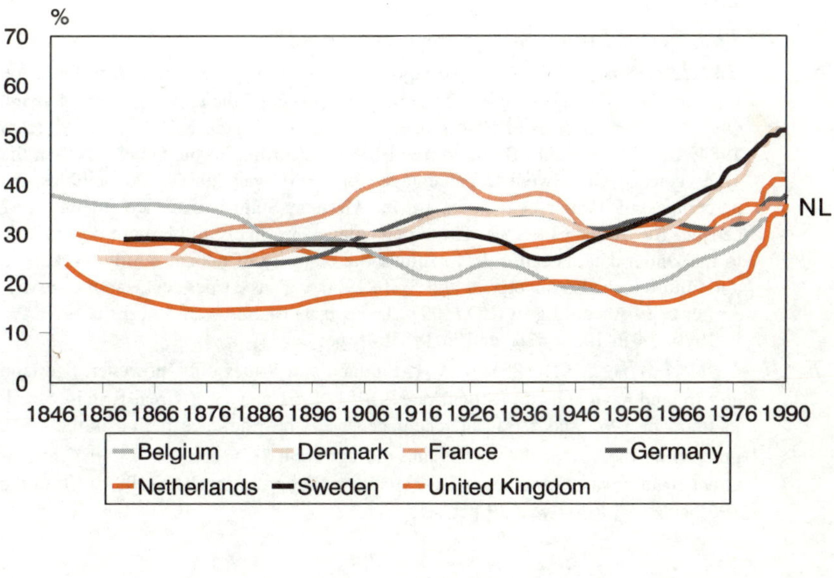

Sources table 2.2:

See bibliography; in addition to the censuses, labor force surveys and specific sources mentioned in the bibliography for each individual country, sources concerning all seven countries are for 1930, also: ILO, 1936; for 1950: OECD, 1979: Demographic Trends 1950-1990; for 1960-1990: OECD, 1971, 1973, ... 1991a, 1991b, 1992b.

1 - 7 ***All seven countries:*** - indicate that no data are available because no census was held in that decade.
According to OECD (1991b and 1992b, the percentages for Belgium since 1970 are lower than in previous publications, because series have been revised. For most countries previous published figures are only one to two per cent higher or lower; for Germany the most recently published figures from 1979 - 1987 were two per cent higher than the earlier published figures.

1 ***Belgium***: Methods and estimates were revised in 1959 and 1970. Age limit in last censuses is 14 years and the reference period one day.

2 ***Denmark***: Labor Force Survey figures since 1971, from 1976 onwards annually. Short (week) and long (year) reference periods. In 1981 both were applied to all persons aged at least 16 years. According to other sources, e.g. the Dutch Central Bureau of Statistics (CBS, 1899), the figure in 1890 was 21 per cent, and according to my own calculations the percentages for 1880 and 1901 were 19 and 27 per cent respectively.

3 ***France***: Sample surveys since 1969 in addition to the censuses of 1968, 1975, 1982 and 1992. Age limit 15 years. Reference period is the day of the census.
According to the census of 1921, the given percentage of 42 applies to 90 départements, when (as in previous censuses) 87 départements are taken, the percentage is 43. The 1926 and 1936 (not in table) rates have been 38 and 34 per cent respectively. According to ILO (1936) the figure in 1931 was 37 and in 1936: 35 per cent. According to OECD (1985) the figure in 1967 was 28 per cent.

4 ***Germany***: Last censuses 1950, 1961, 1970 and 1987. Age limit 15 years, reference period is the day of the census.
According to the *Statisches Jahrbuch* 1930 the figures in 1882 and 1895 were 22 per cent. According to Sullerot (1969) the rate was 30 per cent in 1925, while according to Zimmermann (1985) the percentages were: 1940:37, 1960:36, 1975:37, 1977: 38 and 1979:38 per cent.

5 ***The Netherlands***: See comments on table 2.1.

6 ***Sweden***: Since 1960 sample surveys, from 1970 onwards monthly, at the same time the minimum age changed from 14 to 16 years and the upper limit to 74 years. OECD figures previous to 1984 represent all persons aged 16 - 74 years old, from 1984: 16 - 64 years old. Break in trend 1987. According to the Dutch CBS (in the 1899 census) the Swedish percentage for 1890 was 20. This resembles the percentage of 19 per cent given by the German Statistical Office (in the 1882 census) for Sweden in 1880. These percentages are likely to be more comparable to the Dutch data, because they exclude the majority of unpaid family workers in agriculture (see also chapters 4 and 5). In 1960: census 31 per cent, sample survey: 33 per cent. According to ILO (1991:106) census figures were lower, in 1960: 26, in 1970: 34 in 1980: 43% and in 1985: 48 per cent.

7 ***United Kingdom***: 1861 to 1931, England and Wales only, however, Scotland and Ireland have almost identical rates; 1951, 1961 and 1971 Great Britain. Break in trend in 1961 and 1971. In recent censuses the reference period is the week preceeding the day of the census and the age limit 16 years. In 1931 the rate for Great Britain was 27 per cent (ILO, 1936) and according to ILO (1991:110) in the 1961 census 1961 it was 29 per cent.

2.4.2 Male labor force participation rates, 1850 - 1990

The international long-term trends in male labor force participation rates are given in figure 2.5 and table 2.3. It is obvious that the participation rates for males show much less variation than those for females, both internationally and over time. Moreover, there is a strong similarity in the trends for all these countries.

Dutch male activity rates are not exceptional, although they were relatively low between 1910 and 1981. Another striking feature of the Netherlands, compared with the other six countries, is the relative stability of both the male and female labor force participation rates (and therefore also the total labor force participation rates) for more than a century after 1859. This is especially remarkable given that the same period saw a tremendous increase in the population, from 3 million people in 1849 to 13 million in 1971 (see chapter 7, which also gives a comparison with the other countries), as well as dramatic changes in economic structure (see chapter 4). The 1987 changes in the definition of labor force participation and in the method of sampling (again as with females) produced a sharp apparent increase in labor force participation.

The decline in Belgian female labor force participation rates, which started in 1846 and reached a relatively low level in 1920, was not mirrored by any decline in male activity rates in that country. Between 1910 and 1930, the male activity rate increased from 62 to 69 per cent. After World War II the rate shows a secular decline, bottoming out in 1988 at a level of 50 per cent, where it remained in 1989 and 1990. Denmark's male labor force participation rates reached a peak in 1940 and 1950, after which the rates declined until 1977. Levels in 1990 are similar to those a century earlier.

French male activity rates, like female ones, started to decline after 1921, but failed to recover after World War II. In 1990 the male labor force participation rate is 20 percentage points lower than in 1921. The German male labor force participation rate similarily reached a peak in the 1920s, although levels around 1990 are 2 percent lower to those a century earlier at 61 per cent. The same applies more or less to Sweden, except that the peak in the male activity rate was reached in 1940. The rate in 1990 is between those of France and Germany and equal to the Dutch rate.

The British trend is similar to the German, except that over the last few years German rates have gone up slightly and those in the United Kingdom slightly decreased.

However, the main conclusion is that the difference between Dutch activity rates and those of other countries is much smaller for the male rates than for the female. This suggests that the low activity rates for women in the Netherlands were indeed specific to females.

Table 2.3 and figure 2.5 *Male labor force participation rates: male labor force as a percentage of the total male population, a seven-country comparison, 1850 – 1990*

	Belgium	Denmark	France	Germany	Nether-lands	Sweden	U.K.
1850	61	60	–	–	59	–	66
1860	65	60	58	–	58	50	65
1870	66	61	55	–	–	50	65
1880	66	59	60	61	–	51	61
1890	64	62	64	61	58	55	63
1900	66	63	66	–	59	56	67
1910	62	64	68	63	59	58	67
1920	65	65	71	68	61	61	68
1930	69	64	69	65	61	66	69
1940	–	67	65	65	–	69	–
1950	64	67	65	63	61	65	65
1960	58	64	63	64	57	63	65
1971	54	60	60	59	55	59	60
1973	54	58	55	58	54	58	60
1975	53	58	55	57	52	58	59
1977	53	59	54	57	53	57	60
1979	53	59	54	58	53	57	59
1981	53	59	54	58	55	57	60
1983	54	59	53	59	53	57	59
1985	52	60	53	60	53	56	60
1987	51	60	51	61	56	57	60
1988	50	62	51	60	56	56	59
1989	50	62	51	60	56	56	59
1990	50	62	51	59	57	56	58

1 According to OECD (1991b:38), for Belgium in 1979, 1981, 1983 and 1987: 53, 53, 53, 52, and 51 per cent; and for Germany in 1981, 1983, 1985 and 1987: 59, 60, 61 and 61 per cent. France, 1926: 70 per cent.

Sources and actual census years: see table 2.2.

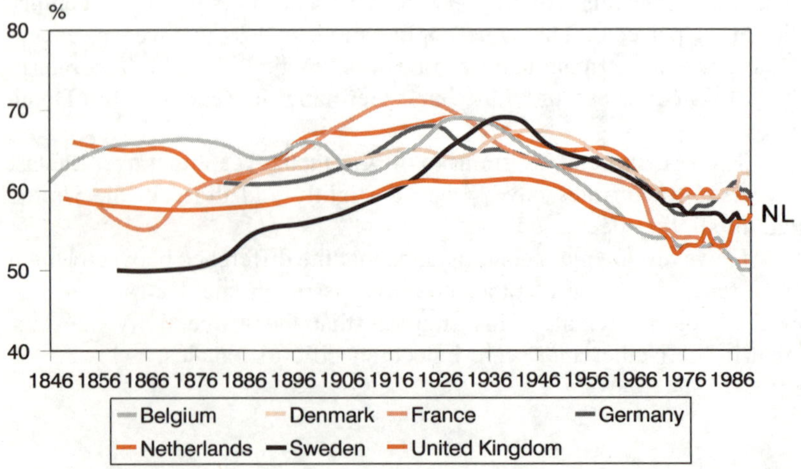

2.4.3 Total labor force participation rates, 1850 - 1990

If both the female and the male labor force participation trends differ, the total trend in activity rates is likely to do likewise. As figure 2.6 and table 2.4 indicate, some countries show a decrease in the total labor force participation rate while other countries do not. The differences between countries are smaller.

In the period between 1846 and 1930, Belgium reaches its highest total activity rates in 1856 and 1866 (51 per cent), in 1910 the lowest (44 per cent), while at the beginning and end of the period the rates are almost equal. After World War II the rates become relatively stable with any variation being limited to a few percentage points.

Denmark's total labor force participation rates show a very gradual increase over the whole period from 1855 to 1990, but the greatest increase occurs after 1960: from 47 per cent that year to 57 per cent in 1990, an increase of 10 percentage points, and one of the sharpest increases recorded in any of the seven countries.

As was expected, the highest total level in France was reached in 1921 at 56 per cent. Since 1960 the French total activity rate has been remarkably stable at around 43 per cent. Again Germany displays the same general trend, although again the pattern is less evident than in France before 1940, and after 1960 there was an initial decline followed by an increase since the end of the 1970s, eventually resulting in the same level of total labor force participation in 1990 as in 1960: 48 per cent.

Total labor force rates in the Netherlands follow a trend similar to those in Denmark, but at a lower level. However, the rise between 1960 and 1990 shows the same spectacular record as Denmark: an increase of 10 percentage points, from the low level of 36 right up to 46 per cent. Sweden is the only country where total labor force rates never declined from the beginning of the period right through until 1990. There is a remarkably rapid increase of 6 percentage points between 1910 and 1920, but unlike the rates in France and Germany those in Sweden never again declined. Since 1960 the increase has been modest compared with Denmark 6 percentage points, but the 1990 level is the second highest in any of our seven countries at 53 per cent. The total labor force participation trend in the United Kingdom is not very spectacular. Before 1940 there was a steady increase, after 1940 first a decline, as in Germany, then a slight increase. The total increase between 1960 and 1990 was only 2 percentage points, from 48 to 50 per cent.

Table 2.4 and figure 2.6 *Total labor force participation rates: total labor force as a percentage of the total population, a seven-country comparison, 1850 – 1990*

	Belgium	Denmark	France	Germany	Nether-lands	Sweden	U.K.
1850	47	43	–	–	41	–	45
1860	51	42	51	–	38	35	45
1870	51	43	40	–	–	35	45
1880	49	43	44	42	–	35	42
1890	47	43	50	43	37	35	43
1900	48	46	51	–	38	37	46
1910	44	48	53	46	39	38	46
1920	45	48	56	51	40	44	46
1930	46	45	52	49	40	47	47
1940	–	50	49	49	–	47	–
1950	41	48	45	46	40	48	48
1960	40	47	43	48	36	48	48
1971	39	49	42	44	37	49	45
1973	39	49	42	44	37	49	46
1975	40	49	42	44	37	50	48
1977	40	50	43	44	37	51	47
1979	41	51	43	45	37	52	47
1981	41	52	43	46	40	52	47
1983	42	53	43	47	40	53	47
1985	42	54	43	47	40	53	49
1987	42	55	43	48	44	53	49
1988	42	56	43	48	45	53	50
1989	42	56	43	48	45	53	50
1990	42	57	43	48	46	54	50

Sources and actual census years: see table 2.2

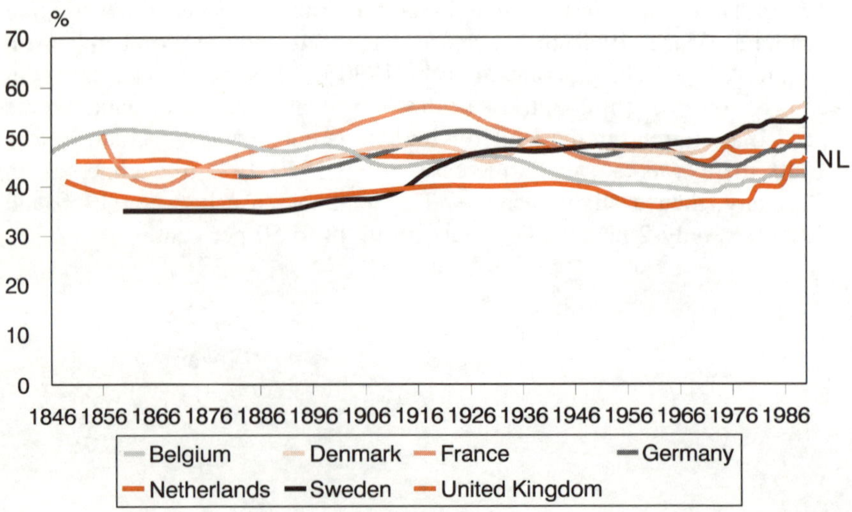

2.4.4 Refined activity rates, 1960 - 1990

The figures given in this section reflect the refined activity rates over the period from 1960 to 1990: that is, the labor force related to the population aged between 15 and 65 years. As mentioned above, refined activity rates are considered to offer better comparisons between countries. Comparability is further enhanced by the fact that the rates presented here are nearly all taken from the same source: the *Organisation for Economic Coordination and Development (OECD).*

Since October 1961, the *OECD* has issued annual "Labour Force Statistics", representing data from 1958 onwards. The earliest data have to be considered as provisional. For several countries data previously published could afterwards be partially revised, but breaks in the series frequently occurred due to changes in the national statistics. Standard definitions are recommended by the OECD for such concepts as: *Population, Total Labour Force* and *Wage Earners and Salaried Employees*. These concepts match the *International Labour Office* (ILO) concepts.

The sources used by the OECD to construct their labor force statistics are:

1 Data collected in national surveys, using national concepts and definitions of the countries considered.
2 Answers to the annual questionnaires sent out by the OECD manpower committee.
3 Demographic Yearbook (United Nations).
4 Monthly Bulletin of Statistics (United Nations).
5 Yearbook of Labour Statistics (International Labour Office). (Since 1980 separate statistics for women have been presented by the ILO in this Yearbook on a systematically basis).

Besides the OECD, the *Statistical Office of the European Communities*: *Eurostat* and also the U.S. *Bureau of Labor Force Statistics, BLS*, both publish comparative labor force participation rates (for details of comparability, see Moy, 1988). The Eurostat (and also the BLS) participation rates are fundamentally different from those calculated by the OECD in that they are based on a European Community wide survey which uses common concepts and definitions. The data are processed and tabulated centrally by Eurostat. These statistics are disregarded in this monograph, because the OECD series closely reflect the national series of the countries considered, and may present a better continuous overview of the long-term trends. Moreover, they also include Sweden.

Table 2.5 and figure 2.7 *Female labor force participation rates: female labor force as a percentage of the female population aged 15 to 64, a seven-country comparison, 1960 – 1990*

	Belgium	Denmark	France	Germany	Netherlands	Sweden	U.K.
1960	36	44	47	49	26	51	49
1967	39	55	47	48	27	55	50
1971	40	59	49	49	30	61	51
1973	41	62	50	50	31	63	53
1975	43	64	51	51	31	68	56
1977	45	65	53	51	31	70	57
1979	46	70	54	52	33	73	58
1981	48	72	54	53	38	75	57
1983	49	74	54	53	40	77	57
1985	49	75	55	53	41	78	61
1987	51	77	56	54	[2]49	79	63
1988	51	78	56	55	51	80	64
1989	52	77	56	56	51	81	65
1990	52	78	57	56	53	81	65

1 According to OECD (1991b:39) the percentages for Belgium in 1979, 1981, 1983, 1985 and 1987 are 46, 48, 49, 49 and 51 resp.; for Denmark in 1987: 77; for France in 1979: 54; for Germany in 1981: 52, in 1983: 52, in 1985: 52; for Sweden in 1968: 51 and 1974: 54 and for the United Kingdom in 1960: 46.

2 This OECD figure differs from that given by the CBS; according to the old Dutch definition, the figure for 1987 is 43 per cent and according to the new definition 50 per cent; the corresponding CBS figures for 1988, 1989 and 1990 are 52, 52 and 54 per cent respectively.

Sources: See table 2.2.

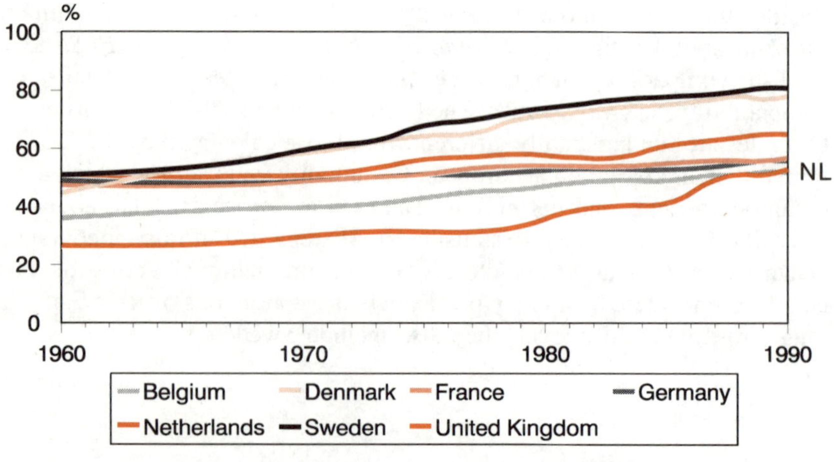

Female refined activity rates

Figure 2.7 shows the female refined activity rates over the period between 1960 and 1990. It is based on table 2.5.

Remarkable features are the virtual equality of activity rates for France, Germany, Sweden and the United Kingdom around 1960, the divergence thereafter, the almost identically strong growth in Denmark and Sweden, the stability in France and Germany and the slight increase in the United Kingdom. Until recently Belgium and the Netherlands have lagged behind.

As with the crude activity rate, the Netherlands had the lowest refined rate until it surpassed Belgium in 1990. The increase in Belgium and the United Kingdom over the whole period from 1960 was 16 percentage points, in France and Germany only 10 and 7 percentage points and in Denmark and Sweden 34 and 30 percentage points. However, the rise in the Netherlands has been almost as spectacular at 27 percentage points.

Male refined activity rates

Figure 2.8 and table 2.6 present the male refined activity rates. Again, it is obvious that there is less variation than across female activity rates, although the trends do differ. Belgium, France and the United Kingdom show a continuous decline between 1960 and 1990, whereas in Denmark, Germany, the Netherlands and Sweden the decline stops in 1985 and there is some recovery thereafter. Belgium and France have lower participation rates for men than the Netherlands and Germany in the 1980s. Denmark, Sweden and the United Kingdom have the highest participation rates for men in 1990.

Total refined activity rates

The corresponding *total labor force participation rates* or *total refined activity rates* are given in figure 2.9 and table 2.7. This figure and table show even more clearly the spectacular increase in Dutch activity rates since the recent change in definition in 1987. The trends in the total labor force participation rates resemble those in the female rates: Denmark and Sweden grow in tandem (though less spectacularly than the female rate), while developments in France and Germany are comparable, with their total rates showing a slight decline between 1960 and 1990.

Table 2.6 and figure 2.8 *Male labor force participation rates: male labor force as a percentage of the male population aged 15 to 64, a seven-country comparison, 1960 – 1990*

	Belgium	Denmark	France	Germany	Nether-lands	Sweden	U.K.
1960	88	100	95	95	98	98	99
1971	84	91	88	92	85	89	94
1973	83	90	86	90	83	88	93
1975	82	90	84	87	82	89	92
1977	80	91	84	85	80	88	92
1979	79	90	83	86	78	88	91
1981	79	88	81	84	81	87	90
1983	77	88	78	83	77	86	88
1985	75	87	77	82	76	84	89
1987	73	88	76	83	79	86	88
1988	72	90	75	82	79	84	87
1989	72	90	75	82	80	85	87
1990	73	90	75	82	80	85	86

According to OECD (1991b:39), for Belgium in 1981, 1983, 1985 and 1987: 78, 77, 75, 73 per cent and for Germany in 1981, 1983 and 1985: 85, 84 and 83 per cent respectively.

Sources: See table 2.2.

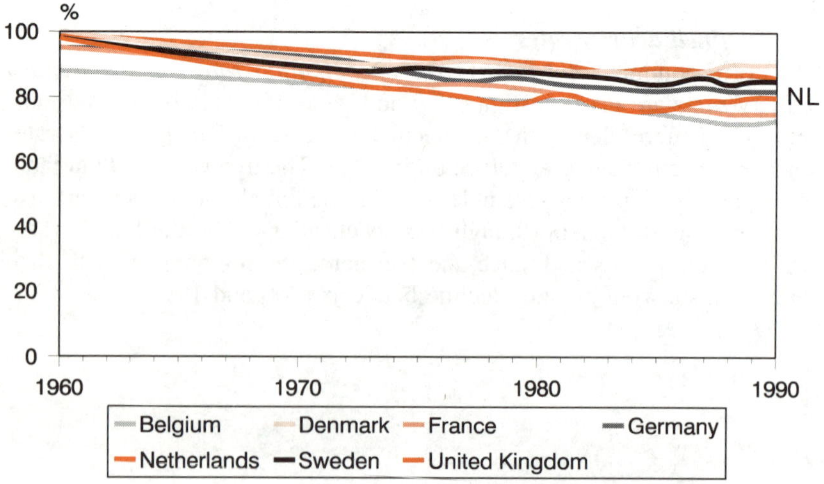

Table 2.7 and figure 2.9 *Total labor force participation rates: total labor force as a percentage of the total population aged 15 to 64, a seven-country comparison, 1960 – 1990*

	Belgium	Denmark	France	Germany	Netherlands	Sweden	U.K.
1960	62	71	70	71	62	74	72
1971	62	75	68	69	58	75	67
1973	62	76	68	69	58	76	73
1975	63	77	68	69	57	79	74
1977	63	78	69	68	57	79	70
1979	63	80	68	68	57	81	72
1981	63	80	68	68	60	81	74
1983	63	81	66	68	59	81	72
1985	62	81	66	68	59	82	75
1987	62	83	66	69	59	82	75
1988	62	84	66	69	65	82	75
1989	62	83	66	69	66	83	76
1990	63	84	66	69	67	83	76

1 According to OECD (1991b:38), the rates for Germany in 1981, 1983 and 1985 are all 68 per cent; differences for other countries are limited to less than 2 per cent.

Sources: See table 2.2.

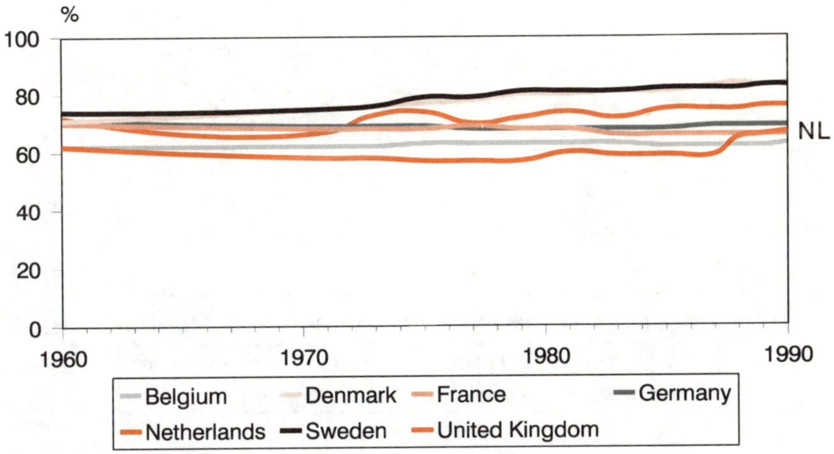

2.5 Women's share in the labor force, 1850 - 1990

Rather than as participation rates, international comparisons can also be expressed in terms of the share of women in the labor force (as a percentage of the total labor force population, males and females together). These percentages are presented in figure 2.10 and table 2.8. The advantage of using participation shares is that these figures are less sensitive to differences in definition between countries, since such definitions affect both men and women.

As expected, the female shares in the Netherlands are still low as compared with the other countries, but the difference is now much smaller. This may indicate that differences in definition play a role to the extent that such differences affect females and males alike. It also reflects the fact that male labor force participation rates have also been relatively low in the Netherlands, especially between 1910 and 1981 (as pointed out in subsection 2.4.2).

Figure 2.10 *Women's share in the labor force: female labor force as a percentage of the total labor force, a seven-country comparison, 1850-1990*

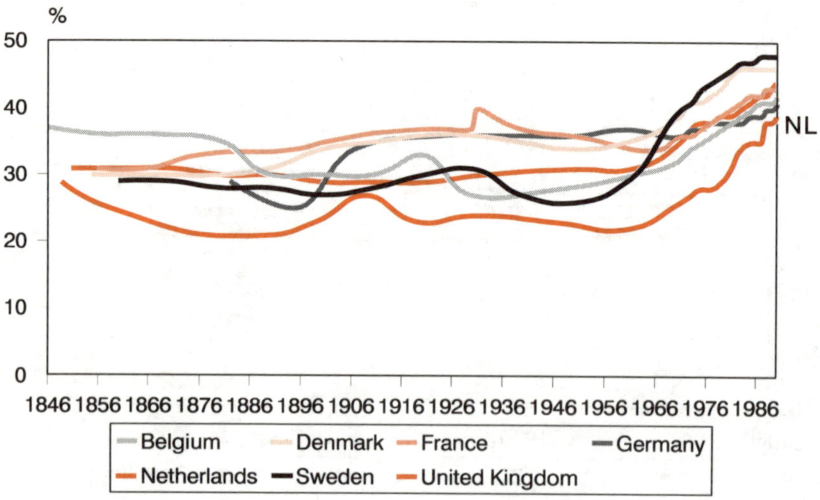

Table 2.8 *Women's share in the labor force: female labor force as a percentage of the total labor force, a seven-country comparison, 1850 – 1990*

	Belgium	Denmark	France	Germany	Nether-lands	Sweden	U.K.
1850	37	30	–	–	29		31
1860	36	30	31	–	25	29	31
1870	36	30	31	–	–	29	31
1880	35	30	33	29	–	28	30
1890	30	31	34	29	21	28	30
1900	30	34	35	–	23	27	29
1910	30	35	37	34	27	28	29
1920	33	36	40	36	23	30	29
1930	27	36	37	36	24	31	30
1940	–	35	37	36	–	27	–
1950	28	34	36	36	23	26	31
[1]1960	30	35	34	37	22	29	31
1971	32	39	36	36	26	40	35
1973	34	41	36	37	27	41	37
1975	35	41	37	37	28	43	38
1977	36	42	38	38	28	44	38
1979	37	43	39	38	29	45	39
1981	38	45	40	38	31	46	39
1983	39	45	41	38	34	47	40
1985	40	46	42	39	35	47	41
1987	41	46	42	39	35	48	42
1988	41	46	43	40	38	48	42
1989	41	46	43	40	38	48	43
1990	42	46	43	41	39	48	44

1 According to OECD 1991b:37, the shares for Denmark, France, Sweden and the United Kingdom in 1960 are: 31, 33, 34 and 33 per cent respectively.

Sources and actual census years: see table 2.2.

2.6 Conclusions to chapter 2

Changes in labor force participation up to the period of industrialization are difficult to quantify. Since that period, statistics are available but imperfect. Using these statistics for the seven countries, the following conclusions can be drawn.

Female labor force participation rates in the Netherlands were constantly lower than those in the other six countries from the first census in 1849 to 1987, except for 1947 when Belgian female activity rates were one percentage point lower. The increase between 1987 and 1988 was relatively sharp, due to a change in definition, particularly with respect for small part-time jobs. International compatibility remains a problem (this will be addressed again in chapters 6 and 8). If this change had occurred earlier, the Dutch statistics would probably have equalled those for Belgium, France and Germany a few years earlier.

For about a century between 1849 and 1960, in the Netherlands as in Sweden and the United Kingdom, the figures hardly showed any trend at all and the female labor force participation rates remained roughly stable. Since then, as in all seven countries since 1970, the trend has been upwards.

The long-term trend in Belgium was downwards until 1947, after which it started to rise again. By contrast, there has been a persistent rising trend in female economic activity in Denmark ever since 1855 except for the 1950s and 1960s. France showed a strong increase in female labor force participation rates at the beginning of the century, reaching a high level in 1921. The levels declined thereafter until 1967. Despite the increase since then, the 1921 percentage has in 1990 still not been surpassed. Germany also reached a relatively high level of female economic activity at about the same time as France, in 1925, and this level was equalled in 1983. In the Netherlands, the female economic activity rate was not only the lowest in all the seven countries between 1849 and 1987, but the difference was sometimes quite considerable (as much as 26 per cent compared with France in about 1920). However, it should once again be emphasized that these long-term developments must be regarded with caution and that apparent differences may have been due to different methods of statistical measurement.

The male participation rate in the Netherlands was also relatively low, and in fact the lowest between 1920 and 1977, but the differences with the other countries were much smaller. That suggests that the low participation rate for women in the Netherlands was indeed more specific to women. This is also confirmed by the long-term trends in women's share in the labor force. The Dutch female shares remained for over a century lower than those in any other country.

CHAPTER 3

WOMEN'S WORK HISTORY

"Dreams of a past Golden Age are beautiful but misleading."
Alfred Marshall, 1936:11

The background sketch of *women's work history*[1] given in this chapter, adresses the question of gender-specific patterns in the division of labor and the development of women's work in relation to men's work in Europe since the Middle Ages. The history of women's work deals mainly with questions concerning the improvement or deterioration in the economic and social position of women over past centuries. The answers to these questions as well as to those about women's market work are ambiguous and often phrased as might-have-beens. Much room is left for nuance. The interpretations of the changes described are subjective and history often seems to be (mis)used as a *"Tummelplatz der eigenen Träume und Wünsche"*[2].

Despite numerous books about *women's work* and *the history of women's work*, *women's work history* has until recently been unexplored. This chapter contributes (particularly in combination with chapters 9 and 10) to all three areas. The focus in this chapter's discussion is on the differences in developments between the Netherlands and Belgium, Denmark, France, Germany, Sweden and the United Kingdom. The description of the Dutch nation before the French Revolution is based mainly on the Western provinces (Holland), and that of the United Kingdom on England.

Section 3.1 gives a brief outline of the history of women's work since the Middle Ages. Special attention is given to the development of towns, guilds and specialization of labor in section 3.2 and to the Dutch Golden Age (the seventeenth century) in section 3.3, with subsections introducing long-term trends in marriage, family and labor in the Dutch Republic and the other six countries. Section 3.4 describes the period in between the seventeenth century and industrialization. Section 3.5 discusses developments in the cotton and textile industries and during the period of conversion of home-based industries into mechanized and heavy

---

1 The neologism '*women's work history*' refers to the (initial) consciousness-raising strategies of feminism. For debates on the shifting emphases between the standard expression '*history of women's work*' and the use of '*women's work history*', see Offen, et al., 1991. Because section 3.1 deals not only with feminist historians but also with traditional historians, the title '*history of women's work*' has been chosen.

2 "Playground for the individual's own dreams and wishes". See Rita Bake, et al., 1983:150, "Zur Stellung der Frauen in mittelalterlichen Handwerk. Schreibtisch-mythen und Realitäten", in: Feministische Studiën 2: 147-155, quoted by Kloek, 1991:32.

industrial production. Subsection 3.5.3 describes the late Industrialization in the Netherlands.

3.1 History of Women's Work in Western and Northern Europe, a brief introduction

Women's work varies over time and across societies. Nowhere has there been complete equality in the status and division of labor between women and men, with the sole possible exception of the field work done by slaves on plantations or in the industries of nineteenth-century America: "In the fields, the slaves were classified as "hands" [...] Once hands were classified, they all did the same work, just different amounts." (Matthaei, 1982:88).

Blau and Ferber argue that the greater the share of the necessities of life[3] provided by women, the more modest the difference in status between the sexes (Blau and Ferber, 1986: 22). In pre-industrial economies most of these necessities for survival are produced by both sexes working together. This means that women tend to enjoy a higher status in horticultural societies than in pastoral and agricultural ones, where women's activities tend to be increasingly centered within the home (Blau and Ferber, 1986:25). Of course, the distinction between men's and women's tasks in the area of Europe considered in this volume has traditionally depended heavily on local geographical features and opportunities for animal husbandry, agriculture and horticulture.

In pre-medieval Western Europe, there was less difference between female and male status in Gaul and among the Teutonic (Germanic) peoples than within the Roman Empire or Greek culture (Sullerot, 1969, Badinter, 1990). The division of labor also differed tremendously between these cultures and was in Gaul and among the Teutonic peoples "exactly the opposite of that among the Greeks and Romans" (Strabo, quoted by Sullerot, 1969:48). These different cultures, with their conflicting approaches to the division of labor between the sexes, merged together in the Middle Ages, producing a period in which distinctions between men's and women's occupations were for a time less strict[4]. It was, for example, possible for women to study (and lecture) at the university of Bologna (Italy) and to be admitted to the early universities of England, France and

---

[3] This is not an unambiguous statement. Apparently the term necessities means only food, shelter and clothing (housework). Otherwise, the statement "equal shares in necessities, equal status" is a tautological one; although those producing are not necessarily doing so for their own consumption.

[4] A considerable debate has developed about the economic and social status of women in the centuries before industrialism developed (see Bradley, 1989 for a discussion and see below).

Germany. Gradually, however, from the end of the fourteenth century onward, gender inequalities once again seem to have increased (Sullerot, 1969). It was set against this background of increasing inequality that Christine de Pisan wrote between 1404 and 1405, using arguments which could still be employed today, what are probably the first two feminist books about the position of women: *Le Livre de la Cité des Dames* (The book of the City of Ladies) and *Le Livre des Trois Vertus*"[5] (The Treasure of the City of Ladies or The Book of the Three Virtues). In *Le Livre de la Cité des Dames* the writer uses dream and allegory as an indirect means of expressing criticism of male prejudices concerning female vices. In her dream, three crowned ladies of the highest stature, Virtue, Reason and Justice by name, command her to build a City of Ladies in which women will be safe from the false allegations of men. Digging and delving with the mattock of her intelligence, she asks questions for the three virtues to answer - questions concerning the education and intellectual abilities of women. Lady Reason, for example, replies that if girls were taught the same things as boys they would not remain at home and that they would be found just as capable of understanding as the boys. She criticizes the double moral standard entertained by men and the unequal regard accorded to men and women. The second book "complements the earlier work in that is supposed to be the cardinal possession of the ladies now securely sheltered in their allegorical city, it is a book of a very different character. The reader seeking feminist polemics will not find them here" (Lawson, 1985:21)[6].

According to Sullerot, the mentioned increasing gender inequality is reflected in the changing ratios of female to male wages, declining from a position of broad equality during the high Middle Ages to a ratio of about 3:4 at the end of the fourteenth century. Over the next century, female wages were to decline still further to less than fifty per cent of male wages (Sullerot, 1969:59).

Both during the Middle Ages and in the period immediately thereafter, the nobility displayed a more rigid division between male and female occupations than was prevalent among the peasantry and townspeople. Labor did not then have the high moral value attached to it in later centuries. In contrast to what is generally believed, however, there was a high degree of specialization in productive activities connected with clothing and textiles. Sullerot (1969:53) mentions fifteen exclusively female oc-

5 The first book has been translated into Dutch from the original medieval French by Tine Pontfoort, see references: De Pisan, Christine (1404/1984). The second book is translated in English by Sarah Lawson (See references: De Pisan, 1405 and Lawson, 1985)

6 The Treasure of the City of Ladies is part etiquette book, part survival manual. It is a practical social advice to women ranging from those with power and authority to the poorest peasant women, including widows, spinsters, prostitutes and nuns (Lawson, 1985: 21,22).

cupations, involving highly specialized and repetitive work such as reeling, and carding and combing wool, existing between 1292 and 1300[7].

For the people on medieval farms, labor was mainly domestic, being carried out for the family by the family, with each family supplying its own wants first and then disposing of the residue. In rural communities, the activities and division of labor continued largely unchanged until far into the nineteenth century.

Work entered a new phase through the emergence of industries in monasteries and convents. In many cases such communities not only made everything they themselves needed, but also worked to supply the outside world. And, of course, within these single-sex establishments no sex-specific division of labor was possible, although it did to some extent exist between them.

3.2 Towns, guilds and specialization of labor

3.2.1 Towns and guilds

During the Middle Ages there was a gradual increase in the differentiation and specialization of labor, which was accelerated in the growing medieval towns of the thirteenth century onwards. Townspeople and town councils replaced the feudal system, particularly in those activities producing for the local markets. The towns, islands in an largely agricultural society, offered the former feudal dependent peasants personal freedom if not reclaimed by a feudal lord within a year and a day (Uitz, 1990:14) and new economic possibilities in terms of the independent small-scale production of goods and exchange of goods with other settlements. Both the merchant and the craftsman were offered various opportunities of making profits.

Female inhabitants achieved a recognized position in the economic life of the town, limited legal competence, and the possibility of acquiring the right of independently citizenship. The women in the lower strata of town life contributed to the family income by working for the family workshop or by finding work in small-scale trade or as wage earners. Women from the wealthier levels of urban society found work in trade, in currency exchange offices and in craftwork (Uitz, 1990:177).

The guilds[8] were a major factor in these changes. The objective of a craft guild was to maintain for its own members a monopoly of local

---

7 Noordegraaf (1992:6) also mentions extensive labor specialization particularly in the textile industry in the fourteenth century.

8 *Guilds* is a term applied to various types of associations - whether commercial, professional, social or religious - formed to promote the common interests of their members (Collier, 1966:522).

production and trade in a particular industry and at the same time to ensure good workmanship and fair and equal competitive conditions for everyone within the group.

In Western and Northern Europe, merchant guilds preceded the craft guilds by half a century. The top urban economic centres were those towns which had acquired an important role in sea and transit trade (Uitz, 1990:23). By the thirteenth century, craft guilds were fully organized in every town in Western and Northern Europe and over the next two centuries they reached the peak of their importance (Collier, 1966).

In both merchant and craft guilds, the social and religious functions of the association were important, although subordinate to the economic. Members had to contribute to a common fund for the care of the sick and needy, for the decent burial of those who died, and for the care of widows and orphans. The members were told to love and help one another, and the good name of the association was safeguarded by regulations.

3.2.2 Specialization of labor

In general, written documents hardly mention the participation of women (Uitz, 1990:19). However, "(t)he female town dweller was initially most active and contributed to the greatest extent and most consistently to economic prosperity in trade and finance." (Uitz, 1990:24). Independent female merchants were recorded in Italian notary registers at the beginning of the thirteenth century, and appear in corresponding French sources only a little later (Uitz, 1990:24). In the fourteenth and fifteenth centuries independent female traders are found in German towns. Impressive achievements by the women of Cologne in controlling large portions of the sugar, wine and steel imports, illustrate how far opportunities had increased for female citizens to be professionally active in the medieval communities (Uitz, 1990:39). To avoid the guild regulations, however, many women were involved in the various branches of minor trade for which no guilds existed.

In the case of merchants, there are many sources of information available, such as notary registers, account books and business letters. For the craft worker, there are no such sources, but the customs and ordinances of the craft guilds do provide important information on, for example, the legal conditions for women's participation in the crafts. Unfortunately, this tells us nothing about the actual participation of women, not even of professional women working in the crafts organized by guilds. Moreover, the ordinances of the guilds were mainly concerned with rules and customs not automatically respected. Supplementary sources, such as sentences passed in court proceedings are just beginning to be explored and analysed (Uitz, 1990:51).

In Paris[9] at the end of the thirteenth and the beginning of the fourteenth century, many female inhabitants were actively participating in the production of craft goods and services within the framework of guilds. Their conditions, however, may have been relatively favourable compared to the rest of Europe (Uitz, 1990:53).

Specialization and differentiation continued to increase in various industries, with new guilds splitting off from the old. The late thirteenth century in particular saw a marked specialization in the crafts, while the second half of the fourteenth century experienced another distinct boom in this sector (Uitz, 1990:23).

A world-famous textile industry was established in medieval Flanders, centered on the cities of Bruges, Ghent and Ypres. These crafts attracted others, and for more than three centuries manufacturing activity was higher in Flanders than anywhere else in Europe (De Raet, 1914:119). The scarce research indicates that women were involved in the economic activities of their families, in religious institutions and beguinages (semi-religious communities), but women are seldom mentioned explicitly in the regulations and statutes of the craft guilds. Women's work was certainly seen as inferior and the detailed rules of the guilds imposed a strict prohibition on most work being done by the master's wife or "*maerte*" (maidservant) (De Raet, 1914:59). In the English guilds, attitudes towards women compared badly to, for example, those of the Paris guilds in around 1300. In some cases it was strictly forbidden to take on women as auxiliary workers unless they were the wives or maids of masters (in the belt-makers' guild for example) (Uitz, 1990).

Over the whole of England, Flanders, France and Germany, there were only a few separate guilds for women. Most of these female guilds were associated with the production and distribution of food and clothing (Tilly and Scott, 1987:49). In the Netherlands there was only one female guild, for bakers, although the clothing guild in Amsterdam also had a special division for women, which had its own female masters and apprentices after 1539. Only a few (late) examples are known of girls being admitted as full members in their own right to otherwise male guilds in the Netherlands. Judith Leyster, was admitted in 1633 as a female painter to the Haarlem Guild of St Luke (Schama, 1988:415). She had her own apprentices.

---

9 For Paris, the duties and rights of 100 craft guilds are described in 1270. The trades were compared with the Paris tax registers of 1292, 1300 and 1313, which also list the number of independent working women. One occupation practised exclusively by women was the beating, teasing, and carding of flax and hemp for textile manufacture. The production of linen yarn took place under a mixed guild, with both men and women. Apprentices had to undergo a six-year training. Flax and hemp spinning was also carried out under a mixed guild. Among the clothmakers, widows were the only women to have the status of masters (in 1300, 10 compared to 350 men). Women masters or workers were also a rarity among feltmakers. On the other hand, the ribbon and braid-weaving guild was in 1300 exclusively female, as was the Parisian silk-manufacturing trade and purse-making guild (Uitz, 1990:51-53).

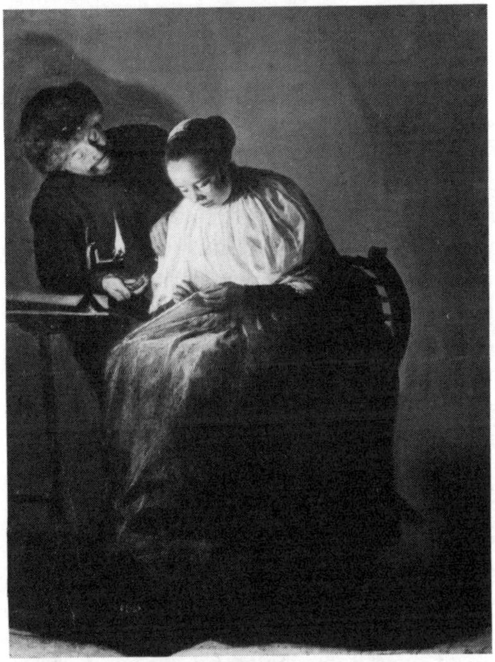

Judith Leyster (1609-1660)
Man offering money to a young woman, 1631
Mauritshuis, The Hague

The sewing of the woman probably symbolizes her virtue, underlining her refusal to acquiesce to the older man.

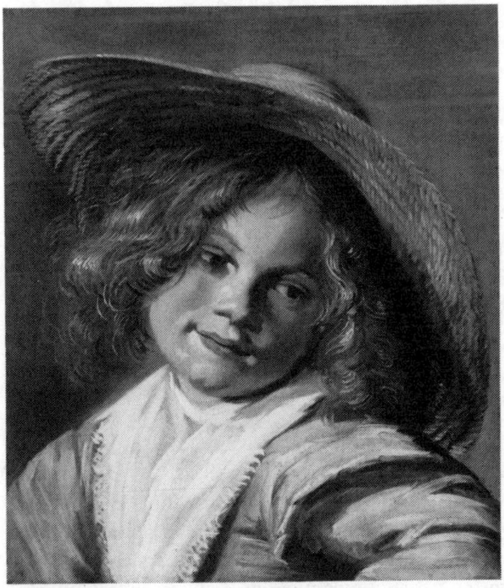

Judith Leyster (1609–1660)
Girl with straw hat, between 1633 and 1635
Foundation Dr. Rau pour le Tiers Monde,
Embrach, Switzerland (photo: Peter Schälchi)

Likewise, Anna Maria van Schuurman[10], an extremely talented woman both intellectually and artistically, was admitted in 1641 to the Guild of St Luke in Utrecht (Schama, 1988:412). In general, however, although women participated in nearly all the guilds, they did so at a secondary level. In certain guilds widows, and sometimes unmarried daughters, of members were specially privileged by being granted full membership after their husbands' or fathers' deaths, or were allowed to continue the business of the deceased so long as they did not (re)marry. For widows this practice also existed in Denmark, England, Flanders, France, Germany and Sweden. In France, Turgot's edict of 1776 abolished the guilds (Hepple, 1986). In the Netherlands guilds continued at least as late as the nineteenth century (Wichmann, 1917:78), similarly in Denmark and Sweden. In Denmark the guilds were abolished in 1857; in Sweden in 1846, at which date single women simultaneously acquired limited rights to practice certain occupations[11] (see also chapter 9). In the other countries guilds were abolished around Napoleonic times.

3.2.3 Professional and economic life of women

Besides participating in the kind of work represented by the guilds or in small-scale trade, women bore their share of the production of agricultural products, peat, bricks, or various luxuries for wealthy citizens and (less importantly in the Netherlands) the nobility. They also worked in cottage industries and in domestic service in manors, on large farms etc. Besides domestic work, women were responsible for tasks such as spinning (weaving being done mainly by men), bleaching, dyeing, making clothes, washing and so on. Women were also represented in the retail trades and in inns, restaurants and other such places. The most vulnerable fell prey to prostitution. In cases where demand for labor exceeded supply, women from the lower strata of urban society often took on heavy physical work in mining, smithies and construction (Uitz, 1990:177).

At present we have only a very sketchy idea of the professional and economic life of women in the medieval towns. Little is known of the reasons for the (also much debated) gradual retreat from the positions women seem to have occupied during this period. This retreat seems to be a general accepted conclusion in comparisons of this period with the next: until the second half of the fifteenth century, in some cases to the end of the sixteenth century, there seems to have been a series of

---

10 spelled by Schama as Schurman.

11 The publication of ***Det går an*** (Common decency), by Carl Jonas Love Almqvist in 1839, in which a plea was made for the economic independence of women, contributed much to the debate preceding the changes. In this novel, a very capable and well-qualified daughter of a deceased glass manufacturer runs her father's business, but is aware that she can do so only as long as her dying mother, who has taken over the official guild membership, stays alive.

favourable conditions encouraging independent female professional work, some of which disappeared in early modern times (Uitz, 1990:177).

The women's history debate among historians seems rather to be dominated by arguments about how **the** position of women and **the** role of women in history developed for better or for worse (Kloek, 1991:178), without there being any clear criteria as to the quality or possible quantification of such changes.

The mainstream of (feminist) historiography draws the conclusion that after the Middle Ages, but especially in the eighteenth and nineteenth centuries, women's contribution to economic life declined from one period to the next[12], female (productive) labor became more and more restricted and this decline in economic opportunities was accompanied by a loss of freedom in political, cultural and sexual life. This conclusion would mean that following the Middle Ages women's position consistently deteriorated.

This 'critical pessimistic tradition' of a gradual deterioration in women's position has recently come under criticism (Bradley, 1989, Kloek, 1991; Offen, et al., 1991). It now seems unlikely that women ever enjoyed any important economic role. Even in the Middle Ages, women seem to have had more limited privileges than men. And without clear criteria for the evaluation of women's economic position or well-defined measurements of the changes, the outcome of the debate can only remain uncertain.

It certainly seems obvious that in places and periods enjoying relatively high prosperity and an excess demand for labor, women had relatively more opportunity to perform market activities and could claim their share in the social and economic revival and upsurge. No clear trend for all women and all types of work can be distinguished, however, and it is difficult to conclude that there was any.

3.2.4 Developments in Holland prior to the seventeenth century

There is no easy answer to the question of whether the circumstances of Dutch women were any different from those in the rest of Europe. The history of women in the Netherlands before (but also during) the seventeenth century is virtually unexplored territory. An exception is Els Kloek's study (1991). She has tried to answer the question "Was Female Labour Restricted" (from about 1380 to 1580) on the basis of the ordinances of the cloth industry, and the correction books in which violations of the ordinances were recorded, in Holland's textile city of

---

12 For this reason the scheme of periodization has also been called into question; see for example "Did women have a Renaissance?" by Joan Kelly-Gadol, and Fox-Genovese, Elizabeth, "Women and the Enlightenment", both in: Bridenthal and Koonz (eds.), 1987, respectively: 139-164, and: 251-278.

Leyden. She concludes that there was a strict division of labor, which may have been simply taken for granted and not the result of explicit policies.

In Leyden, combing and spinning was women's work, while weaving, fulling, dyeing, cloth shearing and cloth production were apparently as a rule done by men. This sexual division of labor was not regulated by the ordinances. Only a few of these[13] restricted the type of work women were allowed to do, and these concerned work in the specific context of the production process and were apparently intended to protect the high quality of the cloth. It appears that the work done by women was barely regulated at all, while that done by men was governed by exact rules. The formulation *'wie hij zij, man of wijf'* - who ever he may be, man or woman - was used only occasionally in matters regarding management to make clear that these ordinances applied explicitly to women as well as to men (Kloek, 1991).

Kloek criticizes two studies based on the same sources: those of Posthumus (1908) and of the American historian Martha Howell (1986). "Posthumus frequently refers to the 'army of female workers' which was employed in Leyden's medieval cloth industry in order to prove that the relations were *already* capitalistic then. He emphasizes the poorly paid, unskilled nature of the work then also performed by women. ... Howell sketches a different picture. She highlights the large degree of independence and the high status enjoyed by the women drapers and other female producers in the old cloth industry in order to show that women *still* had plenty of opportunity to work then." (Kloek, 1991:180).

Els Kloek argues for a different interpretation: "what the various female textile workers had in common with each other was the marginal role which they played in the old cloth industry. ... there was no conscious policy of pushing women out of the 'high status jobs' as Howell suggests. An opposite line of reasoning is more obvious: women only functioned at the margin of the old cloth industry, and that is why there were so few regulations involving the work they did." (Kloek, 1991:180).

Whatever the outcome of the debate, the division of labor seems not to have differed in the Low Countries from that in the rest of Europe. It seems likely that the male-dominated sexual division of labor, seen as more or less self-evident and generally respected, existed in the whole of Western Europe. Holland may have differed from areas like Flanders and France in that, except in Leyden, not many women were involved in crafts such as the textile and related industries. This was because Holland remained throughout the Middle Ages a relatively underdeveloped and mainly agricultural country (Van Zanden, 1991:31). However, the feudal system of the surrounding countries was largely absent. This latter fact

---

[13] For instance, it was forbidden to the *'joncwijf, die in dachuyren werckt'* - a maid who works for daily payment - (i.e. not a domestic servant) to produce cloth by herself, while *'vollersvrouwen'* - wives of fullers - were not allowed to trim the cloths. These ordinances seem to have been formulated rather to protect the quality of the cloth than to restrict female labor. In the correction books no violations of these rules were found (Kloek, 1991).

may have contributed to the genesis of the Golden Age in the Netherlands.

3.3 The Dutch Golden Age

3.3.1 Economic Development

The break between the (Protestant) Northern and (Catholic) Southern provinces of the Low Countries became permanent when the seven Northern provinces formed the Dutch Republic in 1579 and declared their independence in 1581. From that time forward, the history of the Netherlands is the history of the Northern provinces; and although the fight for liberty and religious freedom was still far from won (Collier, 1966, 17:322), a period of prosperity ensued. The Southern provinces (Flanders, the Dutch-speaking part of present-day Belgium) remained under Spanish rule, which meant the end of three centuries of relative prosperity. Antwerp, in the sixteenth century the centre of world commerce, lost most of its trade when the Dutch closed the mouth of the Scheldt. This fate had a depressing effect on the other leading cities of Flanders. Many craftsmen and businessmen emigrated to the Dutch Republic causing, for example, the spectacular growth in the population of Leyden from about 12 thousand in 1581 to over 44 thousand in 1622 (Daelemans, 1975). This, together with the introduction of new diversified products, contributed to the establishment of Leyden as a world leader in cloth production for over a century thereafter.

Immigration, the (religious) wars in the surrounding countries, the spectacular rise of the grain trade after the European crisis of 1590, the absence of a feudal system, these are some of the factors which may have contributed to the development of perhaps the first 'modern' urbanised industrial region in the world (Van Zanden, 1991:31[14]). During the seventeenth century, and especially after 1648, the Dutch Republic became one of the great powers in Western Europe. This was largely due to economic prosperity, based mainly on trade. Two large companies[15], the East India Company (V.O.C.) and West India Company (W.I.C.), held the trading monopoly with East Asia and America and were major contributors to the Golden Age. The name Golden Age applied to the seventeenth century refers not only to the economic and political power and glory of the period. It also reflects a remarkable contemporary development in culture and science, due in part to the contribution of

---

14 This publication mentions the year 1570. As was pointed out to me by Leo Noordegraaf, this is a typing error.

15 These companies, the *Verenigde Oostindische Compagnie* (V.O.C.) and the *Westindische Compagnie* (W.I.C.), employed hundreds if not thousands of laborers (Van Zanden, 1991:51).

refugees like the Iberian and German Jews and the Huguenots. This important cultural and social development in the Dutch Republic was closely related to the religious situation. Calvinism, as a specific offshoot of protestantism, encouraged a mentality combining hard work and a modest life-style.

Despite some similarities, seventeenth-century Holland differed in many respects from the surrounding countries. "(T)here was something special about the Dutch situation - its fortune and its predicament - that did set it apart from other states and nations in baroque Europe. That something was its precocity." (Schama, 1988:8). This precocity, this exceptionally early development, seems to have had its roots in the very rapid wage rises of the period 1580-1620. "(T)he rise of the Dutch Republic ... went hand in hand with the bidding up of wage rates to what were probably the highest in northern Europe." (De Vries, 1977:45). This was one of the reasons why labor-saving devices were so widely employed in Dutch industry, and why such intensive use was made of non-human energy sources in the form of windmills and peat. "In short, the Dutch labor force was endowed with per capita energy supplies that had no equal until the coming of the steam engine. This endowment obviously affected the productivity of labor." (De Vries, 1977:46). This suggests that high productivity was important in setting wage rates and that Dutch wages were able to rise in the early seventeenth century because capital investment and the training of skilled workers made labor here more productive than it was elsewhere. Besides, basic wage rates were high because agriculture in the region was productive, and strongly commercialized as a result of the division of labor (Noordegraaf, 1992).

3.3.2 Labor and family

Did Dutch women emerge from their marginal position during the Golden Age? Historians (e.g. Schama, Clark) have occasionally considered the role of Dutch women in the Golden Age, but have usually done so in connection with exceptional Dutch manners and customs, and hardly ever in connection with their economic position. Among the merchant and artisan classes at this time, wives were likely to be partners in the family business. They generally took charge when the men were away on business and often continued trading after their husbands died. The first occupational census in the Netherlands, taken in Leyden in 1581, shows that many[16] married women were then participating in the labor market. However, married women's participation in the labor market is likely to have been rare, except in the circumstances mentioned. Maybe it was

---

16 In later centuries likewise *many* married women are found, even in higher professions. (Posthumus-van der Goot, jrb. II, 1938). Similar statements with the word *many* are used by Schama, 1988; Noordegraaf, 1980; Posthumus-van der Goot, 1937; Leydesdorff, 1991; etc. but none of these authors have quantified the statement.

relatively high in Leyden, because Leyden was well known for its textile industry, a sector in which in later centuries also relatively large numbers of married women were found (see also chapters 4 and 8). The share of (all) women in the total labor force in Leyden was 30 per cent at that time (Posthumus, 1914, quoted by van Deursen, 1978:18). These women were mainly employed in washing, spinning and combing (Van Deursen, 1978:18). This 30 per cent has been regarded as a high figure. Van Deursen explains the high figure by claiming that the textile industry attracted single girls from elsewhere. However, the share is not very high compared with the figures in table 2.8 and, for example, with the total share of women in the Netherlands in 1849, when it was 29 per cent. That means that the majority of women in the labor force in Leyden were probably non-married[17] and that it is likely that only relatively more women than elsewhere have been performing market work.

Evidence is scarce but wives and daughters of the burghers (bourgeoisie) of the Dutch Republic were not generally supposed to earn their own living. The Amsterdam marriage register may support this view, since only the bridegroom's occupation and occupational status were registered, and not those of the bride (registration in church or city hall had been obligatory in Amsterdam since 1578 (Van Zanden, 1991:56)). The proper place of a woman was apparently in the home, preferably as a mother and housewife.

The division of labor, the high degree of specialization, industrialization and the relative prosperity of the Dutch Republic might have contributed to the realization of a family model with this division of labor (and other characteristics of the nuclear, affective family, see chapter 7). In specialized industries production and household activities are separated (e.g. the silk industry in Amsterdam used large workshops (Van Deursen, 1978:18), while in Leeuwarden a factory for the production of wool fabrics existed: 90 feet long, 30 feet wide and 6 stories high (Noordegraaf, 1992:11), but for the majority of craftsmen or minor tradesmen (work)shops adjoined their homes. Noordegraaf (1992:2) mentions large scale fine cloth activities in Leyden, Haarlem and Delft, while the latter two cities had also important beer, luxury production and porcelain industrial activities; in the city of Utrecht three-quarter of the working population was involved in industrial activities.

Unfortunately, no national or regional statistics are available concerning the development of the working population per sector and branch for the seventeenth century to support the statements about the relation between separation of specialized industries and division of labor within households.

What can be traced is the ideal of faithful marriage and close family life (see also subsection 3.3.4). Among the burghers it can be traced back to the fifteenth century but became of paramount importance

---

17 The term *non-married* includes *single* (never married), *widowed* and *divorced* women (see also chapter 8).

during the Golden Age. Marriage was the institution respected by the overwhelming majority of the population, while concubinage was rare (Van Deursen, 1978:18).

Although the reconstruction of the life of the poor and illiterate is fraught with difficulty, it seems likely that in the Dutch Republic their life too centered on the family household. "While the ethos of other seventeenth-century states was built around the aura of a dynasty, or the historic privileges of a city commune, in the Netherlands it was the family household that was "the fountain and source" of authority" (Schama, 1988:385-386). The importance of the family home worked with particular force and intensity within Dutch culture (Schama, 1988:400). Mothers are the guardians of household purity and responsible for the obligatory scrubbing of the pavement in front of the house and for keeping a spotless home. The cultural norms of the bourgeois family probably started to dominate Dutch cultural life at least from the seventeenth century, contributing to a development that made the Netherlands unique in comparison to its surrounding countries. The fragmentation of cultural norms which existed in societies composed of a number of distinct status groups and classes was largely absent in the Netherlands. In England and France, for example, more or less self-contained cultural units seem to have existed, each with its own attitudes and customs. Systems of values and patterns of acceptable behavior which were normal for one class or social stratum were often quite different from those which were normal in another. "The result was less the supersession of one family pattern and set of familial values by another than the provision of a widening number of quite different patterns." (Stone, 1990: 23).

The familial relationships of the rich bourgois middle classes and their behavior may indeed have become the dominant form of household behavior in all European countries in the eighteenth and nineteenth centuries, but this bourgeois family model certainly already existed in the Dutch Republic during the Golden Age.

At the heart of the decisive penetration of this family model into the life-styles of all classes is the fact that the domestic sphere became the central locus of quality considerations. The well-being of all the members of a household was improved if men provided the financial resources and companionship and women were responsible for raising or maintaining the quality of life of the household (Lesthaeghe, 1991:2). This quality-oriented family model gave women working in their own households a higher status, but was based on the same asymmetric gender roles as existed in the labor market. The increasing dominance of this family model is also reflected in the increasing institutional control over marriage that emerged in both Catholic and Protestant areas (especially strongly from the 16th century onwards) and has only begun to decline in recent decades.

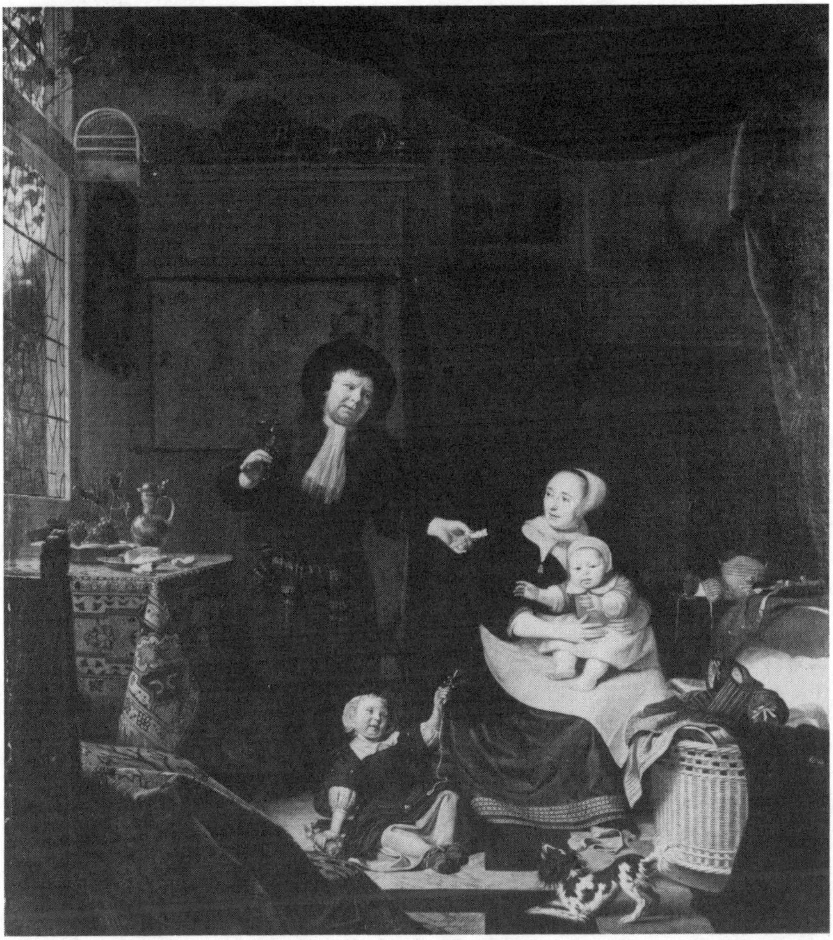

***Ludolph de Jongh** (1616–1679)*
Dutch family in a room, circa 1673
Amsterdams Historisch Museum

3.3.3 Long-term European trends in marriage

Marriage is one of the oldest of human institutions and one of the most universal elements in the social structure. At least as early as the eighteenth century, societies in Western and Northern Europe in particular began to surround marriage with well-defined laws to arrange, sanctify, preserve and dissolve unions between men and women. Before that time marriage was an engagement which could be undertaken in a variety of ways. According to Stone (1990:29), polygamy appears to have been general up to the eleventh century, with easy divorce and much concubinage. In the early Middle Ages, marriage constituted a private contract between two families concerning property exchange, and for those without property was a contract enforced by the community sense of what was right. "It was not until the thirteenth century that the Church at last managed to take over control of marriage law, to assert at least the principle of monogamous indissoluble marriage, to define and prohibit incest, to punish fornication and adultery, and to get bastards legally excluded from property inheritance." (Stone, 1990:30).

Although in the countries studied marriage was by the sixteenth century well defined, there were still numerous ways of entering into it. For persons with property it involved a series of distinct steps, while for the poor any sort of exchange of promises before witnesses followed by cohabitation was regarded as a valid marriage. The Jewish culture, implemented via Christianity, had left its legacy in the Western world in at least three aspects: monogamy, women's dependence on/ obedience to men and the attachment of a high value to the virginity of the bride. Although the Catholic Church had elevated marriage to the position of a sacrament in 1439, it was only in 1563, after the Reformation, that the Catholic Church first required the presence of a priest for a valid and binding marriage (Stone, 1990:30). At the same time it decided - after the Council of Trent (1545-1563) - in opposition to the Reformation, that a marriage could not be dissolved (Van Eupen, 1985:17).

In the Dutch Republic it became compulsory to sign a state marriage contract in 1580 (in Amsterdam in 1578), so that from that date on people could marry before the magistrates instead of or in addition to marrying in a Calvinist, Jewish or Catholic Church.

In Denmark, the Marriage Ordinance of 1582 attempted to make a church wedding "a condition of valid marriage, but despite the peasantry continued for a couple of hundred years to marry according to the ancient custom of betrothal followed by intercourse. Not until 1799 did a church wedding become the only recognized form of marriage." (Dahlsgård, 1980:23,24).

In Great Britain, the Anglican Church did not recognize the Catholic sacrament of marriage, although both the laity and the clergy came increasingly to regard the church wedding as the key ceremony. However, the civil lawyers continued to recognize espousals before witnesses as constituting marriage, until in 1753 Lord Hardwicke's Marriage Act was passed, declaring that only the church wedding was legally binding and that no marriage of persons under twenty-one was valid without the consent of parents or guardians (Stone, 1990:32).

In Germany in 1576, in Rhineland, a secular wedding ceremony was introduced side by side with the religious one because, according to Luther, the registration of marriage was a worldly matter (Van Eupen, 1985:33). The Lutheran faith was introduced in Sweden shortly after the posting of Luther's 95 Theses in 1517 by King Gustav Wasa (1523 - 1560), who became head of the church in Sweden in 1527 (Åberg, 1988:162).

In seventeenth-century France, marriage was regarded essentially as a family concern, not that of two private individuals. The woman's right of choice was very limited; marriages took place not out of consideration for the contracting party, but for the honour and advantage of families. In selecting a prospective partner, negotiators rarely allowed considerations of sentiment: "*peu de mariages succèdent bien, qui sont commencés et acheminés par les beautés et désirs amoureux*"[18] (Gibson, 1989:43). The time taken to bargain for a marriage partner varied from a matter of years to one of minutes. Enlightened thinkers tried to open the eyes of the French to the absurdity of their customs by making pointed comparisons between these and Dutch conventions, which allowed a girl to become well acquainted with her future husband (Gibson, 1989:57).

Among the middle classes, marriage patterns in all the Western and Northern European countries developed along quite similar lines. At least after 1600[19], marriage age was high and a large percentage of adults never married. The economic structure forced men to wait until they owned a farm or business before they could start a family.
Marriage obliged wife and husband to stay together until one of them died. Marriage assumed a life of security, comfort, the provision of stability, mutual assistance, and the nurture and care of children. For women it was the only way to obtain respectable status and a decent living. Single women were treated with contempt. There was hardly any escape from an unsatisfactory marriage. Marriage was based on constraints for both men and women, but for women, and certainly for mothers, the constraints were greater. It nearly always meant the denial of any alternative means of obtaining money, and it meant subordination to their husbands. The different roles of men and women were for centuries accepted as inevitable. Until at least the nineteenth century, only a tiny minority of women and men attacked the idea that the natural destiny of a woman was to be a mother and a housewife or thought that assigning women to domestic functions based entirely on their sex might be unjust or inefficient and unnecessarily constrictive (see also Bergmann, 1986:7).

In general, until the twentieth century, women were prohibited or

---

18 "few marriages turn out well when they start and progress on the basis of physical charms and amorous desires".

19 According to Verduin (1989:5), these marriage patterns can be traced back to the Middle Ages.

discouraged from learning or practicing a profession. These ideas and the marriage patterns that went with them began gradually to change in the second half of the nineteenth century (see chapters 7 and 9). The geographic diversity in household size and composition and the prevalescence of the nuclear, affective family in the seventeenth and eighteenth century will be discussed in chapter 7.

3.3.4 Marriage in the Netherlands

The greater freedom enjoyed by women in the Netherlands as compared to French women has been already mentioned. "*En France où l'on se marie quasi toujours par intérêt, les personnes sont peu examinées et souvent la sûreté des conventions précède la simple curiosité de se voir. ... Quelle belle qu'elle puisse être, ... nous nous engageons indifféremment au mariage, dans un dessein tout formé de nous consoler ailleurs d'un domestique lassant et d'une societé ennuyeuse. En Hollande, où l'on se livre de bonne foi et où la délicatesse de ces réserves est peu entendue, on croit ne pouvoir jamais assez connaître ce qu'on veut toujours aimer.*"[20] (Saint-Evremond (1610-1703) quoted by Gibson, 1989:48).

"Women as a whole and particularly women of rank - whether in religious orders or not - led much freer lives in the Low Countries. This was something on which travellers commented including the fact that women here participated equally in conversation and argument with men" (Frazer, 1984:139).

In 1709 Joseph Shaw wondered why Dutch women seemed both more moral and happier than those in England, and attributed this to their "being better provided for by laws of their country than in other nations (so that they) are not forced to trust to their wits, nor put on those pitiful shifts to jilt mankind and bubble their husbands for money," (Shaw, quoted by Schama, 1988:404).

Some of the legal provisions that enabled women to inherit and bequeath property in their own right had survived from the Middle Ages. Since then, the Humanist and Protestant ethos seems, in the Netherlands as in Germany and the Scandinavian countries, to coincide with their more generous treatment. Dutch women could and did have recourse to legal process, for example to reclaim their share of the marital estate in cases of abuse by the husband or on his death. Unmarried pregnant women could sue the putative father, either to oblige him to marry or, if he was

---

[20] "In France, where marriage almost always takes place out of self-interest, the individuals are rarely considered, and the settling of the formalities often precedes simple curiosity to see one another. ... However beautiful she may be, ... we enter upon matrimony with indifference, fully intent on consoling ourselves elsewhere for a tedious home life and wearisome company. In Holland, where people surrender their freedom in good faith and where the finesse of these reservations is scarcely understood, they think that you can never know enough about that which you want to love forever."

married already, to provide a dowry, costs for the delivery of the child and in some cases funds for its regular maintenance (Schama, 1988:404-405). In Leyden between 1671 and 1795, fifty-seven women won their cases, as against twenty-one who lost (Schama, 1988:405-406). "Women could also make commercial contracts and notarized documents and so had all the formal qualifications needed for active commercial or business dealing, an opportunity of which many availed themselves.... Widows, in particular, especially in the great trading families..., were renowned for their astute handling of the family property. But further down the social scale - at the level of shopkeepers, for example - it was not uncommon for wives to handle business and money affairs during marriage.... In 1742 when a general tax assessment was made, fifteen per cent of all taxable enterprises in Amsterdam and twenty-four per cent in Leiden were those of women. But it also seems that these incomes were those of widows rather than married women trading on their own." (Schama, 1988:407).

These rights were abolished after the French conquered the Netherlands in 1811 and most of them were never restored. As will be described in chapter 9 (about legislation concerning women), the restoration of some of these rights or the introduction of new rights took place relatively late compared to the other countries. For example, in the Netherlands married women acquired the right of full legal capacity only in 1957. Until then, therefore, married women in the Netherlands could not sign labor contracts without their husbands permission (see also chapter 9).

The dominance of the family household as early as the Golden Age had important consequences for women's roles, resulting in some remarkable differences between Dutch women and women in the surrounding countries.

As the guardians of the household, mothers were responsible for the care of their children. This was in contrast with the situation in England and France, for example, where upper-class mothers did not look after their own children but sent them first to wet-nurses[21] and afterwards, from the seventeenth century onwards, to boarding schools. The latter hardly existed in the Low Countries (nor in Denmark, Germany and Sweden).

In the Low Countries as elsewhere, good education for a woman was a matter of individual luck: especially in a (rich) family of brothers she might enjoy the services of their tutor. Because of the dominance of the wealthy bourgois family this may have been relatively more often the case for Dutch women than for women in other countries. Illiteracy was lower as well (the marriage registration records of Amsterdam indicate

[21] The word was introduced in 1620, before that the general term 'nurse' was used. The consequence of this social usage was that richer women enjoyed a higher rate of fertility than their poorer sisters, unaware of the protective value of lactation as the most natural form of contraception (Frazer, 1984:85-87).

this, Van Zanden, 1991:57), compared to England[22] where most women were illiterate. In London around 1600, illiteracy among women was 90 per cent and in East Anglia practically 100 per cent (Frazer, 1984:143).

The greater freedom enjoyed by Dutch women may have been closely connected to the Calvinist marriage doctrine. In Catholic marriage doctrine, the emphasis is on reproduction. *Generatio et educatio proles* - to procreate and educate offspring, progeny - is the first goal of marriage. Mutual faithfulness, loyalty, comes next and the third goal is to regulate passion. Two starting-points formed the basis of that marriage doctrine. In imitation of Greek (Plato, Aristotle), early Christian (Augustine) and medieval (Thomas van Aquinus) philosophers, Catholic theologians drew a sharp distinction between body and mind. Natural processes must not be disturbed by human interference.

In contrast, Calvinist marriage doctrine does not consider marriage as a sacrament: mutual assistance is (was) the most important element; procreation comes (came) second. Procreation is a consequence of, not a reason for marriage. To the Calvinist mind, nature represents sin, therefore nature can never be normative. One of the other differences between Catholics and Calvinists was that among Catholics celibacy had a higher status than marriage, so marriage had a conversely less negative image among Protestants. "Marriage was companionship...At the core of the marriage bond was affection, tenderhearted sentiment, love. Humanists had long held this to be so... Calvinist teaching, at least in Holland, did not at all subordinate love to obedience but rather exalted it as the indispensable quality for a godly union." (Schama, 1988:421). The inferiority of women, subjected to the "*droit divin et humain*" (the divin and human rights) of their husbands, as expressed by the sixteenth century Catholic Benedicti, was absent in Calvinism (Haks, 1985:10).

In short, the relatively favorable economic features of Dutch society in the seventeenth century, such as an important trade sector and high productivity in other sectors, combined with Calvinism, may have coincided with a rather different position for women, compared with that of women in the other countries.

The dominance of the family household, in which married women especially played a central role and in which they were valued as partners or business partners and prized as mothers, came to shape preferred behavior much earlier in the Netherlands than in other countries. All women were expected to be married, to be good housewives, taking care of the cooking, laundry and cleaning (either themselves or supervising servants), and caring mothers, while men grew up expecting to earn the money for the whole household. Married women were not supposed to do any market work. The husband's income or occupation and the wife's

---

[22] In England the existing prejudice against education for girls, and especially its dreaded end- product, the learned woman, derived new impetus after 1603 from the sovereign James I: "To make women learned and foxes tame has the same effect: to make them more cunning". He even forbade his daughter Elisabeth to learn Latin (Frazer, 1984:135).

qualities as a housekeeper determined the status of both. The relative wealth of the Dutch Republic may have guaranteed that many married couples could live up to this ideal. However, despite the relative social liberty, social and economic freedom for women was still limited: only widows enjoyed both to any great extent.

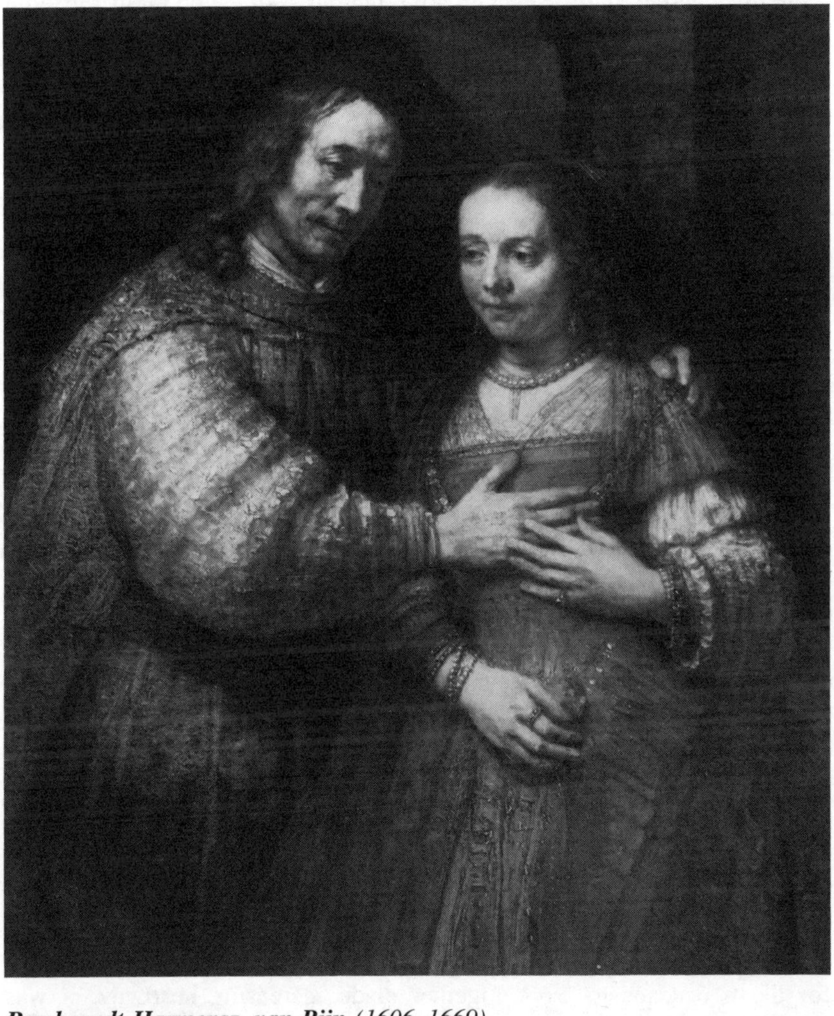

***Rembrandt Harmensz. van Rijn** (1606–1669)*
The Jewish Bride (year unknown)
Rijksmuseum, Amsterdam

3.4 Between the Golden Age and Industrialization

3.4.1 The Netherlands in the eighteenth century

From the 1680s onward, and most especially in the early eighteenth century, the Dutch urban economy experienced a relatively profound economic decline. Industries with a putting out system and industries with a demand for cheap labor were moved from the towns in Holland to the sandy rural areas, textile industries even as early as 1640 (Noordegraaf, 1992:15). Dutch towns lost their function as staple markets for Baltic grain and raw materials, and England assumed the leading role in international trade. The aggregate demand for labor declined markedly over the seventy years after about 1675. Wage rates remained high and remarkably stable until the third quarter of the nineteenth century, making the country less competitive within Europe. Adjustment to the decline in demand for labor probably took the form of population decline, particularly in the industrial cities (Leyden, Delft and Haarlem) and the economically important North-Holland peninsula (De Vries, 1977:49). Household size became unusually small. Another adjustment may have taken the form of decreasing female wages during economic depressions. The remarkable nominal wage stability seems only to have existed for (skilled) male wages, not for female and unskilled male labor (Noordegraaf, 1980:17), indicating a relative deterioration of women's economic position relative to men's in the eighteenth century in the Low Countries. Only the agricultural sector developed favorable at the end of the eighteenth century (Noordegraaf, 1981:361).

3.4.2 Europe in the eighteenth century

The dominant conclusion of historians (Clark, Frazer, Howell and Wiesner) and sociologists (Sullerot and Verwey-Jonker) is that, all over Europe between the seventeenth century and the French Revolution, the position of women and the associated potential for female labor gradually deteriorated. In France and England, increasing numbers of occupations were barred to women, despite heavy resistance from the women themselves (Sullerot, 1969:65). Apparently, the view that it was not decent for the two sexes to work together made increasing headway. It was openly declared to be indecent, improper, scandalous, shameful and disgraceful for a woman to have to perform paid work: it degraded the woman herself, the men in her family and those who worked with her (Sullerot, 1969:66).

During the eighteenth century, this ideology found acceptance all over Europe. Besides, from the eighteenth century on, more attention was paid to the ideal of the family and the importance of a good upbringing for children. Factors influencing this tendency included not only the need for educated and disciplined laborers to work in the new industries, but also the ideas of the Enlightenment then being disseminated throughout Europe. The early romantic ideas on education advanced by Rousseau (and publicized in the Netherlands by Betje Wolff and others) had an even greater influence. Rousseau's emphasis on the natural development of the individual and his or her emotional relationships led to a more responsible and demanding role for women as mothers. The more important the education of children, the more important the role of the mother within the family[23].

The increasing emphasis on bourgois family ideals may, on the other hand, have had something to do with the general economic decline. Women may have had to supplement family income in increasing numbers. It could have been that people were saying and writing that women should not perform market work because more of them were in fact doing so.

3.4.3 The Netherlands in the nineteenth century

Although there are indications that in the early Dutch society of the Golden Age women could be seen for what they were rather than for how they ought to be (Schama, 1988:412), by the nineteenth century there was certainly a strong tendency to consider women mainly as wives and mothers. In the Netherlands, as in the rest of Europe, this was reflected and thereby established in the key legislation of the period.

The French army marched into the Low Countries in 1795, and in 1810 the Netherlands became an integral part of Napoleon's empire. Starting on 1 January 1811, the French administrative regulations were imposed and five codes of law introduced, among them the Code Civil and Code Pénal. These codes remained in force even after the French defeat in 1813. Although the new system of statutory instruments put an end to the arbitrary power of local administrations, for women their introduction meant the loss of certain rights, such as the 'promise of marriage'. This was the right for a pregnant woman right to force the putative father either to abide by his promise to marry her or to pay compensation. This practice also existed in Denmark and Sweden. It gave

---

[23] The same ideology of family and motherhood, comparable developments and a similar decline in the economic and professional status of women is described by Goldin as occurring in the early American republic: "The thesis that women's status deteriorated from a "golden age" in America is best stated by Lerner: "The period 1800-1840 is one in which decisive changes occurred in the status of American women...women were by tacit consensus excluded from the new democracy. Indeed their actual situation had in many respects deteriorated.... Women's work outside the home no longer met with social approval...many business and professional occupations formerly open to women were now closed...The entry of large numbers of women into low status...industrial work had fixed such work by definition as 'women's work'"(1969:5,7)." (Goldin, 1990:237).

women valuable protection, especially in rural areas where it was generally accepted that marriage did not occur until a baby was expected and the woman thus proved fertile.

A new Code Civil was introduced in 1838. Its main provisions were structured around the male individual, who was assumed to be an enlightened property-owner and the head of the family (Sevenhuijsen, 1987:19). Women as active legal agents and citizens were largely absent. Under the new code, married women could not possess property or have an income and they had no legal authority to take decisions, even about the education and upbringing of their children or the disposal of the household budget. The code gave the father almost absolute power, unlimited by any government restrictions. Inheritance and the transmission of property, skills, identity and family tradition were the main characteristics of fatherhood in this old-liberal paradigm, also voiced by John Locke and Thomas Hobbes (Sevenhuijsen, 1987:351). "Unwed mothers were portrayed as cunning and seductive women hunting the family capital of innocent young men. Law had the function of protecting the interests of the family against their lures and lies." (Sevenhuijsen, 1987:351).

The conclusion generally accepted is that, as a result, the socio-economic position of women was even more heavily dominated by the position of fathers, brothers or husbands than before and that it was certainly not determined by women's own position in the labor market or by their market work.

3.4.4 Developments in Europe

The French administrative regulations were likewise imposed in the other European countries except England although the timing of their replacement by other laws proved to be different (see chapter 9).

Most work done by women at this time was more or less associated with the private sphere of the individual household. It is difficult to quantify how many women were restricted and barred from other work.

Moreover, it seems paradoxical that exclusive dedication to the role of wife and mother, widely accepted in all reports written in the nineteenth century as the only proper and fulfilling ones for a woman (Leydesdorff, 1977:17), was in fact an option withheld from many women by the relative shortage of men and relatively low household incomes. Many women never married at all, or if they did so were forced by poverty to work outside the home or to earn money at home by taking in boarders or doing piece work. Especially in the period around 1850, many women in Europe were unable to marry because of the relative shortage of men. This was simultaneously damaging the position of women, because these single women were seen as a threat to marital morals as well as increasing women's economic opportunities (see also chapters 7 and 8).

3.5 Industrialization

3.5.1 The cotton and textile industries

As industry developed, more capital was needed to become a master craftsman and it became usual to spend a period as a journeyman. This eventually became compulsory. The more enterprising masters started to avoid the lengthy procedure of training apprentices by hiring journeymen. A new class of permanent wage earners came into existence, a class socially inferior to the masters who gave orders and who owned the tools of production. The distinction between employers and permanent wage-earners became ever more marked, heralding the breakdown of the guild system. By the beginning of the nineteenth century almost all the guilds had disappeared.

In most European countries during the eighteenth and early part of the nineteenth century, some employers were trying to find ways to free themselves of the restrictions imposed by the guilds. They turned to small towns and villages where there were no guilds and where costs were lower. Peasants were provided with looms or spinning-wheels and paid piece rates for the finished product. This system was well-suited to the textile industry, whose processes were familiar and not as difficult to learn as other crafts.

Demographic expansion in poor agricultural areas caused a surplus of labor and the need for complementary earnings in the form of cottage industries. This *proto-industrialization* (Mendels, 1972, quoted by Vanderpijpen, 1990:123) was visible in all the poor and socially deprived (agricultural) areas, but not in productive agricultural areas such as Holland and the coastal polders in Belgium. Moreover, processes of separating primary and supplementary activities on farms, such as combinations of spinning and farming, or occupational combinations as skipper and peasant, were already signalled in the Dutch Republic during the Golden Age. Industries with a putting out system and industries with a demand for cheap labor were moved from the towns in Holland to the sandy rural areas, textile industries even as early as 1640 (Noordegraaf, 1992:15). By 1670, classic domestic crafts such as spinning had already completely disappeared from the rural areas in Holland (not in the other parts of the Republic), (Van Zanden, 1991:52) and these activities were not introduced again in later centuries.

Britain was the first nation to industrialize. The cotton textile mill was the early symbol of industrialization and the initial focus of the transformation of the domestic into the industrial mode. Family labor was replaced by labor in the mills, by men, women and children. In the early eighteenth century, fewer and fewer farmers were able to support themselves. The enclosure of large areas of land and the gradual dispossession of thousands of small farmers reduced the members of these families to the status of day-laborers or cottage industry workers. "By

1750 land ownership was concentrated in the hands of a limited class of very large landlords, at the expense both of the lesser gentry and the peasants" (Tilly and Scott, 1987:14). These *enclosures* probably forced the inhabitants of small farms to seek a living in workshops or factories in the cities. The plentiful supply of cheap labor - male as well as female - acted as a stimulus to the industrial production of goods to meet growing demand in expanding world markets in Britain, nearly 75 years before Germany, almost 50 years before France and at least a century earlier than in the Netherlands.

By 1763, England had emerged as the victor in a worldwide struggle for possession of the colonies. England's own large supplies of iron and coal and the colonial empire which furnished her with a wide variety of raw materials facilitated the transition to new methods of production, substituting mechanical means of manufacture, transport and communication for their manual equivalents: in short, industrialization. England also largely escaped the convulsions of the French Revolution and the Napoleonic era. All these factors working in concert made England at the dawn of the nineteenth century an important source of supply of manufactured goods. This was despite the fact that British growth before 1815 had been very modest: roughly 0.3 per cent annual growth in per capita income (Williamson, 1990:30). The flight of Dutch capital to England[24] after the French invasion may have been one of the causes of the acceleration in British industry, at the same time aggravating the already serious situation of the Dutch economy.

In continental Europe, the traditional textile centers of Flanders were the first to industrialize. The first textile factory workers were prisoners in Brussels in 1764 (Lis and Soly, 1990:138). To combat increasing pauperism, magistrates worked in close cooperation with textile employers to force proletarians and their children to work in the textile factories, which were rapidly expanding between 1766 and 1780 in Flanders (Lis and Soly, 1990:139,140). A similar close connection between poor aid (and children's homes[25]) and the first factories has also been identified in Sweden (Olsson, 1980).

---

24 "Although we cannot be sure how much capital was transferred from the Netherlands to Britain, the scope of the activities of Continental Bankers in London during the Wars suggests that it might have been quite large. Neal shows that of the foreign holders of British debt sequestered by the Bank of England - an unknown proportion of total holdings - the Dutch held 60.3 % in 1801 and 57.8 % in 1806." (Buyst and Mokyr, 1990:67).

25 In Flanders the orphanages were called *maisons des pauvres* (houses of the poor). In England places where relief was provided for the poor were called 'workhouses'.

3.5.2 Conversion of home-based industries into mechanized and heavy industrial production

The early cotton textile mills in England used water power and the kinetic energy supplied by women and children. Gradually mechanization and steam power took over the simple tasks previously performed by women and children (see also chapter 6). In Belgium, the peak of the process of industrialization is often placed during the French period (1794 - 1814). Although this is largely true for Ghent cotton and Verviers wool, it was the years between 1820 and 1830 which were of decisive importance for the coal and iron industries (Hepple, 1986:13). In France there was an importation of British technology up to 1790, then a slowing down during the French Revolution and Napoleonic Period, with a gradual resumption of industrialization from 1815 to 1850, and a spread after 1850 (Hepple, 1986a:13).

In most countries from 1850 to 1870 onwards there were marked changes in the production of goods generally, largely as a result of technological progress. In England, France and Flanders, the spinning and weaving machines of Vaucauson, perfected by Cartwright, spelt the end of the home-based industry, resulting in increased output and substantial savings to manufacturers.

Although France's economy was to remain predominantly agricultural throughout the nineteenth century, by the 1850s there were cotton textile factories in the cities of Mulhouse, Lille, Roubaix, and Tourcoing as well as in Normandy and Picardy. Germany quickly followed. "It is a matter of debate whether the German Industrial Revolution began around 1833, with the formation of the *Zollverein* (customs union) or between 1842 and 1843, a period of heavy growth or only after 1850" Hepple, 1986a:13). However, by the mid-1870s Germany had undoubtly emerged from relative backwardness to become a strong industrial nation. But the pace of change was uneven: some regions like Saxony had been industrialized before 1850, while others like East Prussia continued to be dominated by the agricultural estates of the landowners (Hepple, 1986a:14).

During the second half of the nineteenth century, however, iron and steel production and the manufacture of machinery and heavy equipment became more important. Sweden, being very poor in the nineteenth century, had iron and coal but could not afford to build railways until English capital financed them in the 1870s. Iron and steel production and the manufacture of machinery and heavy equipment employed almost exclusively male workers.

The Netherlands industrialized late (see next subsection) as did Denmark[26] and Sweden, although Sweden did so earlier and Denmark

---

26 Denmark used to be a primitive country with a subsistence economy and a very low standard of living. Rigid distinctions between town and country were a contributory factor. In 1733, for example, rural inhabitants aged between 14 and

later than the Netherlands. In Denmark it may have been the high productivity of the agricultural land (as in the Northern part of the Netherlands) which prevented industrialization, taking off in effect after 1900 during the *Second Stage of Industrialization*, characterized by electrical power, petroleum fuel, the internal combustion engine, motorcars and science-based chemical (synthetic) manufacture (Hepple, 1986a:14). Up to World War II, however, Danish industry remained predominantly of the small handicraft type (see also chapter 4).

One of the consequences of industrialization generally accepted was that many (cottage industry) tasks traditionally performed within households, such as spinning, weaving, candlemaking and brewing, were transferred from the home or farm to the factory. There was an increasing demarcation between paid market work and unpaid household work. Female family work, performed as part of the family unit, was converted into work with individualized, separate earnings. Another consequence was that it became more and more difficult to combine motherhood and child care with (paid) productive labor. Some historians have seen the transformation of tasks originally performed in the home and on the farm as the end of a '*golden age*' in which women participated fully in 'productive activities' (Clark, 1982). However, what is good and what is bad? Did industrialization really destroy domestic industry and the balance between motherhood, domestic work and market labor (as argued, among others, by Clark in 1919 and Wichmann in 1917) or did it in fact represent an advance for women, providing the male breadwinner with a family wage and opening up a variety of jobs for single women, affording them new opportunities and status (Pinchbeck, 1930)? The first proposition is challenged by the considerable number of women who continued working as outworkers, homeworkers or remained involved in family-based work well into the twentieth century (see chapter 4), while the second is less easy refuted. Improving standards of living for many women offered them various forms of freedom and choice, simultaneously engendering a division of labor which trapped them in a limited range of socially acceptable roles and activities (Bradley, 1989:42). The fear that mothers performing factory labor would neglect the care of children and household tasks certainly was a factor reinforcing the ideology of the male breadwinner as head of the household served by a full-time female homemaker.

As far as the consequences of industrialization for labor force participation of females and males can be quantified (which will be only feasible after around 1850), they will be analysed in chapter 4. As with the other controversies, the outcome depends on particular circumstances

---

36 were forbidden by law to leave the estates on which they were born. This was intended to prevent emigration in years of depression. The measure was relaxed in 1788. By contrast, town-dwellers enjoyed special privileges and an almost absolute monopoly of the production and sale of goods (Andersen, 1977:122).

and the interpretations of the changes, with what is considered 'better' and what 'worse' a subjective matter. Today's interpretations certainly differ from those in the early twentieth century. Considering the low percentage of women, particularly married women working in industry the statements about separating motherhood and productive labor at home certainly have to be doubted for the Netherlands (see also chapters 4 and 8).

3.5.3 Industrialization in the Netherlands

The small open commercial economy of the Netherlands, whose prosperity was built on international trade and freedom of navigation, suffered more than those of the other countries from the French and Napoleonic wars. As the French troops crossed the River Waal in 1795, the Batavian Republic was proclaimed. In the peace treaty that followed (in May 1795), the Batavian Republic had to pay an indemnity of 100 million guilders, to grant a huge loan at a symbolic rate of interest and to maintain a French army of 25,000 men. "Even more important was the disruptive effect of economic warfare on Dutch trade. ... Britain conquered the Dutch possessions overseas and definitively took over the lead in colonial trade. In this respect, the liquidation of the Dutch East India Company (founded in 1601) in 1800 marked the end of an era" (Buyst and Mokyr, 1990:66).

All industrial activities were severely affected by the Wars in the Netherlands. Salt, distilleries, shipbuilding, sugar and tobacco declined due to the dislocations of the Wars. "Fisheries came to an almost complete stop because of the Wars, the notable exception being the year 1802, the year of the shortlived peace of Amiens." (Buyst and Mokyr, 1990:67). "The vulnerability of a small open economy to war became all too clear. It took a number of different forms, all with the same consequence: the loss of markets, the loss of sources of raw materials, and the loss of access to the sea itself (e.g. for fishing). Each of these blows involved further damage to the industries which supplied it or bought from it. Of the seven shipyards in the Zaan area still operating in 1780, only one was active in 1808. The velvet industry in the town of Naarden was completely closed down. The potash and tobacco industries had to curtail sharply their activity due to the scarcity of raw materials. The Leyden cloth industry, the Amsterdam sugarmills, and even the pipemakers of Gouda suffered disastrous declines in output and employment. ... The many technological breakthroughs that took place in the Belgian departments of the French Empire and other areas on the Continent passed the Netherlands by. The net result of the crisis was a severe impoverishment of the population, especially of the urban regions in the Western provinces of Holland. ... Among the working classes, unemployment and declining real wages led to an increasing pauperism." (Buyst and Mokyr, 1990:69). The period of poverty, stagnation and unemployment among the lower classes was followed by a very gradual growth of industrialization from the mid-century onwards, which gathered momentum after 1895.

According to Leo Noordegraaf, these statements are too strong because - in contrast to the stagnation and decline in the other sectors - agriculture developed favorably. However, developments differed geographically as well as chronologically, and the poverty should not be overestimated in comparison with other periods and foreign countries (Noordegraaf, 1981:383). The relative prosperity of the Netherlands, built up during the seventeenth century when the Dutch Republic was a leading world power and founded on international trade and transport and the related processing industries and services, persisted even after Britain had become the dominant naval power. Despite the impoverishment after the French occupation and the failure of the union with Belgium, the Netherlands was still one of the richest countries in the world (Maddison, 1982), although Amsterdam had definitely lost its position as Europe's entrepôt market and the old traffic industries had lost their past glories. Colonial trade, rapidly expanding in the eighteenth century, was the main force behind the recovery of Dutch international commerce (Buyst and Mokyr, 1990:74).

However, the industrialization of the surrounding countries brought a further rapid decline in the importance of Dutch ports for the distribution and storage of foreign products, a decline which had already started during the French wars. The production costs of many products were lower in the industrialized countries and over-land transport improved rapidly in the rest of Europe.

Despite the decline in the position of the ports, it is a remarkable fact that average income (Gross National Product per head of population) remained high in comparison with the rest of Europe (except the United Kingdom, where GNP was also high) during the whole of the nineteenth and the early twentieth century. This high income was due not only to profits from foreign investment and the colonies, but also to the proceeds of the agricultural, trade and service sectors (De Hen, 1985:5).

As mentioned above, the Netherlands industrialized late, decades after most of the other countries which today still make up the main industrial area of Western Europe. Why the Netherlands, situated geographically at the heart of industrialization, lagged so far behind is a mystery which has puzzled generations of economic historians (De Hen, 1985). It is argued that the main obstacles to industrialization were the lack of iron and coal and the absence of infrastructure, except in terms of waterways (Verduin, 1989). It was not until 1880 that a network of cross-country roads and the first railroads were built. It is also argued that after about 1870 economic growth was spurred by the industrial boom in the German Ruhr area (Hepple, 1986a:12). Besides the economic circumstances influencing the late industrialization, and possibly interacting with them, Noordegraaf (1990:33) mentions certain psychological factors (such as lack of entrepreneurial spirit) which might have interacted with the economic factors. Another possible hypothesis is that it was the relative prosperity of the country, especially that of the cities and of the relatively productive northern and south-western agricultural areas, that prevented early industrialization. It was only in the poorer agricultural areas, mainly in '*Brabant*' and the '*Achterhoek*' the areas close to the German and Belgian borders that cottage industries gained a foothold and textile factories were founded. This factory labor replaced the family labor in cottage industries. In Tilburg in 1812, 76 per cent of all laborers in the wool industry were working at home as outworkers, while the remainder were employed in finishing the cloth in separate premises (Noordegraaf, 1981:364). In 1847, however, 90% of the weavers in Twente were still working at home (Schilstra, 1976:33) assisted by their wives and children. These cottage industries were later to supply the labor for the factories, a development similar to that in England, Belgium, Germany and France.

The Netherlands industrialized at a time when steam engines had already replaced the water mills and the early stage of industrialization had passed. Even the second stage of industrialization, with its emphasis on coal, iron and steam, had already been overtaken by new developments by the time the new Dutch infrastructure developed after 1880 could profit from it. However, by the turn of the twentieth century, circumstances in the Netherlands favoured the introduction of the new products important in the next stage of industrialization: crude oil, electricity, the combustion engine, electrical apparatus etc. Dutch internationals like Shell (the Bataafsche Petroleum Maatschappij), Unilever, Philips and AKU (part of what is now AKZO) were all founded during this period. Like the second-stage industries, these newer industries employed almost exclusively male workers.

3.6 Conclusions to chapter 3

The early centuries of the millenium saw a gradual growth in the differentiation and specialization of labor. This found clear expression in the guilds, which came into existence in the thirteenth century. In general women did participate in the guilds, but at a secondary level. Besides the work represented by the guilds, women early bore their share in the production of luxuries, agricultural products, in trade and in domestic work in other people's households.

Women probably never enjoyed an important economic role, either in the Middle Ages or thereafter. The majority of women performed work which was regarded as of lower status than that of men and which, if remunerated at all, was less well paid than men's work.

During the Middle Ages, Holland remained in general relatively underdeveloped and mainly agricultural. However, the feudal system current in the surrounding countries was largely absent here. It is uncertain whether the economic circumstances of Dutch women prior to the Dutch Golden Age were any different from those of women in the rest of Europe. If women functioned in the market at all, for example in guilds, they did so at the margin of the old cloth industry, and that is also why there were so few regulations covering the work they did. This sexual division of labor seems not to have differed in the Low Countries from that in the rest of Europe: it seemed self-evident and was generally respected.

During the Golden Age, it seems likely that life in the Dutch Republic centered on the family household rather than around the aura of a dynasty or the historic privileges of a city commune. The fragmentation of cultural norms which existed in societies composed of a number of very distinct status groups and classes was largely absent in the Dutch Republic. The cultural norms of the bourgeois family contributed to a development that made the Netherlands unique in comparison to the surrounding countries.

The bourgois family model, while bestowing a higher status on women working in their own households, was based on the same asymmetric gender roles as existed in the labor market. During the Golden Age, Dutch women could make commercial contracts and notarized documents and had the formal qualifications needed for active commercial or business dealing. Widows, in particular, used these qualifications. The relative freedom of Dutch women may have been closely connected with the Calvinist doctrine of marriage.

French administrative regulations were imposed in 1811 and remained in force after the French defeat in 1813. For Dutch women, their introduction meant the loss of certain rights. As a result, their socio-economic position became even more heavily dominated by the position of fathers, brothers or husbands. It was certainly not determined by women's own position in the labor market or by their market work.

As industry developed, the distinction between employers and permanent wage-earners became more marked. In most countries the rise of cottage industries in small towns and villages heralded the breakdown of the guild system. This process paved the way for the start of the industrialization: the transformation from mainly manual labor to mechanical methods of production, transportation and communication. Industrialization started relatively late in Sweden, the Netherlands and Denmark, and relatively early in England and Belgium. Everywhere, tasks originally performed in the home and on the farm, such as spinning, weaving, candlemaking and brewing, were transferred to the factory. A generally accepted conclusion is that these changes made it increasingly difficult to combine motherhood with productive labor outside the home. The industrial transformation created the image of a previous 'golden age' in which women had participated fully in productive activities. This picture seems certainly to be idealized. Without clear criteria by which to evaluate women's economic position and without well defined measurements of the changes that occurred, however, all statements will remain vague. In Holland (and probably in some other prosperous agricultural parts of the Dutch Republic), cottage industries had already disappeared by 1670. The ideal of domesticity, even for women without the 'natural' duties of wives and mothers, seems to have been fairly dominant in Holland ever since the seventeenth century. Since then most women in Holland seem to have been excluded from performing market work, except in agriculture and domestic service. This suggests that labor force participation rates of women in the Netherlands may always have been low in comparison to those in the surrounding countries, except in those parts of the country close to what are now the Belgian and German borders (with the exception of the relatively rich agricultural northern province of Groningen). However, prior to industrialization, changes in labor force participation are difficult to quantify.

Finally, it is important to give serious regard to the remark by Marshall that heads this chapter. Evaluating women's position in the past is a tricky matter, if the criteria are not clear. What we now perceive as bad, may at that time have been perceived as good, simply because norms and values differed. For this reason the focus here is on descriptions and quantifications; although these may include descriptions of historical norms and values, evaluating these past values is not the prime goal.

CHAPTER 4

WORK BY INDUSTRY

> *"Industrialization in some industries (especially the sweated trades) came to mean extensive subdivision of the labour process and men fearful of losing skilled jobs and good wages insisted on women taking the less skilled jobs. ...women were excluded by custom not merely from apprenticed trades but from practically every occupation which led to the acquisition of skill."*
>
> *Elisabeth Roberts[1], 1990:24*

In the area of market work, women (and children) have usually performed types of labor entirely abandoned to them by men. The previous chapter showed that this division was seen as more or less self-evident and generally accepted and respected despite the male domination it implied. A pattern of concentration within particular occupations has existed in all seven countries compared: Belgium, Denmark, France, Germany, the Netherlands, Sweden and the United Kingdom. However, this will not contribute much to the explanation of the low labor force participation rates in the Netherlands, nor to differences in activity rates across countries, unless the *sectoral division by occupation* or the *sectoral division by industry* varies or has varied in the past. Here, the term *occupation* describes the economic activity of an individual, whereas the term *industry* relates to the economic activity of a group of economic establishments or workplaces with common characteristics (HMSO, 1971:430,431). The expectation is that these sectoral divisions may have been different across the seven countries. For this reason, analysis in this chapter focuses on the demand side of the labor market, e.g. the sectoral composition of the labor market in terms of activities.

The chapter starts with a short introduction concerning occupational segregation (section 4.1). Subsection 4.1.1 remarks on female occupations and subsection 4.1.2 on the reliability and measurement of the two sectoral divisions mentioned. What is known and what has been measured?

The historical development of the female and male labor force in terms of sectoral composition until 1990 in the seven countries is treated in two sections: 4.2 and 4.4. Section 4.2 discusses these long-term trends in the Netherlands in more detail than the developments in the other countries: Belgium, Denmark, France, Germany, Sweden and the United Kingdom. Section 4.3 presents an historical sketch of the industrial development in the seven countries as an introduction to section 4.4 which

---

[1] Elisabeth Roberts (1990) refers here to two publications: Angela John (ed.), 1980, Unequal Opportunities: Women's Employment in England 1800-1918; and Charles More, 1980, Skill and the English Working-Class 1890-1914.

discusses the long-term trends in the labor force by industrial sector between about 1850 and 1990 in all seven countries. The end of this chapter offers some conclusions on the division by industry.

4.1 Occupational Segregation

Despite the considerable geographical variation in activities within and between the seven countries, there are many occupations where no women are found at all in the early censuses. However, with only a few exceptions such as nun, midwife and charwoman, it is very difficult to list occupations which are confined solely to women, since boys often did women's work as well.

4.1.1 Female occupations

In the nineteenth century the female labor force consisted almost entirely of domestic servants, manglers, laundresses, assisting family members or laborers in agriculture (weeding), in fishing (mending nets) and of women employed in textile industries (knitting, spinning). The poor but genteel woman had an additional choice of three occupations: governess, companion, or seamstress. All female occupations were underpaid and overcrowded. In all seven countries, a woman's only true 'natural' destiny was thought to be 'embellishing the existence of others', preferably as a wife and mother. If a single woman had to earn a living it was preferable to do so (temporarily) as a domestic servant, since domestic servants "fulfill both essentials of woman's being: they are supported by and they minister to men." (Vicinus, 1985:4).

In the nineteenth century the increasing proportion of (middle-class) women who did not marry at all (see also chapter 7), and lacked men (fathers, brothers etc.) to support them, caused what in most countries was called *the woman question.* It is difficult nowadays to believe the solutions generally suggested to this 'surplus' of women[2]. Women, in the general opinion, should certainly not be offered a viable economic alternative "lest they never marry" (Vicinus, 1985:3). However, despite the resistance to the idea, individual single women in all seven countries started to demand the right to education and to better paid and more meaningful occupations; this was *the first feminist wave,* which started

---

[2] In England in 1862, the influential journalist W.R. Greg of the Saturday Review, writing under the title "Why are Women Redundant?", proposed emigration to Canada, Australia and the United States and advised those who stayed behind to learn from upper-class courtesans, so that more men would prefer marriage to their mistresses and clubs (Vicinus, 1985:4).

around the beginning of the second half of the nineteenth century (see also chapter 9).

The occupational structure started to change, but only gradually. Around 1900, despite the creation of new jobs in the educational, health, distributive, catering and commercial sectors, women still tended to perform market work predominantly in *traditionally female sectors* such as *agriculture*, *domestic work* and *textile and clothing*. For example, in England the percentage of women workers employed as teachers, nurses, shop assistants and civil servants[3] increased enormously: from 4 per cent in 1851 to 6 per cent in 1891 and again to 10 per cent in 1911, although even the last percentage was still low compared to that of the traditional occupations at the same date (see also section 4.4). The jobs done by women remained mainly low-grade. Industries and occupations requiring craft and technical skills were dominated by men; the caring occupations and those requiring manual dexterity and simple skills (except in some crafts and in the textile industry) by women. During the early decades of the twentieth century, more and more young women moved into shop-work, office and public sector jobs. As in the unskilled occupations, however, most female clerical occupations turned out to be dead-end jobs.

In 1930, a little over 76 per cent of all women in the Dutch labor force were to be found in a mere seven professions out of the 371 occupations distinguished. These seven occupations were, in order of importance: domestic servant, agricultural worker, clerical worker, shop assistant, seamstress, primary school teacher and nurse (CBS, 1934, part VIII:80). In the same year, 70 per cent of all men in the labor market were spread over 38 occupations, with agricultural and clerical work as the dominant professions, absorbing over 14 and 7 per cent respectively (CBS, 1934:8-0). More than forty years later, the occupational situation had changed only slightly. Van Mourik, De Poel and Siegers (1983) investigated occupational segregation in 1971, 1975 and 1979. They defined an occupation as being 'male' if at least 60 per cent of the workers were men and as 'female' if at least 60 per cent were women. In 1971, 1975 and 1979, respectively 60, 58 and 57 per cent of all working women were employed in a 'female' occupation. More than a quarter had jobs in which more than 90 per cent of the workers were female and which involved activities similar to household tasks. Twenty per cent were employed in occupations such as shop assistant or secretary, typist or telex operator, and more than 50 per cent in a mere 28 occupations out of the 289 then recognized. Similar results are found in the other countries (see OECD, 1988).

Data on occupational segregation should, however, be interpreted with great caution. One reason why more male occupations are recognized than female may be that a greater number of different occupations are

---

3 These figures are based on two of the occupational categories in the 1911 census: *professional occupations and their subordinate services* (including, for example, professional entertainers and nurses) and *commercial occupations* (clerks, typists etc.) (HMSO, 1971:195).

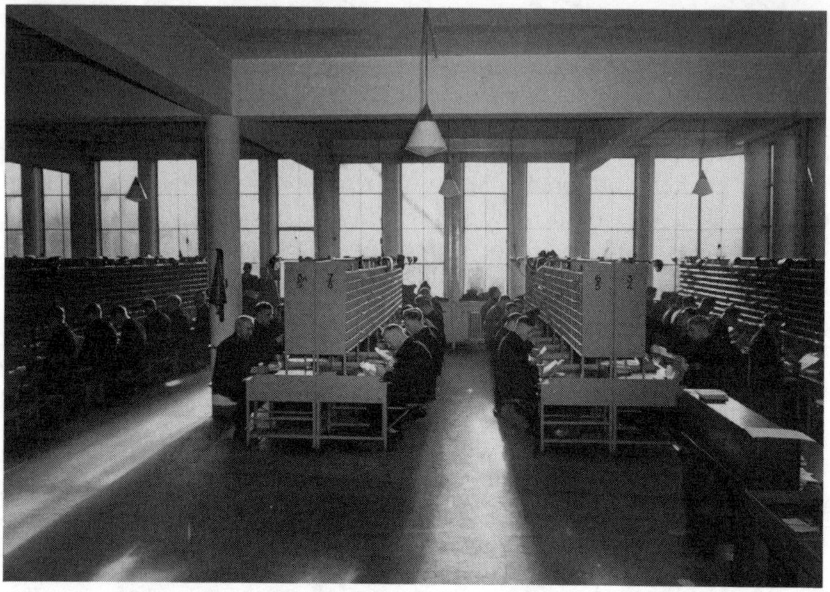

Sorting room for town-delivery in the Utrecht postal despatch office, 1940s
PTT Museum, The Hague

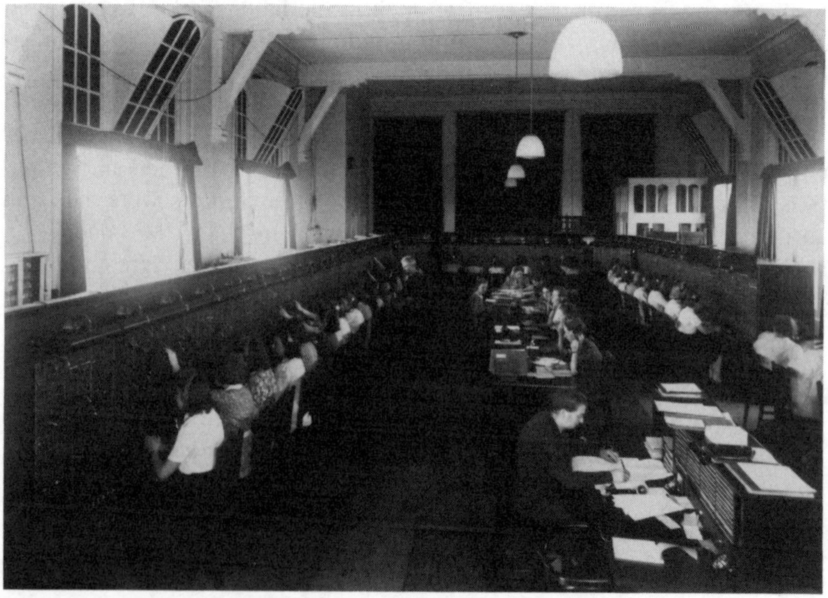

Telephone operators, 1940s
PTT Museum, The Hague

The same segregation still exists today.

recognized in the predominantly male industrial sector than in the mainly female service sector (Van Dijk and Verstegen, 1988:22). There are two reasons for this: the fact that industry was for a long time considered to be the principal sector in terms of economic development, and because the industrial sector does indeed have a high degree of specialization of labor.

The less hierarchical character of female occupations may also have something to do with the comparative scarcity of distinctions between female jobs. Finally, the identity of various female jobs may be less obvious to the - male - investigators than the identity of male jobs; this might, for example, produce a differentiation between different kinds of bricklayers but not between different categories of secretaries (Tijdens, 1990:16). This can be illustrated by the fact that in the Dutch census of 1849 typical female occupations such as 'seamstresses, knitters, manglers, platters, ironers, laundresses, charwomen and netmakers' were lumped together and largely disregarded (Schilstra, 1976:31). Similar problems are known from other countries, with census categories changing not only their names but also their functions. For example, in the census data of 1871 in England and Wales laundry workers replaced washer women. Laundry women could and did include washer women, but laundry workers in the large commercial laundries in existence by the end of the nineteenth century might perhaps be more accurately described as factory workers (Roberts, 1990:29).

Currently, around 1990, in all seven countries, women are employed principally in the *caring* professions (as nurses, teachers and welfare workers), in junior *white collar posts* (as clerks and secretaries), and in *sales and service* occupations (as cooks and cleaners) (see also OECD, 1980 and 1988).

Therefore, despite the fact that the sexual division of labor is extremely variable with a complex and varied pattern over time and across societies, there is a striking consistency in the overall pattern of women being concentrated into certain occupations. However, the emphasis in this chapter is, as mentioned above, on differences in the main trends in sectoral division, not on differences between occupations themselves, which are anyway difficult to measure and compare.

4.1.2 Reliability and measurement of the division

Most of the problems concerning the reliability and measurement of the division into sectors were found to be similar in all seven countries studied. Data on labor force participants by sectoral division are even more beset by measurement problems than are labor force data themselves. The figures vary from one publication to another! The long-term Dutch trends published by the Central Bureau of Statistics, for example, frequently differ from the original figures in the census publications. Comparing different sources - even from the same agency - in the other countries, reveals the same thing. One of the reasons for such discrepancies is the use of two different key criteria to classify the labor force into the various sectors: a *classification by occupation* (called *occupational*) and a division by *economic activity of the industry or business* involved (termed *industrial*, or *division by industry*). Confusion emerges because the same titles are used in both classifications. In one case 'service' refers to the occupation, in the other to the industry. In the latter case, all those working in establishments or workplaces relating to a particular industry are regarded as belonging to that industry, whatever their actual occupation may be. The same occupation may therefore be classified as belonging to several different industries. So long as businesses remain small, the differences between the two criteria will be slight: business or industrial activity and individual occupation will tend to coincide. In larger businesses or industries, however, the same occupation may be found in many different sectors: for instance, a secretary or cleaner employed by an industrial firm will be considered as working in industry, while under the occupational classification she will be regarded as having a service occupation.

Early comparisons between the two classifications in the Netherlands are possible only for 1909, 1920 and 1930 (Posthumus-van der Goot, 1937:87; CBS, 1934:82). In table 4.1 this is illustrated by means of a classification into five sectors.

Table 4.1 *Division of the female labor force by industrial and occupational classification in the Netherlands in 1909, 1920 and 1930 (absolute figures in thousands)*

	division by occupation			division by industry		
	1909	1920	1930	1909	1920	1930
agriculture[1]	112.2	89.7	109.3	112.3	89.7	109.3
industry[2]	111.8	135.4	148.0	114.4	148.1	169.9
trade[3]	59.9	75.5	118.6	62.2	92.6	138.4
dom. serv.[4]	215.0	236.6	268.2	205.4	211.3	234.4
other[5]	42.1	106.6	123.5	43.3	87.0	110.4
total	541.0	631.8	767.6	541.0	631.8	767.6

1 Agriculture, including horticulture and fishing.
2 Industry, including mining, construction and public utilities.
3 Trade and transport.
4 Domestic service.
5 Non-domestic services and other occupations or industries not mentioned earlier.

Sources: Posthumus-van der Goot, 1937:87 and 1938:145

In the industrial division as compared with the occupational classification of the female labor force, relatively more women are found in industry, trade and transport - and in 1909 also in non-domestic services (though this is because the other occupations are added to this sector) - and relatively fewer in domestic service.

Every census involves the use of different classifications as changes and modifications are introduced in the light of previous experience. In the Netherlands, the first occupational classification was made in 1849, incidental to the population census of that year. According to Schilstra, the figures for women are completely useless for purposes such as illustrating changes between agriculture and industry (Schilstra, 1976:5). What is known from other labor counts is carefully documented (see Schilstra, 1976) but the information is not very exact or complete.

Further occupational counts were held in 1859 and 1889, but each used a completely different system of classification (CBS, 1966, part 10:7; Van Dijk and Verstegen, 1988:22-23). In 1899 another, but again purely occupational, classification was devised. In 1869 no questions were asked about occupation, and in 1879 only to verify the answers to other questions (Schilstra, 1976:31).

Although the Dutch censuses of 1909, 1920 and 1930 employed both the occupational and the industrial critera to determine sectoral composition, the 1947 census, by contrast, employed only the industrial criterion and this continued to be the only one used in the two subsequent censuses. In other countries similar problems are found up until the 1960s.

In general in the trends presented below, where two divisions were available (and/or if it was indicated which division), the sectoral division by industry has been used to calculate the figures presented. The main reason is that in the Netherlands only this division was available for all censuses. In the early censuses in most countries, however, only one division was made, and that was frequently the occupational one. The figures are therefore not strictly comparable between one country and another. Moreover, in some countries the classification by industry or occupation excludes certain occupations or industries or certain service groups, such as the liberal professions. Where there are differences in definitions or in tabulation practice, details of the actual composition of the broad groups if available and relevant are mentioned in the footnotes to the tables presented.

The trends the figures reveal are of interest, but great caution should be exercised in interpreting the statistics presented in this chapter and care should be taken not to attach too much value to the absolute numerical data. However, some consistency may be expected in two succeeding censuses within the same country, especially because a high aggregate level of between three and six sectors will be used in this chapter.

4.2 Female and male labor force by sectoral composition in the Netherlands

In order to facilitate comparison over time, the material from the censuses in the period from 1849 to 1960 has been reorganized by the Central

Bureau of Statistics (CBS, 1966, part 10, C:8). This makes the existence of a residual category inevitable. As in earlier publications, the Central Bureau of Statistics again remarks that women are not easy to register, a fact influencing the comparability of the figures, especially as between 1849 and 1930 (CBS, 1966, C:46).

In this 1966 adaptation of the figures, the CBS tried to comply with the *International Standard Classification of Occupations (ISCO)*, and the *International Standard Industrial Classification of all Economic Activities (ISIC)*, introduced in 1958[4] (CBS, 1966, C:8). A revised ISCO and a revised ISIC were adopted in 1968, and both classifications have recently been revised again (ISIC-88). At the level of detail shown in this monograph the differences between the classifications are minor. The ISIC-58[5] distinguishes 9 divisions, the ISIC-68 one more. The 1968 classifications have been applied to the statistics presented by the OECD since 1960. Besides this breakdown of the labor force into 10 (industrial) activities, the OECD uses another major division of only three sectors. In the international comparisons concerning the years after 1960, these OECD figures are quoted, if available.

4.2.1 Female labor force by five sectors, 1849 - 1990

Table 4.2 presents the long-term trends in the Dutch female labor force from 1849 to 1990 by five sectors: *agriculture, industry, trade and transport, domestic service, non-domestic services* and a residual category, *other*, for jobs not covered by the previous five sectors[6]. For comparison, data for males are given in table 4.4 discussed below in subsection 4.2.2 with an emphasis on percentage shares.

Table 4.2 indicates that the relatively high participation of women in 1849 as compared to 1859 is almost completely due to changes in the female agricultural labor force (table 4.9 will confirm that it is completely due to the decline in the female agricultural labor force). Idiosyncrasies in the female agricultural labor force are also noticeable in 1909, 1947 and 1990.

Figure 4.1, based on table 4.2, not only shows the long-term trends in the female labor force between 1889 and 1990 by the five sectors: *agriculture, industry, trade and transport, domestic service* and *non-*

---

4 See International Labour Office, Geneva, 1958 or Statistical Papers, series M, no.4, Rev.1, United Nations, New York, 1958; and ILO, 1991 for ISIC-58 and ISCO-58 as well as ISIC-68 and ISCO-68.

5 The *Minimum List Headings* of the *ISIC-58*, issued by the United Nations in 1958, distinguishes 152 industries, further grouped into 24 industry orders (HMSO, 1971:430).

6 The Dutch data for 1849-1960 given in this table and the following tables are based on the statistics as modified by the CBS; they reflect the classification by economic activity of the business, i.e. by industry.

domestic services (including the residual category), but also the tremendous increase in the female labor force over the period. Female employment in domestic service reached its highest absolute level in 1930 and its lowest in 1981, while the number of female participants in agriculture (and fishing) was greatest in 1947 and declined from then on until 1987.

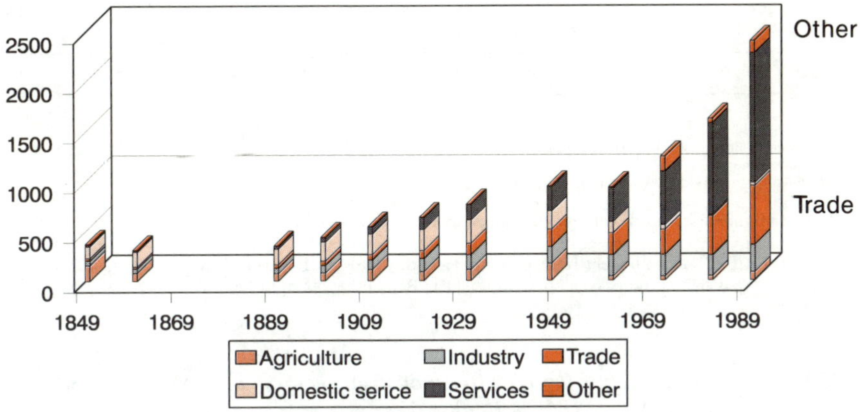

Figure 4.1 *Female labor force by five industrial sectors in the Netherlands, absolute figures in thousands, 1889-1990*

The trend in agriculture (and fishing) is, however, rather irregular, with extraordinary peaks in 1909, 1947 and 1990, unmatched by the male trend (see table 4.4 and figure 4.3), although the highest absolute level for men in the agricultural sector also occurred in 1947. These female peaks coincide with changes in the registration of (married) women in the labor force (see also chapter 8).

Agricultural figures are in general the least reliable, in international as well as in national comparisons. For example, in some communities in 1849 and 1859, all members of the farmer's family down to the smallest children were counted as workers, while in others only the head of the family was counted (Schilstra, 1976:32). Another problem with agriculture is that the counts from 1849 to 1930 were held in winter, when farming activities were at a low ebb. Moreover, detailed research shows that in the early censuses some workers performing agricultural tasks for most of the year are nonetheless counted as workers in the textile industry, work they only undertook during the winter months (CBS, 1966, part 10:13). Because of the small number of women involved, however, this hardly influences the national aggregates.

In industry, 1960 was the year in which (both) the female and male labor force peaked. Since 1981, the female labor force has again increased in domestic services, industry and agriculture. The female labor force in trade and transport shows a secular increase, and this is also reflected in the trend for men. The steady increase in non-domestic services is a striking feature.

Table 4.2 *Female labor force by five industrial sectors in the Netherlands, absolute figures in thousands, 1849 – 1990*

Sector	1849	1859	1889	1899	1909	1920	1930	1947	1960	1971	1981	1990
Agriculture[1]	158	79	73	80	112	90	110	169	41	39	42	81
Industry[2]	48	45	54	74	97	132	148	167	214	217	208	272
Trade[3]	22	19	33	43	52	77	114	175	217	251	391	592
Domestic service	118	147	157	190	205	211	234	183	114	46	12	32
Services[4]	16	14	29	45	73	119	158	246	341	541	925	1307
Other	7	5	3	3	3	6	4	8	10	148	44	121
Total	370	308	349	432	539	630	764	944	928	1226	1590	2405

1 including fishing
2 including mining, construction and public utilities
3 including transport
4 non-domestic services including banking and insurance

Note: In figure 4.1, the category *other* is added to *non-domestic services.*

Sources: CBS, Volkstellingen: 1899, part 2:271; CBS, 1966, part 10, C:11; CBS, 1989, Negentig jaren statistiek in tijdreeksen:76; CBS, Enquête Beroepsbevolking, 1990.

Table 4.3 *Female labor force by five industrial sectors in the Netherlands, in percentages, 1849 – 1990*

Sector[1]	1849	1859	1889	1899	1909	1920	1930	1947	1960	1971	1981	1990
Agriculture	43	26	21	19	21	14	14	18	4	3	3	3
Industry	13	14	15	17	18	20	19	17	23	17	11	11
Trade	6	6	9	10	10	12	15	19	23	21	25	25
Domestic service	32	48	45	44	38	34	31	20	12	4	1	1
Services	4	4	8	10	14	19	21	26	37	44	58	54
Other	2	2	1	1	1	1	1	1	1	11	3	5
Total per cent	100	100	100	100	100	100	100	100	100	100	100	100

1 See footnotes and sources for table 4.2

Table 4.4 *Male labor force participation by five industrial sectors in the Netherlands, in percentages, 1849 – 1990*

Sector[1]	1849	1859	1889	1899	1909	1920	1930	1947	1960	1971	1981	1990
Agriculture	45	41	36	34	31	26	23	20	13	7	7	5
Industry	22	23	24	30	26	28	28	30	33	30	25	24
Trade	13	14	18	18	21	21	23	19	20	19	24	25
Domestic service	2	3	1	1	1	1	0	0	0	0	0	0
Services	8	8	10	9	9	11	11	16	17	19	30	34
Other	10	10	12	13	12	14	15	15	18	25	15	11
Total per cent	100	100	100	100	100	100	100	100	100	100	100	100
Absolute figures in thousands	881	943	1298	1489	1720	2090	2415	2923	3241	3509	3533	3951

1 See footnotes and sources for table 4.2

4.2.2 Percentage shares of the female and male labor force by five industrial sectors, 1849 - 1990

Percentages given in figure 4.2 and table 4.3 show the relative importance of female labor force distribution over the various sectors, with the corresponding percentages for men being given in figure 4.3 and table 4.4.

These percentages confirm the conclusions of the absolute figures. They also show that for female workers the relative importance of *domestic service* has been transferred to *non-domestic services*. *Agriculture* has become steadily less important but seems to have reached the end of its decline in the 1980s, while trade and transport participation shares remained fairly stable. Industry initially increased until 1920 but since 1960 has decreased in importance.

Figure 4.2 also shows that idiosyncratic figures in agriculture influence the percentages in the other sectors. The relatively high percentage in 1947 depresses the percentages in the other sectors. To remedy this, (yet) another presentation of the same figures is chosen in the next section.

Up to 1947, most occupations for women within these sectors were either domestic or semi-domestic in nature, or related to jobs relatively easy to combine with housework, such as work in agriculture and small shops.

Up to the turn of the century, the industrial sector was apparently not the most important source of either female or male employment in the Netherlands. It was not until after 1920 that its importance for men began to exceed that of the agricultural sector. The relative importance of the industrial sector to men as compared to its effect on women is obvious. This confirms the expectation mentioned in section 3.6, to the effect that the late industrialization of the Netherlands had a greater impact on the employment of male than of female workers.

Comparing figures 4.2 and 4.3 for the service sector reveals the opposite effect compared with the industrial sector: this sector is far more important to women than to men, although even to men the service sector does become more and more important.

The overall pattern is similar for both women and men. As compared with the rate of population growth, market work in agriculture and domestic service lagged behind, while in trade and transport and other services the increase in employment was more rapid.

Figure 4.2 *Female labor force by five industrial sectors in the Netherlands, in percentages, 1889-1990*

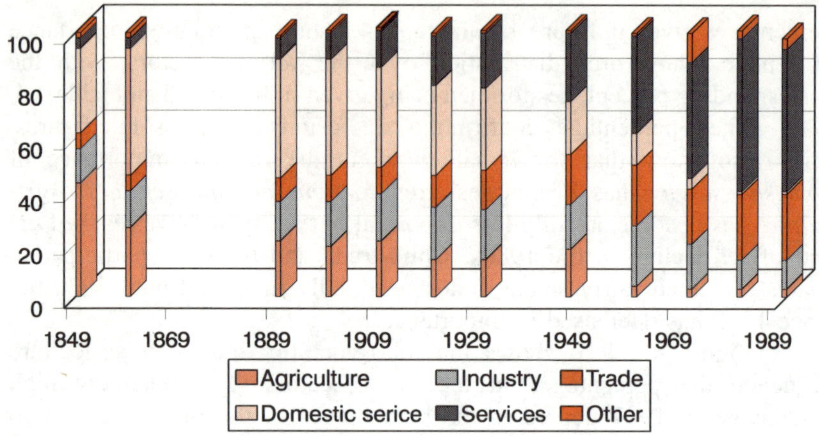

Figure 4.3 *Male labor force by five industrial sectors in the Netherlands, in percentages, 1889-1990*

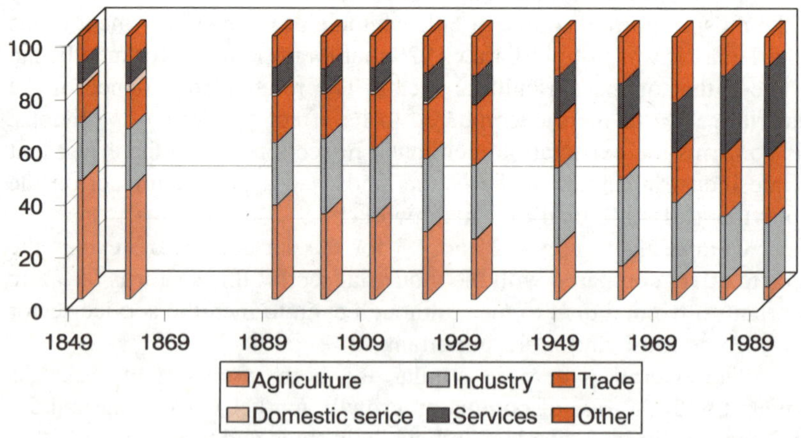

4.3 Economic activity by sectoral division and industrial development in seven countries

Both the sectoral composition of the labor force and its evolution are expected to have been quite different in the various countries examined. To set the stage, the next subsection shows the sectoral division of the total labor force in 1900 and 1990. These figures are (relatively) more accessible than the equivalent data for the female labor force alone.

4.3.1 Sectoral division of the total labor force around 1900 and 1990

The sectoral division of the total labor force in around 1900 in the seven countries considered in this study is presented in figure 4.4. The length of the bars shows the relative importance of different sectors in the various countries considered. The sectors distinguished for 1900 are: *agriculture* (including horticulture, fishing and forestry); *industry* (including mining, quarrying, public utilities - like gas, water and electricity - and construction); *trade and transport*; (*domestic service* and *other) services*.

Figure 4.4 *Sectoral division of the total labor force by five sectors, a seven-country comparison, in percentages, around 1900*

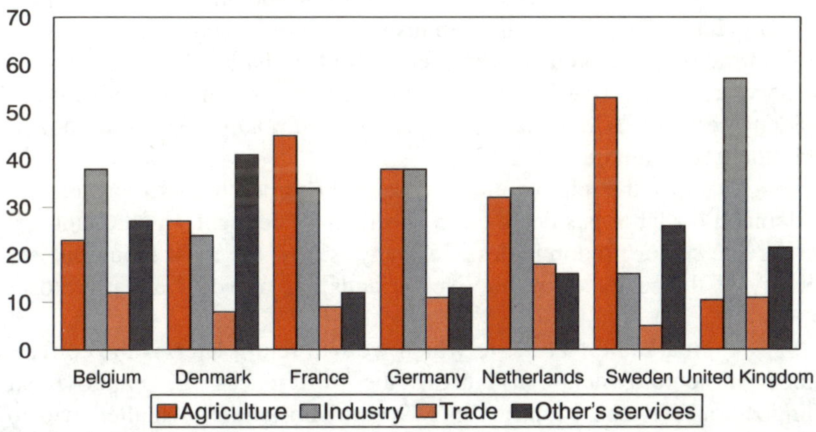

The bars in figure 4.5[7] show the sectoral division around 1990. Because participation in domestic services has fallen in all the countries to a mere few per cent, these are not shown separately but aggregated into one sector *services*.

---

[7] Both figures 4.4 and 4.5 correspond with the data presented in table 4.12.

Figure 4.5 *Sectoral division of the total labor force by four sectors, a seven-country comparison, in percentages, 1990*

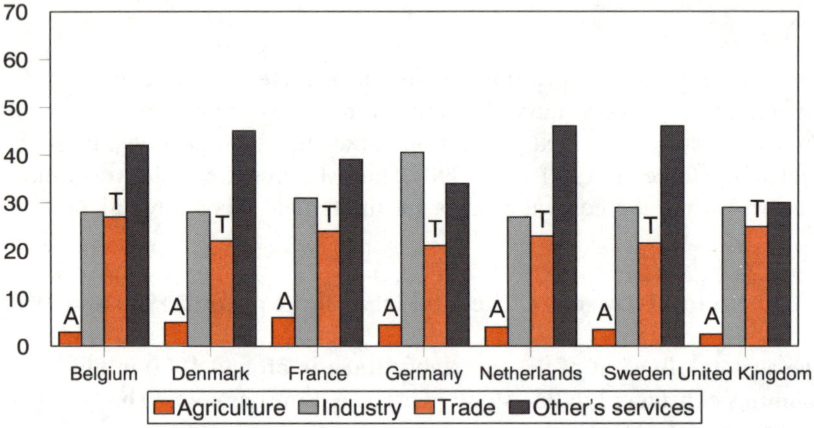

In 1900, a relatively large number of people in the Netherlands were working in *trade and transport*, while in the other sectors the Dutch labor force composition occupies an intermediate position. England was the most industrialized country, Sweden the least; as far as the labor force in agriculture is concerned, the reverse is the case. France at this time displays both a relatively large industrial and a relatively large agricultural sector, while in Denmark and Germany, the proportions of the labor force participating in the agricultural and industrial sectors are about equal. Belgium has a relatively large industrial sector as compared with its agricultural sector. An outstanding feature in Denmark is the large domestic services sector (partly because the figures also include other non-resident servants (*Daglejere, Arbeidsmænd, Tyende*, see Befolkningsførholdene I Denmark, 1905:177).

By 1990, the relative importance of the agricultural sector in terms of demand for labor has declined to less than 10 per cent. In all countries, the service sector predominates. Germany is now the most industrialized country of the seven, while the Netherlands has moved gradually closer to average.

A remarkable feature, to which we will return later, is the convergence in employment structures: the differences in employment composition between countries in 1990 are substantially smaller than in 1900. If we subtract the calculated maximum and minimum percentages, the differences between them for agriculture, industry, trade and for other services are respectively 44, 42, 11 and 22 per cent in 1900 and 5, 13, 6 and 13 per cent in 1990. Thus, we may expect sectoral differences in demand structure to be less important in 1990 than they were in 1900. The range in total female participation rates has also decreased, from about 18 per cent in 1900 to 14 per cent in 1990. But the large gap in 1900 is mainly due to the very low rate for the Netherlands: excluding the Netherlands would generate a range of 10 per cent. This illustrates clearly the extreme position of the Netherlands in 1900.

4.3.2 Historical sketch of industrial development

This section starts with a brief description of industrial development in all seven countries. This description is by no means complete. It merely provides some remarks to illustrate and clarify the movement shown by the numerical data in the tables of the sectoral division on the female labor force in the countries considered and to facilitate the international comparison of the female and total labor force between 1850 and 1990 in all seven countries, presented in section 4.4.

In general, all over Europe around 1850, economic circumstances were depressed. There was a crisis in 1893-94 (after the Paris panic on the stock exchange and the London goldmines crash); 1908 was another year of depression, while the recovery after 1910 was disturbed by World War I in 1914 - 1918. The heavy crash of 1929 caused a severe crisis in all seven countries, with most countries reaching rock bottom in 1934 (the Netherlands in 1936), but it was not until after World War II that recovery really started.

The detailed analysis of the Dutch trends showed that idiosyncrasies in one sector influence the percentages of female labor force participation in another, if the breakdown by sector is shown in percentages of the (total) female labor force (for example see table 4.3). Mention has also been made of the fact that different countries use different definitions and classifications of sectoral divisions.

For the sake of international comparisons, the tables below adopt a different approach from that employed in table 4.3 and figures 4.3 to 4.6, using instead the female labor force participation rate in the sector under consideration. This means that the percentages of the sectors distinguished now add up to the (total) female labor force participation rate, as defined and presented in chapter 2.

Belgium

As briefly mentioned in the previous chapter the Dutch-speaking part of Belgium, Flanders, has a long tradition of manufacturing, going back to the Middle Ages and encompassing many ups and downs. During the sixteenth century, the manufacturing of cloth declined rapidly, mainly as a result of English competition but also due to the increase in products from the rural countryside. Religious strife and the Spanish war finally ended three centuries of relative prosperity. Gradually the manufacture of linen and bobbin lace increased in importance, but the main source of wealth for the nobility and religious foundations was no longer manufacturing but agriculture, though the two were admittedly closely connected with farmers not only growing the flax but also processing and spinning it and weaving the linen fabric (De Raet, 1914:145;164). Wars in the seventeenth and early eighteenth century precluded higher levels of prosperity.

The early industrialization and the rise of the cotton, flax and textile industries beginning in the 1760s and booming after the 1780s has already been mentioned in the previous chapter. Economic crises were experienced in 1808, 1810 and 1814. However, misery really struck

Flanders in the period 1845 to 1847. The introduction of the new spinning machines and the failure of the harvest, occurring just as the newly-established country was recovering from the post-Napoleonic chaos and its separation from the Netherlands, condemned many thousands to hunger and poverty. Many emigrated to the north of France (founding Tourcoing and Roubaix as centers for the textile industry), or to the French-speaking part of Belgium, the Walloon country, where the heavy industries were then emerging. Because of these heavy industries, productivity per worker increased tremendously and the number of workers in industry rose for the whole kingdom from 430 thousand in 1846 to over 1 million in 1896 (Recensement Général, 1896). However, the numbers working in cottage industries declined over the same period from 270 thousand to 118 thousand (see also De Raet, 1914:163).

The 1846 census counted 66 thousand female lacemakers; the 1896 census more than 18 thousand fewer. (The introduction of lace machines in England ruined the hand lace production in Flanders, at the same time introducing boom years in the East Midlands[8].)

The loss of female employment between 1846 and 1896, causing the decline in the female labor force demonstrated in figure 2.4, is analyzed by sector in the next table.

The extent to which women were participating in industry in 1846 and 1856 - even in the heavy industries[9] - is remarkable, 17 per cent in 1846 and 15 per cent in 1856 of all the women were working in industry, percentages higher than in any of the other six countries. However, between 1846 and 1856 the total labor force in the *Industrie Métallurgique* (metal workers) declined from 218 thousand to 138 thousand, and the *Industrie Manufacturière* (manufacturing, especially the linen and cotton industries) decreased from 461 thousand to 282 thousand, whereas in contrast the *Industrie Vêtement* (clothing industry) employed both in 1846 and in 1856 about the same number of people (255 and 253 thousand respectively).

Between 1856 and 1896 female activity rates in industry fell from 15 to 8 per cent. Table 4.5 clearly shows the dramatic decline in female labor in industry between 1846 and 1880, and the fact that this decline in the total activity rate was disguised by the rise in agriculture between 1856 and 1880. The subsequent apparent dramatic decline in female labor force participation in agriculture between 1896 and 1910 is clearly due to differences in the methods of enumeration. In 1910, female unpaid family workers (*les aidantes/helpers*) are not counted. If they are included,

---

8 In 1850, the lace industry in England involved 110 factories and about 500 lace machines in operation. Eighty per cent of England's 4,500 thousand bobbinet machines were working in the East Midlands, turning Nottingham into the lace capital of the world (Lowe and Richards, 1988:27).

9 According to Sullerot (1969:90), besides the 64 thousand women working in the textile factories in 1846, another 71 thousand worked in the heavy industries and 7 thousand in the mines.

Table 4.5 *Female labor force participation rates by five industrial sectors in Belgium, 1846 – 1990*

Sector	1846	1856	1880	1896	1910	1920	1930	1947	1960	1970	1981	1990
Agriculture[1]	16	16	19	13	3	2	3	1	1	1	1	1
Industry[2]	17	15	9	8	11	8	9	7	6	6	5	4
Trade[3]	2	2	2	4	4	3	4	4	4	6	7	7
Dom. service [4]	3	3	3	3	4	3	–	–	–	–	–	–
Services[5]	1	1	1	1	4	2	8	8	8	9	15	18
Total[6]	38	36	34	29	25	21	24	19	20	22	31	34

1 Including fishing
2 Including mining, construction and public utilities
3 Including transport
4 Since 1930 included in services
5 (Non-domestic) services, including banking and insurance
6 See also table 2.2.
Since 1972 the figures for Belgium have been readjusted as closely as possible to the ISIC-68 by the OECD.

Sources: See table 2.2.

Note: addition of the participation rates in all sectors may produce a lower total female labor force participation rate than the one presented here (in tables 4.5 to 4.11) and in table 2.2 because of the long-term unemployed, non-classified and rounding up or down of the figures. The OECD figures (since 1960 if available) concern the *civilian labour force*.

female labor force participation rates in agriculture would rise to 8 per cent, and if these *helpers* are also included in the other categories total female activity rates would have been 36 instead of 25 per cent (Recensement Général, 1910:251). The next chapter analyzes female activities by position in the labor market in more detail. That the method of counting farmer's wives and relatives frequently causes idiosyncrasies can also be illustrated by calculating the share of women participating in agriculture. In 1846 women's share in agriculture was 39 per cent, in 1880 it was 46 per cent and in 1910 only 15 per cent. However, even if these unpaid family workers were included, the figures would still show a drastic decline in the female agricultural activity rate between 1896 and 1910. As will be shown below in this section and in the next chapter, the figures for Belgium since 1910 are probably more comparable to the British, Danish and Dutch figures for women in agriculture, while the earlier data may be more comparable to the French and German data.

In 1920, the industrial sector remained the most important sector to women in the labor force (8 per cent, compared with the second largest sector of domestic services with 3 per cent). Nine thousand women were still working in the mines, a low number compared to the 172 thousand male mine-workers. In absolute figures most women were working in the textile (*industries textiles*: 107 thousand) and related (*industrie du vêtement*) industries (131 thousand), together accounting for 83 per cent of the female industrial labor force. Relatively large shares of women (but of less numerical importance) were found in the tobacco and paper industries.

Since 1930, female labor in the industrial sector has declined continuously. Together with the loss of female labor in the agricultural sector (still continuing, even taking account of differences in registration), this decrease is responsible for the severe overall decline in the female labor force until 1947. The table also illustrates the gradual increase in importance of the trade and transport sector, and the rapid rise of the service sector after World War II. Domestic services were modest in their contribution to the female labor force, remaining fairly constant at 3 per cent.

The table does not show the development of the male labor force. The mining, metal, building and chemical industries were the most rapid growing industry groups, all four employing mainly male workers (Nijverheidstelling, 1947, deel X:77) and contributing to the dominance of industry as the largest sector after 1896. Ever since the first census in Belgium in 1846, more male laborers have worked in industry than in agriculture.

Denmark

Denmark used to be a primitive country with a subsistence economy and a very low standard of living until the second half of the eighteenth century. Rigid distinctions between town and country were a contributing factor. In 1733, for example, rural inhabitants aged between 14 and 36 years were forbidden by law to leave the estates on which they were born. This was intended to prevent emigration in the years of depression. The measure was relaxed in 1788. By contrast, town-dwellers enjoyed special privileges and an almost absolute monopoly of the production and sale of goods (Andersen, 1977:122).

During the eighteenth century, more than 60 per cent of the Danish population worked in agriculture. Productivity rarely exceeded subsistence levels (Andersen, 1977:123). Political reform in the 1780s greatly enhanced economic progress. Not only was the bondage of agricultural workers to the manors relaxed and migration allowed, but land was also redistributed and technological improvements introduced. As a result of these reforms, agricultural production can be seen to have doubled between 1770 and 1800. As in the Netherlands, however, this relatively positive trend changed once Denmark was drawn into the Napoleonic wars in 1807. Between then and 1818 the country experienced an agricultural crisis, caused partly by a diminished demand for goods after the conclusion of the war (Andersen, 1977:126). After this date, trade with England increased and in subsequent years links between the two countries were so close that there was an almost parallel evolution in their national price structures (Andersen, 1977:126). During the 1820s economic recovery was achieved, but there was little reform of government.

Between 1860 and 1880, there was a spectacular development of the Danish infrastructure and the close cooperation with England produced an increasingly marked division of labor between English industry and Danish agriculture (Andersen, 1977:127). During World War I, Denmark remained neutral but suffered economically because trade with Great Britain was interrupted. The cooperative movement started to flourish in agriculture as well as in other sectors. It was not until after World War II that the dominance of the agricultural sector for the total labor force was taken over by industry. Danish industry had remained predominantly of the small handicraft type (Collier, 1966) until after World War II. Since then, heavy industries have developed and expanded and a modern welfare state has been created with one of the highest standards of living in the world.

The sectoral development of the Danish female labor force is demonstrated in table 4.6.

Table 4.6 *Female labor force participation rates by five industrial sectors in Denmark, 1855 – 1990*

Sector	1860	1870	1880	1890	1901	1911	1921	1930	1940	1950	1960	1970	1980	1990
Agriculture[1]	12	11	10	11	12	10	9	8	10	7	4	2	2	2
Industry[2]	4	4	5	5	7	5	5	6	6	7	7	7	7	7
Trade[3]	4	2	2	3	4	3	4	3	5	5	6	7	7	10
Dom. service [4]	2	3	2	2	3	9	12	16	7	4	2	1	0	0
Services[5]	3	4	3	4	4	4	4		6	8	11	17	28	29
Total[6]	25	25	24	26	30	30	34	34	34	30	30	34	46	51

1 including fishing
2 including mining, construction and public utilities
3 including transport
4 see remarks in the text below and in 1930 including other services
5 non-domestic services, including banking and insurance
6 see table 2.2

Sources: See table 2.2.

There are some problems in relation to the allocation of domestic servants in the Danish figures. In the censuses of 1855-1901, the total population is divided by industrial sector. Within each sector a distinction is made between *forsørgere* (breadwinner), *forsørgerde* (dependent) and *tyende* (domestic or other servant). If the females of the first and the last category within each sector are added together (and divided by the female population), this produces the labor force participation rates as presented in table 4.6. If, for example, the *tyende* in the agricultural sector are subtracted from the figures presented in 1855 and 1860, participation rates in agriculture decrease by 9 per cent and the figures increase by the same percentage in domestic services. The percentages in 1870, 1880, 1890 and 1901 are 8, 7, 6 and 6 respectively. Sometimes one of these percentages is found in international comparisons, but the distinction is not clear. Neither division is comparable with the figures for 1910, 1920 and 1930, all three years showing relatively large female activity rates in domestic service. As with the other countries, figures are more comparable since World War II.

Quinquennial censuses were held between 1945 and 1970, while the last two censuses were held in 1976 and 1981. Links to the ISIC-68 and ISCO-68 have been established for these last two censuses (but only to the major division level or major group level) (ILO, 1991:67).

Since 1950, services have clearly been the dominant sector in Denmark. Female labor force participation in industry has been fairly constant since the beginning of the century. Trade and transport are becoming more and more important and, as in Belgium, the increase in this sector has been persistent ever since the first census.

France

Around 1750, agriculture employed 75 per cent of the total French population (Tilly and Scott, 1987:12). Following the industrialization of the rural areas, the industrial sector increased in importance, but France remained predominantly agricultural and the small family farm depending on the labor of the whole family is still relatively important there, certainly compared for example with England. Until the end of the nineteenth century, the peasant class constituted about three-quarters of the population. There was and is a high degree of political and economical concentration in Paris. Large regional differences remain even today.

A remarkable feature in France, but also in England, was the emergence of the rural 'wet-nurse'. Women in the country became wet-nurses, suckling and raising the children of middle-class women, urban artisans and shopkeeping families, especially those of married women participating in the labor force in the industrial urban areas. In the late eighteenth century, close to a third of all babies born in Lyons (famous as the heart of the French silk industry) were being carted off to wet-nurses in the countryside. If such children survived infancy at all, they often remained with their nurses until they were three or four years old (Tilly and Scott, 1987:46).

In France by around 1850 (Sullerot, 1969:89) more men and women were employed in the textile industry than in any other form of industrial work. In 1847, about one million women were working in the French textile and clothing industry, as against 35 thousand in the coal-mines and 38 thousand in the steel industry (Sullerot, 1969:89).

For both sexes participation in agriculture remained important until the 1960s. For men it remained the dominant sector until 1921, for women until 1954. One reason may be that relatively many unpaid family workers are counted in that sector (see chapter 5). To men and women within industry the *Industries Textiles* (textile industry) and the *Travail des étoffes et vêtement* (textile processing and clothing industry) were extremely important sectors until after World War II.

The sectoral development of women's participation in France since 1866 is given in table 4.7.

Table 4.7 *Female labor force participation rates by five industrial sectors in France, 1866 – 1990*

Sector	1856	1866	1876	1896	1906	1921	1926	1931	1936	1954	1960	1970	1980	1990
Agriculture[1]	12	10	12	14	17	20	16	15	14	8	7	4	2	1
Industry[2]	6	7	7	11	13	12	11	11	9	7	10	10	9	9
Trade[3]	1	1	2	3	4	5	5	5	6	4	8	7	8	9
Dom. service [4]	5	6	6	4	4	3	3	3	3	2	–	–	–	–
Services[5]	–	1	1	1	1	2	2	3	3	9	7	9	12	16
Total[6]	25	24	30	33	39	42	38	37	34	30	33	30	32	36

1 including fishing
2 including mining, construction and public utilities
3 including transport
4 added to services since 1960
5 non-domestic services, including banking and insurance
6 See table 2.2.

Sources: See table 2.2

A remarkable feature is the high proportion of women in the labor force in agriculture, higher than in industry until 1954; the proportion of women in the industrial sector has remained relatively high (except in 1954 when it was 7 per cent) ever since the end of the nineteenth century. As in Belgium and Denmark, since 1856, the trade sector shows a secular increase and the service sector an important rise, while domestic services became less and less important over the period.

Germany

Historically, the term 'Germany' has had several different meanings. At first it was used to designate the aggregate of princely territories that made up the Holy Roman Empire (Collier, 1966:17), while in the course of the nineteenth and twentieth centuries, the borders of 'Germany' have changed several times. From 1815 to 1866 Germany meant the German Confederation, which also included Austria. The German Empire of 1871 to 1918 defined Germany as the principal German-speaking area of Europe apart from Austria and Switzerland. From 1919 to 1933, Germany was officially referred to as the Weimar Republic and under Nazi rule as the Third Reich. Following World War I, the Weimar Republic had to cede the territories of Alsace-Lorraine, the Saar and Upper Silesia, while under the aggressive regime of the Third Reich in the 1930s new territories were added. After World War II, the situation described here is confined to that of the Federal Republic of Germany[10].

Germany's economy before World War II was marked by sharp contrasts. Large industrial centers were located in agricultural areas where methods of ownership and cultivation were centuries old. After World War II, the Federal Republic astonished the world by the speed of its economic recovery. In the decade between 1950 and 1960 the gross national product more than doubled. This *Wirtschaftswunder* (economic miracle) was spurred on by the Marshall Plan (1948 - 1952), the industrial pump-priming of American dollars, especially to coal-mining. The structure of the economy was strengthened and foreign trade revived. Despite this, about one third of the population was still engaged in agriculture around this time, within the prevailing system of small land-owners. (Collier, 1966:27). The breakdown of the German female labor force is shown in table 4.8.

Table 4.8 *Female labor force participation rates by five industrial sectors in Germany, 1882 – 1990*

Sector	1882	1895	1907	1925	1933	1939	1946	1960	1970	1980	1990
Agriculture[1]	11	10	14	14	14	13	12	7	4	2	1
Industry[2]	5	6	7	9	8	9	7	10	10	9	9
Trade[3]	1	2	3	5	6	4	4	8	7	8	9
Dom. service [4]	7	6	5	4	3	–	–	–	–	–	–
Services[5]	0	1	1	3	1	8	8	7	9	12	17
Total[6]	24	25	30	35	34	34	31	33	30	33	38

1 including fishing
2 including mining, construction and public utilities
3 including transport
4 added to services since 1939
5 non-domestic services, including banking and insurance
6 See table 2.2.

Sources: See table 2.2

Labor force participation by women in agriculture was slightly lower than in France until the 1930s, but showed the same pattern as in the previous countries mentioned. Women's participation rates in industry reveal a similar pattern, especially compared with France. Again the importance of trade and transport increases slowly and that of the service sector is the same as that in France (exactly so since 1960).

A study comparing the sectoral composition of the labor force in

10 Although the full political unification of the two parts of post-war Germany was established on 3 October 1990, and the monetary and economic accession of the German Democratic Republic (GDR) to the Federal Republic of Germany (FRG) had taken place on 1 July 1990, this three to six-month period is left out of consideration in this study.

Germany and the Netherlands between 1920 and 1960 confirms that in Germany during this period greater proportions of people worked not only in the industrial but also in the agricultural sector[11]. In the industrial sector, female labor force participation rates in Germany were at least twice as high as those in the Netherlands, while those in agriculture were nearly 5 times as high in the 1920s and 1930s and 10 times as high in the early 1960s. This substantial difference in the female agricultural labor forces will be analyzed in more detail in the next chapter. In the Netherlands, trade, transport and (other) services were relatively more important (Van Dijk and Verstegen, 1988:58).

In both countries, mechanization of the textile industry and other major sources of manufacturing employment for women occurred relatively late. German women displayed considerable resistance to the loss of their home-based, cottage industries at the end of the nineteenth century, but as elsewhere had eventually to surrender in the face of competition from the more productive factories.

In Germany between 1925 and 1961, an increasing proportion of women were to be found in services, while in the Netherlands the rate remained constant between 1920 and 1960 (Van Dijk and Verstegen, 1988:58). These differences reflect the lower percentage of women in the Dutch labor force (also illustrated in table 4.9).

One reason often cited for the differences in participation in industry, is the work done by women in the German war industry after 1914. However, a comparison between the female industrial labor force in Germany in June 1914 and that in June 1918 reveals that 200 thousand women left this sector over that period. The same is true of France, with 150 thousand fewer, and Great Britain, with 400 thousand fewer (Sullerot, 1969:141). The census figures before and after the war confirm this. What happened in these three countries was that a reorganization of female work took place during these war years, mainly in the textile industry.

Despite this decline, female employment in industry still showed the same pattern before and after World War II, with female shares in the *Bekleidungsindustrie* (clothing industry) being 72 per cent in 1936 as against 75 per cent in the American zone and 78 per cent in the British zone of Germany in 1948. The figures for the textile industry were 52 per cent in 1936 and 54 and 46 per cent for the American and British zones respectively in 1948. As in the other countries, the highest absolute figures for women were found in the textile industry (Statistisches Jahrbuch, 1952).

The Netherlands

At the turn of the century, the Netherlands differed from the neighboring countries in a number of respects other than, of course, in its geographical position: there were wide regional differences in economic structure,

[11] This study was conducted by Van Dijk and Verstegen (1988). They compiled a completely new classification of occupations.

dialects, population characteristics, long traditions of trade and trade-related processing industries, was late industrialization and relative wealth, due in part to its colonial possessions. All these factors helped to produce an economy more diverse than those of the surrounding countries (Van Zanden and Griffiths, 1989). This has already been illustrated to some extent by the breakdown of the labor force into different sectors.

The Dutch trend in female labor force participation rates by five industrial sectors is given in table 4.9. The table is another presentation of the same figures provided in table 4.2 and table 4.3.

Table 4.9 *Female labor force participation rates by five industrial sectors in the Netherlands, 1849 – 1990*

Sector	1849	1859	1889	1899	1909	1920	1930	1947	1960	1971	1981	1990
Agriculture[1]	10	4	3	3	3	4	3	4	1	1	1	1
Industry[2]	3	3	2	3	3	4	4	3	4	3	3	3
Trade[3]	1	1	2	2	2	2	4	4	3	4	6	8
Dom. service	8	8	7	7	7	6	6	4	2	1	0	0
Services[4]	1	1	2	2	2	4	4	5	7	10	13	17
Total[5]	24	18	15	17	18	18	19	20	16	19	25	36

1 including fishing
2 including mining, construction and public utilities
3 including transport
4 non-domestic services including banking and insurance
5 see table 2.2.

Sources: See tables 2.2 and 4.2.

The table confirms the findings of the previous section, but shows very clearly that Dutch female activity rates in agriculture as well as in industry were very low compared with the countries treated so far: i.e. Belgium, Denmark, France and Germany. The other three sectors show the same patterns as in those countries.

Sweden

Economically speaking, Sweden was a late developer in comparison with the other countries. Although merchants from Lübeck were active in Stockholm from the thirteenth to the fifteenth century, the country's position on the border of two economic worlds, the European and the Russian, without control over the Baltic, remained its main weakness, which they have strived to change. For example, the Baltic was monopolized by the Dutch from the sixteenth century until the increase in English penetration after 1675. Dutch entrepreneurs exploited the coastal areas, exporting sawn timber and woodpulp as well as mining products. These two extractive industries were completely dependent on Amsterdam until the eighteenth century (Braudel, 1979:237). Economic development was also slow because the population increase was insignificant. The end of the Napoleonic era brought a peace to Sweden which has lasted to the present day. Infrastructure improved, the country's natural resources were developed and during the nineteenth century Sweden became a leading country in the production of fine steel. Since World War II a modern welfare state has been created with very high standards of living and high female labor force participation rates. The Swedish female labor force participation rates by five sectors are shown in table 4.10.

Table 4.10 *Female labor force participation rates by five industrial sectors in Sweden, 1870 – 1990*

Sector	1880	1890	1900	1910	1920	1930	1940	1950	1960	1970	1980	1990
Agriculture[1]	14	13	13	11	9	8	3	2	2	2	1	1
Industry[2]	2	2	3	4	5	6	6	6	7	7	7	7
Trade[3]	1	1	2	2	4	5	7	7	8	9	9	10
Dom. service	11	10	10	10	9	7	5	9	–	–	–	–
Services[4]	–	–	–	2	3	3	4	9	14	20	28	31
Total[5]	28	28	28	28	30	29	25	29	33	39	47	51

1 including fishing
2 including mining, construction and public utilitiess
3 including transport
4 non-domestic services including banking and insurances
5 see table 2.2.

Sources: See table 2.2.

There are similar problems in relation to domestic servants and unpaid family workers as in Denmark in the censuses before World War II (see also chapter 5). However, in Sweden nearly all these 'servants' are registered in agriculture. If these 'servants' (called *Tjenstehjon* in 1880 and 1890; *Tjänstehjon* in 1900 and *Tjänare* in 1910 to 1940) are not counted as being in the labor market, female labor force participation rates would have been 19, 21, 22, 26 and 26 per cent for the censuses 1880 to 1920[12]. These figures resemble the female labor force participation rates, mentioned in chapter 2, given in the German 1882 census for Sweden in 1880 and in the Dutch 1899 census for Sweden in 1890.

The resemblance with Denmark is remarkable, except that the decline in agriculture started earlier in Sweden. Industrial participation

12 Without the unpaid daughters the rates are again 6 to 11 per cent lower (Silenstam, 1970; see also chapter 5).

rates are almost identical, and the rates in the trade and transport and services sectors are fairly similar.

Great Britain

Estimates based on scattered local studies indicate that in 1750 agriculture employed 65 per cent of the English population (Tilly and Scott, 1987:12). After that date, the industrial sector increased in importance. By 1850, manufacturing was evidently the dominant form of economic activity in Great Britain, with spinning, sewing, lacemaking, knitting and needlework as major areas of female activity. Weaving was and remained male work and, although it was complementary to spinning, male weavers earned double the wages of the female spinners (Tilly and Scott, 1987:45). Agriculture was to decline rapidly throughout the nineteenth century, and the number of female agricultural workers in England, Wales and Scotland dropped from over 70 thousand in 1851, to under 56 thousand in 1871, 46 thousand in 1891 and 19 thousand in 1911 (Roberts, 1990:43).

Over the same period the number of female textile workers increased from 507 thousand in 1851 to 604 thousand in 1911. The sharp decline in female textile workers following the First World War, to 374 thousand in 1931, is mostly accounted for by the slump in the cotton industry (Roberts, 1990:34). The manufacture of woolens and worsted, as well as the flax, jute and silk industries, had already started to decline much earlier (Roberts, 1990:33).

The labor force participation rates in Great Britain, by occupational sectors between 1851 and 1921 and by industrial sectors between 1931 and 1990, are presented in table 4.11.

Table 4.11 *Female labor force participation rates by five industrial sectors in Great Britain, 1870 – 1990*

Sector	1851	1861	1871	1881	1891	1901	1911	1921	1931	1956	1961[6]	1971	1981	1990
Agriculture[1]	3	1	1	1	1	0	0	0	0	0	0	0	0	0
Industry[2]	14	13	12	11	12	11	11	9	10	12	11	9	7	7
Trade[3]	–	–	–	–	–	–	–	–	1	1	2	–	–	–
Dom. service	12	13	13	11	12	11	10	9	8	7	–	–	–	–
Services[4]	4	2	2	2	2	3	4	8	8	15	23	23	29	34
Total[5]	30	28	28	25	27	25	26	26	27	30	32	31	36	41

1 including fishing
2 including mining, construction and public utilities
3 added to services
4 non-domestic services including banking and insurance
5 See table 2.2 and remarks in table 4.5.
6 According to ILO (1991:386,388) industry both in 1961 and 1966: 10%; in 1971: 9% and in 1981:7%; in all the years mentioned agriculture: 0%.

Sources: See table 2.2.

A remarkable feature is the absence of women in one of the most traditional sectors: agriculture. Despite this, female labor force participation rates were not unusually low, mainly due to the high percentages of women in the industrial and domestic services sectors.

4.4 A seven-country comparison of female economic activity by sector

4.4.1 Female activity rates in agriculture and industry

A comparison of the Netherlands with the other six countries (tables 4.5 to 4.11) reveals that female labor force participation rates in the Netherlands were very low in both the agricultural and the industrial sector. This is once more illustrated in figures 4.6 and 4.7 (both based on tables 4.5 to 4.11).

Figure 4.6 *A seven-country comparison of female labor force participation rates in the agricultural sector, 1846-1990*

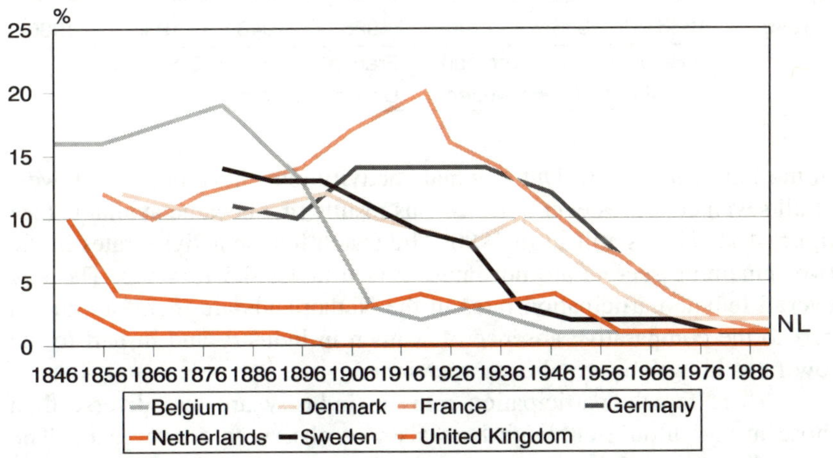

There are several conclusions to be drawn from figure 4.6. Before World War II, agriculture was an important sector of female economic activity. Until recently, there were large differences in participation rates between the seven countries, and even the development over time differed greatly.

After World War II, agriculture disappeared rapidly as a source of employment, and hence also as a source of differences in female participation rates. In 1990, only Denmark had a female participation rate of 2 per cent in that sector, while that in the other countries was 0 to 1 per cent. Throughout the period of observation, female participation in agriculture has been very low in the Netherlands, with only the British rate being even lower. Part of the cause of the low Dutch (and to a lesser extent the

British) rates in agriculture can be attributed to the non-registration of unpaid family labor (see also chapter 5).

A remarkable feature is that Belgium and France show the same patterns in female agricultural activity rates; the difference is that France reached its peak in 1921 and Belgium in 1880. If unpaid family labor had been included over the intervening decades in Belgium, the similarity would have been even more remarkable.

Figure 4.7 *A seven-country comparison of female labor force participation rates in the industrial sector, 1846-1990*

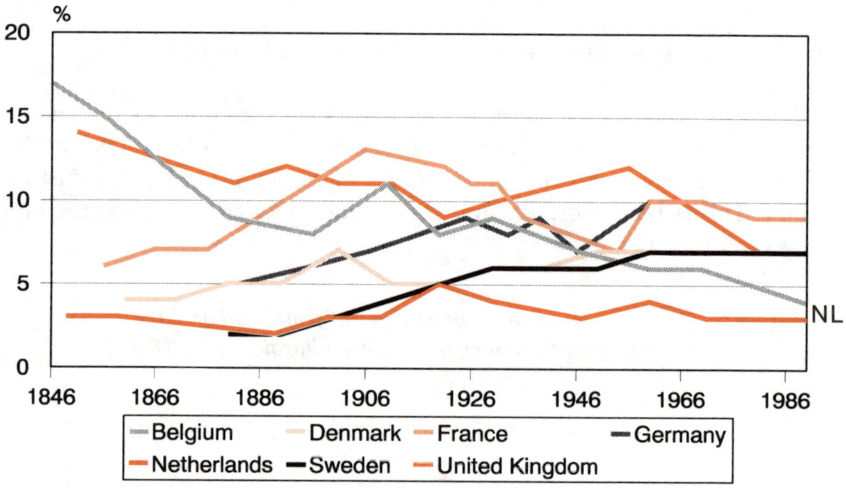

In the industrial sector, Dutch female activity rates have been the lowest of all seven countries ever since census results first became available (see figure 4.7). This is still so in 1990. The Dutch female activity rates in the two remaining sectors are not unusual (see tables 4.5 to 4.11). The low overall female participation rates in the Netherlands are therefore due in part to the comparative absence of women in industry and in part to the low rates in agriculture already mentioned.

The female participation rates in industry are less diverse then those in agriculture, although here also we observe a convergence. The range diminished from 11 percentage points around 1860 to 6 percentage points in 1990.

The transition from textile to heavy industry meant a relative decline in jobs for women in the manufacturing sector in countries with a large textile sector like Belgium, Great Britain and to a lesser extent France. These countries show a loss of female employment in the industrial sector in the second half of the nineteenth century (between 1846 and 1896; and between 1851 and 1881 respectively).

The traditional forms of employment for women in agriculture and domestic service nearly disappeared in all countries after 1980. For lower-class girls domestic services remained an important sector until the 1930s, especially in the Netherlands and Great Britain. Gradually in the years before Worl War II, charwomen or poor immigrant women replaced living-in female servants. A large part of the population of living-in servants was formed in France by girls from Britain, Italy or Spain, in England by girls from Ireland or Scotland and in the Netherlands by girls from Germany. All early censuses pay relatively great attention to participants in the labor force by nationality.

In services, the Dutch position is less extreme than in agriculture and industry. Before the war, services were important in Germany and Britain, but the Dutch rate was of the same level of magnitude as in the remaining countries for the three quarters of a century up to the second World War.

Participation in domestic services was actually relatively high, and in trade and transport, it was comparable to that in other countries. After World War II, participation in trade and transport is fully comparable with levels in other countries. Participation in services is on the low side, putting the Netherlands in the same category as Belgium, France and Germany, while Sweden, Great Britain and Denmark all had substantially higher levels.

To illustrate the difference between the Netherlands and the other six countries, figures 4.8 and 4.9 compare the average trend of the other six countries with that in the Netherlands. Since 1859, labor force participation in agriculture has accounted for an overall female participation rate between 2 and 7 percentage points lower than in the other countries and an industry rate at least 4 percentage points lower.

Figure 4.8 *A comparison between the Netherlands and the six-country trend in female labor force participation rates in the agricultural sector, 1846-1990*

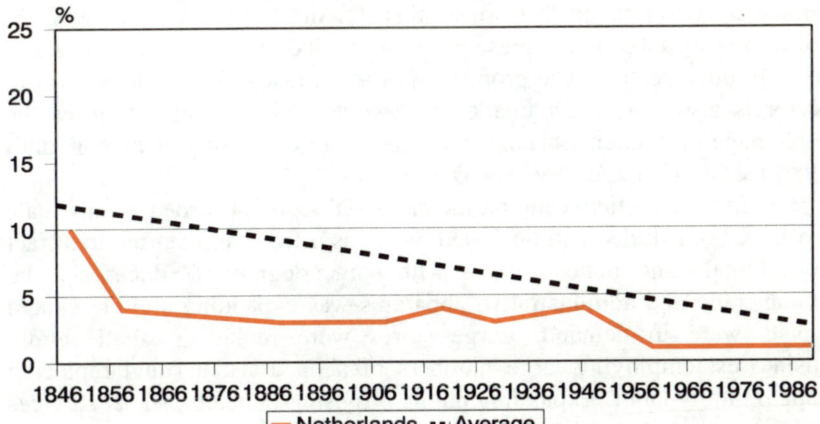

Figure 4.9 *A comparison between the Netherlands and the six-country trend in female labor force participation rates in the industrial sector, 1846-1990*

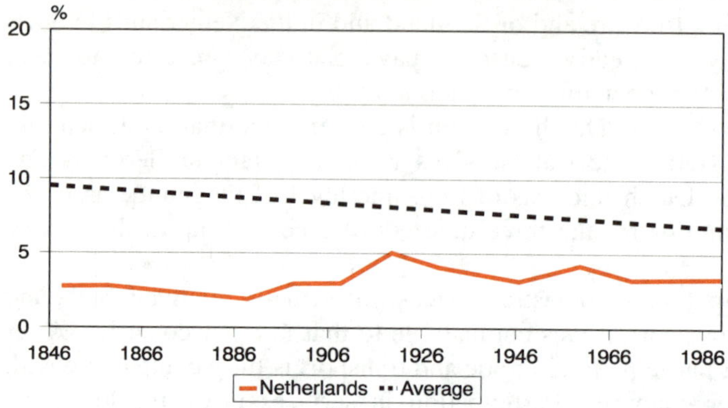

4.4.2 Breakdown of the total and female labor force in three sectors

The main findings of this chapter are once more illustrated by two tables. Table 4.12 presents the breakdown of the total labor force in three sectors, agriculture, industry and other, as percentages of the total labor force (meaning that the three sectors add up to 100 per cent).

The table confirms that Sweden, Denmark, France and Germany all had relatively large agricultural sectors until World War II. The small agricultural sector in Great Britain (after World War II the United Kingdom) was compensated by a large industrial sector. In Belgium, France and Germany, the industrial sectors were also of importance. Compared to the other countries, Dutch industrial shares in the total labor force were not exceptionally low. This confirms the fact that it was only female activity rates in the industrial sector that were low. This is again confirmed by table 4.13, presenting the breakdown of the female labor force in three sectors. The proportion of women working in the industrial sector is also low in Denmark and Sweden, but in both countries the percentage of women working in the agricultural sector was higher (until 1980 for Sweden and 1990 for Denmark).

In the twentieth century, the industrial sector absorbed mainly male workers, both skilled and unskilled, whereas office work started to attract both female and male workers with some degree of education. The bureaucratic and administrative apparatus was expanding and clerks and typists were in demand. Large stores were replacing small family businesses, employing large numbers of shop assistants and replacing unpaid family labor. Expanding public provision in health, social services and education increased the demand for nurses, white-collar staff and teachers, but in all the countries absolute figures remained low until after World War II. For women in the upper and middle classes, the expansion after World War II created new opportunities to obtain paid employment.

In all the countries, structural change has had a significant impact on female participation rates, leading to a pattern of employment growth varying from one sector to another. Over the 1945-1990 period, the service sector has been by far the major source of net job creation for women in all seven countries. The public sector has played the most notable role in this, especially through the creation of part-time employment. There has been a tendency for the public sector to become more female-intensive over time (OECD, 1985:14).

Table 4.12 *Breakdown of the total labor force by three sectors, a seven-country comparison, in percentages, 1880 – 1990*

	Belgium			Denmark			France			Germany			Netherlands			Sweden			U.K.		
	a	b	c																		
1880	43	35	22	54	26	21	48	31	21	42	36	22	–	–	–	68	17	15	13	49	38
1890	42	37	21	49	28	23	45	34	21	36	39	25	33	30	37	62	22	16	11	49	40
1900	23	38	39	40	29	31	44	34	22	–	–	–	31	34	35	55	28	17	9	51	40
1910	22	44	34	38	29	33	43	35	22	34	40	27	28	33	36	45	32	23	8	52	40
1920	15	47	38	37	30	33	38	39	23	30	42	27	24	34	33	44	35	21	10	43	47
1930	17	48	35	32	31	37	36	39	25	29	41	30	21	49	32	40	36	24	6	46	48
1940	–	–	–	32	30	48	36	37	27	26	42	32	–	–	–	34	38	28	–	–	–
1950	12	49	39	27	32	48	26	38	36	29	39	32	19	37	44	25	43	32	6	37	57
1960	9	47	45	19	37	45	22	38	40	14	49	37	12	40	48	14	42	43	4	34	62
1970	5	42	53	11	35	52	13	40	47	8	48	43	7	38	55	8	38	54	3	44	53
1980	3	34	63	7	31	62	9	35	56	5	44	51	5	31	64	6	31	64	3	36	62
1990	3	28	69	6	28	66	6	30	64	3	40	57	5	27	68	3	29	67	2	30	69

a (first column) = agricultural sector.
b (second column) = industrial sector
c (third column) = other sectors

Sources and actual census years: see table 2.2

Table 4.13 *Breakdown of the female labor force by three sectors, a seven-country comparison, in percentages, 1880 – 1990*

	Belgium			Denmark			France			Germany			Netherlands			Sweden			U.K.		
	a	b	c																		
1880	55	26	19	46	19	35	40	27	33	44	24	35	–	–	–	50	6	44	3	44	53
1890	44	23	23	44	20	36	32	30	38	41	24	35	21	16	63	49	7	44	2	44	54
1900	10	40	50	41	23	36	43	32	25	–	–	–	19	17	64	45	10	45	1	45	53
1910	8	44	48	35	17	48	43	33	24	47	23	30	21	18	65	37	12	51	1	46	54
1920	10	39	51	29	16	55	46	29	25	43	25	32	14	21	65	32	19	49	2	33	65
1930	14	37	51	25	14	59	41	29	30	40	24	36	14	20	66	17	21	52	1	38	61
1940	–	–	–	29	18	53	40	27	43	38	28	44	–	–	–	13	24	63	–	–	–
1950	7	39	54	24	20	62	27	24	49	41	22	37	18	18	64	7	26	67	2	24	74
1960	8	30	62	14	24	62	19	26	55	20	34	46	4	23	73	9	24	77	1	19	80
1970	3	27	71	7	22	71	8	24	58	12	34	55	3	17	80	5	19	77	2	28	71
1980	2	17	82	5	15	80	6	24	70	7	28	65	3	11	86	3	15	82	2	20	78
1990	1	14	84	3	15	82	3	23	74	3	24	72	3	10	87	2	14	84	1	16	83

a (first column) = agricultural sector.
b (second column) = industrial sector
c (third column) = other sectors

Sources and actual census years: see table 2.2

4.5 Conclusions to Chapter 4

Following industrialization, the composition of the labor force and the occupational structure changed rapidly. These changes are difficult to quantify exactly, but a survey of the sectoral distribution in the different countries leads to the following conclusions.

Everywhere the role of *agriculture* in providing market work suffered a long-term decline, while the proportion of female workers in (textile) manufacturing showed a variable pattern in each of the countries considered. Frequently it rose initially but declined later. In all seven countries the relative decline in the importance of the *domestic service* for women was compensated by an increase in employment in *non-domestic services*. In general, the trends for men and for women parallel each other, though the participation rates for men are relatively high in *industry* as compared with those for women, while in the service sector the opposite is the case. *Trade and transport* reveals a secular rising trend in all seven countries, while the levels of female activity in this sector are fairly similar.

Occupational segregation appears to have persisted, moving from old sectors to new ones. Agriculture, domestic service and the textile industry disappear as important female employment categories. The new female sectors are the caring occupations, junior white-collaradministrative work, sales and services. The trends are visible in the Netherlands, where the female labor force peaked in *agriculture* in 1947, while participation in *trade and transport* showed a steady increase and in the *service sector* a spectacular one over the period between 1849 and 1990.

Compared with those in the other six countries, Dutch female activity rates in agriculture were extremely low. The one exception is Great Britain, where they were even lower. In Great Britain, however, these low agricultural rates were compensated by relatively high activity rates in industry. In the Netherlands, by contrast, female labor force participation rates in industry have been the lowest of all seven countries ever since 1849.

The main trends in all seven countries are more or less similar, despite the differences in actual activity rates: a decline in agriculture, relative stability in industry (except in Belgium and Great Britain, in both of which there was a declining trend in the second half of the nineteenth century), a slight increase in trade and transport, a decrease in domestic service and a rise in other services varying from the fairly to the extremely spectacular.

The overall conclusion with respect to the Dutch female participation rates is that they have been low because of the low participation in agriculture and in industry over almost the entire period of 150 years. Participation in trade and transport, and in domestic and other services has not been extreme by international standards, although after the Second World War participation was in a group of relatively low rates, together with Belgium, France and Germany. With respect to participation in agriculture, the data are not entirely reliable due to differences in definition. The figures for low participation in industry are probably more reliable. Since 1849, this can be held responsible for producing an overall female labor force participation lower by at least 4 percentage points than the average trend value of the other six countries.

It is possible, therefore, to distinguish some continuity in the long-term development. The early disappearance of the cottage industries in the Netherlands also means that there was no tradition of female labor in these industries in the dominant parts of the country. The late date of industrialization is not a clear factor, because even when industrialization did finally take placc, females did not find much employment in the new industries.

CHAPTER 5

WORK BY STATUS

> *"The bought and the unbought kinds [of services] do not differ from one another in any fundamental respect, and frequently an unbought service is tranformed into a bought one and vice versa. This leads to a number of violent paradoxes ... the services rendered by women enter into the dividend when they are rendered in exchange for wages, whether in the factory or in the home, but do not enter into it when they are rendered by mothers and wives gratuitously for their own families."*
>
> *Arthur Cecil Pigou, 1920*

Measurement of participation in the labor force is complicated by the existence of unpaid family labor and by the combination of paid and unpaid work in the home and on the farm. This has already been mentioned several times in the previous chapters. In particular, the registration of work performed by wives and daughters or sisters assisting in the family business seems to be the cause of many idiosyncrasies in the labor force participation rates, particularly in agriculture. The figures for employed women may be expected to be more reliable and to show less under-estimation (or over-estimation) than those for women assisting husbands, fathers or brothers, especially on an unpaid basis.

The main question examined in this chapter is: to what extent can differences in labor force participation rates between the Netherlands and the other six countries be attributed to differences in classification by *status*? It is hardly surprising if status is not easy to compare between countries, particularly before World War II[1]. Where available, the data presented in the previous chapters is used to create[2] a three-fold distinction in status between:

a) Employers and persons working on their own account.
b) Wage earners and salaried employees.
c) Unpaid family workers.

In the remainder of this chapter a) is abbreviated to *self-employed*

---

1 To improve comparisons between countries, the ILO recommended as early as 1948 the *International Classification by Status in Employment (ICSE)*. This classification was amended in 1958 (ILO, 1991:XVI). The *status* of an economically active person refers to whether this person is (or has been, if unemployed) an *employer*, *worker on her/his own account*, *employee*, *unpaid family worker*, or a *member of a producers' co-operative*.

2 In the annual *"Labour Force Statistics"* of the OECD, the same classification into three categories is published (if available).

(so including *employers* and *workers on their own account*), b) to *employed* and c) to *unpaid family worker*.

Section 5.1 analyses the long-term trend by status and by industrial sector in the Netherlands. Unpaid family labor may be expected mainly to influence the female labor force in agriculture and in trade (shops). Will the trends be any different for men and women?

Section 5.2 compares the Netherlands with the other six countries. Problems of definition appear immediately, even in 1990. Until very recently, an *unpaid family worker* (if defined at all) was defined as a person who works a specified minimum amount of time (usually at least one-third of normal working hours), without pay, in an economic enterprise operated by a related person living in the same household (ILO, 1991:XVI). To improve measurement of the economic activity of women, the 13th International Conference of Labour Statisticians recommended in 1982 the inclusion of all unpaid family workers (if working during the reference period), irrespective of the number of hours worked (ILO, 1987:16). In 1990, this recommendation was applied for the first time in the Netherlands. Most countries nowadays count persons working fewer hours than the former minimum of 13, 14 or 15 a week as belonging to this category. Because the ICSE could not be applied until after World War II, care is required in making comparisons.

5.1 Long-term trends in the Netherlands by status and by industrial sector

Unfortunately, prior to World War II no separate category of *unpaid family workers* was recognized in the Netherlands. This is a reason for subdividing the sectoral division of men and women by status in the labor market merely into *self-employed* and *employed*. *Self-employed* includes managers, employers, persons working on their own account and wives assisting their husbands. *Employed* lumps together skilled and unskilled wage earners, and salaried employees. For some years, the *employed* also include unpaid family workers other than assisting wives.

5.1.1 Trends by status by four sectors, 1899 - 1990

The Dutch censuses of 1889 and 1899 explicitly excluded an assisting wife from the labor force unless she had her own well-defined task or an occupation unconnected with that of her husband. In the 1909 census the instructions were less strict. The censuses of 1899 to 1930 classified the labor force into four different status categories: self-employed, managers, and skilled and unskilled workers. In 1947, these categories were expanded from four to eight: self-employed, small (self-employed) businessman or woman in an industrial firm, director, manager, wife assisting small businessman, child assisting a self-employed person, and skilled and unskilled[3] worker. Although, because of budget cuts in 1947, the results of that census are considered to be less reliable than those of the previous counts, the fact that specific questions were asked about assistance by family members means that figures referring to this category may be more accurate than those in previous counts, especially with regard to women assisting on farms and in shops.

Prior to 1947, assisting wives were regarded as either self-employed or lacking employment. Their children were also awarded a specific status in 1947, whereas previously (as mentioned) they had been counted merely as employed. In 1947, all assisting wives were counted; in the censuses of 1960, 1971 and 1981 only those working more than 15 hours a week. In 1960 the same applied to wage earners (it was estimated to make a difference of about 25 thousand), while in 1971 all wage earners working fewer than 15 hours were counted, unless they were regarded as students or unpaid family workers (it was estimated that about 15 thousand assisting wives were working fewer than 14 hours a week, Berends and Boelmans, 1979:13). In 1990 no such criteria were applied. For these reasons, it is reasonable to expect that more unpaid family workers will have been registered in 1947 and 1990 than in the intervening years.

To compare the censuses and to show the long-term trend, figures on the division of women by industrial sector and by status (self-employed or employed) are presented in table 5.1 and table 5.2 respectively.

---

3 If a distinction is drawn between skilled and unskilled workers, then the increase in skilled workers is found to have been vastly greater among women than among men - so much so that by 1960 the number of female skilled workers (413 thousand) actually exceeded the number of unskilled (382 thousand, equal to 48 per cent); corresponding figures for men in 1960 are 832 thousand and 1,815 thousand (68 per cent) (CBS, 1966, C:20). This compares with an 1899 total of 91 per cent of the girls and women performing unskilled labor, as against 86 per cent of the men. Over the period, from 1899 to 1960, the increase in professional employment requiring skilled labor was relatively greater for women than for men (CBS, 1966). However, since differentiation between skilled and unskilled workers is not feasible for the whole period in all seven countries, and also because this differentiation leads to additional difficulties in the international comparison, a systematic treatment of this distinction is omitted here. Some remarks will be added where appropriate.

Table 5.1 *Self-employed women by four industrial sectors in the Netherlands, absolute figures in thousands, 1899 – 1990*

Sector	1899	1909	1920	1930	1947	1960	1971	1981	1990
Agriculture	21	49	30	51	95	23	31	32	55
Industry	21	22	12	12	15	9	12	14	29
Trade	29	29	23	36	71	54	67	82	86
Services[1]	15	20	20	25	39	29	20	48	33
Total	86	120	84	124	221	115	130	171	299
Assisting wives	–	–	–	–	152	64	86	93	[2]115

1 Domestic and non-domestic services together
2 Includes all unpaid family workers.

Sources: CBS, 1966, vol. 10, C:18 and sources table 4.2

Table 5.2 *Employed women by four industrial sectors in the Netherlands, absolute figures in thousands, 1899 – 1990*

Sector	1899	1909	1920	1930	1947	1960	1971	1981	1990
Agriculture	59	63	60	59	18	18	8	10	26
Industry	54	75	120	137	205	205	205	194	243
Trade	13	24	62	86	190	190	184	309	506
Services[1]	220	257	303	358	400	400	569	889	1308
Total	346	419	545	640	723	813	[2]961	1381	2106

1 Domestic and non-domestic services together.
2 In contrast to the years 1971 and 1981, the category 'other' is not classified as employed or self-employed and therefore excluded.

Sources: CBS, 1966, vol. 10, C:18 and sources table 4.2.

Table 5.2 reveals a steady increase in *employed* women, both in absolute figures and in percentages, but table 5.1 shows that absolute numbers and percentages of women registered as *self-employed* (probably because they perform *unpaid family labor)* fluctuate. The registration of assisting wives (since 1947) is displayed in the bottom line of table 5.1[4].

[4] The tremendous decline in the numbers of assisting wives between 1947 and 1960 will eventually be found to offset the increase in employed married women (chapter 8). For this reason, although there was a very large increase in the number of employed women between 1947 and 1960, it was not large enough to compensate for the decrease in the number of self-employed women. This produces the decline in female labor force participation rates between 1947 and 1960 seen in figure 2.1 of the second chapter.

The same analysis is given for men in tables 5.3 and 5.4.

Table 5.3 *Self-employed men by four industrial sectors in the Netherlands, absolute figures in thousands, 1899 – 1990*

Sector	1899	1909	1920	1930	1947	1960	1971	1981	1990
Agriculture	166	191	191	215	239	219	179	148	130
Industry	113	113	113	128	156	128	80	66	59
Trade	109	123	123	170	193	177	184	156	123
Services	26	28	32	45	64	69	75	82	114
Total	413	454	459	558	651	593	517	451	420
Share of self-employed women in total of self-employed	17%	21%	15%	16%	25%	16%	20%	27%	42%

Sources and footnotes, see tables 5.1 and 5.2

Table 5.4 *Employed men by four industrial sectors in the Netherlands, absolute figures in thousands, 1899 – 1990*

Sector	1899	1909	1920	1930	1947	1960	1971	1981	1990
Agriculture	347	338	360	331	340	187	74	81	77
Industry	420	530	723	883	1102	1426	1436	1298	1321
Trade	172	252	358	420	423	540	614	687	864
Services	137	145	190	224	407	492	866	974	1238
Total	1076	1265	1631	1858	2272	2647	[a]2989	[b]3060	3520

a In 1971, 41 thousand persons were not classified and
b in 1981, 236 thousand.

Sources and footnotes, see tables 5.1 and 5.2.

If the share of self-employed women among the total self-employed is calculated (see the bottom line of table 5.3), then women are found to have formed a relatively large share in 1990 (as expected, because of unpaid family workers). Self-employed women are found mostly in agriculture, in industry and in trade. The shares of self-employed women in agriculture and trade in 1947 are smaller, but also relatively great (again as expected).

5.1.2 Status of men and women in agriculture

Under-counting of women working in the agricultural sector before World War II is almost certain. This is confirmed by Van Zanden (1985). By

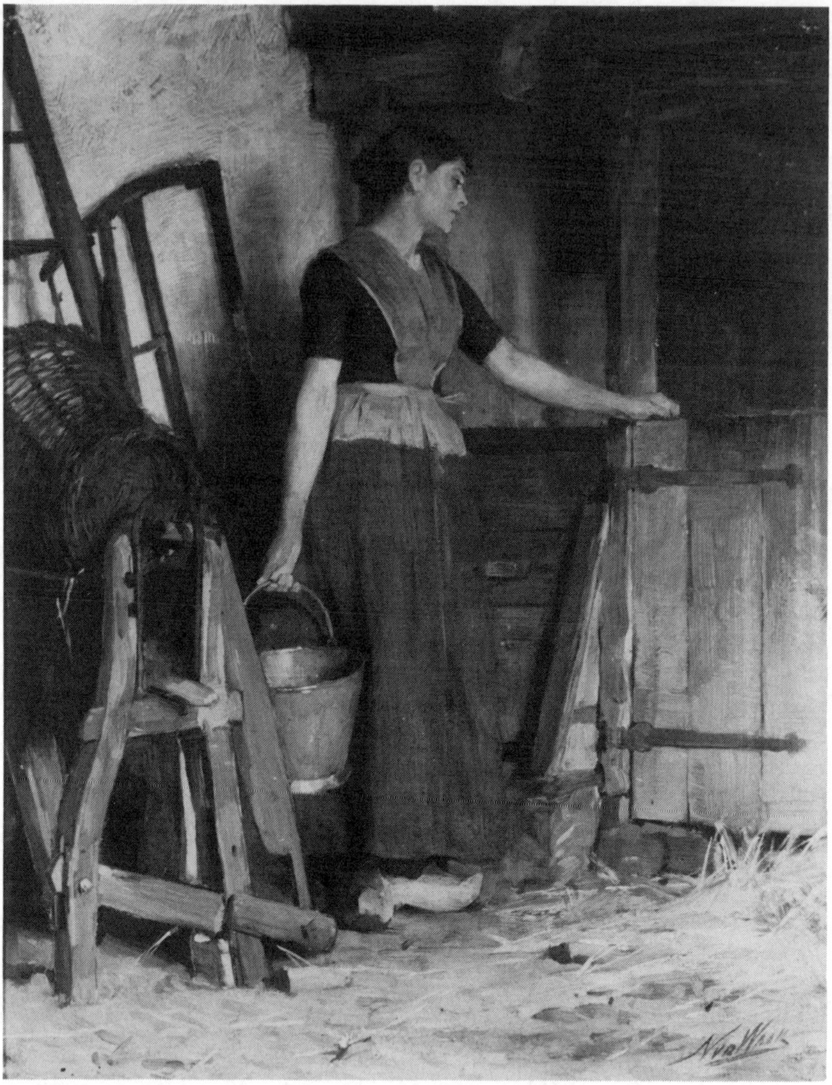

Nicolaas van der Waaij *(1855–1936)*
Country girl (Boerenmeisje)
Amsterdams Historisch Museum

dividing the female agricultural labor force into three groups - *werkbode* (maid), *dag- of weekloonster* (day or week laborer) and assisting family members - he compares the census figures with other sources such as the registers of taxes, which had to be paid for living-in servant girls and maids on farms. These tax figures show a remarkable pattern: between 1807 and 1858 the number of maids increased rapidly; they decreased sharply over the next twenty years and after 1880 more gradually. The tax figures confirm that the census figures are too low. In the province of North-Holland, the total number of maids according to the taxes is actually higher than the whole female labor force in that province according to the census (Van Zanden, 1985:70). Assuming that on each farm there was at least one woman assisting in the daily farm work, Van Zanden estimates that between 1810 and 1850 the Dutch female labor force in agriculture rose by 25 per cent and that it remained stable between 1850 and 1910. Women's share in the agricultural labor force decreased from 57 per cent in 1810 to 37 per cent in 1910. These estimates are higher than the census figures (see table 5.5). The total decrease in farm maids is caused mainly by the fact that many girls went to the urban areas to become living-in domestic servants. This decrease was only partly offset by the increase in assisting wives. After 1850, relatively more farms were established, resulting in more assisting wives and other unpaid family workers. The large number of proletarian women found in the agricultural sector around 1850 largely disappear because of the increase in employment opportunities in the cities, particularly after 1860 (Van Zanden, 1985).

Table 5.5 *Estimates of the female labor force in agriculture in the Netherlands, absolute figures in thousands, 1807 – 1910*

	1807	1849	1880	1910
assisting family members	74	87	101	119
maids	37	42	33	29
day laborers	31	47	38	29
total	142	175	172	176
total census	–	158	[1]73	[2]112
total number of living-in domestic servant girls	52	[3]58	[4]100	[5]125

1 Actually 1889
2 Actually 1909
3 Actually 1846
4 Actually 1878
5 Actually 1896

Sources: Van Zanden, 1985:70,75 and table 4.3.

This confirms the expectation that female labor force participation in agriculture will be difficult to measure. However, the remainder of this section analyzes only census figures and, for the recent years, sample survey data.

Figure 5.1[5] shows the census and sample survey data on self-employed women and men in agriculture.

Figure 5.1 *Self-employed in agriculture, absolute figures in thousands, in the Netherlands, 1899-1990*

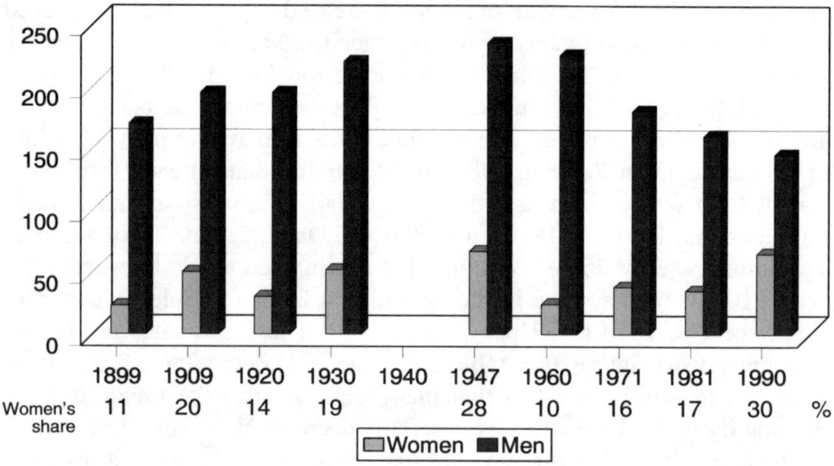

No regular pattern for women is revealed in figure 5.1. As mentioned above, this may be due to differences in the method of registering wives and daughters engaged in unpaid family labor. Of all women working in the agricultural sector in 1947, 84 per cent were working together with their husbands or fathers (CBS, Volkstelling 1947).

Comparing the figures for *self-employed* women with those given for *self-employed* men in figure 5.1, there was an increase in self-employed men until 1947 and since then a decrease, while numbers of self-employed women showed rather large fluctuations. Some similarities between men and women can be noted however: a decline between 1909 and 1920, a more substantial decline between 1947 and 1960, an increase between 1920 and 1930 and another increase between 1981 and 1990. Between 1909 and 1920, the numbers of self-employed men in agriculture - and likewise in both industry and trade and transport, see figures 5.3 and 5.5 - remained more or less unchanged, while the number of their female counterparts in agriculture and industry declined sharply. If women's share is calculated, the share of self-employed women in agriculture was relatively high in 1909, 1947 and 1990, with 20, 28 and 30 per cent respectively, and low in 1899 and 1960 with 11 and 10 per cent respectively.

Figure 5.2 gives the corresponding data for those *employed* in agriculture. Note that the scales of the self-employed and the employed are different, the maximum on the scale of the *self-employed* is 250 thousand, (the maximum of the four sectors) while that of the *employed* is 1.5 million.

---

5 The figures 5.1 - 5.8 are based on the four tables 5.1 - 5.4.

Figure 5.2 *Employed in agriculture, absolute figures in thousands, in the Netherlands, 1899-1990*

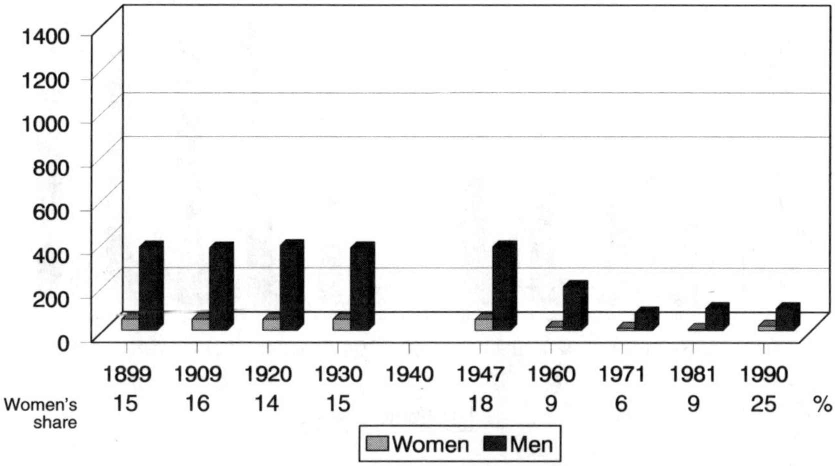

Figure 5.2 shows that the numbers employed in agriculture remained at about the same absolute level during the first fifty years of this century, after which they declined. Since 1970, absolute levels for employed men seem to have stabilized again, but women's employment has increased. The share of women employed in agriculture varied between 14 and 16 per cent prior to 1947, increased to 18 per cent in 1947, then dropped below 10 per cent in the next three censuses; it had, however, shot up to a relatively high 25 per cent by 1990.

5.1.3 Status of men and women in industry

The corresponding figures for men and women registered as self-employed or employed in industry are presented in figures 5.3 and 5.4.

Figure 5.3 *Self-employed in industry, absolute figures in thousands, in the Netherlands, 1899-1990*

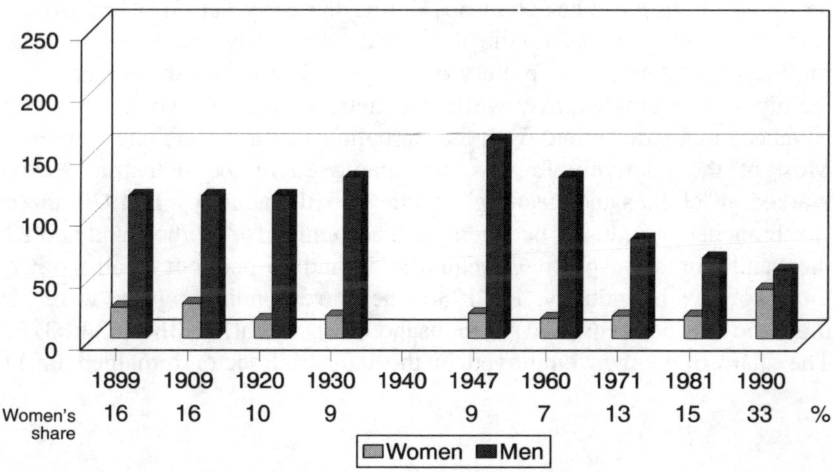

Figure 5.4 *Employed in industry, absolute figures in thousands, in the Netherlands, 1899-1990*

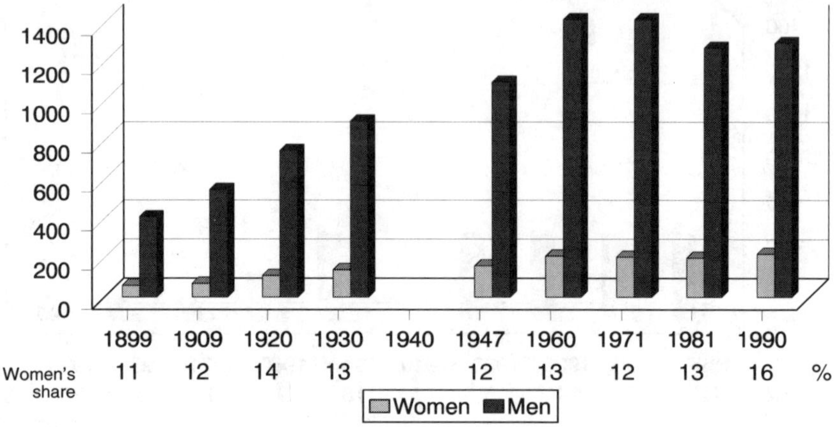

These figures confirm the conclusion that, compared with men, relatively few women were found in the industrial sector. This applies to self-employed as well as to employed women.

The trends for self-employed men and self-employed women differ, while the trends for the employed are rather similar. Self-employed men peak in 1947, self-employed women in 1990. The absolute figures for self-employed men in industry (as in agriculture) in 1960, are only slightly higher than those for 1930. Between 1947 and 1960 the number of male business heads decreased. This decrease is also illustrated by the share of self-employed women, which was never greater than 16 per cent, except in 1990 when it reached 33 per cent.

The aggregate data conceal the sharp division between female and male labor in the different branches of industry. The figures also conceal the large regional differences. If women in the Netherlands were to be found anywhere in the industrial sector a century ago, then they were to be found (as in the other countries during the early period of industrialization) working in the textile mills and other early industries such as millinery, candlemaking, pottery and cigars. These industries employed mainly young single girls, while the new, rapidly growing and more advanced industries relied from the start almost entirely on male workers. Most of the relatively few women employed in the industrial sector worked in "clothes and cleaning" and the "textile industry". In 1920, these two branches of industry between them accounted for 79 thousand and 22 thousand women respectively, equal to 53 and 15 per cent of all women then working in industry. By 1930, the corresponding figures were 78 thousand (46 per cent) and 30 thousand (18 per cent) (CBS, 1934:83). The share of women employed in the industrial sector remained fairly

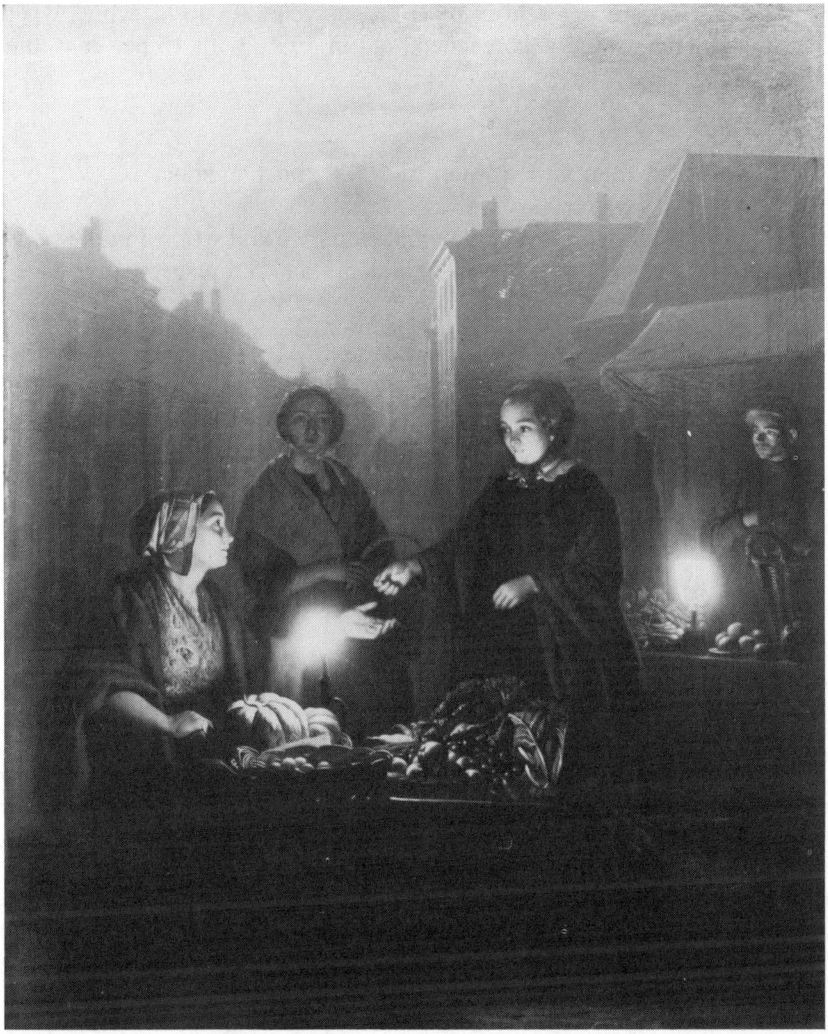

Petrus van Schendel (1806–1870)
Merchant woman selling at night (koopvrouw bij avond), late nineteenth century
Amsterdams Historisch Museum

constant at 12 or 13 per cent in most census years. In 1899, with 11 per cent, the smallest share was reached, and in 1990, with 16 per cent, the largest share.

5.1.4 Status of men and women in trade and transport

The figures for self-employed and employed men and women in the trade and transport sector are shown in figures 5.5 and 5.6 respectively.

Figure 5.5 *Self-employed in trade and transport, absolute figures in thousands, in the Netherlands, 1899-1990*

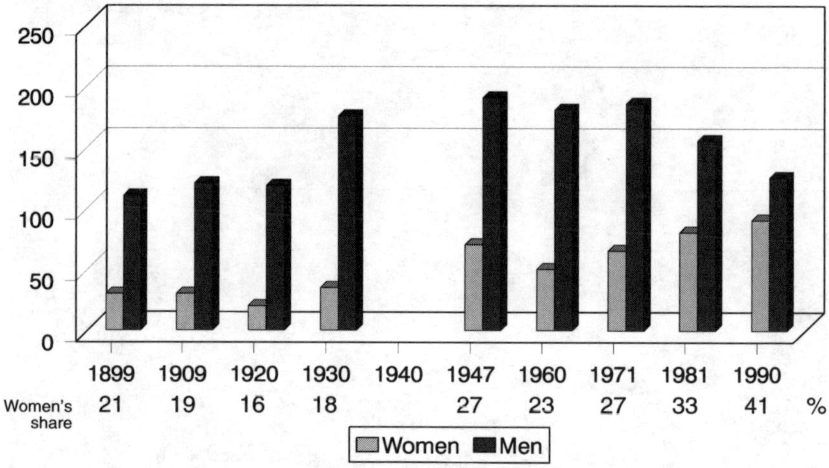

Figure 5.6 *Employed in trade and transport, absolute figures in thousands, in the Netherlands, 1899-1990*

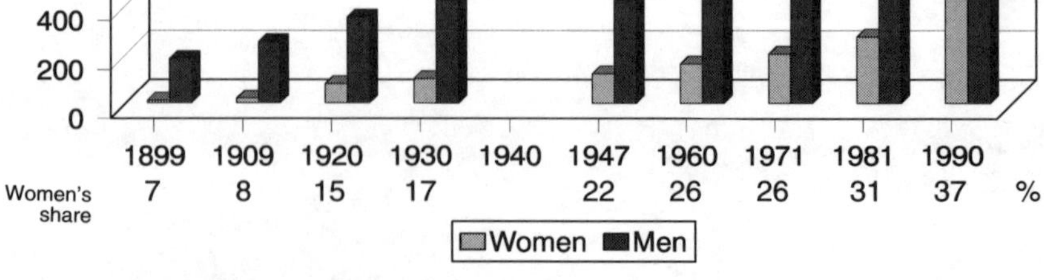

The very slow increase in the total number of self-employed men lags behind the relative increase in the population (more than 1.5 million people) during the first twenty years of the century. Between 1920 and

1930, there was a relatively large increase in trade and transport, due to a boom in the number of shopkeepers. The large increase in female shopkeepers (54 per cent) between 1920 and 1930 is due, according to the CBS (1932:125), to the fact that more care was being taken to register assisting family members. However, the increase in male shopkeepers was also exactly 54 per cent (see also Van Dijk and Verstegen, 1988:77).

Employment in petty trade increased slightly from 13 to 15 per cent of the labor force in the trade sector (Van Dijk and Verstegen, 1988:78). In agriculture in 1930 almost half the number of *self-employed* women were wives assisting their husbands, while in trade and transport the majority of women were either shop or inn-keepers or running boarding houses (CBS, 1934:84).

In 1947, trade and transport included 51 thousand wives working jointly with their husbands in shops, out of a total of 54 thousand assisting wives in this sector. In 1960, 36 thousand assisting wives were counted in trade and transport, with 33 thousand (52 per cent) of them in shops, in contrast to 17 thousand in agriculture (27 per cent). The decline in small shops caused the relative decline in assisting wives in the trade and transport sector. It is obvious, however, that unpaid family workers are a major factor in this sector. In the retail trade, even more than in agriculture, wives assist their husbands. For this reason, the share of self-employed women in the trade and transport sector, although fluctuating, is larger than in agriculture and industry, except in 1947 when the numbers were about equal. The share increased from 16 per cent (in 1920) to 27 per cent (in 1947 and 1971) and reached the high percentage of 41 in 1990.

The number of men and women being employed in the trade and transport sector shows an upward trend overall, with women's share in this sector gradually increasing from a low 7 per cent in 1900 to a high 37 per cent in 1990.

5.1.5 Status of men and women in services

Examination of figures 5.7 and 5.8, relating to developments in the service sector, reveals a steady increase in both men and women employed in this sector, showing that the decline in domestic service after 1930 (see table 4.2) was largely compensated by an increase in non-domestic services.

Again, especially after 1947, no regular pattern can be distinguished for the self-employed in services. In contrast to that of self-employed women in the other sectors, the female share in services was almost identical in 1900 to that in 1990, at 37 and 36 per cent respectively.

Aggregation of domestic and non-domestic services disguises the differences between the various occupations involved. Domestic services are in general lower grade occupations involving hard physical work, while the non-domestic services offer more attractive jobs for relatively better educated workers.

Figure 5.7 *Self-employed in services, absolute figures in thousands, in the Netherlands, 1899-1990*

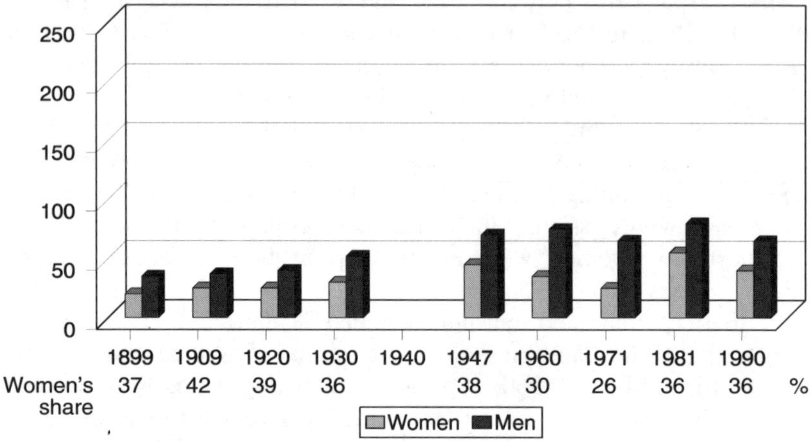

A remarkable feature of the period between 1920 and 1930 is the half million increase in foreign, especially German, workers (and of course in the population as a whole). In 1920 the labor force included 19 thousand men and 12 thousand women from Germany; by 1930 their numbers had increased to 29 and 33 thousand, a respective increase of 57 and 174 per cent. Half of all foreigners in the Netherlands in 1930 were employed in domestic service, this high proportion being influenced by the tremendous increase in German servant girls between 1920 and 1930 (from 9 to nearly 31 thousand, an increase of 233 per cent). There was also a striking increase in male foreigners working in the mines (CBS, 1934:87).

Figure 5.8 *Employed in services, absolute figures in thousands, in the Netherlands, 1899-1990*

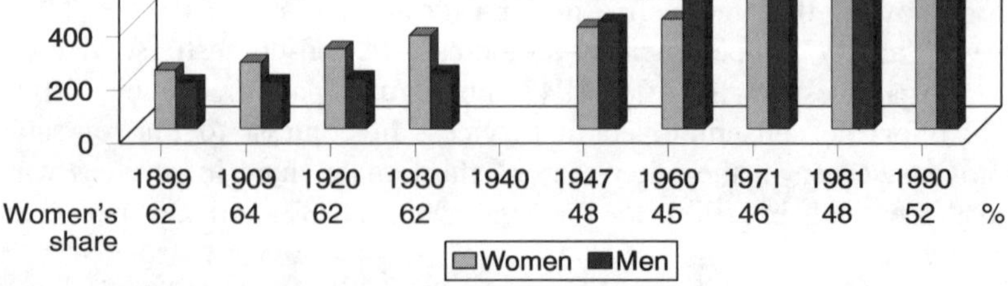

As figure 5.8 displays, the share of women was over 50 per cent in the first half of the period: 62 per cent in 1899, 1920 and 1930 and 64 per cent in 1909; it then dropped to 48 per cent in 1947 and 45 in 1960, rising again to 46 in 1971, 48 in 1981 and 52 per cent in 1990.

5.2 A seven-country comparison of female economic activity by status in the labor market

In the Dutch case, treated in some detail in the previous section, self-employed women formed a heterogeneous group, consisting of inter alia women working on their own account and assisting wives. Even in the 1980s, not much is known about this category in the other countries and statistical enquiries are rare[6].

In 1985, a study was run in the then 10 countries of the European Community dealing both with women who were employers or working for themselves and with women involved in the activities of their husbands (Riffault and Tchernia, 1987). This group consisted of about 13 million women, with one third running their own businesess and two thirds helping their husbands as assisting wives. The three Benelux countries (Belgium, the Netherlands and Luxemburg) had the lowest percentage of married women involved in their husbands' activities, while the Netherlands was the country with the lowest percentage of women working independently on their own account (Riffault and Tchernia, 1987).
Despite the differences between countries, there are many similarities. In the 10 European countries considered, about half of all women working on their own account or running a business are in the retail trade. The rest are spread over a small number of other sectors and occupations. In descending order of importance, 12 per cent are found in beauty care and hair dressing, 10 per cent in professions such as the law and dentistry, 9 per cent in farming and fishing and 9 per cent in arts and crafts. Registered companies are rare. Regardless of whether or not the business is a registered company, the chief executive or managing director is usually the woman herself, either alone or together with her husband.

It might be expected that, as in the Netherlands, salaried workers and wage earners would be a less diverse category. What did the censuses of the other six countries register with respect to status in the labor market?

5.2.1 Breakdown of the labor force by status

Where the total and female labor forces are classified by status at all, at least the same two categories are used as in the Netherlands, but a third category is frequently added: *self-employed, employed* and *unpaid family*

[6] A comparative set of comparative data on the self-employed in OECD countries was published in OECD (1986, chapter 2) and OECD (1992, chapter 4), while the topic has also been widely discussed by ILO (1991). Part of the reason for this recent interest is that self-employment has been growing in several countries, reversing a trend of many decades. These publications are likely to be of particular interest to policy makers.

workers. For the early censuses, such classification turned out to be impossible in all seven countries. For this reason, if distinguished at all, the period chosen in this section is 1910 - 1990.

To compare the seven countries, two tables (5.6 and 5.7) have been compiled. The calculations are based on the same sources as those in table 2.2. Where other additional sources were available (for example, ILO, 1933 and ILO, 1991), the calculations were repeated and checked against the computations based on the original sources.

The censuses before World War II are difficult to compare, even within one country, because different classifications are applied. For example, in Belgium in 1890 and 1900 status is divided into the categories of *maîtres* (employers, masters), *surveillants* (supervisors), *employés techniques* (technicians) and *ouvriers* (laborers), but it is only in the industrial professions that a distinction is drawn between female and male wage earners and employees. In 1910 the whole female labor force is categorized into *maîtresses, employées and ouvrières*. In 1920 the labor force is divided into *patrons, employés* and *ouvriers*, and in 1930 bilingually into *patrons/bazen, employés/bedienden, ouvriers/werklieden*. Moreover, as in 1910, in 1920 and 1930 a separate category of *aidants-/helpers* (unpaid family workers) is registered, although these workers are not counted as part of the labor force (see also chapter 4). These are included in table 5.6. The male unpaid family workers are in the majority (103 thousand males as against 76 thousand females in 1920), most of them working in agriculture (75 thousand men and 56 thousand women). Only 9 thousand women assist in the trade sector[7], a situation different from the Dutch. In 1930, 189 males and 185 females are assisting the head of the household. Besides, in Belgium in the early censuses there is no classification of those gainfully occupied in public administration, in the liberal professions, domestic and personal services, and insufficiently described occupations. In tables 5.6 and 5.7 they are added to the category of employed. For coding status, the 1947 and subsequent censuses used eight groups: self-employed, employer (not bound by labor contract), head of establishment or business (bound by contract), public sector employee, private sector employee, wage earner in private sector, apprentice bound by an apprenticeship contract, and unpaid family worker (see also ILO, 1991:24).

In Denmark in 1901 and 1911, as mentioned in the previous chapter, the labor force is divided into *Forsørgere* (breadwinners), *Forsørgerde* (dependants) and *Tyende ved Husgerning og Ehrververvs-tyende under* (domestic servants in households and businesses). In 1921 and 1930 the division is into *Hovedpersoner* (main persons or self-employed), *Funktionærer* (employees) and *Arbejdere* (wage earners) and in 1940 into four groups: *Selvstændige Næringsdrivende, Direktorer* (self-

---

[7] This means in the *achat, vente et location des produits industriels et agricoles* (purchase, sale and hire of industrial and agricultural products) (Recensement Général 1920:95).

employed and employers); *Medhjelpende Hustruer* (assisting wives); *Funktionærer, Tjenstemænd* (employees and public servants); and *Arbejdere* (wage earners). In 1950, the active population is divided into those working outside the home and at home (*Husmedhjelpere*) and both categories into *Selvstændige*, including *medhjelpende hustruer* (self-employed, including assisting wives), *Funktionærer* (employees) and *Arbejdere* (wage earners). The recent censuses code status into 6 categories: self-employed, assisting wives, employees, skilled and unskilled wage earners and unspecified employees (ILO, 1991:68).

In France, in contrast to the majority of the other countries, the censuses of 1896, 1906, 1911, 1921, 1926, 1931 and 1936 register nearly all farmers' wives as being in the labor force and belonging to the category *chefs d'établissement* (masters), as against the other two[8] categories: *employés et ouvriers* (employees and wage earners) and *travailleurs isolés* (isolated, independent workers). Public administrators, those working in the liberal professions, and domestic and personal services are included in the classification. Most female *chefs d'établissement* are found in agriculture (81 per cent and 83 per cent in 1906 and 1921 respectively). For this reason, in France the *self-employed* category includes assisting wives. The censused conducted since 1954 have used 12 groups for coding status in the labor force, three for non-employees and 9 for employees (ILO, 1991:87).

In Germany, the censuses of 1882, 1895, 1907, 1925 and 1933 employ 5 status categories: *Selbständige* (self-employed); *Mithelfende Familienangehörige* (unpaid family workers); *Angestellte und Beambte* (employees, including the armed forces); *Arbeiter* (wage earners), and Hausangestellte (domestic servants). The *Hausangestellte* are included in the category *employed* in the census tables. In most countries domestic servants are not classified, but in tables 5.6 and 5.7 domestic servants in all seven countries are added to the category *employed*. Since 1925, all farmers' wives in Germany have been counted as belonging to the labor force. The result is that in the 1925 census the male and female labor force in agriculture are about equal. Van Dijk and Verstegen (1988:32), comparing the Netherlands and Germany, conclude that if in 1920 all farmers' wives had been counted in the Netherlands, participation by women aged 15 - 64 would have increased from 23 to 27 per cent.

The recent German censuses (e.g. 1987) have used eight categories for coding status: self-employed (employing paid labor or without paid labor); skilled worker; other wage earner; salaried employee; apprentice; official, judge, soldier, person doing alternative civilian service, and family helper (ILO, 1991:95).

Prior to 1947, three main groups were distinguished in the Netherlands: *bedrijfshoofden, inclusief medewerkende echtgenoten* (business heads, including assisting wives), *employés* (employees) and *arbeiders* (wage earners). In 1947, as mentioned in the previous section, eight

---

[8] Three, if unemployed is counted as a separate category.

groups were used, but in 1990 only three main groups: *zelfstandigen* (self-employed), *personen in loondienst* (employed persons), *meewerkend gezinslid* (assisting family member).

In Sweden, as mentioned already in chapter 4, unpaid family workers and domestic/agricultural servants complicate comparibility. Without the *Tjenstehjon* female labor force participation rates in 1880 and 1890 were 19 and 21 per cent respectively. In 1900, without the *Tjänstehjon* the rates were 22 and 26 per cent. Silenstam (1970) has also calculated the figure of the economically active, without these servants and the unpaid family workers, particularly without the unmarried suns and daughters[9]. Dividing these figures of the *yrkesverksamma* by the total female population gives the following labor force participation rates: 13 per cent in 1880; 12 per cent in 1890, 13 per cent in 1900, 15 per cent in 1910, 19 per cent in 1920, 23 per cent in 1930 and 24 per cent in 1940. Only the last figure closely resembles the figure published in table 2.2 and 4.10. However the figure in 1940 is 30 per cent (according to Silenstam (1970:100), calculated by assuming an equal percentage of unpaid family daughters and assisting wives in 1940 as in 1930).
In 1920 and 1930[10] four groups were used for coding status of *de egentliga yrkesutövarna* (the economically active population without unpaid family workers), *Företagare* (employers and self-employed), *Funktionärer* (employees), *Medhjälpande familjemedlemmar* (family workers) and *Arbetare* (wage earners). In 1940, *Förvaltningspersonal* (public servants) were added, while in 1950 *Företagare* (employers), *Tjänstemän* (salaried employees), and *Arbetare* (wage earners) were distinguished. In the recent censuses, four groups have been used: self-employed in farming/forestry, employer, employee and seaman (ILO, 1991:221).

In England and Wales, the censuses of 1901, 1911 and 1921 distinguished those engaged in certain industries only into: *working at home*, *employers, working for employers, working on own account* and *others.* In 1901, most women working on their own account were dressmakers (110 thousand), while domestic servants (not classified) remained by far the largest group (402 thousand of the total 721 thousand occupied females). Farmers' sons, daughters and other relatives assisting in work on the farm are in general excluded from the labor force, but if included they are registered as *employed*.

In more recent censuses, for example the 1981 census, five basic

---

9 Until 1930 unmarried daughters over 15 years old and living on a farm were counted as being in the agricultural labor force, however, married women not. Registration only improved since 1965 (Silenstam, 1970:100).

10 In 1910, 1920 and 1930 a different classification was also made into: *Självständiga* (independent persons, including retired persons able to take care of themselves, analogous to the *Forsørgere* in Denmark), *Funktionärer* (employees), *Medhjälpande familje medlemmar* (family workers) and *Arbetare* (wage earners).

categories have been distinguished: self-employed (employing others or not), employee (supervising others or not) and apprentice or trainee. For a ten per cent sample, an extended classification has been used (ILO, 1991:241).

Table 5.6 gives the breakdown of the total labor force by status in percentages. The three categories *self-employed*, *employed* (salaried employees and wage earners) and *unpaid family workers* therefore add up to 100 per cent (or approximately so, if the category of non-classified is relatively substantial).

Despite all the changes and inaccuracies in registration, it is obvious that unpaid family labor (if registered) is diminishing in importance, especially since World War II, and that *being employed* (including wage earners) is becoming relatively more and more important in all the countries. Moreover, differences between countries are growing ever smaller. For over half a century, Great Britain had the largest proportion of the total labor force in the category *employed*, while in France this category has been relatively small and the *self-employed* and *unpaid family workers* categories relatively large.

Table 5.7 gives the corresponding percentages for the female labor force. It is obvious that larger percentages of women than of men in the labor force are involved in unpaid family labor. It is also obvious that where no separate category of unpaid family labor was registered, the category to which this work was added is always relatively large in the country in question. So, France and the Netherlands had a relatively large category of self-employed while Great Britain/United Kingdom had a relatively large category of employed. In 1990 France still had the lowest percentage of women classed as employed, followed by Belgium.

A remarkable feature is the relatively high percentage of women employed in the Netherlands prior to World War II and the high proportion of women classed as unpaid family workers in 1947. Over the last four decades, however, the Netherlands has occupied an intermediate position.

Table 5.6 *Breakdown of the total labor force by status, a seven-country comparison, in percentages, 1900 – 1990*

	Belgium a	b	c	Denmark			France			Germany			Netherlands			Sweden			U.K.		
1900	–	–	–	–	–	–	50	50	–	23	68	9	26	74	–	–	–	–		–	
1910	22	46	22	28	64	8	50	50	–	19	66	15	25	75	–	–	–	–		–	
1920	19	75	6	24	69	7	47	53	–	16	67	17	20	80	–	25	53	17		–	
1930	20	56	10	24	70	6	43	57	–	16	68	16	25	75	–	21	67	12	12	88	–
1940	–	–	–	22	72	6				–	–	–	–	–	–	21	71	8	–	–	–
1950	18	71	11	21	73	6	21	64	13				19	68	10	19	75	6	7	93	–
1960	19	74	7	20	70	6	19	72	9	13	77	10	15	80	5	14	83	3	8	92	–
1970	14	82	4	15	79	6	16	75	7	10	84	6	11	85	3	9	89	2	8	92	–
1980	13	83	4	12	85	3	14	79	3	9	87	4	10	81	2	7	93	1	8	92	–
1990	14	82	4	10	88	2	15	76	5	9	89	2	10	80	2	9	91	0	14	86	–

Belgium: data from censuses in 1910, 1920, 1930, 1947, 1961, 1970 and 1981; if unpaid family workers are not counted, in 1910 a) = 22% and b) = 78%
Denmark: census years 1911, 1921, 1930, 1940, 1950, 1960, 1970 and 1980
France: census years 1896, 1906, 1921, 1931, 1954, 1962, 1968, 1975; because of non-classified total does not add up to 100%; non-classified in 1954: 2%; in1968: 2%; in 1975: 4%; in 1982: 9%.
Germany: census years 1895, 1907, 1925, 1933, 1939, 1960, 1970, 1980
The Netherlands: census years 1899, 1909, 1920, 1930, 1947, 1960, 1971, sample surveys 1981, 1990
Sweden: census years 1910, 1920, 1930, 1940, 1950, 1960, 1970
United Kingdom: census years: 1931, 1951, 1961, 1971, 1981

a (first column) = self-employed;
b (second column) = employed;
c (third column) = unpaid family workers

Sources: See table 2.2

Table 5.7 *Breakdown of the female labor force by status, a seven-country comparison, in percentages, 1910 – 1990*

	Belgium			Denmark			France			Germany			Netherlands			Sweden			U.K.		
	a	b	c																		
1910	18	54	18	11	68	21	62	38	–	–	–	–	22	78	–	–	–	–	–	–	–
1920	19	72	9	15	56	31	55	44	–	8	55	37	13	87	–	13	48	39	–	–	–
1930	23	53	25	14	61	25	49	51	–	8	56	36	16	84	–	12	69	19	8	92	–
1940	–	–	–	10	66	24	37	63	–	–	–	–	–	–	–	12	66	8	–	–	–
1950	18	71	11	7	75	19	14	58	26				7	67	26	11	84	5	4	96	–
1960	19	72	9	6	86	17	12	69	19	8	70	22	5	84	10	10	87	3	4	92	1
1970	11	79	10	4	77	11	8	74	15	6	79	15	4	88	8	5	91	4	4	94	2
1980	9	83	8	4	90	6	9	79	7	5	88	7	6	88	6	3	94	2	4	96	–
1990	9	83	8	7	93	–	11	87	–	5	91	4	8	88	5	5	95	–	8	92	–

Belgium: data from censuses in 1910, 1920, 1930, 1947, 1961, 1970 and 1981; if unpaid family workers are not counted, in 1910 a) = 22% and b) = 78%.
Denmark: census years 1911, 1921, 1930, 1940, 1950, 1960, 1970 and 1980, sample 1987: a) includes assisting wives.
France: census years 1906, 1921, 1931, 1954, 1962, 1968, 1975; in 1982 a) + c) = 15% and b = 85%; because of non-classified total does not add up to 100%; non-classified in 1954: 3%; in 1968: 2%; in 1975: 6%.
Germany: census years 1925, 1933, 1960, 1970, 1980
The Netherlands: census years 1909, 1920, 1930, 1947, 1960, 1971, sample surveys 1981, 1990
Sweden: census years 1910, 1920, 1930, 1940, 1950, 1960, 1970
United Kingdom: 1931 census concerns England and Wales only: employers: 1.5%; workers on their own account: 6.5%; census years: 1951, 1961, 1971, 1981 and sample survey 1991 concerns U.K.

a (first column) = self-employed;
b (second column) = employed;
c (third column) = unpaid family workers

Sources: See table 2.2

5.2.2 Female labor force participation rates by status

Table 5.7 does not provide any clear indication of why Dutch female activity rates were so low. For this reason, and because of the inaccuracy in the measurement of the unpaid family workers and the heterogeneity of the self-employed group, figure 5.8 and figure 5.9 have been constructed to show how much the female category *employed* contributed to the overall female labor force participation rate.

Table 5.8 and figure 5.9 show that though low, Dutch female labor force participation rates are not the lowest throughout the period. The Belgium female labor force participation rates in both 1910 and 1930 were even lower and in 1920 and 1961 they equalled the 1920 and 1960 Dutch rates respectively.

In 1920, the Dutch rate of participation of the employed was 80 per cent of the highest in the seven countries, and in 1930 it was 67 per cent. After World War II, this highest-lowest ratio fell to 50 per cent over the period from 1947 to 1981. In 1990 it rose to 60 per cent.

Another remarkable feature of table 5.8 and figure 5.9 are the high rates in Denmark since 1950 and the very high rates in both Denmark and Sweden in 1990. The United Kingdom (Great Britain in the figure before World War II) also had relatively high labor force participation rates of the employed.

Between around 1910 and 1920, if measured, there was an increase in females employed in the countries considered, except in Denmark and Sweden where this increase occurred between 1920 and 1930.

If a similar table is constructed for the rates of participation of self-employed women, it is obvious that the Dutch rates were extremely low before World War II and the French rates extremely high, see table 5.9 and figure 5.10. After World War II, the differences become much smaller, although the rates in France remain relatively high. In 1990 the ratio between the highest and lowest is 2/12, while in about 1920 it was 2/24.

The low Dutch female participation rates before World War II can be attributed almost entirely to the low participation rate of self-employed women. After World War II, participation rates of employed women in the Netherlands are fairly similar to those in Belgium and France. In all countries, the rapid increase in females in employment took place between about 1960 and 1980, leveling off thereafter, except in the Netherlands and the United Kingdom where the increase between 1980 and 1990 was relatively high.

Table 5.8 and figure 5.9 *Labor force participation rates of women employed (employees and wage earners), a seven-country comparison from around 1910 to 1990*

	Belgium	Denmark	France	Germany	Nether-lands	Sweden	United Kingdom
1910	12	–	15	–	14	–	–
1920	16	17	19	20	16	15	–
1930	13	21	19	19	16	20	24
1940	–	16	17	–	–	20	–
1950	14	23	17	–	13	18	25
1960	14	24	19	14	14	24	27
1970	19	24	24	14	14	33	29
1980	27	42	26	27	20	43	31
1990	25	44	26	32	28	47	37

Sources: Actual census years:
Belgium: 1947, 1961
Denmark: 1921
France: 1906, 1921, 1931, 1936, 1954, 1962, 1975, 1982
Germany: 1925, 1933, 1971
Netherlands: 1909, 1947, 1971 and survey 1981
United Kingdom: 1931, 1951, 1961, 1971, 1981

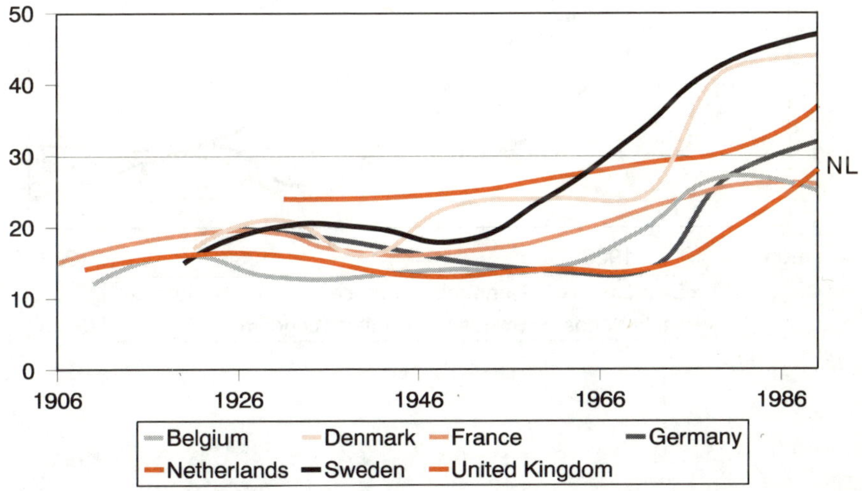

Table 5.9 and figure 5.10 *Female labor force participation rates of the self-employed (including unpaid family workers), a seven-country comparison from around 1910 to 1990*

	Belgium	Denmark	France	Germany	Nether-lands	Sweden	United Kingdom
1910	13	–	24	–	4	–	–
1920	5	17	24	15	2	15	–
1930	11	13	18	14	3	9	5
1940	–	18	17	–	–	5	–
1947	5	7	13	–	7	11	5
1961	6	6	14	3	2	9	5
1970	3	10	14	6	5	6	2
1981	4	4	6	5	5	4	5
1990	5	4	12	3	8	2	6

Sources: see table 2.2 and table 5.8.
Censuses and survey data

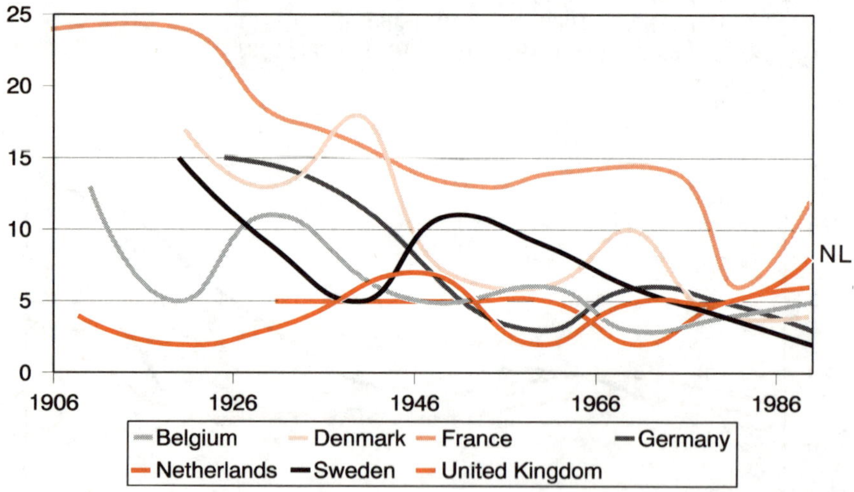

5.3 Conclusions to chapter 5

Differences in female labor force participation rates between the Netherlands and the other six countries can be partly attributed to differences in classification by *status*. Although status is not easy to compare between countries, certainly not before World War II, a three-fold distinction in status is shown (where available):

a) *Self-employed* (including *employers* and *workers on their own account*)
b) *Employed* (including wage earners and salaried employees)
c) *Unpaid family worker*.

The long-term trend by status and by industrial sector in the Netherlands confirms the expectation that unpaid family labor (included in the self-employed) influenced the female labor force in agriculture and in trade (shops). The trends are different for men and for women. In general, the trends for self-employed men and self-employed women differ, while the trends for the employed are fairly similar. There was a steady increase in *employed* women, in absolute figures as well as in percentages, but both absolute numbers and percentages of women registered as *self-employed* (probably because they perform *unpaid family labor)* fluctuate. Women's share in employment in agriculture dropped in mid-century after a long period of stability but rose sharply between 1981 and 1990; in industry it remained relatively low; in trade it steadily increased and in services it remained stable over the first forty years, and lower but also stable over the next forty years. Compared with men, relatively few women were found in the industrial sector. This applies to self-employed as well as to employed women.

In the retail trade even more than in agriculture, wives assist their husbands. For this reason the share of self-employed women in the trade and transport sector, although fluctuating, is higher than in agriculture and industry, except in 1947 when they were about equal.

Self-employed women form a heterogeneous group, consisting inter alia of women working on their own account and assisting wives. In all countries, registration by status proves to have changed several times since the turn of the twentieth century.

Despite all the inaccuracies, unpaid family labor (if registered) diminishes in importance, especially after World War II. *Being employed*, on the other hand, becomes more and more important in all the countries, while differences between countries become ever smaller. On average, Great Britain had by far the largest proportion of the total labor force in the *employed* categorie, while in France this category was relatively small and the *self-employed* and *unpaid family worker* categories relatively large.

Because of the heterogeneity of the group of self-employed and the inaccuracy in the measurement of unpaid family workers, a calculation was performed to establish how much the female category *employed* contributed to the female labor force participation rate. Although low,

Dutch female labor force participation rates over the period from about 1910 to 1990 were not the lowest. In Belgium, female labor force participation rates were even lower in 1930 and in 1961 they equalled the 1960 rates in the Netherlands. In 1920, the Dutch rate of participation of the employed was 80 per cent of the highest in the seven countries, in 1930 it was 67 per cent. The highest-lowest ratio was 50 per cent from 1947 to 1981. In general, the low Dutch female participation rates before World War II can be attributed almost entirely to the low participation rate of self-employed women, while participation rates of Dutch employed women were relatively low during the first three decades following that war.

CHAPTER 6

WORK AND LIFE CYCLE

"Train up a child in the way he should go, and when he is old he will not depart from it."
Proverbs 22:6

The long-term historical perspective on work given in the previous chapters, revealed that there have been major changes in the way market work is recorded and in the type of work that has been done. But fundamental alterations in job opportunities and in the status of women's work did not take place until the twentieth century. It is particularly during the second half of that century that those changes have occurred. However, it is not only job opportunities and status that are important in determining female labor force participation, but also a woman's position within the life cycle, i.e. her age.

This chapter documents the main changes in patterns of female (and for childhood also male) activity by age-group over the life cycle. It is divided into five sections: *Childhood*, *Adolescence and Youth*, *Adulthood*, *Middle Age* and *Old Age*[1]. Have Dutch female activity rates been lower in all age groups?

Section 6.1 defines *Childhood* as the period until the child reaches the age of 15 years (sometimes 14 or 16 years, depending on the available statistics). At the moment 15 or 16 years is the legal minimum age of employment in most countries, but the limit used to be lower[2]. The same demarcation is used to define child labor, although in the nineteenth century labor below the age of 12 would have been more appropriate. However, in order to allow comparisons between the countries over the whole historical period, the demarcation line of about 15 years has been preferred.

Section 6.2 discusses female labor participation during the period of *Adolescence and Youth*. Adolescence is strictly speaking the transitional stage between childhood and adulthood. This period is not constant over time, across countries or between individuals, but in order to compare between countries over a fairly long period, the age limits of 15 to 24 years have been chosen.

---

1 Victor R. Fuchs used identical headings for the chapters in his book: *How we live* (1983). He also used the opening quotation of this chapter.

2 A remarkable feature is that the biological development of *childhood* in the Western world shows the opposite trend. Girls used to reach the age of menarche (their first period) at 15 or 16 years, but in recent decades it has fallen to around 12 years. At the same time, the average age of the climacteric (the beginning of the menopause) has risen since World War II from 45 to over 51 years (Kronjee, 1992).

Section 6.3 covers the rather long period of *Adulthood*, defined as the period between the ages of 25 and 49 years. Section 6.4 discusses female activity rates during *Middle Age*: (ages 50 to 64) and section 6.5 those in *Old Age* (above 65 years of age).

In each section the changes in age-specific participation rates will be described. By analogy to the previous chapters, emphasis is on the development in The Netherlands, as compared with Belgium, Denmark, France, Germany, Sweden and the United Kingdom.

6.1 Childhood

Childhood may be considered as the period of dependence on adults. This period may last until the *child* has finished its education and enters the labor market. No clear demarcation line exists and all seven countries use different definitions. To keep the description simple, *childhood* in this section is defined as the period up to the age of 14, 15 or 16 years, depending on the age limits chosen in the particular census years.

Three aspects of this childhood are considered: child labor, education and the costs and benefits of children to parents and society. The emphasis is on child labor (sections 6.1.1 - 6.1.3) but school attendance (section 6.1.4) and child labor are to a large extent mirror images of each other. Both became more and more regulated by law. In the twentieth century these laws together explain the almost complete disappearance of child labor, while in the nineteenth century developments might be explained by supply and demand in the market for unskilled labor (see chapters 9 and 10).

6.1.1 Child labor in Great Britain, France, Belgium, Germany, Denmark and Sweden

Most children began their working lives assisting the members of the family of which they were a part. They were given small tasks to do as early as possible, but usually not before the age of seven. Daughters assisted their mothers but boys, once they were able, abandoned what was considered women's work and either helped their fathers or started apprenticeships, or became employed elsewhere. The girls preferably remained within the purview of their mothers or other female adults. Children learned almost from birth to construct themselves as little men or little women and to spurn the activities of the opposite sex (Matthaei, 1982:35). In general, the different gender roles took root during childhood and these roles were accepted as 'natural'.

In the eighteenth and nineteenth centuries, in all seven countries considered, if women and children performed paid work at all, such work tended to be concentrated in unmechanized, traditional sectors of the economy. In farming, as well as in handicrafts and domestic work, children's work was predominantly supervised by their parents. The handicraft system in particular was based on the skills of the workers and children acquired these skills gradually, by performing increasingly complex operations. Thereby, children gradually inserted themselves into the labor force.

In the agricultural regions, despite the diversity between and within the seven countries and an equally wide variety of social structures, the great mass of the peasants and agricultural laborers could not allow their offspring to remain idle for longer than seven years. At that age most children started to contribute to the family economy one way or the other. By the end of the eighteenth century, however, various forms of agricultural specialization were gradually emerging and this limited the opportunities for child and female labor.

When - for a variety of reasons - daughters left home to work, they usually entered another household in the main occupation open to young girls, that of domestic servant. This practice seems to have existed for centuries. In Ealing (England) in 1599, for example, almost three-quarters of the girls between the ages of 15 and 19 seem to have been living away from their parents, most often as servants (Tilly and Scott, 1987:35).

The early phases of economic development during the eighteenth century kept more people alive, but led to more poverty. For example, according to Heywood (1988:30) in France in 1787, a third and possibly half of the population was living in poverty. Although Heywood fails to define the concept of poverty, it is obvious that the income of children was indispensable in these hard-pressed families.

Among the poor families, the introduction of mechanized (textile) industry marked in most countries the entrance of women and children into wage labor in factories and workshops, replacing paid and/or unpaid work within the family. Because these factories were concentrated only in certain areas, large regional differences were created in labor force composition, in the use of child labor and in its abuse. The latter gave rise to regulation by law. Where child factory and other industrial labor existed, the living and working conditions were notorious. Working days of 10 to 12 hours were quite common.

Great Britain

The general opinion seems to be that child labor was a ghastly by-product of industrialization. Although the historical literature includes both positive and negative testimonies, the cruelty, mistreatment and immorality survived in the popular imagination and made the employment of children the industrial revolution's most despised feature, especially in Britain (Nardinelli, 1990:2). "Some observers believe that industrialization could not have occurred without the mass employment of small children. To those who hold such beliefs, the well-being of several generations of children was sacrificed to make Britain wealthy." (Nardinelli, 1990:3).

The most striking examples of industrial cities were the English textile and mining towns like Manchester, Stockport and Preston. In Stockport and Preston, most of the labor force was in textile manufacture (Tilly and Scott, 1987:82,83). An ever greater portion of the population had experienced factory labor as a child. The percentages of children working were very high. In Manchester/Salford in 1852, for example, 76 per cent of all 14-year-old girls and 61 per cent of all boys of that age were employed in the mills (Tilly and Scott, 1987:83).

Although large numbers of children certainly were employed in textile factories, the concentration of factories in particular districts meant that the registered 122 thousand child textile workers in 1874 constituted only a fraction of the total child population. According to the census of England and Wales for 1871, children aged between 10 and 14 years and employed in factories and workshops constituted only 8 per cent of the total child population, and most of them were 13 to 14 years old. In the same year, industrial child labor accounted for less than one third of the total employment of the 10 to 14-year-olds. Traditional employment such as in agriculture and (domestic) service continued to occupy more children than the jobs created by the industrial revolution (Nardinelli, 1990:5). For girls aged 10 to 14 years, participation rates declined from 20 per cent in 1851, 1861 and 1871 to 15, 16, 12 and 10 per cent in 1881, 1891, 1901 and 1911 respectively. For boys, the corresponding participation rates were much higher at 37, 37, 32, 23, 26, 22 and 18 per cent, but show the same declining trend[3].

France

The nineteenth century brought major upheavals for various industries. "The calico-printing industry of Alsace was one of the first to assemble large numbers of children.... Mechanized cotton spinning was also remarkable in the early stages for the female and above all the juvenile stamp to its labor force." (Heywood, 1988:101). A survey of factory hands in 1822 and 1823 showed that in the spinning mills children under the age of sixteen made up approximately 30 to 40 per cent of all workers (Heywood, 1988:102).

Textile and garment making were substantial industries employing over 50 per cent of the industrial population during the first half of the nineteenth century in France. The Industrial Enquiry of 1833-45 shows that adult males made up 65 per cent of the total, women 23 per cent and children under sixteen 12 per cent (768 thousand men, 279 thousand women and nearly 144 thousand children), with an exceptionally high proportion of the female and juvenile labor force involved in textile production (Heywood, 1988:105). The spinning industries were

---

3 In the censuses the following numbers (in thousands) of children under the age of 10 were recorded as occupied (HMSO, 1976:196):

	1851	1861	1871
males	26.5	22.8	11.6
females	15.4	13.8	10.2

exceptional: three-quarters of the workers in linen spinning, two-thirds of those in cotton spinning and one half of those in wool spinning were women and children. Cotton and wool weaving, textile printing, hosiery and certain preparatory industries also recruited approximately half of their labor from these two categories. The only two other industries where women and children formed a majority were canning and papermaking (Heywood, 1988:105). The Enquiry also revealed that in mining, basic metallurgy, machine building, chemicals, glass making, printing and grain-milling, women and child workers formed only a small minority of those employed (Heywood, 1988:106).

The most striking example of an industrial city in France was Roubaix. Textile factories developed on a large scale in the 1860s, although in 1843 there had already been some 30,000 persons employed by factories in Roubaix (most of them living in cottages in the countryside). "By 1861, when the total population of the city was 49,000, there were at least 10,000 textile workers living in the city. Opportunities in factories also attracted thousands of Belgian migrants, and by 1872, 56 per cent of Roubaix's inhabitants were foreign-nationals." (Tilly and Scott, 1987:82). However, in 1872, over 50 per cent of the city's labor force was working in the textile industry. Participation by young people under 15 was high at 39 per cent of the girls aged 10 to 14, and 37 per cent of the boys. Almost 50 per cent of all women over 15 worked, 55 per cent of them in textiles. Most of the female textile workers were young and single, some 82 per cent of them being under the age of thirty (Tilly and Scott, 1987:82).

In the French censuses no information is available on the distribution of the labor force by age group until 1896, but "a sample taken in a number of communes from the census registers of 1851 points, if anything, to a slight decline in employment amongst the young." (Heywood, 1988:100). Over the second half of the century, the decline in the proportion of children who worked emerged more clearly and the paths of female and child labor diverged. During the final quarter of the nineteenth century, the exclusion of young children from the workshops was clearly in evidence: the Factory Inspectorate found that the 7800 in 1876 had fallen to a residual 1800 in 1884 (Heywood, 1988:107). By 1896, the participation rate among the ten to fourteen age group was down to 20 per cent. The coal center Anzin, which expanded after the 1850s and consisted of 1727 households in 1866, employed 526 men and boys and 57 females, mostly girls (Tilly and Scott, 1987:84). In general, in the coal-mining and metal working centers employment existed primarily for boys.

Belgium

The same division of labor found in Great Britain and France also applies to Belgium. Girls and women worked in the textile industries and boys and men in the extractive industries, confirming the picture presented in the previous chapters. In 1845, of the 24 thousand males and 2 thousand females working underground in the mines (*à l'intérieur*), 4 thousand boys were younger than 16 years as were almost a thousand girls. Above the ground (*ouvrier travaillant au jour*), girls were in the majority: a thousand, as against 600 boys younger than 16 years. In 1850, the figures were slightly higher. They rapidly increased over the next decades, peaking in 1876 for boys and girls below the age of 16 years: nearly 13 thousand boys and over 5 and a half thousand girls. The figures for girls working underground had itself peaked in 1870 (3.7 thousand). After that year they were replaced by adult men. Adult males in employment increased from 43 thousand in 1876 to 75 thousand in 1896, while employment for adult women decreased (Annuaire Statistique de la Belgique, 1897:307).

The total number of children under 16 employed in industry in 1846 was: 36 thousand boys and 30 thousand girls (Annuaire Statistique de la Belgique 1880:XXV).

Germany

In Germany, statistics show a similar picture. The same saddening cases can be found as in Belgium, France and England, even as early as in the reign of '*Friedrich der Großen*'. He considered child labor very important and in 1766 offered the merchants of Hirschberg/Schlesien a transport of 1000 children aged 10 to 12 years for employment in spinning (Weber-Kellermann, 1974:134)[4]. After 1871 the number of children in industrial labor started to decline[5]. In the cottage industries very young children had to assist in paid work, for example in making dolls in the poor forest areas[6]. It is remarkable that not only in Germany, Belgium, France and England, but also in Denmark, the Netherlands and Sweden, the number

---

4 "*Die Ablehnung dieses Angebotes erweckte sein höchstes Mißfallen.*" (Weber-Kellerman, 1974:134). (The rejection of this offer provoked his greatest displeasure).

5 "*Erst nach 1871 mit dem Fortschritt des Maschinenwesens, als sich Kinderarbeit für den Unternehmer nicht mehr auszahlte, ging die Zahl der arbeitenden Kinder in der Industrie wesentlich zurück, während sie in der Heimarbeit und im Verlagswesen bis in die zwanziger und dreißiger Jahre unseres Jahrhunderts weit verbreitet gewesen ist.*" (Weber-Kellermann, 1974:135). (Only after 1871 with the progress of mechanization, when child labor was no longer profitable for the entrepreneur, did the number of children in industry decline substantially, while those in domestic work and in cottage industries were widespread until the 1920s and 1930s).

6 "*In der Hausindustrie, die volkswirtschaftliche Romantiker gern so idyllisch darstellen, liegen die Verhältnisse für das Familienleben und die Moral nicht viel besser* (compared to proletarian families). *Hier ist die Frau neben der Mann von früh bis in die nacht an die Arbeit gekettet, die Kinder werden vom frühesten Alter zu gleichem Werk angehalten.*" (Weber-Kellermann, 1974:142). (In cottage industries, which economic romantics like to picture as idyllic, the circumstances for family life and morality are not much better. Wife and husband are chained to their work from early morning until late at night and the children are tied to the same work from an early age).

of children in industrial labor started to decline in the 1870s and the number of young children (aged 10-12) even earlier.

In 1882, only 3 per cent of all girls under 16 years of age were participating in the labor force and 4 per cent of all boys. In 1895 the joint figure was 6 per cent and in 1907 only 2 per cent, mainly consisting of boys and girls older than 12 years.

Denmark and Sweden

In **Denmark** and **Sweden**, as in the countries already mentioned, children had been used in work on the farms from the age of 7 or 8 and had taken part in craft work as apprentices. Children's factory work differed from farm or craft work in that the aim was not the training and teaching of skills, but the performance of unskilled labor tasks. They were recruited only to do the most simple jobs. In 1875, the most child-intensive industrial branches in Sweden (as elsewhere in Europe, apart from textiles) were the making of glass, matches and tobacco[7] (Olsson, 1980:169). In general, children were hired at the age of 10, but left their jobs at the age of 13-16, when they were replaced by a new generation of young children (Olsson, 1980:170,171).

In Sweden (as in the other countries) child labor started to diminish when the transition from manual methods of production to the machine system started. This transition period lasted, for the making of cigars and matches, for about fifty years starting from about 1860, while for glass making it did not begin until the late nineteenth century (Olsson, 1980:171).

In Sweden it turned out to be difficult to get "*the proletarians*" to work in the factories. The factories had to be helped by the authorities to get people to work for them as they wanted. It is symptomatic that the first facturies in Sweden were connected to children's homes and other institutions. One reason that the manufacturers had such difficulties in recruiting workers to the factories was, in fact, this close connection between factory work on the one hand and these institutions and poor aid on the other. There was a close connection between child labor and poor aid as late as the beginning of the 19th century. The main reason why people did not want to work in factories seems, however, to lie in the organization of the work, "*which differed from that in the pre-capitalist society*." (Olsson, 1980:168).

---

[7] Again, this confirms the remarkable feature in all countries: that boys and women did the same type of work. During the whole of the nineteenth century only boys were used in tobacco making, while in the industry as a whole more women were employed than men. In 1891 in the "*Tobaksfabriker med minst 1000 arbetare*" (tobacco factories with at least 1000 wage earners), 1648 women and 1262 men were found (and only 7 boys younger than 13 years, and no girls). In the same year in the "*Spinnerier och väverier med minst 1000 arbetare*" (spinning and weaving mills with at least 1000 wage earners), there were 5134 men and 10,350 women (among them 98 boys and 55 girls younger than 13 years) (Olsson, 1980:144).

The total number of children working in industry remained low in Sweden, but even more so in Denmark. In Denmark, of the 57.6 thousand girls younger than 15 years belonging to the labor force in 1901, 50.1 thousand worked in agriculture, while in Sweden among the children younger than 15 years in 1930 (nearly 8 thousand boys and 3 thousand girls), there were relatively large numbers of unpaid family workers, most of them in agriculture and shops.

6.1.2 Child labor in the Netherlands

Since England was the first country to industrialize, it was there that the use and abuse of child labor in the industrial sector was first noticed. To investigate whether the notorious English abuses also existed in the Netherlands, two enquiries were held, one in 1841 and one in 1860. These enquiries into paid labor by children younger than 16 years do not, however, give much insight into the extent of child labor. In 1841 the aim of the investigation was to identify social evils and abuses, while in 1860 the purpose was to investigate the situation only in factories and workshops employing more than 10 children.

The 1841 investigation, did indeed reveal social evils but not to any large extent. In the 490 enterprises which were investigated, about ten per cent of the labor force consisted of children younger than fourteen years. To prevent child labor, the committee recommended not its prohibition but the promotion of education (Neve and Renooy, 1988).

The absolute number of children working in industry was small. This was already shown in the Factory statistics of 1819 and again confirmed by (Brinckman's) statistics of 1871, which claimed to give a complete picture of industrial labor in the Netherlands[8]. Child labor in 1819 was different in character from that in 1871: many industries did not yet exist in 1819 (for example, the cigar and tobacco industries, the flax industries and the potato flour and strawboard industries) while by 1871 many of the craft type of industries of 1819 had disappeared (like the work of tin and coppersmiths) (Brugmans, 1973). The picture is not really different from that in the other countries. No distinction is made by sex in 1819, but in 1871 the share of girls in factories was about 20 per cent overall, although in the textile industries the share was higher: 32 per cent in the province of Brabant, 45 per cent in the province of Overijssel.

Where abuse of child labor was noticed, cases were often concentrated in various factories in a single city or village, as in Moordrecht. This village in South-Holland holds the record for child-exploitation: in the cord and ribbon-weavery, at the rope walk and in the brickwork industry, children were found - one aged five and two aged only four

[8] Although not exactly defined in 1819, it seems likely that in both 1819 and 1871 'children' were persons younger than 16 years of age (Brugmans, 1973:13).

years - working up to 15 hours a day. The Regout pottery factory in Maastricht was another notorious example in the Netherlands. Children started work there at the age of nine and worked 12-hour days; it was also one of the few factories where children worked on the night shift. In general, however, children working in factories were older than ten years and the total number of children was never very high; in 1871, 110 children and 2,338 adults were employed in the Regout pottery factory (Brugmans, 1973:100).

To estimate how many children participated in industry, Brugmans (1973:93) compared the two sources of statistics mentioned above. He concluded that between 1819 and 1871 child labor in manufacturing increased remarkably in all provinces except Zeeland (probably due to inaccuracy of the data (Brugmans 1973:97)), but that the absolute total numbers were low. Child labor in the Netherlands, as in Denmark and Sweden, meant predominantly labor in the agricultural sector and, especially for girls, in the domestic sector. To a lesser extent it was labor in cottage industries or family labor other than in agriculture. Abuse in industrial labor was not as wide spread and as severe as in England. Moreover, the worst excesses in England (as in France and Belgium) were recorded in the coal mines. Beside child miners, chimney sweeps aroused most outrage. The Netherlands had coal mines only in Kerkrade, and no chimney sweeps[9]. However, by 1871 only 141 adult men and 7 boys younger than 16 years were employed in the mines[10]. Under the imperial degree of 1813, promulgated in pursuance to the Mines Act of 1810, labor in the mines was forbidden for children below the age of 10 years (Brugmans, 1973:106).

The late industrialization of the Netherlands meant not only that few children were working in factories, but also that working conditions had by then improved due to technological change as compared with the early stages of industrialization. By the time the Netherlands industrialized, mechanized operations had already replaced the kinetic energy previously supplied by women and especially by young children.

The census data of 1849, 1859 and 1889 confirm the results of Brugman's comparison between 1819 and 1871: child labor increased overall, but decreased for younger children. The trends for child labor in the censuses and in the industrial sector are shown in table 6.1.

---

9 Chimney sweeps, not only in England but also in France, faced a difficult and hazardous life, often involving serious injuries and occasionally ending in the disaster of suffocation (Heywood, 1988:58).

10 In contrast to the textile industries, where 1715 children were counted in 1819 and 2699 in 1871 (Brugmans, 1973:98).

Table 6.1 *Child labor in the Netherlands, absolute figures in thousands by age and sex, 1849 – 1899*

	under 12 years of age		age 12 and 13		under 10 years in industry only	
	girls	boys	girls	boys	girls	boys
1849	2.4	4.9	1.7	3.3	0.3	0.4
1859	1.7	3.3			0.2	0.4
1889	0.6	1.1				
1899	0.6	1.1	6.7	19.0		

Sources: Brugmans, 1973:107 and CBS, Volkstellingen: 1849, 1859, 1889 and 1899.

These figures confirm the results of the investigations showing that the total numbers of children were low. The figures also show that the total juvenile labor force consisted of about 20 per cent girls.

As in the case of women, under-counting of children involved in family labor certainly took place, especially in agriculture where children had to help during the summer months but were not registered because the censuses were held in winter. This is confirmed by the statistics on absence from school. In 1826 large regional differences in school absences are noticed, indicating substantial child and female labor on the small farms in the South and East of the country, though not in the province of Holland and in the North. According to Van Zanden (1991a) in North-Holland absence from school was even higher in winter than in summer. However, in all censuses before World War II, participation rates of children younger than twelve years were below one per cent for boys and girls together (CBS, Volkstellingen, 1849 to 1930). The shares of young persons in the total labor force were also low, see table 6.2.

Table 6.2 *Shares of girls and boys aged under 14 as a percentage of the female and male labor forces, 1899 – 1930*

	labor force shares	
	girls	boys
1889	0.5	1.4
1899	2.3	1.7
1909	1.7	1.1
1920	1.3	0.8
1930	0.1	0.0

Source: CBS. Negentig jaren statistiek in tijdreeksen 1989:77.

The share of girls aged under 14 in the female labor force is higher than the corresponding share for boys, despite the fact that the absolute number of girls is much lower than that of boys.

In 1899, of all the girls aged 12 and 13 years, about 7 thousand (8 per cent) participated in the labor force and of the girls aged 14 and 15, more than 18 thousand (20 per cent) (CBS, Volkstelling, 1899:220). Taken together, the majority (over 60 per cent) were working in domestic service, about 20 per cent in agriculture and about 20 per cent in the industrial sector.

Gradually, the average age of entry to the labor market rose, and after World War II participation rates of children younger than fifteen were reduced to zero.

6.1.3 Child labor, a seven-country comparison

Child labor in Denmark, the Netherlands and Sweden was identical in character. The absolute number of children in the industrial sector was low, certainly compared to Belgium, England, France and Germany.

The scarcity of data on the composition of the industrial labor force by age in the nineteenth century makes it difficult to describe developments accurately. What emerges unequivocally, however, over the broad sweep of the nineteenth century is a decline in child labor (see also Heywood, 1988:98).

Around the turn of the twentieth century, 12 - 13 was accepted as the normal age at which children started to participate in the labor force. During the twentieth century the average starting age gradually rose and by the 1930s child labor in all seven countries had been reduced to about 1 per cent of the total juvenile population.

In all seven countries agriculture was the main employer of children, followed by domestic service where girls were concerned. Many boys and girls may have worked at home in cottage industries and handicrafts, but it seems unlikely that this work has been recorded accurately by the censuses. In all seven countries children tended to assist rather than replace adults, contributing as early as possible to the family household income. Children younger than 10 years were seldom wage earners. "In Caen, France, the lace industry employed girls between ages five and fifteen. They were first apprenticed for two months and their parents paid both for their training and a place at the workbench. When the lessons were completed girls began to earn a daily wage." (Tilly and Scott, 1987:35).

The principal work for young children in the industrial sector, as already mentioned, apart from textiles, was found in the metal, machine, pottery, cigar and tobacco industries, and in the brickworks. It was therefore the prevalence of these types of industries that determined the demand for industrial child labor and the extent of outrage created by it.

Child labor in non-industrial settings, such as that of girls employed in sweatshops in the garment industries, in general attracted less attention. It was also beyond the reach of the factory acts that came into existence during the second half of the nineteenth century (see chapter 9). The same applies to the labor of young farm servants and living-in domestic servants. The burden of their working lives was aggravated by inhospitable living conditions. They often had to survive on a meagre diet, having no more than a bed and a chest and hardly any privacy.

Child factory labor started to diminish when the transition began from manual production to the machine system, because the simple operations performed by children were the first to be mechanized. This mechanization and the corresponding decline in child factory labor began before the child factory acts (see chapter 9) came into power.

6.1.4 Education in childhood

Around 1800, more children were receiving education in the Netherlands than anywhere else in Europe. Literacy was 68 per cent, relatively high compared for example to Belgium and France, both with less than 50 per cent (Knippenberg, 1986). In England, literacy, measured as the individual's ability to sign the marriage register, was estimated between 1799 and 1804 to be 54 per cent[11] (Sanderson, 1991:10).

The relatively favorable situation in the Netherlands was due to the great importance which the Protestants in particular attached to literacy, so that everybody could read the Bible. Accordingly, in the northern provinces - with a homogeneous Protestant population - relatively more children received at least basic education. On the other hand, it is a remarkable fact that a large number of Catholic girls visited special girls-only Catholic schools in the two southern provinces, which were homogeneous Catholic areas. Their numbers differed little from those for the education of boys, but as opposed to the girls, the boys in these provinces were mainly sent to 'neutral' (non-denominational) schools. Obviously, Catholics attached more importance to a Catholic education for girls than for boys. Political and religious motives played an important role in stimulating schooling as a means of socialization to prepare children for their roles in society in the first half of the nineteenth century. After industrialization, in the Netherlands as in other nations, economic motives also became important (Knippenberg, 1986).

Education became an increasingly prominent issue in the Netherlands as elsewhere. Compulsory education, financed by government, was gradually extended during the twentieth century, but the Netherlands lagged behind the other six countries in this respect (Knippenberg, 1986). Its relatively favourable position in education was lost. It was not until after World War II that this situation improved.

For children of compulsory school age, enrollment levels are now near 100 per cent in all seven countries. In 1990, inequalities between the

---

[11] The marked rise in literacy between the late seventeenth and the first half to three-quarters of the eighteenth century is evident, as is the worldwide disparity between male and female rates and between social classes in England (Sanderson, 1991:11).

countries concern only the compulsory age of entry, and this does nothing to explain the low Dutch female activity rates. Childhood inequalities between the sexes are small in all seven countries and appear mainly in the choice of and attainments in different school subjects during the successive stages of education and training (see next section).

6.1.5 Costs and benefits of children

Costs of bringing up children used to be borne entirely by the parents or other relatives of the children. Gradually political intervention, especially via compulsory and collectively financed education, changed the division of costs between parents and society and between the father and the mother. The benefits of the investment in children also changed over time. Children used to contribute to the household income as soon as possible and were expected to support their parents if necessary.

Not much is known about the historical development in the division between the collective and private costs of bringing up children[12]. For this reason this topic will be disregarded in this chapter.

6.2 Adolescence and youth

In many non-European countries, the transitorial stage between childhood and adulthood, coinciding with the biological transition, is marked by special initiation rites. In Europe these rites have been replaced by a political demarcation. In the Netherlands, since the Middle Ages, the age of legal maturity rose to 25 years and declined only in recent decades to 18 years. However, this recent decline of the period of parental power did not reduce parental responsibility. Until the 'child' is 27 years old, parents are supposed to contibute financially to their offspring in educational investments. The demarcation between 'Youth' and 'Adulthood' seems to be increasingly determined by educational demarcation lines: basic compulsory schooling until 15 or 16 years, secondary schooling until 19 or 20 years and tertiary schooling until at least about 24 years.

With mass education introduced first during childhood, then during youth, the transition from childhood to adulthood (adolescence) was postponed for more and more teenagers and their entrance into the labor market delayed even into their early twenties. "In adolescence the individual begins to make significant choices independently, but these choices are heavily influenced by the circumstances of birth and by the

---

12 This, despite the fact that an enormous amount of literature exists, see for a review: Pott-Buter and Groot (1990), see also Bierens and Pott-Buter (1990) and Pott-Buter (1991).

investments made by the parents during the childhood years, as well as by the support they provide at this stage." (Fuchs, 1983:92). The 'choices' made by individuals in this stage, or the 'choices' they are forced to make, play a critical role in the rest of their lives, influencing matters such as the choice of length and level of education, the choice of a partner or marriage and the choice of income-earning activities, as well as the timing of entering the labor market. However, this section concentrates on the changes in participation rates of young persons aged 15 to 24 in the labor force.

6.2.1 Labor force participation rates in youth and adolescence

Participation in the labor market during youth and adolescence is distinguished into two periods: the first (usually) extending from the age of 15 or 16 years (depending on the point at which compulsory schooling ends and on census or survey demarcation age) to 19 years and the second generally between the ages of 20 and 24.

The female labor force participation rates in the seven countries are given in figure 6.1/table 6.3 and figure 6.2/ table 6.4. Figure 6.1 and table 6.3 show the female labor force participation rate for teenagers aged 14/15/16 - 19 years and figure 6.2 and table 6.4 the rate for women aged 20 - 24. Because participation rates by age are not available for all seven countries until after around 1900, only the figures from about 1900 to 1990 are shown.

Figure 6.1 *A seven-country comparison of labor force participation of girls aged about 15 to 19 years, 1900-1990*

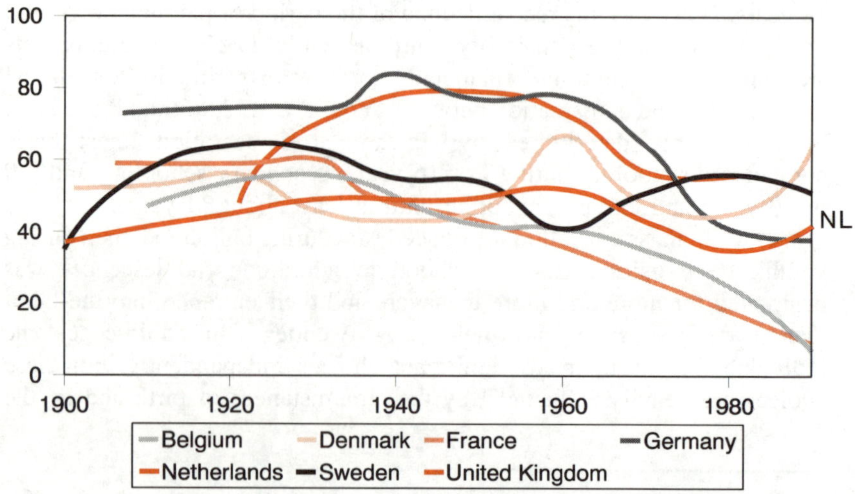

Table 6.3 *A seven-country comparison of labor force participation rates of girls aged about 15 to 19 years, 1900 – 1990*

	Belgium	Denmark	France	Germany	Netherlands	Sweden	Great Britain
1900	a	[1]52	–	[1]66	[1]37	[1]35	a
1910	47	[2]53	[1]59	73	[2]41	[2]57	b
1920	a	[3]56	59	75	45	64	[1]48
1930	56	[4]46	60	75	49	63	[2]71
1940	a	[5]43	51	84	–	55	–
1950	42	46	43	[2]77	49	54	[3]79
1960	41	67	36	78	52	41	72
1970	35	48	27	64	42	[3]51	56
1980	25	45	18	41	[3]35	56	56
1990	7	[6]65	9	38	42	[4]51	c

Belgium:
a not available; figures for 1950, 1960, 1970 and 1980 for the age group 14 – 19 respectively 44, 35, 30 and 19 per cent. Census years: 1910, 1930, 1947, 1961, 1970, 1980; in 1947, 1961, 1971 and 1977, there were still 16, 13, 6.5 and 2.2 thousand boys younger than 15 (2, 1.1, 0.6 and 3.7 per cent respectively) and respectively 9.7, 8.2, 4.2 and 1.4 thousand girls participating (corresponding in these 4 years to respectively 1, 1, 0.4 and 1.8 per cent of the girls aged below 15).

Denmark:
1 1901, these figures concern the age group 15 – 18 years;
2 1911, these figures concern the age group 15 – 17 years, excl. unpaid family labor only 15 per cent;
3 1920: 14 – 17 year old;
4 1930: 15 – 24 year old;
5 1940, 1950, 1960, 1970 and 1980, 15 – 19 year old and
6 the sample survey of 1987, concerning the 16 – 19 year old. According to ILO (1991:82) in 1950 for the 15 – 29 age group: 83 per cent.

France:
1 census years: 1906, 1921, 1931, 1936, 1954, 1962 and 1990; Employment Surveys: 1970, 1980 and 1990; while according to the census of 1968 the figure for this age group was 31 per cent; of 1975: 22 per cent, of 1982: 17 per cent.
In general census figures are lower than survey figures. The French 1990 census is an exception. The higher 1990 census figures are presented in the table. The corresponding survey figure is 8 per cent.

Germany:
1 census years: 1896, 1907, 1925, 1933, 1939;
2 1950, 1960, 1970, 1984 and 1990, concerning the age group 15 – 19 years. However, in 1950 and 1960 still respectively 4 and 8 per cent of all girls and respectively 5 and 8 per cent of all boys aged 10 – 14 belonged to the labor force.

Netherlands:
Census years: 1899, 1909, 1920, 1930, 1947, 1960, 1971.
1 in 1899 age group 14 – 17 years;
2 thereafter girls aged 14 – 19;
3 sample surveys 1981 and 1990, age group 15 – 19 years. According to ILO (1991:99) girls aged 15 – 19 in 1960: 59 per cent and in 1971: 50 per cent.

Sweden:
1 census years: 1900, 1910, 1920, 1930, 1940, 1950, 1960, all concerning the 15 – 19 year old, except
2 1910, this concerns the 15 – 25 age group;
3 1970, 1980 and 1990, 16 – 19 years. According to ILO (1991:107) the age group 15 – 19 in 1970: 30 per cent and in 1980: 29 per cent.

Great Britain:
a and b (censuses 1901 and 1911 respectively): because of uncertainty as to the ages at which the juveniles commenced work, the activity rates cannot be given for these years (HMSO, 1967:206);
1 census 1921: age group 12 – 19;
2 census 1931: age group 14 – 20;
3 census 1951: age group 15 – 19; the same applies to the subsequent census years: 1961, 1971, in census 1981: age group 16 – 19. According to ILO, 1991: the United Kingdom 1961, the 15 – 17 year old: 71 per cent; 1971: the 15 – 19 year old: 56 per cent and 1981: 45 per cent; and
c according to HMSO (1991:147) males and females aged 16 – 24: 22 per cent.

Sources: See table 2.2

In general, the trends are fairly similar in all seven countries, but the levels differ tremendously. Here, more than in the other age groups, the demarcation age matters. In Sweden, for example, the official lower age-limit has since 1970 been 16 years and for this reason the percentages given in table 6.3 for the three years 1970, 1980 and 1990 apply to the 16-19 age group. However, if the age group is extended downward by a single year the percentage is much lower. For example, as mentioned in the notes, ILO (1991:107) presents the economically active population in Sweden for the 15 - 19 age group for 1970 and 1980[13]; these female activity rates were 30 per cent and 29 per cent respectively.[14] The latter (15 - 19) rates are more comparable to the French and Belgian rates, than the figures presented in table 6.3. In other countries similar problems are apparent, but in general only one age group is published.

Despite inaccuracies, the conclusion is clear: teenage participation gradually increased over the first half of the century, but decreased over the second half, especially in the 1970s; the exceptions are that Denmark and the Netherlands showed an increase between 1980 and 1990 and Sweden between 1970 and 1980. However, the levels in Denmark, the Netherlands and Sweden for 1990 may be flattered, because students are to a certain extent counted as participating.

The large increase of young persons in part-time jobs in the Netherlands between 1985 and 1987 (a 309 per cent increase!) occurred mainly in the category of students with an additional job. This increase might be due to changing the rather negatively formulated question *Don't you perform any paid work at all?* into the more positive question *Do you perform paid work, even if it is only for one or two hours a week or for only a short period?* (Paridon, 1989:1032).

The labor force participation rates illustrate the striking development for girls in this age group. Prior to World War II (especially in the Netherlands), the rates increased due to the transfer from domesticity into paid work. After World War II, and in particular since the 1980s, the rates decreased due to the prevalence of mass education for teenagers.

Figure 6.1 and table 6.3 only partly confirm the picture given in the previous chapters and that of the previous section: labor force participation of girls in the Netherlands was indeed low compared to the other six countries up to World War II (although the 14 - 19 age brackets have some influence as well). Since World War II, the rates have certainly not been the lowest of the seven countries: in general the rates in Belgium and France have been lower. Denmark, Germany, Sweden and Great Britain had higher rates until 1990, but in that year only Denmark and

---

13 Remarkably, the ILO presents for 1975 the 16-19 age group (47 per cent; although according to the Statiska Centralbyrån (SCB, 1989:46) sample survey it was 56 per cent).

14 The ILO (1991:108) presents yet another age group for 1985: 10-19 years, with an activity rate of 20 per cent. According to SCB (1989:46), the female activity rates for the 16-19 age group in that year were 49 per cent.

Sweden had higher rates. Moreover, the figures again confirm that even in 1990 there is no international agreement as to how to count the labor force, nor on the lowest age-limit, nor on the minimum or maximum number of hours. Figure 6.2 and table 6.4 present the female labor force participation rates for the next age group.

The trend for women aged over 20 but under 25 years is different from the trend for the 15-19 age group, showing a secular increase in all seven countries until the 1970s; for Belgium, Germany and Great Britain this continues until 1990 and in Denmark, the Netherlands and Sweden, there is even an accelaration between 1970 and 1980. Differences in levels are much smaller than for the 15-19 age group.

There is a remarkable similarity in the 1950s and 1960s in participation rates between the two age groups of tables 6.3 and 6.4, except for France, where in 1954 the rate for the 15-19 age group is lower than that for the 20-24 age group, due to a rapid extension of the period of formal education.

In 1990, France is the country with the lowest participation rate, while the Netherlands shows the highest rates after Denmark and Sweden. Throughout this century, participation rates for Dutch girls in this age group have been at the low end, although not often the lowest. In 1990 the relative rate has increased in the international distribution.

Table 6.4 and figure 6.2 *A seven-country comparison of labor force participation rates of women aged 20 to 24 years, 1900 - 1990*

	Belgium	Denmark	France	Germany	Netherlands	Sweden	Great Britain
1900	–	[1]59	–	46	[1]43	54	57
1910	45	51	60	52	46	[1]57	62
1920	–	[2]63	61	58	47	67	62
1930	[1]31	46	59	61	50	69	65
1940	–	48	55	57	–	58	–
1950	41	64	57	70	51	57	65
1960	52	59	62	76	53	57	[1]62
1970	61	68	64	67	56	56	60
1980	70	86	67	71	70	81	69
1990	57	85	[1]60	74	78	81	–

Belgium:
1 1930, the 21 – 54 age group.

Denmark:
1 1901, the 18 – 22 age group;
2 1921, the 18 – 25 age group.

France:
1 Employment Survey 1990, 57 per cent, so lower than the 60 per cent census figure presented here.

The Netherlands:
1899, the 18 – 22 age group.

Sweden:
1910, the 15 – 25 age group.

Great Britain:
1961, 1971, 1981, identical rates for the United Kingdom (ILO, 1991: 110).

Sources and notes concerning the census and sample survey years: see table 6.3.

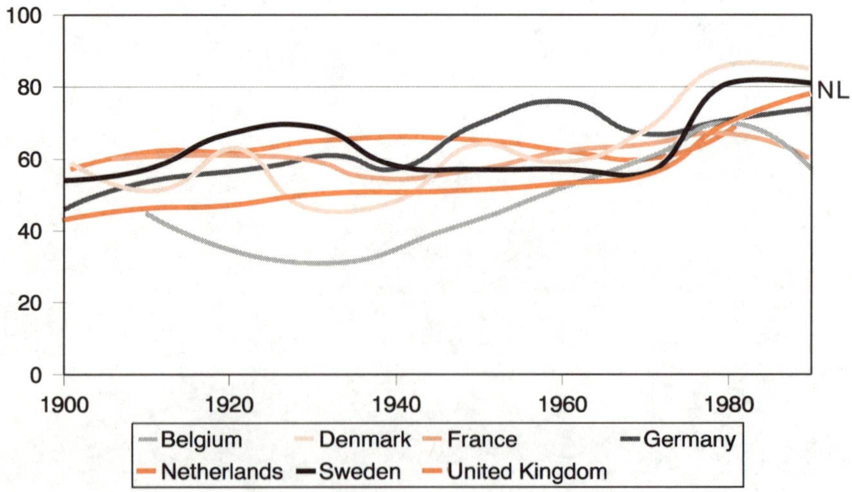

6.2.2 Differences in labor force participation between boys and girls in the Netherlands

Participation rates were quite different in the Netherlands for boys and for girls. The female and male labor force participation rates and the participation shares of boys and girls aged 14/15 - 19 from 1899 - 1990 are presented in table 6.5. The Dutch participation rates for girls shown in table 6.3 are repeated here.

Table 6.5 *Labor force participation rates of women and men aged 14/15 – 19 in the Netherlands, as a percentage of the female population of that age and* ***their share as a percentage of the female and male labor force***

	female		male	
age	14 – 19	**14 – 19**	14 – 19	**14 – 19**
1899	37	**25**	72	**14**
1909	41	**25**	73	**15**
1920	45	**29**	74	**15**
1930	49	**28**	72	**14**
1947	49	**25**	66	**11**
1960	52	**27**	55	**8**
age	15 – 19	**15 – 19**	15 – 19	**15 – 19**
1971	42	**22**	35	**7**
1975	31	**15**	26	**5**
1979	23	**11**	21	**4**
1981	31	**10**	28	**4**
1983	27	**8**	25	**5**
1985	24	**7**	22	**4**
1987	26	**7**	23	**4**

Source: CBS, Negentig jaren statistiek in tijdreeksen, 1989:77,78.

In 1899, 37 per cent of all girls aged 14-17 participated in the labor market (and 43 per cent of the women aged 18 to 22, see table 6.4 and 6.6). Almost all these women were single and belonged to the lowest categories of workers; only a few of them were employees, working either in trade or in clerical services (CBS, Volkstelling 1899:194).

From 1909 to 1960, participation rates of girls aged 14 to 19 increased from 41 to 52 per cent; after 1971 the activity rates decreased again, down to 42 per cent in 1990. However the share of teenager girls in the female labor force had declined since 1930.

In the 1970s this participation rate declined steeply, but 1/3 to 1/4 of all girls aged 15 to 19 still participated in the labor market. The pattern for boys is similar, but the levels of participation used to be different. In the first thirty years of this century nearly 3/4 of all boys aged 14-19 participated in the labor force, but thereafter their participation rates decreased rapidly. In the 1970s they fell below those of the girls. Boys' shares in the labor force are lower throughout the century.

Table 6.6 shows the corresponding participation rates and shares for women and men aged between 20 and 24 years.

Table 6.6 *Labor force participation rates of women and men aged 20 – 24 years in the Netherlands, as a percentage of the female or male population of that age and* ***their share as a percentage of the female or male labor force***

	female		male	
age	20 – 24	**20 – 24**	20 – 24	**20 – 24**
1899	43	**23**	90	13
1909	46	**22**	93	13
1920	47	**22**	95	14
1930	50	**24**	93	14
1947	51	**22**	92	13
1960	53	**23**	91	11
1971	56	**26**	85	15
1975	61	**24**	80	13
1979	66	**24**	76	12
1981	72	**23**	78	13
1983	72	**22**	77	13
1985	71	**21**	74	13
1987	71	**20**	73	12

Source: CBS, 1989, Negentig jaren statistiek in tijdreeksen: 77,78.

Participation rates of women aged 20-24 were slightly higher than those for their younger contemporaries during the first sixty years of this century, but thereafter increased to more than 70 per cent. The share of teenage girls in the female labor force declined continually throughout this century, while the share of young women (aged 20 to 24) remained roughly the same until the secular decline in the 1980s.

Compared with girls aged 15-19, the participation rates of boys were much higher prior to 1960; in the 1970s their participation rates were lower, but during the 1980s boys' and girls' participation rates - steadily converge. Participation rates of women aged 20-24 have always been lower than those of their male contemporaries, but the difference decreased from 47 percentage points in 1899 to only 1.5 in 1987.

In contrast to the participation rates, the share of young girls in the female labor force was much larger than the similar share for boys: despite the slightly lower participation rates of girls in 1960, their share was ever then three times as high. The relative share of teenage girls and boys in the female and male labor forces has declined steadily in this century, becoming relatively more and more unimportant. The share of young men (aged 20 to 24) in the male labor force showed the same relative stability as the share of young women, but at a lower level.

6.2.3 Education in the Netherlands

It is obvious that changes in teenage participation rates are closely related to changes in education. However, except for a few remarks in the next two sections, this topic will be disregarded here. It is extremely hard to establish accurate comparable data on the level of education[15] (or, for example, on in service training of employees), particularly by age group.

Since the introduction of compulsory schooling in the early twentieth century, boys and girls have attended primary schools together until the age of twelve. Secondary education, however, can be divided in general and vocational education. A number of different levels can be reached in each, and vocational education is also divided into different sectors.

Female participation in full-time education at age 15 has risen from 16 per cent in 1930 to 99 per cent since 1983, and the rate for girls aged 20 has increased from 2 per cent in 1930, via 9 per cent in 1971, to 26 per cent in 1990. After World War II and until the 1950s, about 50 per cent of all children opted for vocational training after leaving primary school, but by 1985 this percentage had fallen to 31 per cent. Vocational training is far more segregated by sex than secondary general education (Clason, 1982:42-44).

6.2.4 Post-secondary education in the seven countries

The most remarkable development in all seven countries has been the increase in the mass education of adolescents over recent decades. The trend in upper secondary schools and post-compulsory education is towards higher levels of female involvement, particularly after the 1960s. Inequalities in enrollment levels between the sexes then become smaller and by the 1980s the numbers of women equal or exceed those of men, although in more vocational sectors women still tend to be in the minority.

All seven countries show about equal enrollment levels for boys and girls. Germany is a country which has selective lower secondary schools. The proportion of girls in Gymnasium (the more academic schools) has increased from 42 per cent in 1965/66 to just over 50 per cent in 1980/81. In the intermediate schools, or Realschulen, girls also outnumber boys, the corresponding figures for the same years being 52 and 54 per cent (OECD, 1985:124,125).

The United Kingdom has retained a minority of selective

---

15 The OECD Project on International Education Indicators offers relevant information, but the critical comments concerning recently published figures illustrate the inadequacy and difficulty of interpreting differences between school populations, educational institutions and systems. See for example: Den Broeder and De Moor, 1992 criticizing the outcome of Education at a Glance (OECD, 1992) which concludes a relatively low educational level in the Netherlands.

secondary schools (grammar schools). Girls comprised over half the pupils of compulsory school age at these schools both in 1965 (51 per cent for England) and 1979 (52 per cent for England and Wales) (OECD, 1985:122).

According to Eurostat, in 1982/1983, full-time educational attendance by 20-year-old girls was highest in Denmark (29 per cent of the girls of that age, a figure still much lower than that for the boys: 38 per cent in the same year), while in Belgium 25 per cent of both boys and girls were in full-time education. In France and Germany, more girls than boys of that age were counted (in France 19 and 17 per cent and in Germany 20 and 16 per cent respectively). The largest difference was found in that year in the Netherlands: girls 19, boys 31 per cent. For boys and girls aged 24, similar differences can be found, but participation percentages are much lower (Prondzynsky, 1989:95).

The difference between boys and girls lies therefore more and more not in the extent of educational participation, but in the relevance of girls' education to employment. Girls tend to be evenly or over-represented in the general educational institutions or branches and under-represented in the vocational ones. This difference becomes yet more striking in the subsequent stages of education and training. "In short, it seems that vocational preparation at the compulsory school level is regrettably weak: girls who are school leavers tend to be particularly ill-prepared for the labour market, while girls who stay at school seem in many cases to be responding to lack of job opportunity, although their extra length of schooling does not necessarily provide further preparation for employment." (OECD, 1985:122).

It is a remarkable feature, despite the fact that educational attendance has increased, in some countries labor force participation also increased. To improve comparability, standardization is necessary, for example, via the calculation of full-time equivalents. Not only enrolment levels (particularly in tertiary education) have to be converted to full-time equivalents - as has been done by OECD (1992), but labor force participation as well (see for attempts, chapter 8).

6.2.5 Work by school children and students

Research into paid labor by school children and students after World War II is scarce in the Netherlands. In 1984/1985, 42 per cent of the full-time students had a small job (on average earning 140 guilders a month) and 36 per cent a holiday job. Girls earn less than boys of the same age and educational level (Hagenaars and De Zwart, 1987 and De Zwart and Van Praag, 1990).

Another investigation of 1987 revealed that of the 13-19-year-old students about 28 per cent have some sort of job (Nationaal Onderzoek Jongerenbladen, VNU, 1987).

An inquiry by Neve and Renooy in 1987 revealed a much higher percentage. Of the nearly 2000 students questioned about their various paid activities (at least five days) in the previous year, nearly 75 per cent had had some kind of work, with 25 per cent summer jobs and about 60 per cent more or the less regular jobs, varying from baby-sitting and washing cars to assisting in shops and on farms. Regional differences are large. In the big cities participation is the lowest, followed by urban areas, while in rural areas participation is the highest.

These inquiries confirm the results of an English research project carried out between 1982 to 1983 and involving 1700 students aged 11-16 years. Jobs were held by 41 per cent of the boys and 38 per cent of the girls, both mainly in the service sector. In England as in the Netherlands, delivering papers turned out to be an important student activity[16].

An investigation among students in 1991 (Scholierenonderzoek Nibud, NRC, 18-1-1992) confirmed the 1984 results, but with increased percentages for females. In 1984, 53 per cent of the male students aged 15-19 had a job; in 1991: 53 per cent. In 1984: 37 per cent of the female students; in 1991 also: 45 per cent. Delivering newspapers was the most popular activity (27 per cent), followed by a job in the retail trade (26 per cent) or catering and farmwork (together 12 per cent).

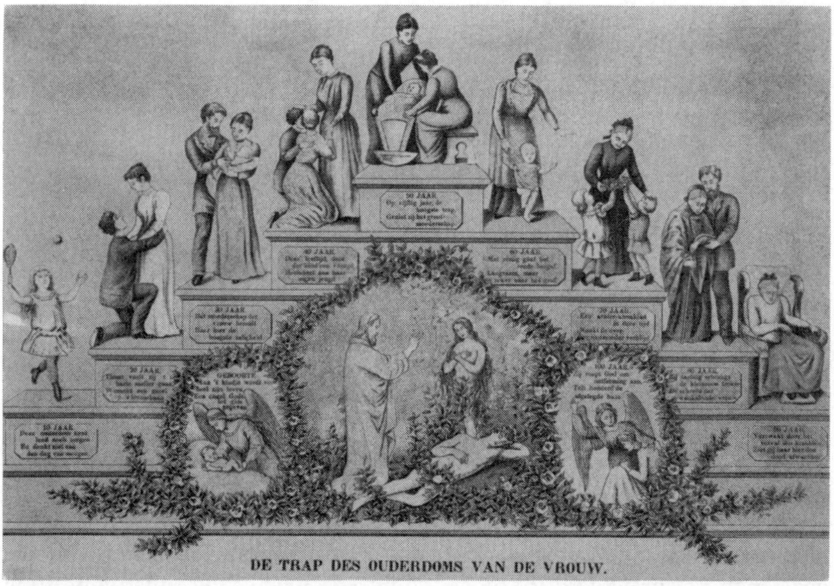

19th century litho (origin unknown).
Double stairway representing the life cycle of a woman
(Photo: Thijs Quispel) Limburgs Volkskundig Centrum, Limbricht/Venlo

---

16 Mac Lennon, E., J. Fitz and J. Sullivan, 1985, Working Children, Low Pay Unit, London, quoted by Neve and Renooy, 1988.

6.3 Adulthood

As with childhood and adolescence, the demarcation of adulthood has changed in the course of history. The biological age of adulthood (for women considered to be the birth of the first child), the juridical (reaching the age of full legal capacity) and the economic demarcation line (entering the labor market) differ from period to period. In this section, however, adulthood is defined as the period between the ages of 25 and 49 years (where available).

Labor force participation rates of women aged 25 - 49 show the same trends in all seven countries, but again the levels differ tremendously (see figure 6.3 and table 6.7). The common characteristic is the steady and continuous increase in all countries. Denmark's and Sweden's increase have been the most spectacular and in these two countries female labor force participation rates in this age group reached average male activity rates.

Figure 6.3 and table 6.7 show that female labor force participation rates for the 25-49 (or 44) age group were lowest in the Netherlands in all years except in 1990, when Belgium showed the lowest rates.

In the Netherlands, women's shares in this age group remained fairly stable until 1971 (34 to 40 per cent) but increased to over 50 per cent in 1990.

For some countries it is possible to assemble data on cohorts of women. An approximation may be constructed by 'synthetic' cohort data[17], combining the experience of successive cross-sections by making use of the fact that the population of women aged 15 - 19 in one year will be the population of women aged 20 - 24 years later. Three broad patterns of participation of age then emerge: one peak at ages 20 - 24; two peaks separated by a valey around age 30; and a broad plateau. At the beginning of the century all seven countries showed curves with a pronounced inflection around the age of 20, just before the peak child-bearing years, recently in Denmark and Sweden the third pattern, a curve in the form of an inverted U or a broad plateau characterizes female participation behavior. This pattern represents the situation where employment is combined with rearing children and the distinction between participation rates of women at different stages of family-formation disappears. The one peak pattern prevailed in those countries where the relatively high participation rates of unmarried women in their early twenties produce the left hand peak, whereas in countries where the presence of young children, rather than marriage, is the major barrier to labor force participation, the two peak pattern prevails. This pattern is seen in the other five countries. (OECD, 1991:133-139).

---

17 A cohort life cycle profile can only be constructed from data following the labor market experience of the same group of women over the life cycle.

Table 6.7 and figure 6.3 *A seven-country comparison of labor force participation rates of women aged 25 to 49 years, 1900 – 1990*

	Belgium	Denmark	France	Germany	Netherlands	Sweden	Great Britain
1900	–	[1]29	–	24	19	27	[1]27
1910	24	27	55	36	21	27	29
1920	–	25	53	39	20	34	28
1930	[1]31	26	55	40	21	37	31
1940	–	35	48	45	–	31	–
1950	25	38	42	43	23	30	36
1960	31	37	42	47	23	38	41
1970	37	57	50	48	24	59	53
1980	53	82	63	57	42	84	59
1990	57	89	73	65	62	91	–

Belgium:
1 1930, the 21 – 54 age group, because only six age groups were distinguished in that year.

Denmark:
2 1901, the 25 – 60 age group: 24 per cent.

Great Britain:
1 the 25 – 44 age group. According to Eurostat 73 per cent in 1989. In HMSO 1993 not available.

Sources and notes concerning the census and sample survey years: see table 6.3.

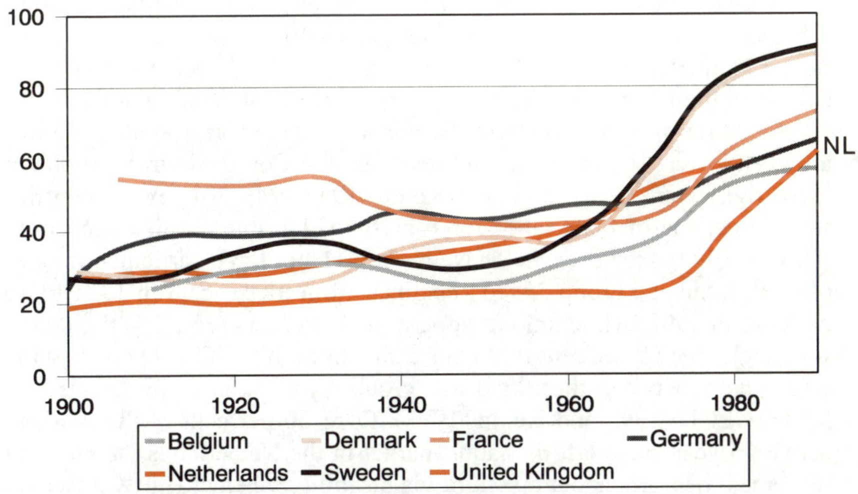

The changes in adulthood are therefore apparently influenced by two important events occurring to the majority of women in this age group: marriage and the birth of children. Because of its importance two separate chapters treat these topics. Chapter 7 discusses marriage and fertility, while chapter 8 describes female labor force participation rates by marital status, particularly by married women, the dominant category in this stage of the life cycle.

6.4 Middle Age

Although, like the limits of the other stages in the life cycle, the age of fifty is arbitrary, to most women it means the inevitable end of child-bearing. There may be major differences in income-generating activities, family life and health. After fifty, life improves for some people, while others begin to feel that their best years are behind them. Inequality of income, health and family situation (children may even have left the parental home), present between women at all stages, become more pronounced in this period of the life cycle than in the previous one (Fuchs, 1983). For the first time in history large proportions of women in this age group are still married, in good health, while at the same time - during this period in particular - their children become independent. As in the previous age group drastic changes are likely to be related to fertility and marital status (and will be treated in chapters 7 and 8).

The aggregated figures of the female labor force participation rates during middle age in all seven countries, presented in figure 6.4 and table 6.8, may conceal two trends of opposite direction: a decline in the activity rates of unmarried women (similar to those of men) and an increase in those of married women.

Total labor force movements in this age group have been dominated by the decrease in male employment. This has been encouraged by a variety of measures, including long-term sickness benefits, invalidity schemes and early pensions (see also chapter 9).
In the Netherlands in 1990, only 27 per cent of all men aged 60 - 64 belong to the labor force, however, only 18 per cent of all men were still employed for over 20 hours a week. For women the corresponding figures are even lower: 10 and 4 per cent respectively! Compared internationally these figures are extremely low (Kemp, 1993:124). All seven countries show a decline of male labor force participation rates in this age group (OECD, 1992). However, in the Netherlands labor force participation rates of men in the age group 55 - 64 declined from 81 per cent in 1971 to 46 per cent in 1990, while among yonger male workers (25 - 54) the deline was negligible (2 per cent to 93 per cent). In no other OECD country the discrepancy between these two age groups is as large as in the Netherlands (OECD, 1992 and Kemp, 1993). Over 50 per cent of the workers above 55 year, have left the labor market in the Netherlands via an early retirement pension, about one third via disability schemes (fairly generous and likely to have contributed to the high figure of people receiving a disability pension - 882 thousand in 1990, 19 per cent of all insured labor years; SVr, 1991).

Figure 6.4 and table 6.8 show that prior to 1980, female labor force participation rates during middle age were lower in the Netherlands than in any of the other six countries (considering part-time employment, see chapter 8). As in the case of adulthood, Belgium is the country with the lowest participation rates in this age group after that date.

Labor force participation rates of women aged 50 - 64 in the Netherlands remained fairly constant throughout this century, at least up to 1980. The census years 1909 and 1960 are (again) ideosyncrasies in the trend (positive and negative respectively). The share of this age group in the female labor force remained fairly constant; it was 11 per cent in 1899 and 10 per cent in 1990, but peaked in 1971 with 13 per cent.

Table 6.8 and figure 6.4 *A seven-country comparison of labor force participation rates of women aged 50 – 64, 1900 – 1990*

	Belgium	Denmark	France	Germany	Netherlands	Sweden	Great Britain
1900	–	a	–	29	17	20	21
1910	31	–	47	38	19	17	22
1920	–	10	47	37	16	21	20
1930	21	20	51	35	15	22	20
1940	–	28	42	38	–	22	–
1950	17	35	41	34	17	26	28
1960	18	31	40	38	14	45	37
1970	18	39	43	44	17	51	50
1980	16	50	43	44	18	63	40
1990	13	51	41	37	26	74	–

Sources: See table 2.2 and table 6.3

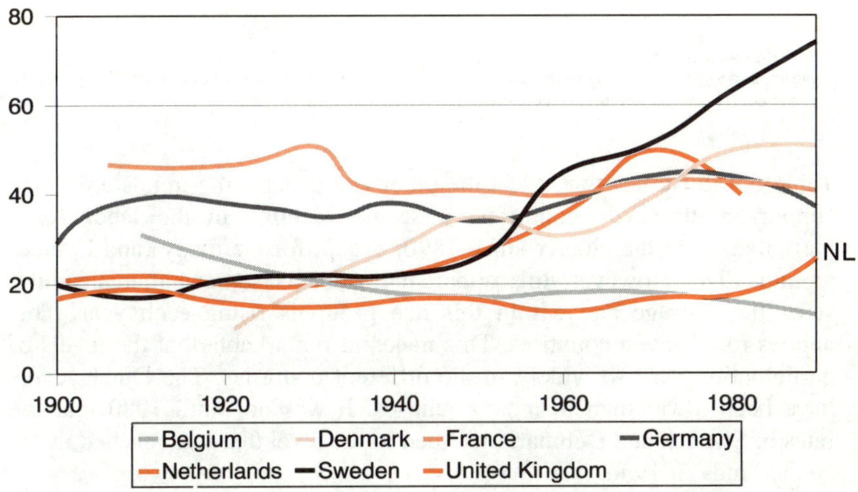

6.5 Old Age

"Historically, one of the strongest of all human aspirations has been to live to a ripe old age - to reach the Biblical 'three score and ten'." (Fuchs, 1983:186). Gradually, more and more people are achieving this goal in all seven countries. The relative number of elderly in the population has increased considerably over recent decades, also partly because fertility rates and therefore the proportion of young people have declined. This has increased the political power of the elderly, and in general their social and economic circumstances have improved tremendously. All seven countries have old age pensions, enabling the elderly to retire from the labor force see table 6.9.

Table 6.9 *A seven-country comparison of labor force participation rates of women aged over 65, 1900 – 1990*

	Belgium	Denmark	France	Germany[1]	Netherlands	Sweden[2]	Great Britain
1900	–	–	–	20	13	–	13
1910	–	–	28	22	13	11	12
1920	–	3	28	18	9	11	10
1930	11	7	31	14	7	9	8
1940	–	6	21	14/17	–	10	–
1950	5	8		10	6	9	5
1960	4	7		8	3	9	5
1970	2	7	7	6	2	9	7
1980	1	7	4	3	1	7	4
1990	0	4	2	2	0	5	–

1 in 1939: bounderies post World War, exclusive Saar, FRG
2 participation in 1930 over 70 years, participation rate age group 60 – 70 = 17 per cent, over 60 years: 13 per cent. Participation in 1980 concerns 65 – 74 age group.

Table 6.9 illustrates that, as in the other age groups, the trends are fairly similar in all seven countries: a secular decline in the labor force participation of the elderly since 1890, except for Germany (and France) around 1920. However, this apparent decline is somewhat misleading, since the average age within this age group is rising each year. This applies to all seven countries. This makes it remarkable that the levels of participation vary so widely in the different countries. The Dutch levels have been lower than in most countries. It was not until 1980 that the rates in Sweden and Denmark declined to the level that was reached in the Netherlands in 1930.

In the Netherlands, labor force participation rates of women aged over 65 dropped below one per cent in the 1980s; and in 1987 the rate was only 0.5 per cent (CBS, 1989:77). Belgium has also reached participation rates of less than a half per cent, and yet again Denmark and Sweden are the highest in 1990.

Since 1899 the share of elderly women in the labor force in the Netherlands has never been higher than 5 per cent; it has fallen to less than 1 per cent since 1977, and was negligible in 1990.

6.6 Conclusions to chapter 6

The small average increase in female labor force participation rates shown in chapter 2 is the net result of participation changes in six different age groups. Child labor, market labor by persons younger than the mid-teens, has almost completely disappeared. So has market labor by the elderly. However, even the rise in labor force participation rates by women aged 15 to 65 years is not reflected equally in the five other age groups distinguished. Teenage participation in the labor force at first increased, but has started to decrease in recent decades; in general this decrease has been compensated by an increase in participation of 20 to 24-year-olds.

The trend for women aged 20 - 24 is different from that for the 15 - 19 age group. It shows a secular increase in all seven countries until the 1970s, and for Belgium, Germany and Great Britain this continues until 1990. In Denmark, the Netherlands and Sweden, there is actually an accelaration between 1970 and 1980. Differences in levels are much smaller than for the 15 - 19 age group. There is a remarkable similarity in participation rates between the two age groups in the 1950s and 1960s, except for France in 1954. In 1990, France is the country with the lowest participation rate for the 20 - 24 age group, while the Netherlands shows the highest rates after Denmark and Sweden. Throughout this century, participation rates for Dutch girls in this age group have been at the low end, although not often the lowest. In 1990, the relative rate has increased in the international distribution.

Almost every generation in the age groups above 25 and below 50 years shows a steady increase in participation throughout the twentieth century. There are, however, a few exceptions.

The 50 - 64 age group, at first increasing after 1960, has started to decline recently in Belgium, Germany and the United Kingdom. This means that labor force participation is being squeezed into an ever shorter period of adult life.

Labor force participation of girls in the Netherlands was low compared to the other six countries up to World War II. After that War the rates in Belgium and France are lower. Denmark, Germany, Sweden and Great Britain have higher rates until 1990, but in that year only the rates in Denmark and Sweden are higher than in the Netherlands.

Female labor force participation rates for the 25 - 49 (or sometimes 44) age group were lowest in the Netherlands in all years except in 1990, when Belgium showed the lowest rates. Prior to 1980, female labor force participation rates during middle age were lower in the Netherlands than in any of the other six countries. As in the case of adulthood, Belgium is the country with the lowest participation rates in that age group after that date.

The labor force participation of the elderly has declined markedly in all countries over the last century, but the levels of the activity rates are very different. This is probably due to assisting wives and mothers, since the levels are relatively high in France and Germany. The Dutch levels have been lower than in most countries. It was not until 1980 that levels in Sweden and Denmark matched that reached in the Netherlands in 1930. In Belgium and the Netherlands, activity rates of women aged over 65 dropped in the 1980s below one per cent.

The low Dutch female activity rates shown in chapter 2 are therefore due mainly to the low activity rates during adulthood and middle age. Moreover, this chapter again confirms that even in 1990 there is still no international agreement at to how to count the labor force, nor indeed as to either the lower or the upper age limit.

CHAPTER 7

MARRIAGE AND FERTILITY

> *"For an individual, the timing and circumstances of birth significantly affect the character, quality and duration of life. For a society, the birth rate is a major determinant of its economic, political, and social development."*
> *Victor R. Fuchs, 1983:15*

The previous chapters have considered various aspects of the female labor force, but not the fact that the labor force participation rates presented disguise a number of changes in the population structure. This chapter therefore describes the demographic developments in the seven countries. If demographic developments in the Netherlands have differed from those in the other six countries over the last century and a half, how have they differed? Was it developments in households and families that differed, or marriage patterns, or fertility?

Section 7.1 describes the population trends of the seven countries. Because it proved difficult, if not impossible, to describe changes in family structure over the whole period in all seven countries, the focus of the remainder of this chapter is on two main events in the life of the family: marriage and reproduction. Their interaction with labor force participation will be examined in chapter 8. Section 7.2 presents definitions and a few remarks on developments in the family and in households. Section 7.3 describes marriage patterns and the composition of the population by marital status in the seven countries. Section 7.4 looks at dissolution of marriage, while section 7.5 considers fertility patterns and trends and section 7.6 identifies Dutch peculiarities in family formation and fertility.

7.1 A seven-country comparison of population trends

In only a few of the seven countries it is possible to trace the population back accurately to the early nineteenth century. This is because borders often changed. The most recent example of such a change is the reunion of the two Germanies in 1990 (disregarded in this study). Including these sudden population changes due to loss or gain of territories, the developments in population size between about 1850 and 1990 are presented in figure 7.1. In general the population size is determined not only by the natural growth rate, i.e. fertility minus mortality, but also by the difference between outward and inward migration. A short description of population developments in each country is given first.

Belgium

In 1830, when Belgium and the Netherlands became separate countries, Belgium had 3.7 million inhabitants and the Netherlands 2.6 million. Infant mortality was high and remained until 1890 relatively higher in the Netherlands than in Belgium. After that year, infant mortality decreased more rapidly in the Netherlands than in Belgium. By the turn of the century, Belgium had 7 million inhabitants, in 1930 about 8 million, around 1960 about 9 million and in 1990 nearly 10 million. The industrial and coal-mining districts in the centre and west of the country have the highest population densities, followed by the semi-agricultural region of Flanders, where rural and urban life are closely intermingled.

Denmark

The Danish[1] population can be estimated relatively far back: it numbered 600 thousand in 1670, and approximately 718 thousand in 1735: a yearly average rate of population growth of around 0.3 per cent. A declining mortality rate, together with an unchanged fertility rate, resulted in a higher rate of population growth - between 1 and 1.5 per cent - from the end of the eighteenth century until about 1850. Because both immigration and emigration had been until then extremely limited, the Danish population could be regarded as a closed population (Andersen, 1977:9). In the second half of the nineteenth century emigration started to increase and the fertility rate began to decline. Population increased from nearly 1.5 million at that time to about 2.5 at the turn of the century, and again to over 5 million in 1990.

France

France, with 28 million inhabitants in 1800, had at that time the second largest population in Europe - Russia with 40 million being largest - and therefore the largest population of all seven countries considered in this study. A century later France occupied fifth position, with a population of nearly 39 million, being overtaken by Germany half-way through the nineteenth century and by Great Britain at the beginning of the twentieth century. In 1990, France's population was estimated at about 56 million, only twice that of nearly two centuries earlier. This relatively slow growth can be partially attributed to the wars of the Napoleonic Era, and the two World Wars of 1914-1918 and 1939-1945 and partially to birth control[2]. It is estimated that 1.5 million Frenchmen died in World War I and that they would have fathered some 2 million children if they had lived

---

[1] The demographic developments for Denmark are limited to the southern part of Denmark and therefore exclude those in Greenland and the Faroe Islands.

[2] According to Haks (1985:26) birth control was spreading among the French population since 1750. France signalled a steep drop of 10 per cent in marital fertility around 1800, nearly a century earlier than most European countries, but according to Yaukey (1981:192) early nineteenth century differentials in marital fertility were caused only to a minor degree by voluntary family size limitation.

(Collier, 1966:254), causing the tremendous decline in fertility after that war (see figure 7.2).

Germany

The area of what in 1990 was still the Federal Republic of Germany, accomodated only 13.5 million persons in 1816, but 62.7 million in 1990. The population grew rapidly during the nineteenth century. As in France, the large number of deaths in World War I - nearly 3.8 million soldiers and half a million civilians - altered the balance between the sexes and the age groups tremendously and a large proportion of the women of that generation remained unmarried. This did not, however, retard the growth of the German population as much as the same factor in France. At the outbreak of World War II in 1939 the German Reich, including Austria, had almost 80 million inhabitants. Within the 1937 frontiers, the population numbered 69.3 million.

Between 1946 and 1953, migration from East Germany brought over 10 million persons into the Federal Republic. In 1956, 396 thousand refugees fled to West Germany (and although during the 1950s many doctors, engineers and artists went in the opposite direction to East Germany, this migration was far less: 49 thousand in 1954, 47 thousand in 1956 and 39 thousand in 1958) (Collier, 1966:21). In 1990, after the reunion Germany had about 79.6 million inhabitants.

The Netherlands

From 1840 to 1990, the Dutch population increased 5 times over, from 3 to 15 million inhabitants. After 1800 it actually multiplied by a factor of 7.5. This rate of increase is particularly remarkable given that during the nineteenth century and up to World War I the Netherlands was predominantly a country of emigration[3]. During the period from 1880 to 1893 it was mainly farmers and agricultural workers who went overseas. Non-agricultural workers living in the border provinces tended to emigrate to Germany. During World War I, many Belgian refugees fled to the neutral Netherlands. In the 1920s and 1930s more immigrants entered the country than emigrants left it, partly because of the relatively favorable economic situation. From the second half of the thirties onward there was a change, resulting in net emigration until the beginning of the 1960s[4].

---

[3] Between 1865 and 1913, however, fewer than 200 thousand persons left the country. Therefore, the effect of migration on the total population was small (as in Belgium). This applies to the whole period between 1860 and 1970.

[4] Extensive repatriation from Indonesia took place in the years 1946, 1950 and 1958. At the same time there was a renewal of interest in countries such as the United States, Australia, Canada and New Zealand, encouraged and partly financed by the Dutch government. In the record year of 1952, 52 thousand persons emigrated to these countries. In the 1960s and 1970s, 'guest workers', at first from Southern European countries - Italy, Spain and Turkey- and later on from North African countries, particularly Morocco, together with the large number of repatriates arriving from Surinam in the second half of the 1970s,

One of the reasons why the population increase was much higher here than elsewhere was that after 1880 the Dutch death rates declined comparatively rapidly, and more rapidly than the birth rates.

Sweden
Population statistics going back more than two centuries allow a reliable description of the country's demographic development. In 1750 Sweden had an estimated population of nearly 1.8 million, in 1800 nearly 3.4 million, in 1850 about 3.5 million, in 1900 over 5 million and in 1990 over 8.5 million. Natural increase was relatively slow. Before 1700, both birth and death rates were high (35 per 1000) and natural increase insignificant. The somewhat lower death rate in the next century resulted in a low natural increase. From 1815 to 1880 the death rate continued to decline, but after 1880 the birth rate declined fairly rapidly. This, combined with emigration, caused a slow growth in population (see figure 7.1). On average 4.4 children per woman were born to the female cohorts of 1735/36 to 1850/51, declining to below 2 for the 1905/06 cohort (see also section 7.5 and Hoem, 1992). In the 1920s the population passed 6 million, at the end of the 1940s it was 7 million, while in 1990 it was 8.6 million.

United Kingdom
The population in England and Wales, according to the 1801 census, was 8.9 million; in 1841 it was 15.9 million and in 1990 over 50.5 million. The average birth rate began to fall in the late 1870s.

Except for London and its immediate environs, the population of the south-east was fairly evenly distributed, whereas in the north and the west there were heavy concentrations of population in the old mining and industrial areas and their adjacent sea ports.

Early in the 1930s there was a halt to the age long drain on the population caused by the excess of emigration over immigration, and between 1931 and 1947 the tide definitely turned in the opposite direction. During this period there was a net gain of 750 thousand due to migration (Collier, 1966: 183).

All seven countries
The changes in population described above are shown in figure 7.1. Because of the relatively large number of breaks in the trend in Germany, this country shows a peculiar pattern.

The figure shows that between 1840 and 1990 the rate of population growth was higher in the Netherlands than anywhere else (a 5-fold increase).

---

caused an immigration surplus amounting to over 650 thousand between 1961 and 1988 (Van der Erf, 1989:19).

Figure 7.1 *A seven-country comparison in population developments, 1840-1990*

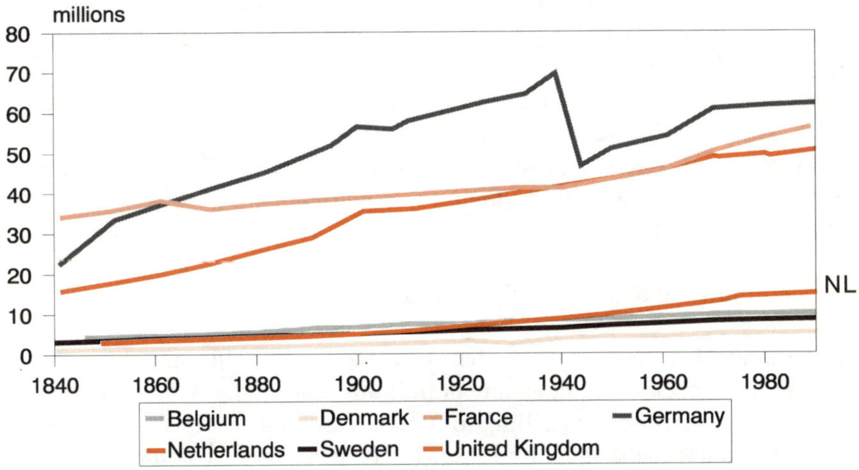

By comparison the Belgian population increased 2.3 times, the Danish population 4 times, the British population 3 times and the Swedish 2.7 over the period in question. The increase was least of all in France (1.6 times).

7.2 The family and the household

Scientific research on and interest in the family started only about 25 to 30 years ago[5]. Controversial statements about social, political, economic and cultural changes in the family can be found since then within various research disciplines, such as historical demography and sociology of the family. The history of the family is also subject to continuing debate and criticism, although the longer the historical period under consideration, the smaller the changes within the family are generally seen to be and the more emphasis is given to continuity. As in the history of women's work, there is much room for many shades of opinion. The various interpretations of changes in attitudes, modes of thought, norms, feelings and

---

[5] In the Netherlands by the sociologist Hofstee (1954) (see also Kooy, 1985:2), in the United States by the sociologist Goode (1963) and in Germany by König (1974). The history of the family flourished as never before since Ariès (1960), Flandrin (1974), Shorter (1975) and Stone (1977), while economist's interest accelerated after Becker (1960).

relations between members of the family are not easy to judge, and certainly not without studying the available historical sources. The point of view (including changes in affectional relations, economic values and size) from which changes in the family are studied seems important. Whatever point of view or discipline is chosen, however, the method of research is indirect and the evidence inconclusive, disputable, incomplete and patchy.

In order to identify some known demographic facts in the various countries and to avoid misunderstandings, subsection 7.2.1 starts with a definition of the concepts of *family* and *household.*

7.2.1 Family and household, definitions

International comparisons of families and households are difficult or impossible, because of the many definitions that exist. "A *household* is ... what a census is able or willing to record." (Schmid, 1988:14). A number of persons under the same roof seems to be a common denominator found in all current definitions of a household (Schmid, 1988:14). This requirement of the same roof often seems to be combined with the requirement of shared meals[6]. Households may also be subdivided into *non-family households* and *family households. A family household*, or *a family*, consists of an adult with at least one additional person in the household who is related by blood, marriage or adoption (Wetzel, 1990:5)[7]. The term *family*, can be applied to the more specific *nuclear family (or conjugal family)*[8]: a married couple with or without children who live together under the same roof; to the *extended family*, which consists of a nuclear family living together with relatives other than offspring or with servants; and to the *multiple family household*, which comprises all forms of domestic groups (Schmid, 1988: 15-16). Sometimes the concept of the *traditional family* is also used. This concept is not without controversy: sociologists use it mainly for what was defined above as the *extended family*, economists for the *nuclear family* with a male breadwinner and a female homemaker who cares for the children

---

6 As, for example, nowadays in the Netherlands and Denmark. In the latter country up to 1950 boarders and lodgers were regarded as members of the household with which they were lodged. Since that date, a lodger has been regarded as a one-person household if he/she provides his/her own food (Andersen, 1977:71).

7 An alternative definition is that a family household consists of a married couple with or without children, or a man or woman with child(ren), or any other combination of relatives living together (Schmid, 1988:15).

8 Some historians of the family distinguish between these two concepts, with conjugal being the general term and the modern nuclear family being used for families with affective relations (e.g. Haks, 1985:2). Others (e.g. Noordam, 1987:87) attribute affective relations to the conjugal family, characterizing it by love between spouses, care and attention for children and a cosy domesticity.

and/or the domestic needs, and demographers for the first definition given above. In contrast, economists define the *modern family* as a nuclear family with both man and wife earning an income. The economists' (and demographic) interpretation will be adopted here, thereby a *nuclear family* can be *traditional* as well as *modern*.

However, economists also contribute to the confusion by quoting the views of historians emphasizing emotional relationships rather than demographic composition or economic relations. For example, Blau and Ferber state that the genesis of "the traditional family is in fact comparatively recent in origin, dating back only to the mid-nineteenth and early twentieth centuries" (Blau and Ferber, 1986:31). This statement has gained wide acceptance, particularly since Clark (1919) and Stone (1977). However, it is the development of affective relations, rather than size (or number of income earners) that is seen here as central.

This trend from cool, unemotional relationships in the direction of free choice and affectional relationships has been described by, amongst others, four famous historians of the family: Phillippe Ariès (1960,1973), Edward Shorter (1975), Lawrence Stone (1977,1990) en Jean-Louis Flandrin (1974). Each of them signals, with differing emphases, great changes in the course of history contributing to the development of the nuclear family, caused partly by economic changes (Shorter, 1975:259) and partly by social and religious changes contributing to the 'rise of affective individualism' (Stone, 1977).

Stone distinguishes several different stages in the development of the family in England. Between 1450 and 1630 the "open lineage family" dominates, "a structure held together not by affective bonds but by mutual interests" (Stone, 1977:118), and it was only between 1640 and 1800 that the "closed domesticated nuclear family", or traditional family, gained ground.

These views have been challenged[9] with regard to the situation in England by Keith Wrightson and Ralph Houlbrook, who emphasize "enduring structures and patterns against the patterns of change from Stone" (quoted by Haks, 1988:55). More recent historical demographic research indicates that views on change and the recent origin of the affectional nuclear family have to be corrected for the whole of Western Europe (Peeters, 1988).

It seems likely that despite fluctuations and geographical differences there is more long term stability than generally expected (see also Haks, 1985:4) and that at least since the Middle Ages the nuclear family (although sometimes with additional family members or servants) remained the dominant household type all through Europe (see also Kronjee, 1991:30).

---

9 The views of Stone, Shorter and Ariès concerning a similar change in parent-child affectional relationships from cool to intimate have also been criticized (among others by Donzelot (1979), Mcfarlane (1979) and Stearns and Stearns (1985), see Haks (1988)).

7.2.2 Family and household in the Netherlands

Whatever the international disputes about changes in the family, the theory of the recent origin of the nuclear family seems certainly inapplicable to the Netherlands. The nuclear/traditional family is likely to have been important and to have existed in this country at least since the Golden Age (as already mentioned in chapter 3). Demographically, the family household was also relatively well defined in the Dutch Republic. "As far as figures permit construction, it seems that Dutch homes were, on average, smaller, more tightly organized and more independent than elsewhere in seventeenth-century Europe" (Schama, 1988:386). Mean household size in that century was 4.75[10], but in towns households were smaller; in Gouda, for example, mean size in 1622 was 4.3 and in 1674 only 3.6 (Schama, 1988). On average, household size was smaller in the Western provinces during that period than in the rest of the country: 3.7 persons, with an average of 1.7 children (Van der Woude, 1970). In 1960[11] mean household size was 3.6 persons (Verduin, 1985:72). Although circumstances were different in seventeenth century Holland and in the mid-twentieth century Netherlands, differences in household size are small. This is also because the percentage of homes with living-in relatives in the Western and Northern provinces in the seventeenth century was only around five to six per cent (Schama, 1988:386-387). The household structure in the rest of the country was quite different. The fact that a remarkably large proportion of the population lived in cities - in 1695 about 42 per cent (Verduin, 1989:5) - where one-family households were dominant, may also have contributed to the small household size[12]. Two or three-generation households were exceptional, even on farms. Parents and their single children frequently left a farm once a newly married son and his wife could take it over (Faessen, 1987:24). Only on small farms in the eastern regions (especially, *Salland* and *Achterhoek*, but also *Drents plateau*) and the south-eastern parts (*Brabant*) of the country did multi-generation households exist to any extent; in these areas, about 31 per cent of the households included one or more living-in relatives and about 50 per cent included relatives and/or others. The other parts of the country (*Zeeland* and north-west *Brabant*, *Utrecht* and *Veluwe*), showed an intermediate pattern. It is remarkable that these three different regional patterns which could be distinguished in the Netherlands in the seventeenth century still existed in 1956 (Verduin, 1985:76). Close to the

---

10 It is a remarkable feature that Laslett (1972) finds the same figure for England and Wales during the period 1574 to 1821 (see subsection 7.2.3).

11 In 1971 it was on average 3.2 persons, with an average of 1.3 children (Verduin, 1985:72; and Kronjee, 1989:324).

12 Kronjee (1991:29) quoting Wall (1983), shows that mean household size in England was 4.4 between 1650 and 1749, 4.8 in the period therafter until 1821, in 1947: 3.7 and in 1970: 2.9 persons.

German and Belgian borders, therefore, the extended and multiple family household existed to some extent. This was the dominant type of household across the borders in Germany, especially on farms and among the richer property-owning class (Verduin, 1985:88).

Average household size remained small throughout the eighteenth and nineteenth centuries in the Netherlands, partly because the proportion of the population living in as domestic servants was only 6 to 10 per cent prior to industrialization, and never more than 5 per cent after 1880 (Faessen, 1987:24). In the first three censuses, of 1829, 1839 and 1849, data about households were collected, with households defined as housekeeping units of *single persons or two or more persons* living together; the average size of households in those years was respectively 4.9, 5.0 and 4.9. In the subsequent censuses households were defined as units of *two or more persons* living together and, although not many single-person households may have existed, household size must have declined sharply between the census of 1849 and the next two of 1859 and 1869, because the average size of (the now multi-person) households dropped to respectively 4.6 and 4.7[13]. In the next three counts it increased slightly to 4.8, an increase due mainly to declining infant mortality, leading also to more exceptionally large families in this than in any other period.

The subsequent steady and continuous decrease in average size of (multi-person) households, to 3.6 in 1971[14], was caused not only by declining infant mortality but also by decreasing fertility (Faessen, 1987:24) and, since World War II, also by new patterns of household formation.

In the period before World War II, only household size was recorded and no more detailed figures about families exist, but it might be expected that in the Netherlands the percentage of households consisting of a nuclear family has always been relatively high. In 1947, family data were also recorded: 76 per cent all households were then nuclear families[15]. The percentage of nuclear families increased to 78 by 1960, but started to decrease over the next decade to 74 per cent in 1971, while 70 per cent of all households in 1980 were nuclear families without

---

13 The Asiatic Cholera epidemics of 1834, 1849 and 1866 may have contributed to this decline as well.

14 In 1920, 1930, 1947, 1960 and 1971 the figures were respectively 4.6, 4.4, 4.0, 3.9 and 3.6 (Faessen, 1987:24). According to the CBS (1989), average household size in 1899 was: 4.5; in 1909: 4.4; in 1920: 4.3; in 1930: 4.0; in 1947: 3.7; in 1960: 3.6; in 1971: 3.2; in 1975: 3.0; in 1977: 2.9; in 1979: 2.8; in 1981: 2.75; in 1983: 2.6; in 1985 and 1987: 2.5 and in 1988: 2.45.

15 This figure would have been higher without World War II. In 1947 relatively large numbers of married couples were living temporarily with their parents because of the post-war housing shortage. In the public allocation of houses, married couples living in with their parents were given the highest priority, indicating the exceptional nature of these situations.

other persons (Faessen, 1987:17). This increase in nuclear families is also due to the fact that the average marriage now lasts longer than at the beginning of the century. In the nineteenth century the average marriage lasted 23 years (Noordam, 1987:115), in 1990 nearly 35 years (excluding divorce even 43.6 years) (CBS, 1992/6:34). In 1900 only 8 per cent of all marriages lasted longer than 50 years; in 1984 the figure was already one in three, a fact due mainly to declining mortality (Kronjee, 1991:56). In the latter year nearly all children under the age of 18 lived in a two-parent family and 5.5 per cent with a single parent (Kuysten and Voets, 1986:48). Also in 1984, of all adolescences between 18 and 24 years, only 5.5 per cent of the girls and 2.6 per cent of the boys had not lived during the whole childhood with both parents, while all the others had (Kronjee, 1989:323).

Since 1981, households and families have been surveyed by the CBS every 4 years in the *Woningbehoeftenonderzoek* (Housing Needs Survey). According to this survey, the percentage of households consisting of married couples with or without children was 72 in 1981, 67 in 1985/1986 and 64 in 1989/1990. In absolute numbers these families increased. The relative decline is mainly due to the remarkable increase in elderly one-person households. In 1989 only 3 per cent of peoples aged over 65 years lived in households with other relatives, while in 1956 this percentage was still 15 per cent. Relatively many elderly people live in institutions, in 1989; about 10 per cent of the whole population over 65 years; this in contrast to, for example, France where only 4 to 5 per cent of the elderly were living in institutions in that year (Esveldt and Van Solinge, 1992:50).

7.2.3 International household trends

Most censuses in all seven countries publish only household size and no further data about families. Throughout Western and Northern Europe an increase in household numbers is reflected in the decline in the size of the average household since national registration started[16]. The number of three or even four-generation households (if recorded) has fallen dramatically. In West Germany, there were still over one million such households in 1961, in 1972 about 770 thousand and in 1982 half a million (Schwarz, 1988:74). Differences as well as common trends can be identified in all seven countries. However, the information about average household size is too inaccurate and too difficult to compare to contribute much to the explanation of low Dutch female labor force participation rates. The only tentative conclusion seems to be that household size in

[16] Between 1970 and 1980, most countries experienced a decline of between 0.3 and 0.5 persons (Hall, 1986:22). The average number of persons per household in Denmark has declined from 4.3 in 1901 to 2.6 in 1970 (Andersen, 1977:70).

Holland was on average smaller until the nineteenth century and that the nuclear family remained of importance in the Netherlands until at least the 1990s. To permit comparison over time and space, allowance must be made for the way in which definitions vary from one country to another and from one period to the next, and - even more importantly - the data must be standardized for the age distribution of the population[17].

Because it is not easy to study the dynamics of the household and especially of the (nuclear) family in the same way that births, marriages and deaths can be studied (Murphy, 1983:50-70), the next two sections will explore differences between the countries in marriage and fertility patterns rather than households and families. The introduction of the Register of Births, Deaths and Marriages, which occurred in most of the seven countries under the Napoleonic regime (in the Netherlands in 1812), made these demographic data available from that period onward.

7.3 Marriage trends

7.3.1 The Netherlands

Due to the poor economic situation in rural areas in the mid-nineteenth century, marriage became even more delayed[18] and a relatively large proportion of the population remained permanently unmarried (Grever & Van der Veen, 1989:9). Of all the men and women born in the middle of the nineteenth century, about 85 per cent ever married (a figure not to be confused with the proportion of married women in the population: see table 7.1). For the subsequent cohorts the probability of marriage increased for men and decreased for women. This development coincided with the emigration of (mainly young) men at the end of the nineteenth century (Tas, 1989:21). Marriage rates for women increased again for women born after 1880, mainly because of the natural surplus of baby boys over girls. The cohorts of men born between 1920 and 1924 enjoyed a historically high probability of marriage: 93 per cent married, a figure exceeded only by that for the female cohort born between 1936 and 1940,

---

17 Schwarz (1988) has done this by using the index of the overall headship - the higher the index, the smaller the average number of adults per household - in order to compare household developments in 19 European countries over a period starting around 1960 and ending around 1980. Finland, the Netherlands, Bulgaria and Portugal show the largest decreases in average household size; Ireland and Greece the smallest. The Soviet Union was the only country showing an increase, due to the growing share of its Asian population (Schwarz, 1988:69).

18 The relatively late age on first marriage in Europe was already mentioned in chapter 3.

with a record 95 per cent. For the more recent cohorts born between 1955 and 1959, the probability of marriage is expected to be 78 per cent for men and 86 per cent for women (Tas, 1989:21).

Table 7.1 gives some additional figures concerning marriage in the Netherlands.

Table 7.1 *Long-term marriage trends in the Netherlands, 1849 – 1989*

	marriage absolute figures × 1000	marriage relative per 1000 of population	percentage married women age 20 – 44	average age on first marriage men	average age on first marriage women
1849	–	–	49.3	–	–
1850/54	–	–	–	29.1	27.2
1855/59	–	–	–	29.4	27.7
1859	–	–	51.5	–	–
1860/64	–	–	–	29.4	27.5
1869	–	–	55.0	–	–
1879	–	–	58.9	–	–
1885[1]	–	–	28.0	28.0	26.0
1889	–	–	56.9	–	–
1899	39	7.7	56.6	29.3	26.7
1909	43	7.3	58.7	29.2	26.8
1920	65	9.6	60.1	–	–
1930	59	7.4	61.5	–	–
1947	99	10.2	65.4	30.3	27.2
1960	89	7.8	75.2	28.3	25.4
1971	122	9.3	78.8	26.1	23.6
1981	86	6.0	73.4	27.5	24.6
1985	83	5.7	67.1	29.1	26.3
1989	88	6.0	62.3	30.1	27.3

1 Sources: 1849 - 1889, Faessen (1987:20)
1899 - 1989, CBS (1989:27).

Table 7.1 conceals the large regional and religious differences in marriage patterns (for which see e.g. Van Poppel, 1981 and 1992). It also conceals the long-term stability of these regional patterns.

The table shows that the percentage of married women aged 20 to 44 years, increased continuously from 1849 until 1970, but since that time has decreased steadily. The total absolute number of marriages reached a peak in 1971. The average age on first marriage of both men and women first declined slightly and following World War II rapidly, reaching historically low levels in 1971, but has since increasing again (see also Noordam, 1987:115, for long-term trends). The percentage of married women in the total population increased steadily until the early 1980s.

Around 1850 about 75 to 80 per cent of all marriages concerned first marriages, since then the percentage increased and around 1900 it was 90 per cent. Second marriages often involved widowers with women who had not been married before (Van Poppel, 1992:275).

Scarce resources indicate that the marriage patterns were not radically different in the seventeenth and eighteenth centuries (Van Zanden, 1991:39) from that in the nineteenth century, although the average ages fluctuated slightly over time[19].

7.3.2 Marriage trends in the other six countries

The changing pattern of marital status within the Dutch population is mirrored by that in the other six countries. Because differences in the marriage trends between the seven countries are slight, no detailed data are presented here[20]. Since the turn of the century all countries including the Netherlands show an increase in the percentage of married, widowed and divorced women and a decline in the percentage of single persons who have never married. The only difference is that the latter decline continued until about 1950 in Sweden and about 1970 in the Netherlands, while in the other countries the turning point occurred somewhere in between. Since these dates, the percentage of single never-married persons has again increased. The question is whether this increase is genuine. The legal registration of the population by marital status does not reflect the percentage of the population living in consensual unions. Official statistical data on such unions do not exist; the researcher is restricted to sample surveys, which are often limited to specific groups. Comparison is difficult. However, one conclusion is clear: in all countries cohabitation outside of legal marriage is increasing, as are births outside wedlock. Denmark and Sweden have been the pacesetters in this development. Three out of four couples aged between 20 - 24 years cohabit in Sweden, while the figure in Denmark is 60 per cent, in the Netherlands[21] about 50 per cent, in France 30 per cent, in Belgium 25 per cent, in Germany

---

19 In 1626/27 average age on marriage in Amsterdam was 25.7 years for men and 24.5 for women. During the economic decline in the second half of the seventeenth century, age on marriage increased: in 1676/77 to 27.7 years for men and 26.5 years for women. At the end of the eighteenth century, it was 28.7 years for men and 27.8 for women in 1776/77 and 28.3 for men and 26.1 years for women in 1796 (Van Zanden, 1991:39).

20 In addition, the problem of comparibility occurs. Two publications, national or international, hardly publish the same figures (e.g. in CBS, 1992/8 the average ages on first marriage from 1970 to 1989 were 1 to 2 years lower than the figures published in table 7.1).

21 In 1981, about 5 per cent of all households consisting of a man and a woman in a stable relationship and both younger than 65 years, were the result of consensual unions. Of all couples living together in a non-marital relationship in 1977, 5.5 per cent were of the same sex, 63 per cent were not married to anyone and 4 per cent included at least one partner who was still married to someone else (Ploegmakers and van Leeuwen, 1983:138).

15 per cent and in the United Kingdom only 7 per cent in 1989 (Van Nimwegen and Moors, 1990:62).

In the Netherlands this development meant a clear break with the past. In the seventeenth and eighteenth centuries cohabitation was illegal and hardly existed. In the city of Haarlem, between 1829 and 1839 less than 1 per cent of the women aged over 25, living together with a man were not married to that man, while in Sweden in the nineteenth century percentages of 20 per cent were not uncommon (Kok, 1992).

Consensual unions are often a temporary arrangement: younger cohabiting couples in particular tend to marry once a baby is expected or wanted. Only in Denmark and Sweden is the percentage of children born out of wedlock high, at nearly 50 per cent (Sorrentino, 1990:44), while in Germany and the Netherlands it is less than 10 per cent (Gustafsson and Bruyn-Hundt, 1991). Births out of wedlock were always extremely low in the Netherlands until the 1980s[22]. A relatively high proportion of births out of wedlock in the United Kingdom are to teenagers: 29 per cent (Sorrentino, 1990:44).

The downward trend in the marriage rate was evident in Denmark, Germany and Sweden in the 1960s, while in Belgium, France, the Netherlands and the United Kingdom the decline began in the 1970s (Sorrentino, 1990:43). In Sweden, a remarkably high number of marriages took place in 1989, due to changes in the law concerning widows' pensions. In 1983, 36 thousand marriages were recorded in that country, a figure slightly increasing in every subsequent year to 44 thousand in 1988; in 1989, by contrast nearly 109 thousand marriages were registered (SBS, 1991:44).

Average age on first marriage fell in all seven countries up to the 1970s, when the trend began to reverse. In general, in Belgium, France, Denmark and the United Kingdom, average age on first marriage has been between one and three years lower than in the Netherlands, while in Sweden it has been slightly higher and in Germany about the same. Sweden and Denmark showed the lowest age on first marriage between 1966 - 1968 and Germany in 1975. The higher age on marriage influences the percentages of married women in the age category 25 to 29, but hardly those in the age category 45 to 49. The majority of women is married and differences between countries are slight. In 1984 the percentage of married women in the age group 45 - 49 was in Belgium, France and the United Kingdom 85 per cent, in Denmark 82, in Germany 83, in France 85 and in the Netherlands 86 per cent (Kronjee, 1991:69).

---

22 In the years following the abolition of the promise of marriage right in 1818, the number of babies born out of wedlock increased. Probably due also to the bad economic situation in rural areas, the percentage of live births out of wedlock increased yet further to 4.3 between 1850 and 1859. In the period 1900 - 1909 this figure was 2.3 per cent and from 1950 - 1954 only 1.4 per cent (Van Poppel, 1981:8).

Some of the trends in marriage patterns may have emerged later in the Netherlands than in the other countries and the percentages of married women may have been higher, but they do not indicate that the Netherlands was unique or even very different from the other six countries in these respects.

7.4 Dissolution of marriage

In the late seventeenth and eighteenth centuries, divorce and remarriage were in practice only possible by law for the rich, and sometimes by folk custom for the poor[23].

Up to the end of World War II, dissolution of marriage took place almost exclusively through the death of one of the partners. The text of Matthew 5:32 "Whosoever shall put away his wife, saving for the cause of fornication" was interpreted by the Roman Catholic Church as meaning that the only way of separation was a *divorce from bed and board* and by the Calvinists as justifying divorce after adultery[24]. This ground for divorce was again confirmed in the 1838 law in the Netherlands and some other grounds introduced as well. Despite these reforms divorce rates remained low during the nineteenth century.

In the Netherlands divorce accounted for less than 2 per cent of all dissolutions up to the end of the nineteenth century, the other 98 per cent being due to death; this increased to 10 per cent of all dissolutions by the mid-1960s, with a sharp increase directly after World War II. More liberal divorce legislation came into force in 1971, accelerating the trend in divorces. It is currently expected that about 30 per cent of recent marriages will end in divorce (Tas, 1989:22).

Divorce rates show a long-term increase in all seven nations since around the turn of the century, with an acceleration in the 1970s (see Sorrentino, 1990:43 for other OECD countries), due to liberalization of divorce laws, in all seven countries beginning in the 1970s. The pace of increase abated at the end of the 1980s.

---

23 Besides simply running away and never being heard of again, eighteenth century England seems to have known a second method of separation: the unofficial 'wife-sale'. The husband put a halter around his wife's neck, led her to market and there put her up to auction to be sold to the highest bidder. This elaborate ritual freed the husband of all future responsibility for his wife and allowed both parties to marry again. Very often, perhaps normally, the transaction was pre-arranged with the full consent of the wife, both purchaser and price being agreed beforehand. This procedure was confined almost exclusively to the lower classes and centred mostly in the big towns and the west of England. The last recorded case was in 1887. (Stone, 1990:35).

24 However, prior to the 1971 divorce law it was not possible when divorced on these grounds to remarry with the adulterer or adulteress.

National statistical offices usually publish divorce figures per 1000 married women[25]. However, other sources, for example the United Nations (Demographic Yearbook), define divorce rates as the final divorce decrees granted under civil law per 1000 of the mid-year population[26]. In addition most statistics refer only to causes of legalized dissolution. For these reasons, caution should be exercized in comparing the divorce rates between countries. The same applies to the rate of increase in divorce; year to year changes in the timing of divorce by duration of marriage produce changes in the total divorce rate, reflecting time changes as well as the ultimate incidence of divorce; these are particularly striking when there are legislative reforms (see Ermish, 1991:28-33). French divorce rates were relatively high and higher than those in Denmark and England and Wales. Dutch divorce rates, by contrast, were relatively low until recent decades. This might indicate that a high value was attached to marriage. As with marriage patterns, however, the behavior in this respect has increasingly converged with the average of all seven countries.

7.5 Long-term trends in births and fertility

With marriage delayed and a large proportion of the population not marrying at all, fertility rates remained fairly constant and populations fairly stable until the nineteenth century in all seven countries. However, although age on first marriage started to decline in the second half of the nineteenth century, surprisingly enough, fertility rates also declined.

The first distinct change in demographic developments is described by the concept of *demographic transition*, which can be characterized by a transition from a state involving high birth and death rates to a state

---

25 This rate was, for example, in:

	France	Germany	Netherlands	Sweden
1981	9.4	5.1	8.3	11.5
1983	10.4	7.2	9.3	12.0
1985	10.8	8.1	9.8	11.7
1987	10.6	8.6	8.1	–

Source: Bronsema, 1986

However, according to the CBS, 1992/8 this rate was in:

	Belgium	Denmark	France	Germany	Netherlands	UK
1970	2.6	11.2	3.3	5.1	3.3	4.7
1980	5.6	12.6	6.3	6.1	7.5	12.0
1989	8.6	13.7	8.4	8.5	8.1	–

26 The rates in 1985 and 1987 are then: (in both years) for Belgium 1.9, Denmark 2.8, France 2.0 and Germany 3.1; for the Netherlands 2.4 and 2.0 respectively; in Sweden 2.4 and 2.3; and the United Kingdom both years 3.0.

involving low fertility and death rates. In all the countries considered here, this transition took place mainly during the nineteenth century, but it occurred rather late in the Netherlands, where the birth rate started to drop only after 1880 (Verhoef, 1989:15). Probably in all countries there was a growing (though unreported) use of birth control. This first fertility transition was a silent one, occurring in the privacy of the family (Lesthaeghe, 1991:4).

7.5.1 Definitions and measurements of fertility

Fertility, actual reproduction, may be distinguished from *fecundity*, the ability to reproduce. In contrast to *fertility*, *fecundity* cannot be observed or measured[27]; the most important measurements of fertility are discussed below.

The *Total Fertility Rate* (TFR), popularly defined as the average number of children born per woman per calendar year, is nowadays the measure most frequently used to compare various populations or sub-populations (see other definition below).

The *General Fertility Rate* (GFR) is the total number of births in any given year divided by the fecund female population in that year, conventionally defined as all women aged between 15 and 45. The rate is expressed per thousand women.

Another measure frequently used is the *Crude Birth Rate* (CBR), this being the number of births in each year per one thousand of the mean total population in that year. In contrast to the Crude Birth Rate, the General Fertility Rate takes into account changes in the number of women of childbearing age. For this reason the GFR is preferred to the CBR as an indicator of fertility. More satisfactory still is the *Age Specific Fertility Rate*, which has become available in the Netherlands only in more recent years, but for example in Denmark was already being used at the beginning of the twentieth century. This rate is defined as the number of live births in individual age groups for women divided by the mean population of women in that age group (again per thousand women). These rates provide the basis for, the *Total Fertility Rate* (TFR) this being the expected average number of children per woman, equivalent to the number of children the average woman would have during her lifetime if her reproductive behavior matched the population's fertility rates by single years of age in any particular year[28]. In a country without inward and

---

27 Research into and knowledge of in vitro fertilization may change this in the near future. Fecundity declines rapidly after the age of 30 years. Childlessness was rare among women who were married before the age of 24 less than 5 per cent in the last quarter of the nineteenth century (Van Poppel, 1981:5).

28 Therefore the Total Fertility Rate shows how many children a thousand women would have if the birth rates were in accordance with the Age Specific Fertility Rates and no woman died before she was 50 years of age (Andersen, 1977: 18).

outward migration a *Total Fertility Rate* of about 2.1 is required to keep the population at a constant level. Around 1900, this replacement level was about 2.7, but it has gradually declined since then, due to declining mortality rates.

With the TFR, the influence of the age composition of the population is limited: 'young' and 'old' populations can be compared with each other. However, an increase between one year and the next might be the result of people postponing the timing of the first birth rather than a change in the intensity of birth (the total number of children). The *Total Cohort Fertility Rate* (TCFR) will reveal if this is the case. Fertility calculations on a cohort basis give the exact level of fertility for a given age group. This is disregarded in this study, because reliable information on the present birth cohorts will be available only about 30 years from now. (To distinguish between the Total Cohort Fertility Rate and the Total Fertility Rate, the latter is sometimes called the *Total Period Fertility Rate*, or TPFR).

7.5.2 A seven-country comparison of fertility

As mentioned above, fertility rates started to decline in the majority of the seven countries in the middle of the nineteenth century, although between 1866 and 1880 fertility remained fairly stable in Belgium. After that it declined steadily, but from 1930 to 1964 slowly increased again. In the second half of the 1960s, however, the same remarkable reduction in fertility took place as in the other six countries.

In France, the birth rate had begun to decline by the middle of the eighteenth century, but birth rates have varied considerably in the different regions. Traditionally it was low in the south, especially the south-west, high in the northern part of the country and very high in Brittany. By the end of the nineteenth century, the birth rates among French working class families had declined dramatically (Tilly and Scott, 1987:167). Infant mortality remained high until the twentieth century. In the other countries similar regional differences can be distinguished. Moreover, social differences in fertility and child mortality can be identified. For example,

---

Two other measures regularly published are the *Gross Reproduction Rate* and the *Net Reproduction Rate*. The Gross Reproduction Rate is based on the same suppositions as the Total Fertility Rate, but counts only the number of girls who would be born; the Net Reproduction Rate also takes Age Specific Mortality Rates into account. Finally, two less commonly used terms. The *total marriage cohort fertility rate* is the cumulative number of births occurring up to the most recent calendar year to one thousand married women aged 15-49 in a specified year (CBS, 1988:21). The *parity-progression ratio* is the fraction of females presently without children who will eventually have at least two children, three children, etc., assuming no mortality and the age specific fertility rates of the given calendar year (CBS, 1988:21).

in the Netherlands around 1890, the highest income families had an infant mortality similar to the national average in 1950, while the lowest income families had infant mortality rates four times as high (Van Poppel, 1981:8).

British studies at the turn of the twentieth century showed that birth rates were falling more rapidly among the upper classes than among workers (Tilly and Scott, 1987:167). "Within the working class a decline in marital fertility was most apparent among textile workers, least among miners and agricultural laborers. Nonetheless, as compared with earlier figures, a decline in working-class fertility was evident. The average number of children ever born to British manual wage earners was 4.9 per couple married in the decade 1890-99, for those married in 1915 the figure was 2.9." (Tilly and Scott, 1987:167).

The long-term trends in the *Total Fertility Rate* in the seven countries since 1900 are given in figure 7.2.

Figure 7.2 *A seven-country comparison of total fertility rates, 1900-1990*

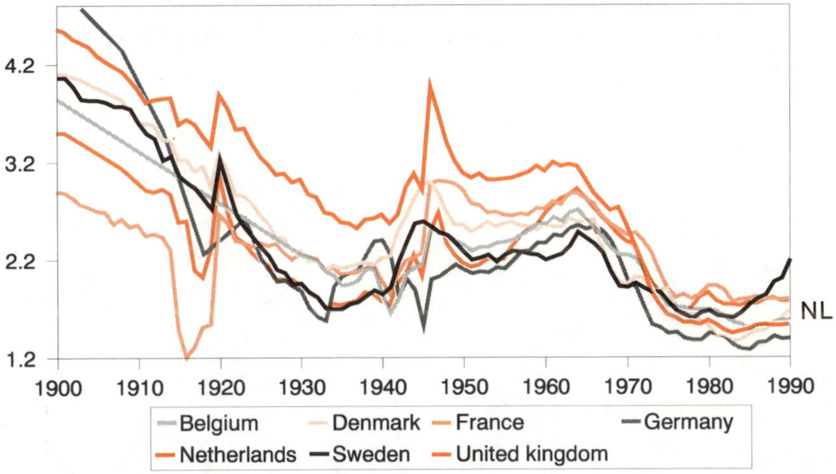

It is remarkable how similar, on average, the patterns for the different countries are, but the levels differ tremendously. In all seven countries the initial years of the two World Wars and the Great Depression produce a drop in fertility, the end of the wars a baby boom. After 1910[29], Dutch Total Fertility Rates were higher than those in the other six countries and the baby boom after World War II was relatively exceptional. Since the

[29] Before 1910, fertility rates were higher in Germany than in the Netherlands. Crude birth rates, available since about 1840 in all seven countries, were the highest in Germany over the period 1840 - 1910 and the lowest in France until 1925, after which date Sweden had the lowest rates (INED, 1971:12).

1970s Dutch fertility rates have been in between those of the other countries. There was a dramatic decline in France during World War I, but since 1946 French TFRs have been relatively high and the highest of all seven countries from 1973 to 1988. Since then, Sweden has taken the lead, reaching a high 2.1 in 1991 (not shown). The Total Fertility Rate dropped below 2.1 in Belgium in 1972, in Denmark in 1969, in France in 1974, in Germany in 1970, in the Netherlands in 1973, in Sweden in 1968 and in the United Kingdom in 1973.

As mentioned above, this study disregards the large regional differences in fertility within a single country or those between socio-economic groups. Differences in abortion[30] and (infant) mortality rates[31] are disregarded as well.

Comparing figure 7.2 with figure 2.3 shows that a decline in fertility precedes the rise in labor force participation by women, this being especially obvious in the French case. Moreover, high fertility rates coincided with low participation rates. More recently the relationship seems less obvious, e.g. in Sweden, where in the late 1980s the highest female labor force participation rate of the OECD countries was combined with the highest total fertility rate (see also Sundström and Stafford, 1991). The relationship will be discussed further in chapter 10.

Table 7.2 gives some additional figures concerning Dutch fertility patterns.

---

30 Figures for legally induced abortions only recently became available. The abortion rate in a given year is defined as the number of abortions divided by the average number of women aged 15 to 44 in that year multiplied by a thousand. In the Netherlands abortion rates are low despite very liberal abortion laws.

31 As with fertility rates, many measurements can be distinguished, making comparisons between countries difficult. Nowadays the following concepts are used: *perinatal mortality*, the mortality rate of babies within 28 weeks of pregnancy or in the first week after birth; *neonatal mortality*, the mortality within 28 days after birth; and both related to the total number of births; *infant mortality*, death within one year; and *child mortality*, death within 5 years, i.e. of children aged 0 to 4 years. These last two rates are related to the total number of live births.

Table 7.2 *Live births (absolute figures in thousands); ratio boys/girls; age specific fertility rates and total fertility rate (tfr) in the Netherlands, 1899 – 1990*

	absolute figures	ratio boys/girls	age specific fertility rates per 1000					
			15–19	20–24	25–29	30–44	15–44	tfr
1899	163	1.058	–	–	–	–	–	4.4
1910	169	1.060	–	–	–	–	–	3.9
1920	193	1.063	–	–	–	–	–	3.9
1931	177	1.063	–	–	–	–	–	3.9
1947	267	1.059	15.0	109.4	206.2	137.3	121.5	3.7
1960	239	1.056	16.3	120.3	208.4	93.5	102.0	3.1
1971	227	1.055	22.3	132.1	172.0	50.4	82.7	2.4
1975	178	1.050	12.6	97.9	137.6	30.0	60.8	1.7
1977	173	1.055	10.1	87.9	136.6	30.9	57.3	1.6
1979	175	1.050	8.9	81.7	139.2	32.0	55.9	1.6
1981	179	1.043	9.0	74.6	139.8	33.4	55.1	1.6
1983	170	1.046	7.7	65.7	129.4	32.9	51.2	1.5
1985	178	1.045	6.8	60.6	131.4	36.5	52.2	1.5
1987	187	1.055	6.7	54.3	132.1	41.0	53.5	1.6
1990	198	1.056	6.4	42.0	122.1	54.1	67.2	1.6

As mentioned above, the age specific fertility rate = number of live births to women in a certain age group (age at last birthday) divided by the average number of women of the same age category multiplied by 1000; and the total fertility rate = sum of the age specific fertility rates divided by 1000.

Source: CBS, 1989, Negentig jaren statistiek in tijdreeksen:24, CBS, 1992.

The decline in the rate of fertility has coincided with a change in the age of women giving birth. After World War II, births became more and more concentrated in the younger age groups and declined markedly for women in the highest age group, over the age of 30, especially in the 1960s. Age Specific Fertility Rates for teenagers started to decline again in the 1970s, while the fertility rates for women above the age of 30 have risen again since then.

The same trends, although not given here, are more or less witnessed in the other six countries. A remarkable feature in the Netherlands is the high average age of the mother at the birth of the first child at 27.6 in 1990 and the highest in the world. In 1970 the average age was still 24.3 and in 1980 only 25.6 years. Since 1970 the average age of the mother at the birth of the first child has been the highest of all seven countries, see figure 7.3.

Figure 7.3 *A seven-country comparison of the average age of the mother at the birth of the first child, 1970-1990*

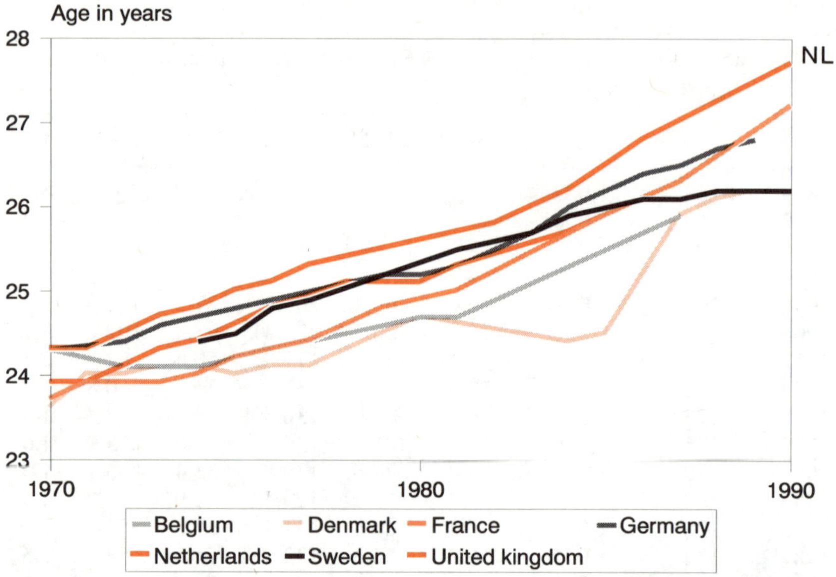

The pattern of childbearing in the Netherlands with respect to the total number of births is the same as in the other countries. The total number of births is higher in the 1980s than in the 1970s, but lower than in the two decades after World War II.

As shown in table 7.2, the number of births decreased from 181 thousand in 1980 to 170 thousand in 1983 but then increased again to 198 thousand in 1990. The number of first children decreased from 78 thousand in 1980 to 73 thousand in 1982 but started to rise again in 1983 to reach 89 thousand in 1990. The years 1983 and 1982 were turning points in the downward trends in both the number of births and the number of first children, trends dating from the 1960s. The development is not unique to the Netherlands. In France, Denmark, and Sweden, total births started to rise in exactly the same year. The Federal Republic of Germany followed two years later (De Beer, CBS, 1989). In all these countries this was due to postponement of the birth of the first or second child.

In all seven countries the decline in the total fertility rate was due to the decline in third and subsequent children. In the Netherlands, the monthly number of third live born children has risen again since the summer of 1988, following the increased number of children born in the period 1985 - 1987, especially among protestants and higher educated couples (CBS, 1990/9:5). However, while about 50 per cent of the women born in 1929 gave birth to a third child, it is expected that less than 25 per cent of those born in 1959 will do so (CBS, 1990/9:4). It may be surmised that the average number of children born to recent generations is more in accordance with the personal preferences of the parents than was the case with the older generation. For example, a 1951 survey concluded that the preferred number of children was 2.77 per family. The parents questioned had, however, an average of 4.26 children (Blok, 1989:45) (see also theories in chapter 10).

To summarize: the main difference between the Netherlands and the other countries was the continuing high Total Fertility Rate in the Netherlands up to the 1970s, producing a greater population increase than elsewhere. In 1990, Sweden had the highest Total Fertility Rate of all seven countries. The proportion of married women in the population, marriage rates and average age on marriage were all fairly similar in the Netherlands to those in the other six countries. Divorce rates were low, as were births out of wedlock and abortion rates. In 1990, the average age of the mother at the birth of the first child was higher in the Netherlands than anywhere else in the world. The trends in marriage, fertility etc. since the 1960s are fairly similar in all seven countries. Sweden and Denmark have been the pacesetters in recent developments. The question is why fertility was so high in the Netherlands and why the value of marriage and the importance of the nuclear family apparently remained higher here than in the other six countries.

7.6 Dutch peculiarities in marriage, family and fertility

Chapter 3 showed that the traditional nuclear family was already important in the seventeenth century and probably, if not the dominant form of household, at least the preferred one. One reason why marriage and the family may have retained their importance longer in the Netherlands than in the other six countries is the influence of the mixed Protestant-Catholic composition of the Dutch population at the turn of the century[32].

For centuries, Catholics had formed a minority which was barred from practicing certain occupations. After the restoration of the episcopal hierarchy in 1853, the emancipating catholic part of the nation developed a battlefield mentality which, especially after the rise of neo-

---

[32] In 1899, the religious distribution of the Dutch population was (in percentages): Roman-Catholic 35.1; Dutch Reformed (Nederlands Hervormd): 48.4; Calvinist/Reformed (Gereformeerd): 8.1; others (mainly Protestants): 6.1 and no religion: 2.3. Nearly a hundred years later it differs substantially. Only the Roman Catholics and the Calvinist/Reformed kept their shares with respectively 35.8 and 8.0 per cent in 1988. Dutch Reformed declined to 18.6 per cent and the other 5.6 per cent no longer consist only of small Protestant religious groups, but also of Muslims and Hindus/Buddhists; those without a religion now account for 32 per cent (CBS, 1989:46 and Beets, 1989:32).

malthusianism in about 1880 (see below), encouraged a strict adherence to Catholic doctrine with regard to marriage, sexuality, the family, procreation and family planning. Another factor was the ambition of some Catholic leaders to achieve a Catholic majority within the total population (Niphuis-Nell, 1987:2).

Episcopal influence was sometimes unexpectedly effective. In the nineteenth century, class differentials were rising, also because the increasingly impoverished bourgeoisie tried to distinguish itself from the lower classes by demonstrating good manners and a modest and prudish life style. This increasing prudishness led around 1850 to an episcopal prohibition on breast-feeding in public. This caused a decline in breast-feeding and a corresponding increase in births. The average interval between births declined from nearly four years to only 16 months (Van Eupen, 1985:23). Fertility also increased because direct birth control was forbidden.

In 1881, the Neo-Malthusian Association (Neo-Malthusiaanse Bond) was founded for the purpose of disseminating knowledge about the possibble means of birth control, such as condoms, creams and Dutch caps (diaphragms). The latter method (described by the german Mensinga in 1880) was improved and introduced in 1881 by the first Dutch female medical doctor, Aletta Jacobs, also one of the most famous Dutch feminists (see also chapter 9).

The Catholic church strongly opposed the Neo-Malthusian Association and soon meetings and propaganda of the Association were forbidden in Catholic communities. The opposition to Neo-Malthusianism seems nowhere else to have been as fierce as in the Netherlands (Verwey-Jonker, 1985).

In addition to contraceptive knowledge and scientific progress in general, the rise of socialism and feminism also scared not only the Catholics but also many other (religious) groups. Together with the marriage doctrines it caused and also strengthened what is called *pillarization collumnization* or *compartmentalization*: the co-existence throughout Dutch society of parallel organizations of all kinds with similar or identical goals but serving each of the different ideological or denominational bases: Protestant, Catholic or Socialist (Niphuis-Nell, 1987:3). All institutions, organizations, schools, shops and means of communication, were divided in at least three compartments: Protestant, Roman-Catholic and Socialist. This pillarization or compartmentalization continued until the 1960s, and even today still exists for example in primary schools and television and radio programming.

Besides the strong cultural value attached to the concept of the family, this pillarization may be one of the reasons fertility remained relatively high until the 1960s (because of particularly high rates among Protestants and Catholics). It is remarkable that the main factor deciding fertility was denomination rather than social class or economic status. Catholics of all social classes had the highest rates and the relatively small group of people without any religion had the lowest (Van Poppel, 1980). Despite differences, reproduction within marriage was in practice throughout history emphasized equally by Calvinists and by Catholics. In discussions about birth control up to the 1960s, Calvinist theologians used the same 'natural' arguments as the Catholics.

After the discovery of the contraceptive pill in 1960 and the wide discussion of it in the very popular weekly family magazines, female demand forced doctors to supply it and the churches to accept its use. In 1963 the Calvinist church synod (gereformeerde synode) decided to allow birth control by means hormonal contraceptives (the pill). On 21 March 1963 a Catholic bishop, Monsignor Bekkers, declared on television in a debate with Mary Zeldenrust (pioneer of the Dutch birth control movement) that family planning was a matter for the conscience of the married couple itself and that nobody should interfere. "The moral innovators were attempting to provide their pillar with a new foundation. Unknowingly however, they were pulling it down"[33].

Fertility started to decline. In the same year that the pill began to be prescribed free of charge, in 1972, fertility rates and the number of births dropped steeply (see also table 7.3). This development was a major factor eliminating the uniqueness of the Dutch situation.
As elsewhere, sexuality became increasingly separated from marriage and procreation, a fact bringing great changes in the formation of families and households and hence in the position of the housewife and mother.

The increasing autonomy of the family may have influenced the first demographic transition; the rising importance of the individual autonomy of women certainly brought about the second (see also chapter 9).

Now, in 1990, there are still some reminders of the long period in which motherhood and fertility were of utmost importance: the national health system provision for pregnancies, deliveries and medical child care is one. The majority of babies used to be born at home; in 1975 the figure was reduced to about 50 per cent, and by 1991 this percentage had fallen to 35, internationally still a high percentage. The father is and always has been usually present at the delivery.

---

[33] "De vernieuwers van de moraal wilden hun zuil van een nieuw fundament voorzien. Onbewust haalden zij hun zuil om." (Koos Schwartz, Trouw, 8-11-1988:27).

7.7 Conclusions to chapter 7

The most striking difference between the Netherlands and the other countries is the very high fertility rate sustained in this century until the 1970s. The fertility trends between 1900 and 1990 showed a fairly similar pattern in all seven countries (except in France during World War I), but the levels of the total fertility rate differ tremendously. Since the 1970s Dutch fertility rates have been in between those of the other six countries. French total fertility rates have been relatively high and the highest of the seven countries from 1973 to 1988. Since then, Sweden has taken the lead. However, in 1990 the Netherlands remained exceptional in the fact that the average age of the mother at the birth of the first child was higher here than anywhere else in the world.

The high total fertility rates in the Netherlands up to the 1970s produced a greater population increase than elsewhere over the whole period. The proportion of married women in the population, marriage rates and average age on first marriage were all fairly similar in the Netherlands to those in the other six countries, but divorce rates were relatively low, as were births out of wedlock and abortion rates.

On the development of the family household, many speculative statements can be made. The demographic development of households in the Netherlands, relatively well known, shows that household size was relatively small until the end of the nineteenth century, partly because living-in servants were comparatively scarce and three-generation households exceptional. The scarce evidence available suggests that the nuclear family was relatively important in the Netherlands until at least the mid-1980s and that the affective family model, based on mutual assistance, seems already to have existed in the seventeenth century. A remarkable feature, specific to the Netherlands, is that the ideals of marriage, motherhood and family life were apparently strengthened by the pillarization or compartmentalization: the existence throughout society of organizations of all kinds with similar goals but different denominational bases. To guarantee its future, each denomination (pillar) emphasized motherhood and child care.

However, the trends in all seven countries are in the same direction. All seven countries have seen a decline in household size from an average of four to five members per household in 1900 to an average of only two to three in 1990. Recently, many new non-traditional household forms have come into existence, or have at least become more common, in particular cohabitation outside of legal marriage and one-person households. Marriage rates first increased during this century, but declined again in the 1960s or 1970s. Average age on first marriage declined up to the 1970s, when postponement of marriage and cohabitation reversed this trend. The Scandinavian countries have been the pacesetters in the development of many of the changes in family life.

CHAPTER 8

MARRIED WOMEN

"The husband must be on the street to practise his trade
The wife must stay at home to be in the kitchen
The diligent practice of street wisdom may in the man be praised
But with the delicate wife, there should be quiet and steady ways
So you, industrious husband, go to earn your living
While you, O young wife, attend to your household."
Jacob Cats (1577-1662) in 1645[1]

The previous chapters have shown that women's role within the family interacts with female labor force participation in many different ways. The changes signalled within the life cycle (chapter 6) and the family (chapter 7) may be expected to connect closely with women's labor market position. This chapter delves deeper into the analysis of the behavior of women in the labor force by investigating the long-term trends in married women's activity rates in the seven countries.

As in the previous chapters, one of the main questions is whether the development in the Netherlands differed from those in the surrounding countries and, if so, in what respect?

Section 8.1 describes the labor force patterns by marital status in the Netherlands. Section 8.2 those of married women in all seven countries. Subsection 8.3.1 discusses the increase in part-time work subsection 8.3.2 other reasons of flattered labor force participation rates and subsection 8.3.3 temporary work. Section 8.4 contains the conclusions.

8.1 Female labor force participation by marital status in the Netherlands

In the Netherlands, Catholics, Calvinists and other Churches were unambiguous about the role of women and about the value placed on marriage and the family. Once married, the only proper place for a woman was in the home, preferably as a mother, housewife and spouse. Daughters had to be trained for this role. From the beginning of the twentieth century, the government tried to enforce this ideal by attempting

---

1 Translated and quoted by Schama, 1987:400. See also the remarks about 'Father' Cats in chapter 3.

to restrict, and even to forbid, all work by married women outside the home[2].

Table 8.1 shows the Dutch female labor force by marital status (absolute figures in thousands) and the corresponding labor force participation rates from 1899 - 1990.

Table 8.1 *Female labor forces and female labor force participation rates by marital status in the Netherlands, 1899 – 1989*

	married			non-married			total
	a	b	c	a	d	e	a
1899	43	5	5	388	22	39	432
1909	74	8	8	465	24	–	539
1920	–	–	–	–	–	–	630
1930	98	6	7	666	27	58	764
1947	198	10	11	727	26	55	925
1960	173	6	7	755	24	56	928
1971	483	15	17	743	22	58	1226
1975	723	22	24	645	18	50	1368
1977	805	24	26	645	18	48	1450
1979	881	25	28	696	19	52	1578
1981	987	29	32	807	21	53	1794
1983	1079	32	35	884	24	54	1963
1985	1068	32	42	996	25	60	2052
1987	1295	37	43	1180	30	62	2475
1988	1341	38	45	1246	33	62	2587
1989	1366	39	45	1256	32	62	2622
1990	1430	41	47	1313	33	64	2743

a absolute numbers in thousands
b married women in the labor force as a percentage of the female married population
c married women in the labor force as a percentage of the female married population aged 15 – 64
d non-married women in the labor force as a percentage of the female non-married population
e non-married women in the labor force as a percentage of the female non-married population aged 15 – 64

Sources: CBS, 1849–1971: Volkstellingen
CBS, 1975–1985: Arbeidskrachtentellingen
CBS, 1985–1990: Enquête beroepsbevolking
(percentages own calculation)

The table shows the tremendous increase in absolute numbers of women in the labor force between 1899 and 1990, with an increase of 33 times the number of married and 3 times the number of non-married (defined as single, widowed and divorced women together). The increase in the

2 This policy may have been due, at least in part, to the increasingly powerful position enjoyed by Catholics within the government. Yet it is a remarkable fact that in 1930, before the marriage bars in the Netherlands became almost absolute (see chapter 9), Roman Catholic women participated more in the labor market than other women (Posthumus - van der Goot, 1938:146). Unfortunately no distinction by marital status and religion was made in any of the censuses before World War II in the Netherlands.

labor force participation rates of the two categories differed; for non-married women (all ages, so including children) it was modest - from 22 per cent in 1899 to 33 per cent in 1990 - in contrast to the spectacular increase in the labor force participation rates of married women - from 5 per cent in 1899 to 41 per cent in 1990.

The rates for married women aged 15 - 64 years rose from 5 to 47 per cent and for non-married women in the same age category from 39 to 64 per cent between 1899 and 1990, but it was not in fact until 1960 that this increase occurred: between 1899 and 1960 the subsequent increase was only one percentage point. For married women aged 15 - 64, the increase between 1960 and 1971 was about 10 percentage points, while for non-married women in the same age category the rate remained about equal. The corresponding increases between 1971 and 1981 and over the next decade until 1990 was 15 percentage points for married women, while for non-married women there was an initial decrease of 4 percentage points, followed by an increase of about 11 percentage points within the last decade. Despite the tremendous increase in the labor force participation rates of married women since 1899, however, particularly since 1960 the majority of married women were still not participating in the labor market in 1990.

Without the self-employed women (mainly assisting wives in their husband's business), the activity rates of married women would have been even lower and extremely low up to 1971. Until that date married female employees or wage earners were exceptional. In the censuses of 1899, 1909 and 1947 the rate was only 2 per cent, while in 1930 and 1960, labor force participation rates of employed married women were slightly higher at 3 and 4 per cent respectively. In 1971 the labor force participation rate of married female employees and wage earners had increased to 12, in 1979 to 22 and in 1990 to 37 per cent. The underlying values attached to marriage and the family, which tended to dominate the whole of Dutch society, are reflected in low participation rates of married women, especially in paid employment.

In the past, the period of - often full-time - market work tended for a woman to end with marriage. Gradually, through the 1960s and 1970s more and more married women remained in the labor force after marriage, although usually in part-time work, while in the 1980s the advent of the first child began to act as the boundary between the initial phase of full-time and the subsequent stage of part-time market work. Because of the increase in education and the initial decline in the average age on marriage and on the birth of the first child, the length of time spent by the average woman in the labor market before marriage or the birth of the first child decreased over these two decades. In the 1980s, however, more and more women delayed marriage and childbirth (see chapter 7), while at the same time more and more mothers remained in the labor force although nearly always part-time (see section 8.3).

As mentioned above, the labor force participation rate of married female employees or wage earners remained very low until 1971. In the Netherlands, marital status more than any other characteristic determined a woman's economic role. This remains to a large extent, although not completely, until today. During the Great Depression in the 1930s the already small number of married women in employment declined. Although exact numbers over that period are not known, the number of work permits issued to married women gives some impression. In order to work outside the home married women needed, in addition to their husbands permission, a work permit (*arbeidskaart*) from the mayor of the town in which they lived. In 1930, 14.9 thousand married women were issued with such permits; in 1931: 11.6 thousand; in 1933, 1934 and 1935 8.5 thousand and in 1939: 13.7 thousand (Blok, 1989). In general women were dismissed on marriage (see chapter 9).

During World War II, from 1940 to 1945, married women could remain in employment if their work was essential, for example because of the shortage of men. (During the war many men were deported for forced labor in Germany.) However, these women could only remain on a temporary contract, which meant they were sent away as soon as someone else was available. During the war not many extra women were employed in this way, partly because this was seen as a betrayal of the country (Verwey, 1951, cited by Blok, 1989:30). The number of work permits issued to married women seems to confirm this, with certainly fewer married women being registered than before the war. In 1940 the figure was 12.0 thousand; in 1941: 11.0; in 1942: 3.9; in 1943: 10.9; and in 1945 only 2.7 thousand[3]. In 1946 the number increased again to 9.0 thousand, still a very low number compared to the nearly two million married women then living in the Netherlands.

Not all married women participating in the labor market were registered however. According to a study conducted by Schellekens-Ligthart in 1957 among married women in the labor market, the majority of registered married women were only recently married and still childless, while non-registered married women were often older and working in unprotected occupations such as charwoman or laundry woman, or were seasonal workers or on piecework at home. These low numbers of working permits do, however, support the findings of the censuses with regard to the low participation of married women.

It is a remarkable feature that although in 1899 married women hardly participated in the labor market, nearly 50 per cent of all widows were participating in that year. Young widows were mainly employed as domestic servants, while older widows were usually self-employed (small shopkeepers, dressmakers, seamstresses). The married women in the labor market in 1899 were fairly evenly distributed between the industrial sector, the trade and transport and the agricultural sector[4].

---

3 The figure for 1944 is unknown, due to destruction of the data.

4 Of the total of 43 thousand married women in the labor force in 1899, 15 thousand were working in the trade and transport sector and 12 thousand in the agricultural sector.

In the agricultural sector large regional differences existed, in relation both to productivity and products, and to the division of labor. In the Northern provinces on the wealthy farms, the farmer's wife did not have to work in the fields. These large farms employed many laborers to do the field work and had domestic servants to assist in the households. They produced mainly for the market and for export, unlike the peasants on the mixed or small dairy farms elsewhere in the country, where women often made the butter and cheese and sold these products themselves. As mentioned in chapter 5, they were then counted in the census as an assisting wife participating in the labor market. The increase - also already mentioned - in married women's labor force participation rates between the 1899 and the 1909 census can be attributed almost completely to a less strict registration of these assisting wives in agriculture.

The extremely modest labor force participation of married women in the last year of the nineteenth century and the first 30 years of the twentieth century is once again illustrated by subtracting the labor force participation of women in agriculture. Participation in these years is then only about 2 per cent, see table 8.2.

Table 8.2 *Labor force participation share*[1] *of married women by sector without agriculture in the Netherlands, 1899 – 1930*

	1899	1909	1930
Industry	1.2	1.1	0.9
Trade	7.1	5.4	6.0
Transport	2.2	3.2	2.5
Domestic Service	3.1	2.8	2.2
Other	1.2	1.3	–
Total	2.3	2.2	2.2

1 Labor force participation share is here defined as the number of married women participating in that sector divided by the total number of persons (male and female) in that sector times 100.

Source: Posthumus, 1938:147.

The majority of married women in the labor force are (again) wives assisting their husbands in shops etc, explaining the relatively high percentage of married women in trade.

In 1930 about 51 thousand women (out of the total of 98 thousand) were assisting wives. The other married women in the labor force (including divorced women a total of 49 thousand), were predominantly laborers, of whom 16 thousand domestic servants (CBS, 1934:86). Industry employed 11 thousand married women, which means that the share of married women (including assisting wives and self-employed women) in this sector was less than 1 per cent.

In 1947 a total of 152 thousand assisting wives were counted, 77 per cent of all the married women participating in the labor market. Without these assisting wives, therefore, the labor force participation rate of married women would have been a modest 2 per cent. Between 1947 and 1960, labor force participation of married women declined in absolute numbers from a total of 198 to 173 thousand. This was caused mainly by a decline in assisting wives, since by 1960 only 64 thousand assisting wives were registered, i.e. 37 per cent of all the married women in the labor force. The absolute decrease of married women in the labor market between 1947 and 1960 is remarkable, given that the total population and the number of married women within it both increased; yet the labor force participation rate of married women decreased from nearly 10 per cent to below 7 per cent and the share of married women in the labor force dropped from 5 to 4 per cent. This decrease occurred in a period of economic expansion and boom, with labor in short supply. The decrease was so large that it could not be off-set by the slight increase in the participation rate of single women over 15 years of age. This rate rose from 56 to 60 per cent (the total number increasing from 672 to 698 thousand) while the total female labor force participation rate actually fell.

Therefore, the ultimate decline in the absolute level of the female labor force between 1947 and 1960 was the result of two opposing tendencies: the decline from 152 thousand to 64 thousand in married women assisting their husband and the increase from 47 to 108 thousand of married women in employment, see figure 8.1.

The figure reflects some structural changes which occurred between the 1947 and 1960 censuses. In agriculture of all the men involved in 1947, 34 per cent had an assisting wife; in 1960 only 8 per cent. In trade, a similar dramatic decline was recorded among shop owners, with 71 per cent had an assisting wife in 1947 and in 1960 only 46 per cent (Hilte, 1965:1328). However, there is some doubt as to whether the change in work and life patterns was really so drastic as figure 8.2 suggests.

As mentioned in chapter 5, the apparent decline may be predominantly caused by the method of recording unpaid family labor. In 1947 all assisting wives were counted as being in the labor force, while in 1960 registration was restricted to those who said that working in the spouse's business was their main occupation and that they worked for at least 15 hours a week. Of course with household and farm work performed in the same place, the division is not easy to define, but the change in questioning may have resulted in under-counting in 1960. The same under-counting probably occurred in the next census and in the early labor market surveys[5]. Another possible reason for under-counting and the apparent decline between 1947 and 1960 might be the higher status

5 In 1983, of the 404 thousand married women in the Netherlands performing market work for less than 20 hours a week, 84 thousand considered working in their own household as their most important occupation (CBS, AKT, 1983:17).

Figure 8.1 *Assisting wifes and other married women in the labor force in the Netherlands, 1947 and 1960 (absolute figures in thousands)*

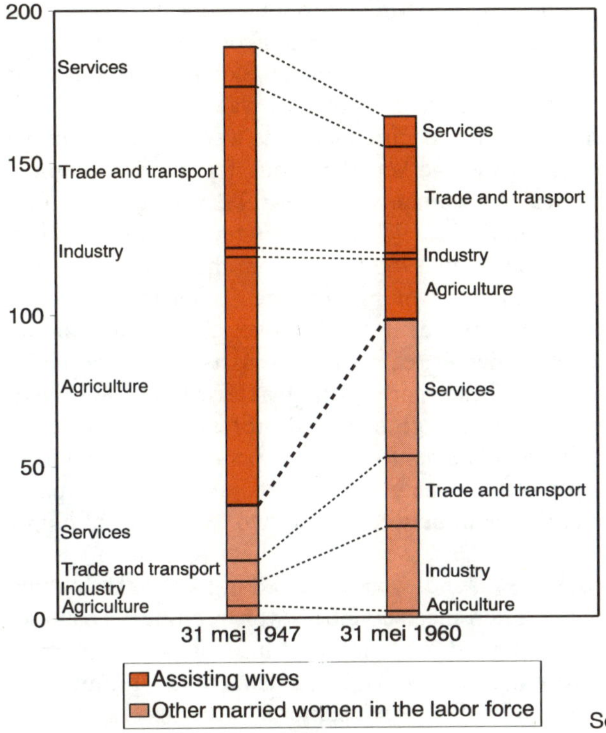

Source: Hilte, 1965: 1326

then accorded to the role of mother and wife compared with 'being in the labor force' (see also chapter 9). In all the agricultural magazines and the publications of the unions of farmer's wives (*plattelandsvrouwenbonden*) at least until the 1980s, the farmers' wife's role as mother and housewife was constantly emphasized and little attention was paid to the reality of her long working hours on the farm.

The under-counting of farmer's wives can also be demonstrated by comparing the labor force statistics with other figures. For example, in the 1962 Income Statististics (of the CBS), about a hundred thousand farmers are recorded as having an assisting wife. The CBS agricultural counts for 1962 also reveal under-counting, with 31 per cent of the farmers listed as having an assisting wife. In 1965 these counts registered a percentage of 36, in 1970: 42 and in 1975: 50 per cent (Loeffen, 1984).

The increase in the supply of non-married women between 1947 and 1960 appears to have been modest, but the increase in the demand for female labor was tremendous. Female labor in the Netherlands had traditionally been synonymous with labor by girls and to a lesser extent by non-married women. After World War II there was a relative decline in the potential supply of girls due to increased compulsory education, the decline in age on marriage and a reduced surplus of women over men (in

1950 the surplus was only 0.3 per cent as a percentage of the total population). The shortage of women in traditional female occupations became so severe that in 1947 compulsory education for girls was reduced by a year. Moreover, there was particular public concern about two specific categories in which there were labor shortages: the domestic girls (not available) and factory girls (not a suitable moral preparation for motherhood). (SER advies, 1952). Because it was thought that the shortages would be temporary, no specific measures were taken to remove existing barriers or improve the market conditions for married women. The primary duty of a married woman was still to be a good (full-time) housewife and mother (see Blok, 1989:70). The few married women participating in the labor market in 1960 (apart from the assisting wives) were either childless (52 per cent) or had children older than 6 years. Only 15 thousand (about 0.6 per cent) of the over 2.5 million of the married women in the labor market (excluding the assisting wives) had a young child or children. These participating married women were relatively often found working in high educated professions. Their share among female medical doctors and dentists was 40 per cent, among nurses and midwives only 4 per cent. Female pharmacists and women in para-medical professions had shares in between these two extremes: 22 out of 100 were married.

Excess demand persisted and even increased in the 1960s. In male jobs guest workers from Mediterranean countries were recruited. To attract more women, employers started offering part-time jobs for married women, while the government introduced tax deductions (for married women employed part-time) in 1962 (see chapter 9). Bruynzeel N.V. was one of the first large companies to try to attract married women to work part-time. The company began this policy as early as 1955, prefering the wives of men already employed, since it was certainly not the intention to discourage the (married) men or to suggest that the women could in any way compete on equal terms with the men (Blok, 1989:137; see also chapter 9).

Since the 1960s, more and more women have stayed in the labor market after marriage. By 1971, married women's labor force participation had increased to 25 per cent, with assisting wives now accounting for 98 thousand of the 483 thousand married women in the labor force (i.e. reduced to 20 per cent). Without these assisting wives, the labor force participation rate of married women would still have been a modest 12 per cent. In 1973 a partly individualized tax system was introduced, comparable to the tax system introduced in Sweden in 1971 and replacing the German tax system introduced in 1941 (see chapter 9).

By 1979, the labor force participation rate of married women (excluding assisting wives) was 22 per cent. Successive years show higher and higher participation rates of married women, at first produced by (young) women without children, but increasingly also by mothers remaining or re-entering the labor market.

8.2 Labor force participation rates of married women, a seven-country comparison

8.2.1 Labor force participation rates of married women

At the beginning of this century the labor force participation rates of married women were relatively low in all seven countries, except in France. Women left the labor force on marriage, except when poverty forced them to enter or remain in the labor market or when they became assisting wives. Their exit was often final unless the marriage ended, usually in widowhood. This subsection draws on a number of studies to point a general picture of married women's labor force participation. The next subsection discusses the statistical time series.

Studies by Labor Inspectorates (and others) at the beginning of the twentieth century in Belgium, France, the Netherlands and the United Kingdom show that married women tended to be wage earners when other household income was low. By the first decades of the twentieth century, the large families meant that married women's childbearing and domestic responsibilities were very demanding and time consuming. The time they spent in wage earning activities was diminishing in countries where this existed to any large extent, such as France. In general, in all seven countries during the first decades, of this century wage earning activities lasted only until marriage. Marriage was seen as the natural destiny of women. In fact in many occupations there were upper age limits for the employment of single women (For example, French telephone operators had to be single and between the ages of eighteen and twenty-five (Tilly and Scott, 1987:184). In teaching and nursing - the two occupations involving relatively long training periods for a substantial number of women - there were usually systems of training and salary increments over a period of years, encouraging women to enter only when they wanted to devote themselves to lifetime careers. Married teachers and nurses were exceptional and could only be found where shortages existed. In France, for example, there were not enough single teachers to meet the demand and in 1922 as many as 56 per cent of all female teachers in France were married (Tilly and Scott, 1987:185). However, in the other countries, the single older nurse and unmarried schoolteacher were familiar figures and for a long time these two professions were the only ones with a certain status in which women participated to any real extent. "The age structure of the teaching and nursing professions was more mixed than in sales and clerical jobs, turnover was lower and the social and economic status higher than in most other female white-collar jobs." (Tilly and Scott, 1987: 185). Training for these professions was available only to daughters of those families who could afford to support them during it.

Working-class daughters (like working-class boys) had to contribute to the family income at the earliest possible moment, and certainly directly after compulsory schooling. Gradually, however, occupational choices increased for working-class children in all seven countries, although regional differences were large. For girls, factory employment (where available) diversified, increasing choice and low-skilled positions became available in the sales and service sector. Particularly after World War II, choice increased and the shorter and more regular hours, as well as the relatively higher wages, drew young girls into other paid work than the traditional domestic service or needlework. Of course, the general increase in household income also reduced the need to contribute to the family income and improved the entitlement of daughters to retain some or most of their own earnings.

In all seven countries before World War II the wife was more frequently employed when the husband's wage was low. Many studies confirm this (see also chapter 10). For example, the results of a large and detailed study conducted around 1900 in Gent (Belgium), a city with a relatively favorable demand for women's jobs (Van den Eeckhout en Scholliers, 1990). Male cotton laborers, flax laborers and metal workers earned on average BF 17.99, 15.70 and 19.64 per week respectively. Of the cotton laborers, 48 per cent had a wife participating in the labor market (usually also in factory work), while 58 per cent of the flax laborers had a working wife and 43 per cent of the metal workers (the majority working in the more flexible, but lower paid service sector). Among the cotton laborers, diversity in income was greater than in the other two categories of workers. Accordingly, the labor force participation rate of wives of relatively badly paid carders (BF 15 per week) was 64 per cent and that of the relatively well paid spinners (BF 25.60) 26 per cent.

In general, participation in the labor market declined with age (and increasing husband's income), while nearly all wives stopped when children began to participate in the labor market, although they sometimes had to start working again when the husband's income declined at an older age. The complementarity in incomes is clear, with labor force participation of members of a family depending heavily on the wage of the father or husband, like *communicating vessels*. It would appear, moreover, that the employment of one's children did not undermine male pride in being the breadwinner to nearly the same extent as the employment of a spouse (Van den Eeckhout en Scholliers, 1990:199). These results are confirmed by studies in France, England (see Tilly and Scott, 1987: chapters 6 and 8), and the Netherlands (Posthumus-van der Goot[6], 1938; Van Zanden, 1985:73). All these studies concerned industrial (textile) cities or areas, but in other areas the influence of

---

6 In this study Posthumus-van der Goot compares two enguiries held in the Dutch textile city Enschede among married women participating in the labor market. The first was conducted by the labor Inspectorate, the second by herself in 1938. The answers given are remarkable similar. Bad economic circumstances force married women into paid employment, which the majority would not perform given any choice.

husband's (or family) income was probably just as strong. Poor married women (like widows and divorcees) had to depend on what jobs they could find. "The miscry of these women stemmed from the fact that they had no choice. Their families' subsistence and its survival demanded that they worked. Their desperate cicumstances, moreover, left them little choice as to what kind of job they would take and little room to negotiate for wages or decent working conditions. The continuing pressure on these women to earn wages was a sign of need in their households. It is no wonder, then, that working-class culture adopted the image of the married woman at home as the sign of the health, stability, and prosperity of a household. The expression of this ideal was less a result of the *embourgeoisement* of the working class than it was a statement about the realities of working class experience". (Tilly and Scott, 1987:196). On small farms and in shops where home and market labor merged, family and market responsibilities were shared and difficult to distinguish from each other.

In England as well as in France, there seem just before World War I to have been fewer married women employed than there had been fifty years before (Tilly and Scott, 1987:196). However, French labor force participation rates of married women were much higher than in England, although the very high labor force participation rates of married women in French agriculture make comparison difficult (see also next subsection).

If women in agriculture are left out, as being a source of ideosyncrasies everywhere, the share of married women in percentages of all other persons in the labor force, is around 1930 in France 13.4 per cent, in Belgium 10.1, in Great Britain 5.0, in Sweden 4.4 and in the Netherlands 2.2 per cent. So in Sweden the share is twice as high and in France six times as high as in the Netherlands (Posthumus-van der Goot, 1938:139). The share of married women both in the total labor force and in the female labor force in France remained high. In 1954 the proportion of married women in the female labor force was 49 per cent, whereas in 1951 in the United Kingdom it was 41 per cent, and in Sweden in 1950 it was still 30 per cent (Klein, 1961:21). By 1965, however, the proportion of married women in the labor force in Sweden exceeded 50 per cent (Sundström, 1991:174).

8.2.2 Long-term trends

Table 8.3 gives the long-term trends in labor force participation rates of married women in all seven countries, from about 1900 to 1990. Because it turned out that often it was not certain whether the number of married women in the labor force was related to the total number of married women or to the number of married women of the working-age population, two tables are constructed. Table 8.3 concerns all married women, table 8.4 married women of working age (about 15 to 65 years). With hardly any married women below 15 or 16 years of age and a relatively small number of women still married above 65 years, the difference is small at the beginning of the century. With increasing life expectancy, declining participation in agriculture and an increasing 'normal' retirement age of married women at about 65 years, differences between the two tables increased.

Table 8.3 and figure 8.2 *Labor force participation rates of married women as a percentage of the total female married population*

	Belgium[1]	Denmark[2]	France[3]	Germany[4]	Netherlands[5]	Sweden[6]	Britain[7]
1900	–	35	56	12	5	–	–
1910	18	23	49	26	8	(3)	10
1920	–	19	50	29	–	(4)	9
1930	16	21	44	29	9	(8)	10
1940	–	24	46	34	–	(9)	–
1950	15	27	41	25	10	14	22
1960	20	28	32	33	6	23	30
1970	26	43	34	36	15	48	43
1980	40	63	41	41	29	70	47
1990	± 60	72	44	47	41	79	53

1 Actual census years: 1947, 1961 and 1981.
2 Actual census years 1901, 1911 and 1921. The corresponding rates for salary workers and wage earners were 6, 4, 3, 5, 11 and 13 per cent from 1901 to 1950.
3 Actual census years: 1901, 1906, 1911, 1931, 1936, 1946, 1954, 1968 and 1982.
4 Actual census years: 1895, 1907, 1925, 1933, 1939. Rates for salary workers and wage earners in these years 7, 9, 9, 9 and 12 per cent. In 1882 this rate was 6 per cent and for all married women 9 per cent.
5 Actual census years: 1899, 1909, 1947 and 1971. Rates for salary workers and wage earners in the first three years 2 per cent, while in 1930 this rate was 3 per cent.
6 The figures for 1910, 1920, 1930 and 1940 exclude unpaid family workers. These figures are probably more comparable with the percentages given for Denmark, Germany and the Netherlands in the notes 2, 4 and 5 and with Britain as presented in the table.
7 Actual census years 1911, 1921, 1931, 1951, 1961, 1971, 1981 and 1991.

Sources: See table 2.2

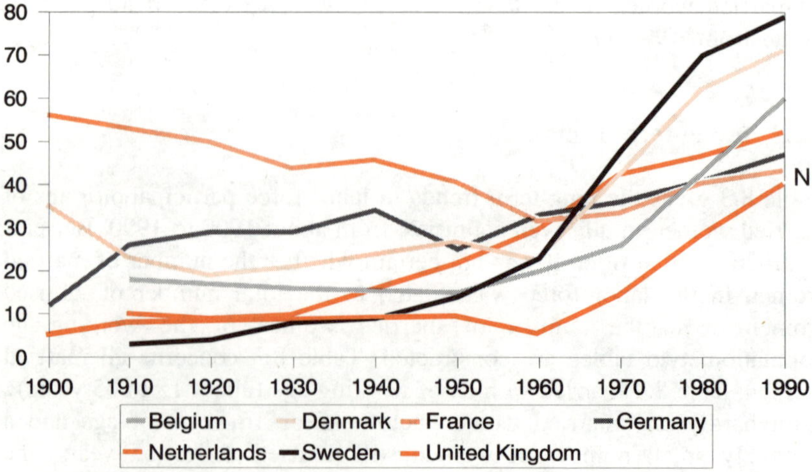

Compared with that in the six other countries, female labor force participation in the Netherlands was low overall, but particularly so in the case of married women. As table 8.3 and figure 8.2 show, prior to 1950 married women's labor force participation does not conform to any simple pattern.

Table 8.4 and figure 8.3 *Labor force participation rates of married women as a percentage of the female married population of working-age.*

	Belgium[1]	Denmark[2]	France[3]	Germany[4]	Netherlands[5]	Sweden[6]	Britain[7]
1900	–	–	(20)	12	5	–	13
1910	19	24	(21)	26	8	4	11
1920	–	20	29	29	–	5	9
1930	19	22	26	30	7	10	11
1940	–	25	–	35	–	10	–
1947	17	28	(28)	28	11	15	23
1961	24	31	(31)	36	7	26	32
1970	29	46	38	40	17	56	46
1980	48	66	50	47	32	76	54
1990		76	53	54	47	86	59

For actual census years, see table 8.3

2 According to the sample surveys 1967 for the age group 15 – 74 years: 45 per cent, in 1970 for the same age group 49 per cent, in 1973: 56 per cent and in 1977: 61 per cent.

3 Age group 15 – 69 years and non-agricultural for the year 1906, age group 15 – 64 years and non-agricultural for the years in 1911, 1921 and 1931; in 1954 and 1961 only salary workers and wage earners and in 1968, 1982 and 1990, all married women aged 16 to 64.

Sources: See table 2.2

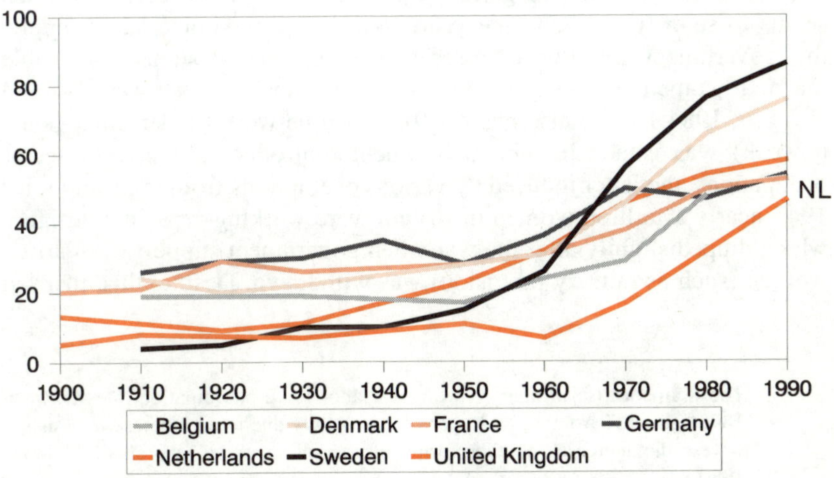

In most countries there was little or no increase; in Germany[7] and Sweden it was slow and evolutionary for married salary workers and wage earners (see notes table 8.3), while in Belgium, Denmark and France there was an actual decline until after World War II. After 1960, however, labor force participation rates of married women increased in all seven countries. The relatively high figures for Denmark, France and Germany are strongly influenced by assisting wives in agriculture. Without these assisting wives the rates in 1921 and 1930 in Denmark, and in 1925 and 1933 in Germany are about equal to those in the United Kingdom, the latter a country without a substantial agricultural sector and excluding assisting wives in the censuses.

The conclusions to be drawn from table 8.4 before World War II are similar to those of table 8.3. Remarkable are the high participation rate of married women in France outside agriculture before World War II and the very high participation rates of employed women directly thereafter. These rates are even higher than those for all married women of working age in Sweden in 1960. These high French rates makes the rise in Sweden since then even more spectacular, closely followed by Denmark, while differences between the other countries are not spectacular. The Netherlands is still the country with the lowest rates for married women, but differences become smaller. The increases in all seven countries are most striking from the 1960s onward. The measured participation rates among married women have risen in all seven countries with every subsequent decade since then.
Remarkably, even without agriculture, French labor force participation rates of married women were already 20 per cent in 1906 and 21 per cent in 1911 for all married women, but 28 per cent in 1911 for the working age group outside agriculture, about twice as high as those in England. In England the decline in married women's labor force participation (from about 25 per cent in 1851) continued throughout the first decades of the twentieth century.

In Britain, although no census was taken in 1941 because of the exigencies of war, the change in the participation rate of married women seems to stem from about that year. In order to maximize labor supply, the government introduced a series of measures designed to enable married women and mothers to enter the labor market (Atkins and Hoggett, 1984:19; see also chapter 9). Part-time work (under thirty hours a week) was established in government-controlled and private sector occupations, the latter induced by various exemptions from legislation. By 1945 nearly 1 million women in Britain were working part-time, a figure which dipped slightly after the war when government support for married women (such as nursery provision) was withdrawn. Despite this, married

---

[7] The dramatic rise in married women's labor force participation rates between 1895 and 1907 from 12 to 26 per cent is mainly due to an increase in assisting wives; the increase in other forms of market labor is very small (Willms, 1980:83).

women continued to remain in the labor market, although to a lesser extent mainly part-time. Female part-time workers increased from 748 thousand in 1951, to 3,152 thousand in 1971, and 3,543 thousand in 1981 (Atkins and Hoggett, 1984:19). The same pattern was more or less followed in the other countries. On average, girls work full-time until marriage; some remain in the labor market thereafter, either full-time or part-time, until the birth of the first child; some women do not return to paid employment until childbearing is completed; others never return.

In all seven countries participation rates of married women are closely related to family composition. However, it is not only married women who have family responsibilities, and other family members besides children may be in need of care. Traditionally, aged parents counted on their unmarried daughters to look after them. Nowadays, apart from married women many single women, as well as widows and divorcees, combine market work with family responsibilities.

8.3 Part-time work

8.3.1 The increase in part-time work

The apparent rise in labor force participation of married women may be much less spectacular once the other dimension of labor supply is considered: that is, hours of work. In a context where (married) women are seen as having primary responsibility for the household and particularly for child-care, we may expect that many women who want to participate in the labor market will be able to achieve these two objectives only by taking a part-time job.

In all seven countries part-time work is predominantly female and likely mainly to be performed by married women. Unfortunately, no regular statistics are published concerning part-time work, and where any such statistics are available they usually concern all women (distinguished from men) without differentiation by marital status. International comparisons are published only occasionally, but with increasing frequency (see below). The comparison is further complicated because definitions of part-time work (less than full-time work[8]) are not standardized. They vary from country to country, with the demarcation between full and part-time work being set variously at 25 hours (in the Netherlands in the 1971 census and various studies, such as: Renes, 1991), or 30 hours (in the Netherlands in the 1960 census and in Britain, HMSO, or see Dex and Shaw, 1986) or 35 hours (OECD, Sweden). This demarcation may itself be based either on usual hours worked or on actual

8 Full-time work, being equal to the normal weekly hours, also varies from country to country.

hours. Sometimes the statistics are simply based on a statement by the individuals concerned that their contracts were part-time, or in other words on the respondent's own assessment of her/his employment (OECD, 1991).

Working part-time has increased everywhere, most notably in the service sector, particularly the public sector. However, in the Netherlands - as in Great Britain before 1940 - marriage bars prevented married women entering the public sector until 1957. For this reason, as a 1957 study shows, it was easier for married women in the Netherlands to enter the private sector than the public sector (Schellekens-Ligthart, 1961). In all seven countries there was a marked increase in part-time work after World War II. In general few men work part-time, with only Denmark and the Netherlands showing some significant proportions in the EC.

The trend over the 1983 - 1990 period is certainly one of increased part-time working (EC, 1992:22,23). In the case of the EC it is difficult to take the observation period further back than 1983 due to lack of harmonized data (OECD, 1990:124). In Sweden the proportion of part-time employed women among female employees rose from 38 per cent in 1970 to 47 per cent in 1982 (a maximum) and then fell back to 41 per cent in 1988 (Sundström, 1991:174; Jonung and Persson, 1992). About half of all actual worked hours by women in Sweden between 1963 and 1988 were devoted to the public sector (especially public services, teaching, health and social services), where part-time work is most prominent. In Britain the number of part-time workers was 5 million in 1984, as compared with 3.2 million in 1971, a period in which full-time employment decreased by 2.5 million, with married women constituting three-quarters of all part-time employees (Hepple, 1986:118). Of the 47 per cent of married women in the British labor force in 1981, 52 per cent worked part-time, or 54 per cent in the 25 to 44 age group (OECD, 1983: 33).

In general, high shares of part-time work coincide with high labor force participation rates (OECD, 1983, 1991). But comparison of participation in terms of numbers of persons may be misleading due to variation between part-time workers. To correct for this, it is possible to calculate *labor force participation rates expressed in full-time equivalents*. Van Paridon (1990) has calculated these for 19 OECD countries in 1987. If all persons worked full-time (assumed to be 40 hours a week), these rates would equal the labor force participation rates; if everybody worked 20 hours a week they would equal half these rates.

Table 8.5 gives the labor force participation rates for all persons aged 15 to 64 (as given in tables 2.5, 2.6 and 2.7), *net labor force participation rates* (i.e. labor force participation rates excluding the unemployed)[9] and the rates in full-time labor force equivalents[10] for all

---

[9] These were published by the OECD in *Historical Statistics*.

seven countries in 1987. The table also shows the proportion of part-time workers among all workers (in persons).

Table 8.5 *Proportion of part-time workers, labor force participation rates of the working age population, net labor force participation rates and rates in full-time equivalents: a seven-country comparison, 1987*

	total				men				women			
	pt	lfpr	nlf	fte	pt	lfpr	nlf	fte	pt	lfpr	nlf	fte
Belgium	10	62	57	54	2	73	70	71	24	51	44	37
Denmark	24	83	77	61	9	88	83	73	42	77	71	49
France	12	66	59	53	4	76	69	67	23	56	48	38
Germany	13	69	61	58	2	83	74	75	30	54	47	39
Netherlands[1]	25	59	53	47	9	79	69	65	55	49	37	26
Sweden	25	82	80	71	7	86	82	–	45	79	78	–
Great Britain	22	75	68	56	5	88	78	75	26	63	58	37

pt = share of part-timers as a percentage of all persons in the labor force
lfpr = labor force participation rate
nlf = net labor force participation rate
fte = full-time equivalents

1 According to the Dutch Ministry of Social Affairs and Employment *(Ministerie van Sociale Zaken en Werkgelegenheid)*, 1990:39 (with data based on Eurostat 1988) the share of the total population of the Netherlands working part-time is 30 per cent, and the percentages for the other mentioned countries in this source (France, Germany and Great Britain) are identical. For men, this source quotes 3 per cent for France and 15 per cent (!) for the Netherlands, while for women the percentage for France is given as 24, for Germany 31 and for the Netherlands 58.

Sources: Own calculations according to data from van Paridon (1990:23,25,26) and tables 2.5, 2.6 and 2.7.

The Netherlands seems to be the exception to the rule as regards the high correlation between labor force participation rates and part-time work, both for men and for women: high shares of part-time employment coincide with low net labor force participation rates. This means that of the potential labor force (all persons aged between 15 and 65 years) expressed in full-time equivalents (of 40 hours per week) labor force rates were only 65 per cent of all potential male working time and that only 26 per cent of all potential female market working time was actually utilized (men and women together 47 per cent) in 1987. Recalculations for 1990 show an increase in Dutch full-time equivalent labor force rates (men and women together) to 50.5 per cent; the corresponding figure for the EC was 55 per cent (Paridon, 1992:803)).

---

10 Based on Van Paridon's (1990) calculations. He uses the Eurostat Labor Force Sample Survey and the net labor force participation rates of the OECD mentioned above.

Table 8.5 shows that, looked at this way, women in the Netherlands no longer have labor force participation rates close to those in Belgium, but 11 per cent lower! Expressed in full-time equivalents, female labor force participation rates in Belgium and Great Britain are 37 per cent, in Denmark 49 per cent, in Germany 39 per cent, in France 38 per cent - and in the Netherlands a mere 26 per cent (OECD, 1991, Paridon, 1990). Again, the Netherlands is the lowest of all seven countries, and by a broad margin.

This very low Dutch full-time equivalent rate is caused mainly by the prevalescence of small part-time jobs (while in Sweden relatively large part-time jobs prevail). Of all women participating part-time in the Netherlands in 1988, one third had a job of less than 10 hours a week (Min.SoZaWe, 1990:38), while 40 per cent worked more than 10 but less than 20 hours a week. 73 per cent of all Dutch women were therefore working less than 20 hours a week, and most of these were teenagers and mothers of small children.

International comparison is difficult because of lack of data but in all countries the presence of children reduces labor force participation rates as well as labor force hours of mothers. Unfortunately, figures available are either only time series on labor force participation rates of mothers with young children or time series on part-time work, and seldom a combination of the two.

The 1988 Dutch Fertility Survey proves that the age of the mother as well as the age of the youngest child and the number of children are influencing the participation decision. For example, mothers born between 1955 and 1959 with one child younger than 5 years had a participation rate of 41 per cent, and mothers born between 1945 and 1949 with two children under 5 years of age a rate of only 20 per cent. Of all participating (married) mothers in the Netherlands, about 75 per cent have a part-time job. In the OSA 1988 sample, only 10 per cent of Dutch mothers with a child under 5 years of age were performing more than 20 hours' market work per week.

In 1985, the majority of mothers in the Netherlands and the United Kingdom with children under 4 years of age participated, if at all, for less than 20 hours a week, while in Belgium, France and Germany the majority worked for more than 30 hours a week (Moors and Koesoebjono, 1990:53). In Denmark in 1974, 16 per cent of all mothers with a child under 6 years of age worked less than 25 hours (the labor force participation rate of all mothers being about 53 per cent and 2 per cent unemployed); the corresponding figure in 1985 was 13 per cent (and 88 per cent; 17 per cent unemployed) (Soren, 1990).

The participation rate of Dutch married women (in 1982) was higher than that of Flemish women (1985/86) before the birth of the first child, but lower during every subsequent stage of the family formation process (Mertens, Van der Meer, Schippers and Siegers, 1992:107). There seems to be a general convergence in the labor force participation rates of married women without children in all seven countries, but very large differences still exist in the behavior of women with small children.

Among older British women with children, by far the most common pattern up to 1980 was to remain at home from the time the first child was born until childbearing was completed. Among younger British women, however, there appears to be a growing trend towards working between births (Dex and Shaw, 1986:28,29). More children lower the labor force participation rate, and the age of the youngest child is also important (see also Dutch Fertility Survey, 1982 and 1988).

A major characteristic of the Swedish labor market in the 1970s was the rapid increase in market work among mothers of pre-school children. Between 1965 and 1980, the labor market expanded by 573 thousand women, of whom 35 per cent had children under 7 years of age and 34 per cent had children aged from 7 to 16 years. Married women accounted for 60 per cent of the expansion (Sundström, 1991:174). The increase in the number of women employed part-time was three times that of the number employed full-time and during the 1970 - 1980 period three-quarters of the employment growth for Swedish women was part-time.

Recent figures for Denmark and Sweden tend to indicate that mothers are increasing their working hours and fathers reducing theirs. In Denmark, at the end of the 1980s, both the father and mother were working at least 38 hours a week in 40 per cent of the families with children aged 0 - 11 years (Soren, 1990:41). In Sweden between 1963 and 1973 there was very little change in actual hours of market work per woman, but the increase in actual market hours between 1973 and 1983 was about three hours per woman aged between 20 and 64. Male market hours, however, decreased by about 8 hours between 1963 and 1988, with most of the dedrease occurring in the period 1963 to 1973 (Jonung and Persson, 1992).

Part-time employment is not only common among employed females; many self-employed women also work part-time. Part-time self-employment is particularly common among women in the Netherlands and the United Kingdom, where respectively 71 and 55 per cent work under 30 hours a week. Average usual weekly hours worked by the self-employed women in 1990 were the lowest in the Netherlands: 28.5 hours a week. The corresponding working hours for self-employed women in the other countries are for Belgium 49.2, Denmark 46.9, France 47.9, Germany 42.5, Sweden 40.3, and the United Kingdom 37.6 (OECD, 1992:161). Self-employed women work on average more hours than employed women in all seven countries, and sometimes the difference is substantial (Belgium, Denmark and France), but - just as with employed women - Dutch self-employed women are trailing far behind in weekly working hours.

8.3.2 Flattered labor force participation rates

The tendencies to count and include in the labor force statistics people who are unemployed or women who are working part-time in very small jobs, are not the only reasons that labor force participation rates have increased recently. Other provisions, such as sickness and disablement benefits or - particularly for married women - maternity leave provisions, also inflate the female labor force participation rates. So, another logical step would be to correct the labor force participation figures for these factors and calculate the full-time equivalent actual market rate, or *on-the-job-rate*. Such a rate has not been calculated yet.

Statistically, many women are now registered as being in the labor force while in reality they are at home taking care of the children. This effect is well documented for Sweden. In 1970, for example, 12.6 per cent of Swedish women with children under 7 years recorded as employed had in fact been absent for the whole of the survey week, a figure which increased to 26.1 per cent in 1985. Corresponding figures for men are 5.2 per cent in 1976 (earliest figure available) and 5.9 per cent in 1985 (SCB, 1986:27; see also Gustafsson and Jacobsson, 1985:table 1). Of all the women with children younger than 1 year, 77 per cent were registered as being employed in 1988, but only 11 per cent were performing market work (Sundström, 1991:177). The difference between the labor force participation rates of Swedish men and women in 1988 amounted to only 5 percentage points, but the difference in their *at-work rates* was 12 percentage points; and while the labor force participation rate of women with children under seven years of age was 86 per cent, according to the labor force surveys, their at-work rate was 55 per cent (Jonung and Persson, 1992). Clearly there is still a marked division of labor in Sweden, even though the position of women is of course different with a job to return to after the period of absence and with entitlements to transfer and pension schemes. Calculating these rates for all seven countries (preferably in full-time equivalent percentages) might show that differences in labor force participation rates between Sweden and Denmark (with similar provisions as Sweden) on the one hand and the remaining 5 countries on the other are much less than presumed, while those between the Netherlands and the other 6 countries might even be more.

8.3.3 Temporary work and married women

In most OECD countries, part-time work and temporary work overlap a great deal and - like part-time workers - temporary workers are more often women than men. France is one exception (OECD, 1987). In 1987 more than 10 per cent of women employees in the Member States had temporary jobs. However, temporary work is much more common amongst the young.

Part-time work and temporary work generate atypical employment relationships, as do putting-out systems, homeworking and sub-contracting. In contrast to the more visible character of temporary and part-time working, outworking (including homework) has a lower profile in the labor market. Outworking encompasses work at home or outside the employer's or organizer's premises. It can take the form of piecework or a combination of piecework and fixed payments. Intrinsic to outwork is the dependent, subordinate and isolated position of the almost always female (married) worker isolated from the sale or marketing of her output (EC, 1989:90). Homeworking is highly concentrated in clothing, textiles, leather goods, toys and novelty goods and regionally concentrated. It has the advantage of offering women the opportunity to become economically active, but is the least protected type of employment. Of course the same applies to domestic servants working part-time in private households. Domestic service and homeworking are two of the more constant features of the position of women in the labor market. Family workers share with home workers many features of their position on the labor market, although they tend to work in different sectors. The proportion of women in the category of home workers seems to have increased. Like unpaid family workers (other than the assisting wife in some countries), home workers are poorly protected by social or labor laws. This type of employment can, however, constitute a buffer against unemployment.

8.4 Conclusions to chapter 8

For a long time, the period of - often full-time - market work for Dutch woman used to end with marriage, except for assisting wives. Labor force participation rates of married women were very low throughout the whole of the twentieth century until the 1970s. In 1960 the labor force participation rate for married women was still only 6 per cent (7 per cent for married women aged 15 - 64 years), while the labor force participation rate of married female employees or wage earners was even lower: 4 per cent. In the Netherlands, it was marital status more than any other characteristic that determined a woman's economic role. This has remained to a large extent, although not completely, the case up to the present day, and while gradually in the 1960s and 1970s more and more married women began to remain in the labor force after marriage, they usually did so in part-time work.

The registered decrease of married women in the labor market in the Netherlands between 1947 and 1960 is remarkable. This decline (from nearly 10 per cent to below 7 per cent) was the result of two opposing tendencies: the decline in married women assisting their husbands and the increase in married women in employment. The few married women (excluding the assisting wives) participating in the labor market in 1960 were either childless (52 per cent) or had children over 6 years of age. Only about 0.6 per cent of the mothers of young children were employed. The married women participating (excluding assisting wives) were relatively often found working in high educated professions.

By 1971, married women's labor force participation had increased to 25 per cent, or to 12 per cent not counting assisting wives. In 1979, without assisting wives, the labor force participation rate of married women was 22 per cent. Successive years show ever higher participation rates of married women, at first by (young) women without children, but increasingly also by mothers remaining in or re-entering the labor market. Compared with the situation in the other six countries, female labor force participation in the Netherlands has always been low, especially as regards married women. But at the beginning of this century the labor force participation rates of married women were relatively low in all seven countries, except in France.

In England as well as in France, there seem just before World War I to have been fewer married women employed than there had been fifty years before. In England the decline in married women's labor force participation continued throughout the first decades of the twentieth century. French labor force participation rates of married women were much higher than in the other six countries, partly due to their very high participation rates in agriculture. However, even without agriculture, French labor force participation rates of married women were still very high right up to World War II. Although lower thereafter, the share of married women both in the total labor force and in the female labor force remained high in France, while in other countries it increased rapidly. The proportion of 49 per cent of married women in the French female labor force (in 1954), was equalled in Sweden in 1965, and eventually in the Netherlands in 1975.

Up to 1950, married women's labor force participation does not conform to any simple pattern. In most countries there was little or no increase. Only in Germany and Sweden was it slow and evolutionary, while in Belgium, Denmark and France there was an actual decline until after World War II. After 1960, however, labor force participation rates of married women increased in all seven countries, although participation was often part-time.

In general, high shares of part-time work coincide with high labor force participation rates. The Netherlands seems to be the exception to this rule, both for men and for women: high shares of part-time employment coincide with low net labor force participation rates. Recalculating labor force participation rates in full-time equivalents (40 hours a week) for the female population aged between 15 and 65 years shows that female labor force participation in the Netherlands is still the lowest in all seven countries, with 26 per cent in 1987. Looked at this way, Belgium and the Netherlands no longer have about equal labor force participation rates (as shown in chapter 2), but female activity rates in Belgium are actually 11 per cent higher (37 per cent), resembling those in France, Germany and Britain, while Denmark and Sweden have far higher rates still. The difference is probably due mainly to the low participation hours of Dutch married women. Of all women participating part-time in the Netherlands in 1988, one third worked less than 10 hours a week, while 40 per cent worked over 10 but less than 20 hours a week.

Participation rates of married women in all seven countries are closely related to family composition. In all countries the presence of children reduces labor force participation rates of married women, but less so in Denmark and Sweden, where there was a rapid increase in market work among mothers of pre-school children in the 1970s and 1980s. Recent figures for Denmark and Sweden tend to indicate that mothers are increasing their working hours and fathers reducing theirs.

It is not known how many women in all seven countries are now registered statistically as being in the labor force while in reality they are still at home taking care of the children. In 1988, the labor force participation rate of women in Sweden with children under seven years old was 86 per cent, while their at-work rate was 55 per cent. Clearly there is still a marked division of labor in all seven countries, even in Sweden.

CHAPTER 9

WOMEN, WORK AND POLITICS

> *"Struggles for equal pay, child care, abortion rights, health care and countless other issues, all have their roots in the nineteenth century. ... The strengths and weaknesses of the nineteenth century live on, even when changed beyond immediate recognition."*
>
> *(Vicinus, 1985:8,9).*

This chapter investigates the norms, values and constraints operating with respect to women's position in society. It describes key pieces of legislation in the seven countries and again stresses the international differences. Is there a link between changes in female labor force participation and legal arrangements? It may be doubted whether the law constrains female behaviour in this respect, but it seems plausible that if it does, it does so at the level of ideology and cultural values. Legislation may be expected to reflect cultural values and vice versa cultural values to influence legislation. Changes in female labor force participation may be interrelated both with these regulations and with cultural values. For this reason, this chapter broadens the focus on women's work to include a brief examination of the most important pieces of legislation with a possible bearing on women's labor market position. In all seven countries a century and a half ago, women were deemed to be dependents both in marriage and law. Gradually, in the context of the legal subordination of women, positive and negative sanctions have changed. When did these changes take place?

Legislation influences the position of women in the labor market at three stages. First before entry, second during participation in the labor market and third on leaving the labor market. Before entry, educational opportunities are essential to women's position in the labor market. For this reason, this chapter starts with the main educational developments in the seven countries since about the mid-nineteenth century (section 9.1). Three developments in the struggle for education have been singled out and highlighted in this section. The first and most spectacular achievement was gaining admission to universities and to professions such as medicine and the law (subsection 9.1.1). In all seven countries, nursing and teaching were considered as skills naturally possessed by women, but even in these areas training was denied. However, these activities gradually became recognized as suitable female professions and provided with special training facilities. The second trend towards secondary schooling, vocational training and access to new occupations is discussed in subsection 9.1.2. The third trend, probably the most important in establishing the equal status of women and men, was compulsory schooling; this was and is the basis for guaranteeing the availability of further and higher education to all girls, not only to those in the middle and upper classes (subsection 9.1.3).

Section 9.2 concentrates on principal labor laws and equal treatment policies, legislation regulating women's work once they have entered the labor market. Early labor legislation started with the protection of children and women (subsection 9.2.1). The restriction of working hours was the next step (subsection 9.2.2), often coinciding with maternity protection (subsection 9.2.3). The same section discusses legislation such as maternal/parental leave and other legislation influencing absenteeism. The development of equal treatment and equal pay policies is discussed in subsection 9.2.4: Gender equality.

Section 9.3 discusses legislation influencing departure from the labor market, subsection 9.3.1 directly relevant legislation such as pensions, early retirement and marriage bars, and subsection 9.3.2 indirectly relevant legislation such as financial (dis)incentives to employment in terms of social security, taxes etc.

Labor legislation influences the position of women in the labor market directly, while some other legislation influences it indirectly. This indirect legislature is discussed in section 9.4. Subsection 9.4.1 gives a short overview of the achievement of suffrage, a milestone in terms of political power. The other two subsections of 9.4 address key pieces of legislation with respect to marriage and the family. Subsection 9.4.2 answers the question: when did women assume control over their own affairs and their own earnings, so gaining financial and legal independence? Subsection 9.4.3 considers arrangements interrelated with female market labor, such as child care provisions, family policies in general and family support.

As in the other chapters, the emphasis here is on developments since about 1830 - 1850. Before that date the inferior legal status of women was clear and relatively unchallenged (see below), despite some fluctuations over the previous centuries. Time and space do not of course allow any extended treatment of these highly complex issues, and this chapter provides no more than a simplified outline summary of events.

9.1 The struggle for the right to education and meaningful work

The first feminist wave

During the nineteenth century single women in all seven countries began to tackle their marginal positions ideologically, economically and socially.

The struggle for the right to education and the corresponding right to decent jobs was characteristic of the *first feminist*[1] *wave*. From the late 1920s until the 1960s when the common goal of *the second feminist wave* - suffrage - was realised in many countries, the energies of feminism were dispersed across many activities. *The third feminist wave* started in the 1960s when large numbers of women realized that - despite progress - political, social and economic equality with men had not been yet established.

Before the emergence of the organized women's movement[2], individual pioneers in the ideological battle for women's rights can be named in all seven countries, especially around the time of the French Revolution[3] (starting in 1789). The publication in France in 1791 of the *Déclaration des droits de la femme et de la citoyenne* by Olympe de Gouges (1748-1793) and in England in 1792 of Mary Wollstonecraft's (1759-1797): *A Vindication of the Rights of Women*, both subsequently translated into many languages, inspired thousands of men and women all over the world. So did John Stuart Mill's (1806-1873) *The Subjection of Women*, published in 1861 (inspiring among others the young Aletta Jacobs[4], the first Dutch female doctor and an important feminist, see her *Herinneringen* (Memoires), 1924).

In Belgium, Denmark and Sweden storms of controversy were raised over *the women question* (see below). In Belgium after the publication of Zoé Gatti de Gamond's letters in 1834, in Denmark after *Tolv Breve* (Twelve Letters) by Mathilde Fibiger (1830-1872), writing under the nom de plume of Clara Raphael in 1848, and in Sweden after *Det går an* (Common Decency) by Carl Jonas Love Almqvist, published in 1834. The list is by no means complete, but indicates that change was in the air at about the same time all over northern Europe.

The women question

The previous chapters have mentioned the fact that economic and demographic changes caused increasing poverty in the lower as well as the middle and upper classes in the mid-nineteenth century. The further

---

1 Feminism is defined as the movement opposed to the systematic social injustices suffered by women because of their sex (Richards, 1982:17).

2 Becoming visible especially after the first Women's Rights Convention in Seneca Falls, U.S.A., initiated by Elizabeth Cady Stanton in 1848.

3 This earlier movement was partly organized (see next section). For this reason some historians prefer to date the beginnings of the first feminist wave from around this time. However, the more commonly accepted origin of the *wave*, in the mid-nineteenth century, is adopted here.

4 Her remarkable library, with an extensive feminist collection on the social, political and legal status of women, most of it already collected by her husband Carel Victor Gerritsen (since 1892) was sold to the John Crecar Library in Chicago in 1903 (De Wilde, 1982:250).

delay in marriage and the demographic shortage of men (already mentioned in chapter 7) gave increasing visibility to the problem of poor middle-class women with no means of subsistence. Single middle and upper-class women had always been socially invisible, except for a few examples of individual women who rebelled - although even then they often did so only in private correspondence (as, for example, did Belle van Zuylen[5]). Such women were supposed to adopt artistic pursuits and help the poor[6], not to become professionals or to be interested in unladylike subjects like mathemathics.

Poor single lower-class women performing market work had always existed, but their long working hours and physically exhausting work aroused little interest: they were fulfilling their accepted social destiny and were not seen as a problem so long as they performed traditional unskilled jobs or worked as domestic servants. What became recognized as a problem in all seven countries in the middle of the nineteenth century was *the women question*: what to do with single 'redundant' (middle and upper-class) women? Allowing women access to education and occupations other than seamstress, governess, lady-companion, domestic servant or worker in an unskilled job would have been a solution. However, the creation of this viable economic alternative was generally rejected in all seven countries in the mid-nineteenth century (see subsections 9.2.1 and 9.2.2).

The large supply of single women needing to earn a living in the few jobs to which they had access meant that the status and remuneration of those jobs remained low. In England in 1851, for example, two million adult women were forced to earn a living for themselves (and their children or parents) because they had no man to support them (Sullerot, 1969:90-91). About 25 thousand of them were registered as governesses (Sanderson, 1991:62). In Prussia, of the 3.8 million women aged between 20 and 40 years in 1867, only 2.2 million were married (Von Soden, 1979:11). Many of the 'spinsters' were condemned to idleness or to marginal positions in the home, church or workplace, while others were fighting an unequal battle for sufficient work at reasonable pay to support themselves and dependent relatives. For this reason, in Prussia between 1825 and 1861, the supply of governesses increased from 705 to 7366 (Sullerot, 1969:116).

---

5 Isabella Agneta Elisabeth de Charrière-van Tuyll van Serooskerken (1740 - 1805) grew up in the Dutch Castle Zuylen, which still exists. Her correspondence (originally written in French, but recently translated into English) with contemporaries such as Constant d'Hermenches, James Boswell, Benjamin Constant and Madame de Staël shows an independent, highly educated and gifted literary woman, critical of the social rules subordinating women.

6 Organized private female charity among the poor and prisoners was founded in the Netherlands in 1821 and flourished especially after the end of the 1830s (Brok-ten Broek, 1968:28).

9.1.1 Admission to University

The coincidence in the dates at which women were first admitted to university in all the seven countries is remarkable. In all seven countries, the first woman was admitted to university in the second half of the nineteenth century and in five of the seven countries women were admitted within a few years of each other: in the Netherlands in 1871[7], in Sweden in 1873, in England in 1878[8], in Denmark in 1875 and in Belgium in 1876. Of the other two countries, Germany was relatively late[9] in 1896 and France relatively early, with the first woman receiving a PhD in Lyon in 1861, but in contrast the first woman being admitted to the medical faculty only in 1886.

These brilliant women paved the way for other women[10]. In the Netherlands, a year after Aletta Jacobs, Catharina van Tussenbroek follow-

---

[7] Aletta Jacobs, the 8th of 11 children, daughter of a general practioner in a small rural village in the North of the country, was only 17 years old when she received permission to study for one year at university on the condition that 'her father supported her'. Her father did, although her mother disapproved. After passing her examinations with excellent marks she received permission to continue her studies in 1872.

[8] Different sources give different years. 1870 is frequently mentioned because it was a turning point in elementary and other education. The new grammar schools included girls and "(t)he 1870s also saw the reception of women into the ancient universities" (Sanderson, 1991:69). However, they were only admitted to its "Local Examinations", a system of middle-class (secondary) examinations not used by the better schools "for their best pupils whom they still directed towards university entrance examinations." (Sanderson, 1991:40). According to Bradley (1989:196), a few pioneering women like Elizabeth Blackwell and Elizabeth Garrett (the first female doctor in England) obtained medical degrees abroad but were then able to practice in England and also according to her, women won admission to the British medical schools of London University in 1878 and Edinburgh in 1886. Boekholt and de Booy (1987:191) also mention the University of London in 1878 as being the first to admit women. Oxford admitted women in 1920, while it was not until 1947 before men and women were admitted to Cambridge on more or less equal terms. Nevertheless, quota's and bars against women continued to exist in British universities, limiting women's choice.

[9] On the other hand, four women gained university degrees in Germany in the eighteenth century: in 1733, 1750, 1754 and 1787 respectively. However, they did so without attending lectures at the university and passed their examinations after private tuition (Von Soden, 1979:9).

[10] Aletta Jacob's younger sister Frederika was the first girl to receive permission to attend the boy's grammar school (*Hogere Burger School* or *HBS*, regulated by law since 1863) on the same terms as boys in 1872. The special permission was only granted to the village school, but soon other villages with only a HBS and no special secondary school for girls followed. After 1906, no special permission to admit girls was required anymore. Aletta Jacob's elder sister Charlotte became the first Dutch female pharmacist.

ed to become both an obstetrician and gynaecologist and a famous feminist, and in Amsterdam alone 34 female medical doctors graduated between 1897 and 1909, among them Cornelia de Lange the first female professor (in pediatrics) from 1927 - 1938.

Nevertheless, the total figures for female graduates remained low in all seven countries throughout the remainder of the nineteenth and early twentieth centuries. The developments in the Netherlands were fairly similar to those in the other countries. In 1909 there were 13 female lawyers, 17 dentists, 14 mathematicians/physicists, 2 engineers and 177 medical doctors and midwives (Polak, 1909)[11].

The gradual nature of the developments makes the international comparison more complicated than might be expected at first sight. Admission of one woman did not always mean that other women could also be admitted, or would be admitted to other disciplines, nor did it necessarily mean the right to practice the relevant profession[12]. In Belgium, for example, the first female doctor in law, Marie Popelin, demanded the right to practice as a courtroom lawyer in 1888, but died in 1914 without ever achieving her ambition. Also in Belgium, women were officially admitted to universities (with the permission of the examination board) in 1890 (unofficially in 1876) and in the same year women were for the first time allowed to practice medicine and pharmacy (*artsenijbereidkunde*). Although the first high school for girls was opened as early as 1864, the first high school preparing for university entrance was opened to girls in Brussels only in 1891. It was not until 1925 that women could be admitted to universities without special permission (de Weerdt, 1980).

In the other countries there were similar historical developments before women and men were admitted finally on more or less the same terms. In Denmark, Nielsine Nielsen applied to the Minister to sit the entrance examination to study medicine in 1874. She received no reply but in 1875 a Royal decree was issued that women were to be admitted to university, though with two important special provisos: no examinations or academic degrees were to qualify women for admission to public office, and female students could not receive scholarships or similar benefits (Dahlsgård, 1980:108,109). Nielsine Nielsen graduated in 1885, but the first woman to graduate in law in Denmark did so only in 1905.

---

11 By 1911 there were 477 women doctors in Britain (382 of them unmarried), rising to 1253 in 1921, a rise from 2 per cent to 7 per cent within the whole profession (Bradley, 1989:196).

12 In the Netherlands, Aletta Jacobs, who had received a PhD in 1879, founded the first birth control clinic in the world (1882), supplying the *pessarium occlusivum*, originally described in a scientific artical by a German medical doctor called Mensinga. She contacted him, perfected the original device and introduced the "Dutch cap". Two days a week female workers and prostitutes could get free consultations (Jacobs, 1978:82).

In Sweden a similar development took place: female admission to university in 1873 did not include law or theology.

In Germany in 1893, a petition signed by 60 thousand persons in favor of admitting women to study medicine was disregarded by the Reichstag. But from 1896 onwards women were allowed to attend lectures (though not to sit examinations) at the University of Prussia (Arons, 1979:43). In 1899, the first woman entered the University of Gießen. From that year onward women were in principle allowed to participate in examinations in medicine and pharmacy and to become dentists. Between 1900 and 1908, more and more states admitted women (always with the special consent of the Minister), and from 1908 onward women were formally allowed to enter universities throughout Germany. In 1909 the first woman was admitted to a technical university.

Germany was not only relatively late, but suffered a serious relapse in 1933, when Hitler after his election changed the Constitution. Women were officially allowed admission to all areas of general education, academic studies and vocational training (except religious), but the proportion of female students at universities had to remain below 10 per cent. In 1934 of the 10,000 *Abiturientinnen* (women qualified to go to university) only 1500 were actually admitted[13].

To summarize, differences between the countries are in general fairly small in this respect. Women gained access to universities in six of the seven countries within a relatively short period and they did so mainly in the disciplines of medicine, pharmacy, dentistry and (often later) law, and to a lesser extent in chemistry, physics and philosophy. In all countries, however, their numbers remained low throughout the rest of the nineteenth and early twentieth centuries.

9.1.2 Nursing and teaching, nice professions for a woman

The passion and struggle for education and meaningful work was expressed by many women in the nineteenth century. For example, Florence Nightingale, born in 1820 and despairing of finding work to meet her talents and energies, cried out at the age of thirty-two years "Why have women passion, intellect, moral activity - and a place in society where no one of the three can be exercised?" (Vicinus, 1985:2).

Pioneering women like Florence Nightingale, opened up for women respectable alternatives to marriage in the form of nursing and teaching. They laid the foundation for the extension of educational opportunities for girls and, together with technical and economic progress, created access to new occupations for women. "The distrust of formal

---

13 In England the interwar period also saw a resurgence of exclusionary policies. In 1933 the Royal Dental Hospital decided to bar women and women in general had to be highly talented and determined to fight their way into medical professions in which they were clearly unwelcome (Bradley, 1989:196).

training and paid work for ladies was combined with a belief in woman's innate abilities to teach and to nurse; special education for either occupation was considered unnecessary. Anna Jameson pointed out that no one suspected that a trained soldier would be less brave than an untrained one, so why distrust the training of woman's instinctive feelings? But the edict against professionalism laid a heavy hand upon all efforts to educate and train girls." (Vicinus, 1985:24).

Nursing

In all seven countries the tasks of nursing and tending the sick had historically been women's work. Women learned techniques of healing, along with all sorts of herbal remedies, unguents, salves, potions and tonics, from older women, and in turn passed them on to their daughters. In England, nursing had from medieval times been an area of independent female employment. London hospitals in the fourteenth and fifteenth centuries employed women as nurses, while other women practiced nursing as casual work, helping sick people in their homes. The eighteenth century saw the slow crushing of female skills and lore in medicine, a process not completed until the nineteenth century (Bradley, 1989:191).

Although women were considered to be natural nurses, they could not before the mid-nineteenth century receive any sort of formal training. In most countries professional nursing was performed by women of doubtful reputation. They were considered prone to intemperance, idleness and theft. In Denmark, Ilia Fibigir (sister of the above-mentioned writer Mathilde Fibiger) caused a sensation when she enrolled as an assistant nurse during the cholera epidemic of 1853. It was considered scandalous that an unmarried woman of good family should undertake the nursing of strangers. Her efforts opened the way for a new type of nurse[14].

"Few women had the determination of Florence Nightingale, whose self-confidence was unassailable once she had broken away. She established her own living quarters and used illness with the same ruthlessness and creativity as her sister and mother to keep all distractions at bay. After her return from the Crimea (1854-1856) she spent the remainder of her life fighting behind the scenes for reforms in military and hospital administration." (Vicinus, 1985:20).

The first nursing organizations in England were all founded upon the principle that women had a natural aptitude for helping the poor. In England in 1840 Elizabeth Fry started the *Institution for Nursing Sisters*[15] and throughout the 1840s and 1850s numerous high-church[16]

---

14 The *Diakonissestifelse* was founded in 1863 to train ladies in nursing, but it was not until 1899 that the *Dansk Sygeplejeråd* (Danish Nurses' Council) was established, offering a systematic theoretical and practical professional training (Dahlsgård, 1980:104).

15 To attempt to raise the status of nursing, Fry's Institute "employed doctors to train 'ladies' as nurses. The essentially domestic duties were now redefined as *scientific* with stress on the medical aspects of hygiene, ventilation, regulation

residential sisterhoods were founded to work with the poor (Vicinus, 1985:11).

In Belgium, Constance Teichmann, active in charity work among the poor, opened a children's hospital in 1846 (only 6-12 cradles). The Teichmann women, especially Constance herself, nursed thousands of sick people during the cholera epidemics of 1848, 1853, 1859 and 1866 (De Weerdt, 1980:26). Many women took up nursing during the Franco-German war, with the first going to the front lines in 1870 (De Weerdt, 1980:26).

In the Netherlands, the first private nursing institute (financed by a charity fund) was founded in 1843 to employ "persons with a certain accurate knowledge of all that relates to the decent care of the sick, and also distinguished by a satisfactory moral and religious education" to nurse in particular the less fortunate in society (Brok-ten Broek, 1968:33). This Amsterdam hospital was founded on a non-denominational basis and was the first to acknowledge the decent character of nursing as a profession.

The German nursing home run by Protestant lay sisters (deaconesses) in Kaiserswerth, founded in 1836, was the first in the world. This example was followed the Netherlands in 1844 in Utrecht and in 1865 in the Hague. In France, religious orders continued to dominate the field, hence this line of work was a far less important form of lay female employment (Tilly and Scott, 1987:161).

After 1870 important improvements in nursing were achieved in all seven countries and nursing was accepted as a decent occupation for women. Developments since then have been remarkably similar in all seven countries.

Teaching

In general, it was uphill work improving the status of single (middle-class) women: young women and their families assumed that they would marry, until at last it was too late to seek skilled training. However, if women wanted or were encouraged to obtain vocational training it was often in teaching, fairly early considered a decent profession for a woman in all seven countries. Again, differences in developments regarding admission to the labor market for female teachers are negligible, although demand varied from one country to another (special girls schools instead of co-education).

In the second half of the nineteenth century, the educational standards of female teachers gradually improved. Compulsory schooling

---

of temperature and so forth." (Bradley, 1989:193). According to the 1851 census, over 39 thousand women working as servants carried out nursing duties and about 25.5 thousand were nurses outside domestic service (plus a handful of men) (Bradley, 1989:192).

16 I.e. belonging to that part of the Anglican church closest to the Roman Catholic church.

increased the number of teaching posts and the demand for female teachers in all seven countries.

In the Netherlands, female teachers have needed a formal qualification (diploma) since 1806 (Vrouwenlexicon, 1989:275). As early as 1827, examinations and training facilities with special government grants were introduced to improve the quality of female teachers (Brok-ten Broek, 1968:27). However, until 1857 the level of their training lagged far behind that of men (Vrouwenlexicon, 1989:275). With the 1878 Elementary Education Act, needlework became compulsory for all girls at primary schools. Schools were therefore obliged to appoint at least one female teacher. The same law established the preferability of appointing women to teach the younger children (the concerning article was lifted in 1981). With the introduction of compulsory schooling in the Netherlands in 1901, teaching opportunities increased, partly because the maximum number of children in a class was reduced to 29. With the 1920 Elementary Education Act the distinction between different types of primary school disappeared: rich or poor, all children had to attend school for seven years (Bakker, 1982:122). However, the status of female teachers deteriorated. A special form of training was introduced for women teaching the younger children[17] and their salaries reduced, while those of the male teachers in the higher classes remained unaffected. The distinction also prevented women from replacing men. Another saving was achieved by the re-introduction of classes of up to 50 pupils, while a law was introduced in 1925 laying down that female teachers should be dismissed on marriage (see next section).

In most countries the introduction of compulsory schooling meant that the female teachers were appointed to teach the younger pupils in the lower classes in co-educational schools. In Sweden, female teachers only gained the right to teach in publicly run schools in 1858 (Qvist, 1978, quoted by Gustafsson, 1984:133). By 1914 in England, the number of women far exceeded that of men in primary school teaching. Women accounted for nearly 75 per cent of all elementary school teachers as compared with about 55 per cent in 1875 (Tilly and Scott, 1987:159). In France the tradition of separate schools for boys and girls meant that there were equal proportions of male to female teachers. In the second half of the nineteenth century, the replacement of nuns by secular teachers and the creation of more schools for girls after the 1882 Act created new opportunities for women. The proliferation of pre-primary schools for very young children, staffed exclusively by women, also increased female employment. (Tilly and Scott, 1987:160).

Both the nursing and teaching professions often trapped single women in a paradox: the price of independence was the reinforcement of sexual stereotyping. Often, after having turned down offers of marriage or

---

17 Except for some catholic schools exclusively for girls (about 12 per cent of all schools in 1930), the majority of schools were co-educational (Bakker, 1982:111).

decided that they had no interest in children, they had to spend the rest of their lives strengthening the nuclear family by teaching and caring for its younger or frailer members (Vicinus, 1985:16). Only at the end of the nineteenth century did training become available for other occupations with a certain standing (training facilities for seamstresses and household servants already existed).

Access to new occupations

Throughout the first decades of the twentieth century there was a growth of jobs not only in the occupations of teaching and nursing, but also in clerical and shop work and organized philanthropy. However, jobs in business and industry were difficult for most women to train for and then to find. Moreover, these jobs were in general accessible only to unmarried women. In the Netherlands, for example, women could be employed in the postal, telegraphic and telephone services from 1900 onward, but were dismissed on marriage (by law from 1904). This practice became normal in the public as well as in the private sector (see subsection 9.3.1: Marriage bars).

From the beginning of the reform of middle-class employment down to the present day, women have clustered in the service occupations, all of which were and largely remain low-paid and overcrowded. This has often been explained to a lack of scientific qualifications among girls but, for example, some university-level courses (notably medicine) in some countries continued to be rationed by quota right up until the time when Sex Discrimination Acts were introduced (in most countries not before the 1970s). "The predominance of women in the second-tier professions is not due to any natural course but is the result of a long-established education policy. In England as elsewhere, marriage and particularly motherhood have been used to control the female workforce..." (Atkins and Hoggett, 1984:15).

Although the choice for (middle-class) women expanded once training opportunities were created for entry to government service or clerical jobs, the most striking feature of the decades between 1880 and 1950 is how firmly the pattern of segregation persisted once established (Bradley, 1989:183). The total number of middle-class women who remained unmarried and in need of work was small in comparison with that of working-class women. Even of the middle-class women, only a minority were able to take advantage of the new educational developments. After the introduction of compulsory schooling, however, there was a gradual expansion of opportunity for all women.

9.1.3 Schooling

Compulsory schooling

Again, developments in all seven countries are fairly similar, despite differences in the dates of the introduction of compulsory schooling and in the ideologies concerning the education of children.

In Denmark, compulsory schooling was instituted as early as 1739, starting at the age of 6 years. In 1814, statutes were promulgated to the effect that elementary schools were to be established in all urban and rural districts (Calvert, 1946:346). Sweden and Belgium were also relatively early: six years of compulsory schooling were introduced in 1842. France[18] had an elementary education act in the same year but it was not until the 1880 School Act (*Lois Scolaires*) that schooling became free and compulsory for all children aged under 13, and free also for all children between the ages of 13 and 18 years; England[19] got a new act in 1870. By 1876, domestic science had become one of the subjects that earned grants for schools; cookery was added in 1882 and laundry in 1890; in 1902 these subjects became compulsory, not only in state elementary schools but also in secondary schools in receipt of grants from the Board of Education (Atkins and Hoggett, 1984:14).

In the Netherlands, the 1801, 1803, 1806, 1857 and 1878 Elementary Education Acts (*Lager Onderwijswetten*), of which the 1857 Act was the first establishing good quality general primary education for all children, were without compulsion. Compulsory schooling was introduced only in 1901[20]. It then started at the age of seven and lasted at least six years. The law did not apply to religious and privately run schools until 1920. However, the total impact of the 1901 law on school attendance was actually slight: before the law, 90 per cent of all children between the ages of 7 and 13 went to school; after the law, 95 per cent. By contrast, the consequences of the 1857 and 1878 acts were fairly spectacular, leading in particular to a shortage of teachers (in 1884 estimated at about 2900 at publicly run schools alone) (Boekholt and de Booy, 1987:160).

---

18 In France, the education clauses in the Child Law of 1874 (see also section 9.2), required children under the age of twelve to attend school for a minimum of two hours per day if classes were held within the factory, whilst children up to the age of fifteen were restricted to six hours of work per day if they could not produce a certificate to prove that they had received elementary primary instruction (Heywood, 1988:265). Tilly and Scott (1987:160) mention the 1882 Ferry Act as the start of compulsory schooling.

19 From 1833, when central government took control of the education of the working classes, through until the 1870s, the emphasis was on fitting girls for domesticity. The Education Act of 1870 extended this control and provided extra money to reward examination successes in this area (Atkins and Hoggett, 1984:14).

20 This was relatively late. It was the fear that children would have to be sent to publicly run schools without the preferred denominational basis that prevented the establishment of compulsory schooling before 1900; for the history of this *schoolstrijd* (school funding controversy) see Boekholt and de Booy (1987:chapter 8). Around 1900 only 30 per cent of all schools were denominational. By the 1980s the situation had been reversed, with only 30 per cent of all schools being publicly run (non-religious) schools. All schools are publicly financed.

For these reasons, the date of introduction of compulsory schooling does not itself contribute much to the explanation of differences in labor force participation between countries. In all seven countries most children under the age of 12 were receiving primary education by around the turn of the century. In the majority of countries compulsory schooling was extended in the 1930s. In the Netherlands, it was extended by one year to a total of seven in 1929. In Denmark[21] in 1937 - a year later than the reforms of the elementary school systems in England, Germany and Sweden - legislation laid down that compulsory schooling should start at the age of 7 and end at 14 (Calvert, 1946:346). In England, the 1936 Education Act raised the school-leaving age to 15, with certain exceptions.

After World War II, compulsory schooling was again extended in all seven countries. The Netherlands, however, reduced it by one year in 1947, but increased it again in 1950 to at least eight years, starting at the age of six or seven, while in 1970 it was extended to nine years and in 1971 to ten years. In 1974, attendance became compulsory up to the age of 16, with the additional obligation to attend school two days a week for the first year thereafter and one day a week for the second year. In 1985, the compulsory age for entry was lowered to five years[22].

Recent developments at pre-primary level, sometimes considered as - partly or at least as closely related - educational, sometimes as child care, are discussed in section 9.4.

Secondary and higher education

Pioneers can again be named in all seven countries. In Belgium, for example, Isabelle Gatti de Gamond (daughter of the above mentioned Zoé) founded the first girls' secondary school in 1864. The foundation for secondary education in Denmark, especially for female teachers, was laid by Pauline Worm (1825-1883) and Nathalie Zahle (1827-1913), while in Germany, it was Hedwig Dohm who early recognized the importance of education and who was one of the founders of the *Deutsches Frauenverein Reform* in 1888, promoting admission to secondary school examinations and universities. In all seven countries, special girls schools were introduced and admission to secondary schools was more or less obtained during the second half of the nineteenth century.

When girls were granted secondary or higher education, however, they could only receive it with the permission (and pecuniary support) of their parents. In most of the seven countries access to means to continue

---

21 However, it was only instruction, not school attendance that was compulsory in Denmark.

22 Younger children can be sent to the Kindergarten (now the nursery classes of primary schools) at the age of four and to 'play-groups' at the age of two or two-and-a-half. Both are voluntary but, in contrast to the situation in around 1950, when only circa 45% of the children went to Kindergarten (then for 4 and 5-year-old children), the figure since 1980 has been nearly 100%.

education independent of the parental income became only (partially) available in the 1980s.

The education of the boys in the family always had higher priority (although most boys also had to earn a living immediately after completing compulsory schooling in order to contribute to the family income). Girls also lagged behind boys in their freedom to choose the education they preferred. In addition they were subjected to moral pressure (more than boys) or even forced to choose an education considered appropriate to their sex (for example, to study pharmacy instead of chemistry, or French instead of mathematics). This pre-market social conditioning remained common practice until at least the end of the 1960s in the Netherlands, and still exists to a lesser extent.

Generally speaking, therefore, the right to choose their own education was granted somewhat later to girls than to boys, particularly at the secondary and higher levels.

Vocational education and training

Despite progress, there remain differences between boys and girls particularly in the area of vocational education and training. These still reflect the main arguments adduced in the mid-nineteenth century discussion concerning the efficiency of early differentiation in the education of boys and girls, on the grounds of the (generally assumed) differences in talent and mature destination of the two sexes[23]. Vocational training still reflects traditional ideas about the natural destiny of girls. Where apprenticeships are available, girls frequently enrol for traditional women's occupations, which often require a shorter period of training. For example, of all pupils in the Netherlands leaving elementary vocational training with a certificate in 1971, 68 per cent of the boys and only 8 per cent of the girls joined apprenticeship schemes; similarly 18 per cent of the boys and only 2 per cent of the girls took up further part-time education. In the United Kingdom in 1970, there were 110 thousand females apprenticed to skilled crafts as against 112 thousand males, and of the girls going into training three-quarters chose hairdressing (Nuss, 1989:4). Clear sex differences regarding vocational training are also noted in Germany (Franz, 1985:S222).

Legislature differences between countries at the level of secondary schooling and vocational training are difficult to identify and compare, but it is obvious that discrepancies between boys and girls at these levels have been similar in all seven countries. Some progress could be observed after World War II, especially in the 1960s and early 1970s. In 1978, OECD Education Ministers declared the equality between the sexes in education and training to be an objective (OECD, 1985:121). In 1988, the European Community launched IRIS: a programme of women's vocational training schemes promoting access to all types and levels of training (EC,

---

[23] For a discussion of the legislation concerning separate higher education since the 1863 Act in the Netherlands, see Boekholt and de Booy (1987: chapter 10).

1991:22). More and more girls and boys are now motivated to make educational and occupational choices based on their own interests without reference to traditional sexual stereotyping.

International comparisons of the conditions of schooling and education are difficult to perform. The OECD has presented a first set of international educational indicators in 1992, showing marked differences in classification (based on the differences in the education legislation). For example, some countries regard courses leading to qualifications in teaching and nursing as university programs, while others do not (OECD, 1992:76). In the Netherlands upper secondary education or tertiary education is often classified as non-university, one of the reasons why the OECD study shows low university enrolment levels in the Netherlands. The same applies to Sweden, where the enrolment ratio[24] for non-university courses is almost three times as high as that for university programs (OECD, 1992:76).

To summarize: despite differences between school systems and educational institutions, the data available do not suggest remarkable differences between the seven countries. The accuracy and validity of the available data and of that presented in this paragraph are such that more rigorous analytical work is needed to draw specific conclusions. The Netherlands was certainly not particularly late with training for nursing, teaching and with entry to certain occupations, or admission to university; in fact, the country was even relatively early (first female professor, first female pastor (see next section), first female medical doctor, etc). School-leaving age (i.e. the end of compulsory schooling) from 1929 until the 1970s, was frequently one year lower than in the other countries (and entrance one year earlier). These findings would lead one to expect a higher rather than a lower labor force participation of women in the Netherlands than in the other countries. However, as was shown in chapter 6, compared with the other six countries figures for child labor were low, while differences in the 15 - 19 age group have not been remarkable.

9.2 Labor laws

Labor laws directly influence the position of women in the labor market and with these even more than with other pieces of legislation the relationship with economic circumstances is evident. Developments in all seven countries accelerated after the introduction of industrialization, which changed the character of labor relations between employers and the employed.

---

[24] Ratio of number of students enrolled at a level of education to the number in the population in a certain age category (see OECD, 1992:68).

Labor law[25] can be seen as the law of dependent labor. The essential subject-matter of labor law is all forms of regulation which seek to order or control the worker's subordination to the employer's authority; an indicator of the development of labor law is the extent to which all classes of 'dependent' workers are brought within its ambit (Hepple, 1986:11). In all seven countries, labor laws began to be passed some time after the process of industrialization had begun (Hepple, 1986:14). But there seems to be no direct link between early industrialization and the first protective measures, as for example the cases of Belgium and the United Kingdom illustrate[26] (see below and the chronological list of selected legislation in the Appendix to chapter 9).

Early legislation in all seven countries was aimed at preventing exploitation of young children in factories, mines and so on. By the end of the nineteenth century, child labor laws had been passed prohibiting employment of 'minors' in all seven countries[27]. The inclusion of women in the protected category was in general the next step in this evolutionary process of protective measures and legislation[28] imposing statutory restrictions upon hours and conditions of employment.

It is a remarkable feature that this legislation was implemented only in those sectors where women and children were working together and in direct competition with men. The fear that women might undercut male wage rates seems to have been the main reason for the devotion of considerable legislative effort to ensuring that women remained at a competitive disadvantage in the labor market (Creighton, 1979:3). The official reason usually given was the need to protect women against the physical[29] and moral[30] effects of industrial employment (this was used,

---

25 Labor law can also be divided into individual and collective labor law. The latter (including such subjects as trade union freedom, institutionalized relations between employers and employees and collective bargaining (Blanpain, 1986:53)) is disregarded here.

26 A problem in attempting to establish this link and to examine time-lags in labor legislation is that industrialization is generally confined to particular regions within and across national boundaries, while labor law is linked to nation states as entire and independent entities.

27 In chronological order: Great Britain, 1802; Germany, 1839; France, 1841; Denmark, 1873; the Netherlands, 1874; Sweden, 1875; Belgium, 1884.

28 Other early legislation, such as that protecting all workers from industrial hazards and abuses in the payment of wages' is disregarded here.

29 According to Lamers, Sloot and Veldt (1989:2), this argument was often used in the Netherlands. Meijers (1968) and Heringa-van Ruth, Pothumus-van der Goot and de Waal (1968) emphasize the moral arguments.

30 As the report and debates related to the Mines and Factory Acts in England show, it was not the gruelling work which outraged Victorian society but the perceived immorality of women engaged in such work (Atkins and Hoggett,

for example, to prohibit women and girls from working underground in the mines).

In Britain, certainly from the 1850s onwards, legislation for women tended to relate to the desire to prevent undercutting and to reinforce (male) perceptions as to the proper role of women (Creighton, 1979:25). In most countries, protests and debates followed early legislation and between the latter part of the nineteenth century (in Britain) and the early part of the twentieth century (in the Netherlands) there emerged a strong undercurrent of opposition to the principle of protective legislation for women[31]. The fact that the effect of such 'protection' was to move women out of well-paid and into poorly paid jobs is hardly ever mentioned.

Whatever the reasons for the legislation, it (almost) completely ignored the category of domestic servants (with their long working hours) or home workers, while protective legislation for agricultural workers was very late in developing. The attention of legislators was concentrated on the factory system. Employment relationships in agriculture were considered to be of secondary importance compared with the contractual model developed in industry, while in domestic service, legislators were reluctant to interfere with the patriarchal authority of the master within his own household (Hepple, 1986:49,47). Another exception in labor law is made for labor in the public sector. In many respects public service in all countries is regulated by a type of law distinct from that operating in the private sector. It is only since the beginning of the twentieth century that the European States have started seriously to consider the problem of public employment by comparison with contracts of employment in the private sector (Hepple, 1986:50).

9.2.1 The beginnings of labor law: protection of children and women, a seven-country comparison

The early child laws in Britain (1802), France (1841) and Germany (1839) are often written off as dead letters. However, the decision to regulate child labor paved the way to the extension of labor legislation.

The earliest protective measures were enacted in Britain: the *Regulation of Chimney Sweepers*, and the *Health and Morals of Apprentices Acts* of 1788 and 1802 respectively. However, it was not until *Althorp's Act* of 1833 that legislation began to be effective in terms of

---

1984:12).

31 The workers' own resistance to the threatened loss of income is seldom mentioned. For example, the female piece-workers of the flax spinning mill Dumonceau went on strike for this reason in 1890, while the comments in the oldest Dutch economics journal *De Economist* suggests that the provisions "may be a blessing to the working people" (see Gustafsson, Bruyn-Hundt and Pott-Buter, 1992:253).

enforcement against defaulting employers and that extended provisions were introduced as to hours of work etc. The main importance of the 1833 Act was, however, that it provided for the appointment of independent salaried factory inspectors (Creighton, 1979:19). This example was later followed in the continental countries. The inspectors' reports caused growing public concern about the effects of industrial labor. In particular, the first *Report of the Committee on the Employment of Women and Children in Mines and Collieries*, published in 1842, outraged public opinion. An Act was passed almost immediately prohibiting the employment of women and girls underground (Creighton, 1979:21). The report also "helped to create a climate of opinion which was receptive to the idea of regulating the labour of women in factories" (Creighton, 1979:21), and so led to the 1843 Bill and the 1844 Act. By 1854, the *Ten Hours Movement*[32] had achieved all its principal aims in relation to women, children and young persons employed in textile factories. The second half of the century saw the extension of this protection to an increasing range of employments, and a parallel increase in emphasis upon the safety aspects of protective legislation as applied to all employees, irrespective of age or sex. (Creighton, 1979:23). By 1878 the evolutionary process of protective legislation was more or less complete and the principles embodied in the Factories and Workshop Act of that year are clearly recognizable as the forerunners of the provisions contained in the Factories Act of 1861, the only significant modifications being concerned with shift work and associated exemption procedures (Creighton, 1979:26).

In France, the 1841 Children's Act regulated rather than abolished child labor and tried to safeguard the production capacity of French industry as much as to protect children against abuse (Heywood, 1988:258). Numerous silk mills (for example in the Ardèche) completely ignored the legal obligations to restrict working hours and allow children to attend school (Heywood, 1988:255). However, despite the fact that the minimum age of entry to workshops was held at eight years, the records show that, particularly during the 1840s, there was some move to eliminate the very young from the labor force and to encourage the primary education of children remaining in the workshops (Heywood, 1988:257). The 1841 Act remained in force for thirty-three years. The 1874 Child labor Act (*Loi sur le travail des enfants et des filles mineures dans l'industrie*) raised the minimum working age from 8 to 12 years, though in a number of specified industries it could still be 10. Children and female minors aged 16 to 21 (*filles mineures*) could not be employed in '*manufactures, fabriques, usines, mines, chantiers et ateliers*'

---

[32] Much of the pressure which led to the passing of the 1833 Act came from the 'Short Time Committees' of the North of England. Their principal aim was the implementation of a ten-hour day. The committees were bitterly disappointed that Althorp's Act did not go further towards meeting their demands (see Creighton, 1979:20,21).

(essentially, factories, mines, quarries and workshops) except under certain conditions, nor could they be employed at night, or on Sundays and public holidays. Adult women were also forbidden to work underground in the mines. To avoid intervening in family businesses, no attempt was made to define precisely what was meant by a factory or workshop (Heywood, 1988:259).

As early as 1818 there was some recognition of the problem of child labor in Prussia, but the first Prussian child law of 1839 was ineffective in forbidding the employment of children under nine in mines and factories and of illiterate children under sixteen (Nardinelli, 1990:127). After Prussia was granted a liberal constitution in 1850, child labor legislation began in earnest in 1853. The law established 12 as the minimum age of employment in industry. Children were limited to six hours' work per day and were required to receive three hours of schooling daily. Other German states followed the Prussian example, but enforcement provisions were weak or non-existent (Nardinelli, 1990:127). The North German Confederation (formed in 1866) introduced a uniform trade law in 1869, including a unified industrial law (Hepple, 1986:18), with essentially the same child labor laws as in Prussia; the legislation was not consistently enforced until after 1878, when mandatory inspection was established by law. Both the law and its enforcement were made more stringent in the Industrial Code of 1891. The minimum age was raised to thirteen, and children over that age could work only if they had received primary education (Nardinelli, 1990:128).

In the 1870s, protective legislation for children was achieved in Denmark (1873), the Netherlands (1874) and Sweden (1875). However, it was only in 1884[33] that the first protective legislation was enacted in Belgium: it was henceforth forbidden for boys under 12 and for girls under 14 to work underground in the mines. By 1884, therefore, child factory labor was prohibited in all seven countries for children under 12 years (in Germany under 13 years). This age limit rose gradually over the first half of the twentieth century to 15 years.

In France industries permitted to employ children under the age of 12 years were specified by 1875, and included all the major branches of textile production, glassmaking and paper milling. Boys of 12-16 years were allowed to work during the night or on Sundays in four industries: paper, sugar refining, glass and metallurgy (Heywood, 1988:265).

In some countries women were included under the protective legislation, as in France in 1874, in Germany in 1876 and in Britain already in 1854. Special legislation for women was introduced in

[33] Other sources (as often) mention other years as the start of labor law in Belgium (see for example Lamers, Sloot and Veldt, 1989:127, who mention 1889; or 1887 the year in which abuses in the payment of wages were controlled (Hepple, 1986:14)).

Belgium[34], Denmark and the Netherlands in 1889 and (again) in Belgium, Denmark and Sweden in 1911. In all these countries, labor at night and on Sundays was forbidden to women[35] and children. Only in Denmark were the protests of women against the loss of their relatively high wages[36] successful: the prohibition on night-time labor for women was lifted again in 1911 (Humanitas[37], 1912). After that, no special protective rules for women were ever again introduced by law in Denmark, but only in collective agreements. Women in most other countries had to wait until the 1980s before the special measures were lifted.

In all seven countries child labor was especially restricted in the textile industry. In 1922 the minimum age for textile workers was 14 years in Belgium, Denmark, Germany, the Netherlands and Sweden, 12 or 13 years in France and 13 or 14 years in Great Britain. Moreover, part-time schooling was obligatory for one or two years thereafter in France, Germany, Great Britain and the Netherlands (Phillips, 1922:32).

It is uncertain how much the laws actually influenced female employment opportunities. In the Netherlands, during the exhaustive discussions in parliament preceding the introduction of the 1889 restrictions for women, factory owners, particularly owners of brick-works, argued that the law would mean the end of their businesses and that the male workers would be worthless without the assistance of their wives and children. Advocates of the law argued that a woman's place was in the home, taking care of the children and her husband. When the law came into force, exceptions were granted for married women working with their husbands in the brick-works and for married women working in the textile, cleaning and food industries (see also van Kessel, Kuperus and Pott-Buter, 1986: 16-18).

In 1899, some 31 thousand married women were counted as working in these 'non-protected' occupations. Of the total of 17 thousand other married women working in industry, only 5.3 thousand fell under the protection of the law. The results of the investigations and the discussions certainly influenced the general opinion expressed by male contemporaries in numerous publications (see van Kessel, Kuperus, Pott-

---

34 This law prohibited night-time labor for women (and children), and restricted working days to 12 hours and the working week to a maximum of 6 days.

35 In the Netherlands it was also forbidden for married women to work on Saturday afternoons. Moreover, the 1889 law prescribed compulsory unpaid maternity leave lasting four weeks.

36 Relatively high wages are also mentioned by an anonymous correspondent from Sweden in 1907: "*in die Gewerbe wo Frauen jetzt bei Nacht arbeiten, kommen relativ hohe Löhne vor*" (in industries where women work at night there are relatively high wages) (Humanitas, 1912:6).

37 This is the only source making special mention of adult women being prohibited from working at night in Denmark; most sources say that there was no special legislation for adult women (e.g. Dahlsgård, 1980).

Buter, 1986). Even more strongly than before, factory work for women and especially married women was condemned, mainly because of the assumed adverse influence on the care of children and the household. The relative decrease in married women working in factories between 1889 and 1899, shown in the census figures, was also noted by the Labor Inspectorate in the factories which they visited between 1890 and 1900 (Schilstra, 1976:113). Whether this decrease was voluntary or imposed by the employers as a result of the labor law is not known.

9.2.2 Restrictions on working hours

By 1922, restrictions on working[38] hours had been introduced in all seven countries for children and women in industry. The maximum working day became eight or nine hours (the latter in Belgium and France) and the maximum working week was (in general) 48 hours (exceptions were the Netherlands with 45 hours between 1919 and 1922 and Germany (from 1918) with 46 hours in occupied territories or for children younger than 16 years and for such children in the occupied territories 36 hours). In some countries, legislation on working hours differed for men (usually longer maximum working hours) and women, while in others there was no distinction.
The principle of a maximum 8-hour working day and a maximum 48-hour working week was introduced in Belgium in 1921. As mentioned above, Denmark had no statutory legal protection for women with regard to maximum working hours (only after 1873 for young persons by an Act renewed in 1975 (Lamers, Sloot and Veldt, 1989:138)). As in Sweden, most regulation took place via Collective Labor Agreements and it still does.

In France, working hours for children under 12 years were limited in the 1874 law to 6 hours per day, broken by a rest period, as opposed to the 8 hours allowed by the 1841 law (Heywood, 1988:264,265). In 1892, maximum hours of work were for the first time prescribed for all categories of workers, with the maximum for adult men set at 12 hours per day. The law enacted in 1919 introduced the 8-hour working day and 48-hour working week and the 1936 law introduced the principle of 40 hours, reduced to 39 hours per week in 1982. In 1987 the restrictions on night-time labor for women and on Sunday working were lifted (Lamers, Sloot and Veldt, 1989:143).

In Germany, the principle of a maximum 8-hour working day for both men and women was introduced in 1918, together with the same protective measures as in the other countries for children, young persons and women.

---

[38] In this section *working* excludes (productive) labor in the home, usually it means *blue collar employment*; sometimes in the rest of this chapter it also includes white collar employment.

In the Netherlands, the 1874 *Children's Law* was extended in 1889. For children aged 12-16 years, the maximum working day became 11 hours, including one hour's rest, working hours were restricted to the period between 5 a.m. and 7 p.m. and Sunday working was banned. The law also prohibited all women, married or not, from working longer than eleven hours a day. In the law of 1911, the minimum age was raised to 13 years and the restrictions extended to the age category 13-17. With the replacement of this law in 1919, these limits became 13-18 years. However, the law covered only 30 per cent of the male and 19 per cent of the female labor force (Lamers, Sloot and Veldt, 1989:8). Special amendments allowed various categories of workers to work longer hours: nursing homes (1928), shops (1929), pharmacies (1932), offices (1937), and others in 1954 and 1958. In principle the 1919 law still stands[39], but the minimum age was raised to 14 years in 1960, to 15 years (for girls only) in 1965, and to 15 years for boys as well in 1970 (Neve and Renooy, 1988).

The rise of large department stores led to increasing employment of women as shop assistants, a very strenuous job, with normal working hours lasting from 8 o'clock in the morning to 9 o'clock at night. Physical complaints caused by excessive standing inspired Aletta Jacobs to place an announcement in the newspapers in 1896 asking the public to boycott shops providing no opportunities to sit down during working hours. This started a public discussion, resulting in 1902 in a law regulating this provision. (The law has never been lifted but was and is to the present day violated everywhere). The example was followed in Britain (Shop Act) in 1899 (demanding the provision of one seat for every three women) (Bradley, 1989:179) and in Belgium in 1906 (De Weerdt, 1980). The long working hours were not reduced until the Labor Law of 1919: a 10-hour working day and 55-hour working week became the maximum for shop assistants (in Great Britain not until 1932). This 1919 Dutch law also introduced an 8-hour working day for men and women in factories and offices, and the principle of a maximum 45-hour working week, 3 hours less than the norm introduced at about the same time in France, Germany and Sweden! The law also extended maternity leave (see subsection 9.2.3). With the deterioration of the economic situation between 1920 - 1923, the working week was again extended by law to 48 hours in 1922.

In the United Kingdom, the hours of women's work were limited for the first time in the 1844 Factory Act to 12 hours per day, and in 1847 to 10 hours per day. Since the end of the 1950s, the trend towards shorter contractual working hours has continued through to the present.

---

39 Exceptions to the ban on paid labor are made for light family labor below the age of 15, and for light labor during school holidays, for artistic, scientific or cultural forms of labor, and for delivering newspapers for no longer than two hours a day (Neve and Renooy, 1988).

France had introduced the standard 40-hour working week as early as 1936 (cut to 39 hours in 1982) but allowed longer working hours for a period during the post-war labor shortage at the end of the 1940s.

In Sweden, the principle of a 45-working week was introduced in 1957, and in the Netherlands in 1959. The principle of a 5-day working week was introduced in the 1960s: in 1961 in the Netherlands, in 1964 in Belgium and in 1970 in Sweden. In Denmark and Great Britain maximum working hours have not been regulated by law, but average maximum working hours do not differ from the other five countries.

At the end of the 1980s a new trend emerged towards more flexibility. Maximum working hours could be longer or shorter during certain periods depending on the economic circumstances, while rules for working overtime, shift work or on Sundays and religious holidays, as well as concerning night-time labor for women were either lifted or relaxed. Only restrictions on child labor remained intact. Working hours over the whole year and over the entire life cycle have on average been drastically reduced, partly because of holidays, paid leave and other days of permitted absence from the labor force and through early retirement schemes (see subsection 9.2.5 and section 9.3). The results are fairly similar in all countries, but only in Denmark and Sweden have the arguments used to shorten working hours and to introduce more flexibility been dominated by social objectives and gender equalizing issues, while elsewhere economic arguments have been more important (Lamers, Sloot and Veldt, 1989:18).

Again it is not certain what influence the laws have had on women's employment. In the Netherlands, according to Anna Polak, the protective measures often resulted in dismissal, decline of employment opportunities and lower wages (Polak, 1921, 1929). On the other hand, the working conditions of the women who were employed in the protected industries improved, partly because of the pioneering work of the female labor inspectors, who stimulated social policies, schooling and improvements in working conditions (Bousardt, 1991:32). However, in all countries, the absolute numbers of women falling under the protective legislation were relatively small. For example, the 1911 Swedish law only applied to 2,407 women (Humanitas, 1912:6). According to Atkins and Hoggett, in Britain, the legal interventions appear not to have affected work opportunities of women, but the restrictions on hours lowered women's pay rates and led to higher rates for men (Atkins and Hoggett, 1984:13). "The more powerful effect of the law was related to its definition of women workers as different, with greater sensibilities. Men, through their organized labour, simply took advantage of these sentiments to counter the threat of undercutting by segregating work on the criterion of physical strength." (Atkins and Hoggett, 1984:14).

In professional life, men proved equally unwilling to admit women into their midst. The justification of physical strength, often used to prevent women from blue collar work, would have been inappropriate to these professions, but the middle-class women pioneers faced a continual scientific battle to disprove theories of comparative differences ranging from concern for women's moral sensibility to their 'scientifically' established intellectual weaknesses (Atkins and Hoggett, 1984:14). For the whole of the nineteenth century women remained excluded from most of the traditional professions either by social convention or, occasionally, by rule of law (see the 1858 Medical Act in Britain). Women were also excluded from both branches of the legal profession (Creighton, 1979:16). Attitudes, norms and arguments have been similar in all seven countries. The barriers came down only gradually, and mainly during the twentieth century.

9.2.3 Maternity protection and absence from work

There are many different reasons for absence from work: some involve workers rights, others refer to absences that are unscheduled and could be avoided. For the latter, the term *absenteeism* is used (OECD, 1991:177), and this - although difficult to distinguish from other absence from work - is disregarded in this subsection.

Labor disputes, bad weather, illness, variable or reduced working hours, temporary lay-offs, official or private training, vacation and holidays, special leave for family reasons and, military service are just some of the possible reasons for absence from work (OECD, 1991:177). There are many labor laws concerned with regulating these forms of absence and with allocating the costs between workers, employers and the government. When making international comparisons[40] such legislation influences the activity rates directly and indirectly, complicating the interpretation of labor force participation rates. This subsection examines only the legislation on two reasons for absence: maternity protection and maternal/parental leave, although it is illness/injury and vacation/holiday that were the two reasons responsible for the highest percentage of total absences in 1983 and 1988 (see OECD, 1991:180, table 6.1).

Maternity protection

An important contributory factor in the development of factory legislation in the nineteenth century was the desire to protect the function of motherhood. In 1919, the International Labour Organization (ILO) adopted the Maternity Protection Convention[41] which provided that for a period of six weeks after confinement no woman should be permitted to work in any industrial or commercial undertaking other than one in which only members of the same family were employed, and that women should be entitled to pregnancy leave for the whole six weeks before confinement, on production of a suitable medical certificate (ILO, 1991:7). During any

---

40 At the fourteenth International Conference on Labour Statistics in 1987, the ILO proposed a statistical framework for identifying absence from work (see OECD, 1991:178-181 for a discussion on the conceptual and measurement issues).

41 ILO Convention No. 3, 1919.

such period of absence the female employee was to be paid benefits sufficient for the full and healthy maintenance of herself and her child, and was to be entitled to free attendance by a doctor or certified midwife, the costs of which were to be provided out of public funds or by means of a system of insurance (ILO, 1991:7).

The report prepared for the 1919 ILO meeting makes it clear that a period of exclusion from work after childbirth (usually four weeks) already existed in most industrial countries, but maternity benefits (or maternity indemnity) not.

In Denmark, a woman could return at any time within the usual four weeks absence on production of a medical certificate (League of Nations, 1919:9). Some of the the existing laws fixing four weeks or a month as the limit were of old standing. Maternity protection had started in Germany in 1878, with three weeks leave after confinement and had been increased to four (or six without medical certificate) in 1891. The Belgian and Dutch[42] laws dated from 1889, and the British from 1891 (and this standard remained unaltered in the 1901 Factory Act). In 1908 Germany increased the period of 4 weeks to 8 and in 1912 Sweden introduced a new law prescribing six weeks in general, but allowing for earlier return (League of Nations, 1919:9). In France and Sweden the woman had the right to leave work without giving the usual notice when in an advanced state of pregnancy and in France the woman's place had to be kept open for her (League of Nations, 1919:10).

Time had to be allowed for nursing mothers to feed their infants during working hours in Denmark (1913), France (1913), Sweden and the Netherlands (since 1919[43]), and in Denmark and France a special room had to be provided for this in workplaces employing more than 25 and 100 women respectively.

To cover the period of exclusion from work due to childbirth, Danish women without means of support could receive public relief and French women without means could receive a special maternity allowance.

In Great Britain a maternity grant was paid to the wife, on the basis of the husband's insurance, and under an amending Act of 1913 a second maternity grant replaced the weekly sickness benefit for the four weeks following confinement. In the Netherlands under the Sickness Act of 1935 80 per cent of the wages had to be paid for the whole period before and after confinement, this was changed to full wages in 1940. However, every married Dutch woman, entering any occupation coming

---

42 In the summer of 1904 an extensive survey was conducted to monitor observance of this rule (e.g. among midwives). There was not one factory where working mothers were found. Married women, if they had not been fired on marriage, were dismissed once pregnancy became visible. Mothers were not supposed to work in factories and indeed they did not.

43 In the 1919 Act, maternity leave was extended to 8 weeks and the mother was given the right to breast feed the child at work. This right was, however, hardly ever used until the 1980s (Van Amstel, 1986).

under the Maternity Act had to be provided with a labor card by the local authorities (a "control" and legal requirement which was lifted only in 1971), who were under an obligation to keep a record of the cards issued. Each confinement had to be recorded on this card and signed by the authority (League of Nations, 1919:14). I have found no evidence that these restrictions on married women's freedom also existed in the other countries. (For other Dutch bans on married women's employment, see subsection 9.3.1).

Another feature distinguishing the Netherlands from the other six countries is its refusal to ratify the 1919 ILO Convention on the grounds that the provisions also applied to unmarried mothers. In all the drafts of the Sickness Act (e.g. the 1928 one), the proposed provisions on paid maternity leave were explicitly applicable only to married women. When the Sickness Act was finally introduced in 1930, however, there was no such provision at all. It was not until 1935 that paid maternity leave was introduced and then indeed only for married women, while in 1940 it was extended for unmarried women as well.

The ILO Maternity Protection Convention was revised in 1952 to provide an entitlement to at least twelve weeks leave. The Convention also proscribes dismissal on the grounds of pregnancy. It was not until 1975, however, that the United Kingdom took the first tentative steps towards up-dating its inadequate legislative provision in this area. Prior to this, the only significant development (since the four-week prohibition had been imposed in 1891) was the introduction of maternity grants and maternity allowances under the National Insurance Act of 1946, with 90 per cent pay during the first six weeks. Since 1975 a maternity allowance has been payable for up to eighteen weeks (90 per cent pay during 12 weeks), usually eleven before confinement and seven after, during which time the mother is actually away from work (Creighton, 1979:39). Statutory Maternity Pay (SMP) can be paid since June 1987 for up to 18 weeks (with payments depending on the length of tenure and average weekly earnings)[44]. Pregnant women not eligible for SMP can be paid a flat rate Maternity Allowance for 18 weeks, starting 11 weeks before the baby is due.

In Belgium, maternity leave was extended in 1971 to 14 weeks (six before and eight after confinement), changed in 1981 to the same period to be taken at will before or after confinement. In 1991 the pre-delivery period is 1 up to 7 weeks, the post-delivery period 8 to 14 and the total 15 weeks (Dumon, 1993:75). Maternity indemnity is phazed and higher in the first part of the period.

In Denmark in 1983 maternity leave was extended to 14 weeks and in 1988 to 28 weeks (4 weeks before and 24 after delivery). Compensation

---

[44] According to Dumon (1993:76) no statutary obligatory maternity leave yet exists in the United Kingdom, selective rules are applied, varying from up to 11 weeks before delivery until 29 weeks after delivery, with workers entitled to 90 per cent of wages for 6 weeks and 44.5 pounds per week for the next 12 weeks.

is about 90 per cent of average wage. The father is also entitled to benefits up to 2 weeks after the baby is born or has come home (Soren, 1990:45). In 1991 these regulations were becoming more flexible to the effect that the father is entitled to utilize his leave of 2 weeks any time he wants during the first 14 weeks after child birth (Dumon, 1993:76).

In France, maternity leave was already extended in 1945 to 14 weeks and in 1977 to 16 weeks (six before, ten after), on 90 per cent of previous pay or full compensation is applied.

In Germany the 14-week period (six before, eight after) was introduced in 1979, with full compensation.

Sweden has maintained leave at two months since 1939, one before one after (on 90 per cent pay), but has extended the maternal (since 1974 parental) leave period several times (see below).

The Netherlands was, in March 1990, the last country of all seven to extend the twelve-week period. Dutch women are now allowed to work until four weeks before the expected date of birth and to remain on leave until ten weeks after the confinement, maintaining 100 per cent of previous salary. Moreover, the law no longer applies only to employed women but also to women who are self-employed and to assisting family workers if they are insured under the Sickness Act. Maternity benefits for non-salaried such as self-employed also exist in Belgium, Denmark, Germany and the United Kingdom.

In October 1992, European Community Directive prescribing minimum maternity leave of 14 weeks on pay at least equal to sickness benefits was accepted after two years of negotiations. Of the six countries in this study belonging to the European Community, this guideline will affect only Great Britain as far as pay is concerned.

In all seven countries (see time table: figure 9.1) regulation was established and then extended within relatively short periods. The first legislation was introduced about 1889-1891, revised (except UK) or first introduced about 1908-1912 or 1918-1919. Paid maternity leave was everywhere introduced shortly before or after World War II and the leave was again revised and extended between 1971-1983, with the only exception being Dutch legislation in 1990.

Maternal/parental leave

Just recently there has been a move in all seven countries, led by Sweden in 1974 to follow the maternity leave by a period of parental leave, a policy measure encouraging the involvement of the father and reducing the unequal treatment and unequal position of mothers compared with fathers. As with maternity leave two dimensions can be distinguished: the availability of the provision and whether or not any indemnity exists. Four countries provide some form of compensation: Belgium, Denmark, Germany and Sweden. The right of the worker to re-enter the labor market is usually more guaranteed in the public than in the private sector.

In Belgium, all public servants of either sex can remain at home since 1981 for a period of three months during the first year after the birth of a child without loss of contract and in addition up to a maximum of four years (until the child is five years old) unpaid, with loss of contract but the right to return. Part-time work is an option for a period of up to 12 months after the birth. Many collective agreements in the private sector include paternal leave schemes allowing up to two years unpaid leave but with no certain right to return. Since 1990 the period granted is in principle 6 months (paid) up to 5 years (unpaid).

Denmark introduced five months parental leave on 50 per cent of the earnings in 1983[45]. According to Soren (1990:45) after the 14 weeks maternity leave after the birth of the baby, both parents can share a 10 week parental leave, while proposals are made to give the father a total of 13 weeks not to be tranferred to the mother.

France introduced unpaid parental leave for a maximum period of two years in 1977, with the parent receiving a benefit (in 1988, 2400 French Francs a month) in the case of a third child (Schunter-Kleemann, 1990:37). Since 1991 a maximum period of 33 months exists (unpaid) (Dumon, 1993:83).

Germany established a paid (maximum 750 DM per month) maternal leave of four months in 1979. This was extended to 10 months in 1986, 12 months in 1988, 15 in 1989 and 18 months in 1990. The 1990 amount of 600 DM per month is means-tested after the seventh month following the birth of the child. For children born after January 1992 the total period of parental leave has been extended from 2 to 3 years. In addition for children born after January 1993 the parental benefit period will be increased from the current 18 months to two years (means-tested after the first six months) (Wingen, 1993:7). Sometimes Federal States provide local parental benefit in the child's third year, for example in Baden-Württemberg (Wingen, 1993:7).

In Sweden, the total period of maternal absence was extended to six months in 1945 and this period was converted into leave with a cash benefit in 1962. As already mentioned Sweden was in 1974 the first country in the world to introduce parental leave for both parents. In 1978 it was extended to 9 months. In 1980 another 13 weeks of benefits became available, up to 12 months and in 1989 to 15 months. Those without previous earnings receive only a small payment (only 8 per cent of all mothers in 1985). In 1979 parents who worked full-time received the possibility of working part-time up to the time that the child is 8 years old. The design of the system encourages women to be employed full-time (prefarably with a high wage) before having a baby. Part-time workers are eligible for the benefits of the parental leave when working 16 hours a week, while to be eligible for a partial pension at age 60 at least 22 hours a week are obliged (Sundström, 1991:180). A woman who gives birth to another child within 30 months will receive parental benefits at least as high as that received during the previous parental leave, even if she is on

---

45 According to Schunter-Kleemann (1990:34), parental leave in 1988 was 10 weeks which the mother and the father can share. Only about 2 per cent of the fathers actually did so (Soren, 1990:45).

unpaid leave or works fewer hours than before the previous birth (Sundström, 1991:185).

The Netherlands achieved parental leave in 1990, and then only in the public sector. For a period of six months both parents are allowed to work part-time (minimum 20 hours a week) on 75 per cent of full-time earnings.

Periods of leave for child care reasons also have consequences at the other end of the age spectrum. Pensions are often based on contributions, and there is growing acceptance for the view that not only pregnancy but also further child-care-related periods should be considered as contributory periods (ILO, 1987:45).

In France, for example, mothers (not yet fathers) are now granted a two-year insurance period if they have stayed at home to rear a child (under the age of 16) for at least nine years and any insured man or woman who has reared at least three children is granted a 10 per cent pension supplement (ILO, 1987:45). Germany followed with pension grants in 1992, while in Denmark and Sweden women retain their pension rights during their period of absence.

9.2.4 Gender equality

Gradually, principles of gender equality have been implemented in national and international agreements and legislation in all seven countries. In contrast to the developments concerning entry to the labor market or protective measures, however, in this case the historical development in the seven countries differs. Before describing national developments, this section offers some remarks about international developments.

International Organizations

The United Nations and (since 1946) its specialized agencies like the ILO and UNESCO have played a major role in the creation of a legal framework to oppose gender discrimination. The ILO (since 1919) takes initiatives and enforces important treaties in the field of labor, issued as Conventions and Recommendations[46], while UNESCO promotes gender equality in the area of education. The ILO Conventions are the motor behind most of the European and national legislation, especially the three important Conventions: Nos 100, 111 and 156. After ratification, a country is committed to follow the *standard-setting* regulation (Bakels, 1987:286) and the government is required to submit an annual report on its implementation in law and in practice. However, there are no

[46] On 1 September 1991, 156 Conventions had received the number of ratifications to bring them into force, and a total of 5,546 ratifications had been registered, out of a total of 172 Conventions and 179 Recommendations adopted by the ILO Conference between 1919 and 1991 (see ILO, 1992:V, this volume contains the texts of 158 Conventions and 120 Recommendations).

possibilities of sanction, although complaints can be deposited at the ILO and (if the Committee of Experts finds it necessary) observations published in the annual report. The influence of the Conventions and Recommendations are difficult to estimate and probably less important in developed than in less developed countries (Bakels, 1987:286). In addition, there exists in the international literature disagreement with its direct action (Wentholt, 1990:43).

ILO Convention No 100 (1951), relating to equal renumeration for work of equal value, has been ratified by more than 100 countries. ILO Convention No 111 (1958) on discrimination in employment and occupation is further extended by ILO Convention No 156 (1981) on equal opportunities for workers with family responsibilities.

At the European level, instruments have been added, such as the European Declaration of Human Rights (4-5-1950) and the Social Charter[47] (18-10-1961) of the *Council of Europe,* an organisation established in 1949 by 20 member European countries, including all seven in this study (Bakels, 1987:288). So it took eleven years after the treaty containing the civil and political rights before the charter containing economic and social rights was ready and available for signature (Betten and Jaspers, 1987:viii).

In addition, the terms of reference of the ad hoc Committee for Equality between Women and Men (CREG) - now, since 1 January 1992, a Steering Committee for Equality between Women and Men (CDEG) - have been gradually reoriented. The Committee's initial function was to create a general awareness of this question in all the bodies of the Council of Europe, but its approach is now targeted at political questions such as equal participation by women and men in the institutional processes and machinery (ENWS/REEF, 1992, newsletter, nr.6:7).

The European Community (EC) was founded under the Treaty of Rome in 1957. This was signed by six members - Belgium, France, Germany, Italy, Luxembourg and the Netherlands - and came into operation January 1958. Denmark, Ireland and the United Kingdom joined in 1973, Greece in 1981 and Spain and Portugal in 1986. The EC has developed a fairly elaborate structure for dealing with Equal Opportunities Policy through Directives, Resolutions and Action programs. The Directives cannot be directly implemented, but form the legal framework for national policies.

Article 119 of the Treaty of Rome has been the cornerstone for equal opportunities legislation. Without exception, all EC Directives are based on this article (ENWS/REEF, 1992, newsletter, nr.6:3). The purpose of Article 119 of the EC Treaty, in introducing the principle of equal pay for men and women was to prevent the use of cheap female labor from

---

[47] For a treatment of the Social Charter see Betten and Jaspers (eds), 1987.

disturbing the markets (Blanpain, 1991:112[48]). It was to have been put into practice in all the original Member States of the EC by 1 January 1962. Delays in its implementation[49] led to the first *Directive 75/117* of the European Commission[50] relating to the principle of equal pay for work of equal value and adopted by the Council on 10 February 1975 (Banks, 1991:63). In Denmark and the United Kingdom (and Ireland) the date on which Article 119 came into force was that of the Accession Treaty: 1 January 1973.

Equal treatment in relation to such matters as conditions of access to jobs, promotion and vocational training and conditions governing dismissal is ensured by the second *Directive 76/207* (Banks, 1991:69). This Council Directive allows Member States to conduct *positive action* programs, and requires them "to abolish all forms of discrimination both in their national legislation and in their administrative practices and to establish the necessary legislative machinery to ensure observance of the principal of equal treatment in collective agreements and individual contracts of employment" (Banks, 1991:70). The third directive was the *Social Security Directive (EC 78/7)*, which covered statutory social security schemes relating to sickness, workplace health and safety, and unemployment. The directive required that there be no discrimination against women in terms of contributions or benefits. (Addison and Siebert, 1991:602,603). In 1986 two more directives followed. "The directives have had a discernible impact on Member States, all of which were forced to introduce enabling legislation. The United Kingdom, for example was forced in 1983 to amend its Equal Pay Act (1970) to comply with the

---

48 Blanpain quotes as the other purpose of Article 119 the implementation of ILO Convention No. 100 in the European Community.

49 Article 119 defines what is meant by *pay* and *equal pay*, but not what is meant by *equal work*; this was remedied by the first Directive (EC, 1991:36).

50 The **Commission** has three principal functions: first, it initiates and proposes Community legislation; second, it acts as the executive organ of the Community; and, third it has the power to bring legal actions against a Member State via the European Court of Justice. The Commission consists of 17 members, two from each of the five largest countries and one from each of the other seven. The Commission is functionally subordinate only to the **European Council of Ministers**, the supreme decision-making body of the Community. Council decisions are made on the basis of 'qualified majority' voting (defined as 54 votes out of the maximum 76: France, Germany, Italy and the United Kingdom have 10 votes each; Spain has 8; Belgium, Greece, the Netherlands and Portugal have 5 each; Denmark and Ireland 3 each, and Luxembourg has 2 votes. Council regulations are binding in their entirety on all Member States, while Council directives are binding as to the results to be achieved by each Member State, but leave the choice of methods to the national authorities. The **European Council** brings together Heads of State. It offers guidance to the Council of Ministers, but does not posses formal decision-making powers. The **European Parliament** has no legislative power, but only the authority to provide an opinion on Commission proposals. (Addison and Siebert, 1991:598,599,600).

comparable worth doctrine, and in 1986 to amend its Sex Discrimination Act (1975) when this was ajudged to be in violation of the Equal Treatment Directive." (Addison and Siebert, 1991:602). Five Directives have got through, four more are on the way (see Appendix to chapter 9).

The legislation based on the first directive was achieved in France in 1972 (amended in 1975), in Belgium in 1975, in Denmark in 1976, and in the Netherlands in 1975. The second directive was implemented in Belgian and Danish legislation in 1978, in Germany in 1980, in France and the UK in 1983 and in the Netherlands in 1984 (although partly in 1980).

The European Community has also endorsed a Social Charter, a declaration of social - primarily workers' - rights (in December 1989). The proposals constitute the most extensive array of Community legislation yet envisaged (Addison and Siebert, 1991:597). "The articles of the Charter covered, among other things, employment and remuneration, improvement of living conditions, freedom of association and collective bargaining, information, consultation and participation rights, gender equality, health and safety at the workplace, and vocational training." (Addison and Siebert, 1991:597). An Action Program describes the measures to be pursued by the Commission in implementing the Social Charter. However, the "Action Program is not binding and each of its proposals will have to run the gauntlet of Council." (Addison and Siebert, 1991:597).

National legislation in the seven countries

The Scandinavian countries were the pace-setters in Europe in terms of implementing gender equality, although they did so mainly via Collective Agreements while legislation was realized only in the 1960s and 1970s. In Denmark by the turn of the century the tobacco workers' federation[51] was the first to achieve equal pay for men and women doing the same work (Dahlsgård, 1980:94). As early as 1919, a law was proposed providing for equal access to jobs and appointments, except in the armed forces (relaxed since 1971), but when the Act was passed in 1921 the Church was also added as an exception (ending when the first female pastor was appointed in 1946)[52]. The Act also stated that it was illegal

[51] Although there was no place for women in the first unions, and the cigar-makers' trade union had in 1871 even explicitly excluded women - "Any cigar-maker who teaches a woman to roll bunches or cigars, except his wife, may not be a member" (Dahlsgård, 1980:92) - by the end of the century strikes had changed the attitudes of the cigar-makers in this respect.

[52] In the Netherlands the first female pastor was appointed as early as 1911 in the Baptist Church. The Remonstrant Church followed in 1915, the Lutheran in 1926 and the Dutch Reformed Church directly after World War II. Sweden appointed the first female Lutheran pastor in 1939. It was not, however, until 1992 that the Church of England finally accepted the principle of access by women to the priesthood after years of debate (with the Catholic Church in Rome reacting negatively, since it - like Orthodox Jewish and Eastern churches

to dismiss women or refuse them employment on the grounds of their being married or having children. There was a fierce debate on the question of whether the principle of non-discrimination in the law applied to married women as well, a relevant question especially during the periods of high unemployment in the 1920s and 1930s, but a high court judgement of 1942 confirmed that it did (Dahlsgård, 1980:142).

The Public Employees Act of 1919 went further in introducing equal pay for women and unmarried men, but also introduced into legislation the concept of the breadwinner, causing a great deal of trouble (Dahlsgård, 1980:147). A cost-of-living supplement had to be paid to breadwinners[53], defined as all married men, widowers, widows, separated or divorced men and women with households on their own or with breadwinner obligations towards children under 18 years of age (Dahlsgård, 1980:148). This concept of the breadwinner provoked intense dissatisfaction among both public employees and the women's organizations, especially when the turn of economic events caused the cost-of-living supplement to form an increasingly large proportion of the total salary. In 1946, and again in 1954, the Public Employees Act was amended and extended to include specified categories of married women. Equal Pay was introduced in the Public Employees Act of 1958 and the 1976 Equal Pay Act (Dahlsgård, 1980:148, 149).

In Sweden, the principle of equal pay for equal work was accepted in 1937 in the public sector and enshrined in legislation in 1947. In 1960 the employers' organizations and the labor unions decided to abolish all special female wage rates within a period of five years and to introduce equal pay for work of equal value, while in 1962 ILO Convention No 100 was ratified. In 1972 an Advisory Council to the Prime Minister on Equality between Men and Women was instituted and active policies were adopted to improve the situation of women in the labor market (Gustafsson, 1984:144). Equal treatment in the public sector was introduced in 1976, equal pay legislation with regard to market work was implemented in 1980 and Equal Employment and Opportunity were introduced in 1983-1984 by collective bargaining.

In Great Britain, many married women had entered employment for the first time during World War I or had returned to the labor market even if they had young families at home (Creighton, 1979:4). Between 1914 and 1918, an absolute increase was recorded of over one million new female recruits or re-entrants to the labor market. Relaxations in statutory restrictions and craft rules were introduced, but repealed in 1919. The Sex Disqualification (Removal) Act (SDRA) of 1919 provided that no one should be disqualified by virtue of sex or marriage from holding any

---

- still excludes women). In each case the arguments against accepting women have been nearly identical, with the same Bible texts being used in all the various Christian churches.

[53] In the Netherlands this concept still dominates the social security system, although since 1985 it has been sex-neutrally defined.

public office, from entering any profession or from graduating from any university. Despite this wording, the operation of a marriage bar did not contravene the Act's provisions and the marriage bar operated in most public service jobs[54] until World War II (Atkins and Hoggett, 1984:17).

According to Creighton (1979:4) the 1919 Act marked a missed opportunity to effect the long-term re-structuring of the labor market, but the unions were extremely worried at the threat that the weakening of traditional craft rules seemed to pose to the job security of their male members. The effect on women's employment is not certain. After the war, many women returned (probably not unwillingly) to the ranks of the economically inactive, but the total female labor force increased because many women had no other choice than to remain in the labor market as war widows, women with disabled husbands or other male relatives to support, divorced women and single women whose prospects of marriage were diminished by the war. Contractual disadvantages on married women, which may have prevented them from functioning as solicitors[55], were removed in 1935 by the Law Reform (Married Women and Tortfeasors) Act.

World War II again provided the opportunity for women to prove that they could perform work that had formerly been regarded as unsuited to their sex. Statutory restrictions on over-time and shift-working were relaxed and as in the 1914 - 1918 period there was a marked increase in the size of the female labor force. The National Service Act of 1941, which conscripted to the services or to essential war work all single women aged 19-30, did not apply to married women or to mothers with children under the age of 14 living with them. But the Registration for Employment Order of 1941 required all women aged between 18.5 and 49 years to register for work, and all but mothers of young children had to go to Employment Exchanges for direction to appropriate war work (Atkins and Hoggett, 1984:19). Once again, pre-war restrictions were restored after the end of the war. Occupational structures and earnings patterns remained essentially unaltered. "Nevertheless change was in the air. The marriage bar in the public service was removed in 1946, ... (and) the demand for equal pay in the public sector was becoming increasingly strident." (Creighton, 1979:5).

In the Netherlands, as in the United Kingdom, the years after World War II were notable - in contrast to the pre-war years - for the lack of parliamentary concern about women at work. Apart from the question of Equal Pay in the Civil Service and one non-parliamentary report on

---

54 It was lifted only where demand for qualified staff exceeded supply, as in the case of London County Council in 1935, where it was lifted for teachers and medical staff only, while in some industries marriage bars were introduced as a response to recession (Atkins and Hoggett, 1984:17).

55 In 1912 Miss Bebb wanted to become a qualified solicitor after a distinguished career as a student at Oxford but unmarried women were first given the right to practice by the SDRA of 1919.

women in teaching, women workers did not figure as a topic in British public debate until 1968. There was no real debate on the position of married women workers until the Expenditure Committee remarked in 1972 that lack of child care facilities had reduced employment opportunities for mothers. The Government's response stressed the need for mothers to stay at home with their children. The acceptance of the equal pay principle was not accompanied by any acceptance of working mothers or part-time workers. (Atkins and Hoggett, 1984:20).

"The fear that women workers might undercut men and restrict men's opportunities is mentioned in nearly every government report from 1914-1944. The response of Governments has been to placate male workers rather than to treat women fairly. ... It has been suggested that the introduction of equal pay into the Civil Service from 1955 to 1963 owed more to the competition of higher wages for white-collar staff in the private sector than to concern for female workers." (Atkins and Hoggett, 1984:20). And the Equal Pay Act 1970 shows all the hallmarks of the trade union concern for pay protection for men. The principle of equal pay for work of equal value was limited to jobs which had been evaluated as equal by the employers, leaving the initiative for introducing job-evaluation firmly in their hands (Atkins and Hoggett, 1984:21).

The history of gender equality in Great Britain does show some similarities with that in the Scandinavian countries so far as the sequence of the events is concerned. However, the timing differed. Special legislation for public servants and of course the specific relaxations of British statutory restrictions during the two World Wars do not apply to the other countries.

Although the first equal treatment policy had already been adopted by the Belgian *Arbeiderspartij* (Labor Party) in 1894, Belgium had to wait until the 1960s and the implementation of European Community Directives before gender eguality legislation came into force. ILO Conventions Nos. 100 and 111 were ratified in 1952 and 1977 respectively (Van Vleuten, 1986:75). Important improvements concerning gender equality were achieved in 1964, 1968, 1975 and 1978. The Royal Decree of 1987 promoted equal opportunities for men and women in the private sector, while in 1989 it was decided that a portion of the fund for the unemployed could be used for affirmative actions. These actions became compulsory in the public sector in 1990.

France enshrined the principle of equal pay for equal work in legislation in 1950, further implemented it in the 1972 Act on Equal Renumeration for Men and Women and established a Council of Occupational Equality in 1983. An Act on Professional Equality between Women and Men was passed in the same year.

In Germany, the 1948 Constitutions of the Federal States implemented high-sounding principles of equal pay for equal work, but without giving them legal consequences. Treaties and agreements before the 1980 Act implementing the EC Directives were quite varied and inadequate (Pfarr and Eitel, 1984:157,159). In 1986 a Directive was implemented on the professional promotion of women in government services (OECD, 1990:167).

The Netherlands, however, could not be convinced of the principle of equal pay for equal work before the 1970s and it was not until 1971 that it finally (as the last of the seven countries) ratified ILO Convention No 100, nearly 20 years later than - for example - Belgium (Wentholt, 1990:30). The implementation of the minimum wage in 1969 (in 1966 only introduced for men) was the first law incorporating the principle for equal wages for men and women. After World War II, wages were strictly controled and established by unions and employers. Female wages were on average set at about 60 per cent of the male wages. Boys wages increased from 30 per cent at the age of 14 to 100 per cent at the age of 23. Trained persons received 20 per cent more than untrained, and wages were different in different communities (divided into 5 categories in 1945). The basic standard was that the wage of a married blue-collar worker, with two children under 16 years of age had to be sufficient for a certain standard of living (Ney, 1983:152), while the guidelines of 1947 (again) confirmed that the needs of women were lower than those of men, justifying lower wages for women than for men. Mid 1960 this controlled wage system became under increasing pressure, but it was not until 1975 that the first Equal Pay Act was introduced.

The appointment of the *Emancipatiekommissie* (Emancipation Committee) in 1974 brought increased official interest in the position of women. The 1975 Equal Pay Act was followed in 1976 and 1980 by two acts prescribing equal opportunities at work in the public and private sector. The acts have recently been combined (1989) and the Equal Opportunities Commission, the body in charge of enforcement, strengthened. In addition, attempts have from 1978 been made to remove all unjustified sex differences in the Dutch legislation.

To summarize this section: differences between countries as regards private labor law are disappearing and there has been increasing convergence in the 1980s, partly due to international conventions and directives. The Netherlands was relative late to implement gender equality, while Denmark and Sweden were relatively early.

9.3 Departure from the labor market and disincentives to paid work

9.3.1 Marriage bars

In the Netherlands up until the 1970s, female employment meant the employment of girls and non-married women. Married women were not supposed to be employed and any desire or need to perform paid work was discouraged or treated with contempt. Between 1904 and 1924, there were ten legislative proposals attempting to forbid all employment to married women in the public service and in factories (Kessel, Kuperus, Pott-Buter, 1986). The 1904 Royal Decree was the first to be passed: women employed in the postal and telegraph services had to be dismissed (with honor) on marriage (a provision officially scrapped again in 1907 but in practice applied until the 1970s). In 1909, another Royal Decree prescribed that female teachers were to be dismissed on marriage (except when over the age of 45). The 1910 proposal to dismiss all female public servants on marriage was withdrawn, although in practice commonly applied, but finally in 1924 accepted. Under this 1924 Act it became possible to dismiss female civil servants in central government on marriage, and this was applied in 1925 under the same order to local government.

In the 1930s measures were intensified: all women were excluded from higher functions in the public sector and restrictions were even placed on paid activities performed by married women in the home, with the activities allowed being carefully defined. Moreover, employers had to register wages of married women in special books etc. In the mid-1930s, with the economic situation getting worse, married women could be found in public sector employment only if they were *breadwinners* and in the private sector only in occupations such as artists. In 1935, legislation was proposed to forbid all girls under the age of 16 from working in factories, workplaces and offices. Such proposals were usually withdrawn because of the protests of employers who did not want to lose their cheap labor, particularly in view of the fact that female wages had been reduced in the 1930s. For example, in 1932, wages in the Amsterdam laundries (jobs not performed by men) were reduced by 10 per cent.

In 1936 a law was passed to dismiss (on the first of January 1937) the last 98 married women teachers still in public service (in the whole country!). A proposal in 1936 that only a small percentage of females should be employed in certain factories and workshop was withdrawn, after initial acceptance, by the *Hoge Raad* (Supreme Court). At the same time, measures were introduced to encourage and even force girls to work as domestic servants (on pain of reduction of the father's already low unemployment benefits), domestic service being the only sector with a shortage of labor. It is notable that in the most notorious Dutch proposal in 1937, the one to forbid all employment to married women, the only sector excluded was domestic service[56].

After World War II, in the Netherlands as elsewhere, the growth of the service and public sectors in particular increased the demand for female workers. However, the supply of girls was declining due to extended education and earlier marriage. Because of this excess demand, the school-leaving age was lowered by one year. Moreover, the Ministry of

---

56 However, even in this sector few married women were counted by the 1930 census: 5,284 out of the total of 234 thousand women employed in it.

Home Affairs decided (in January 1946) that teachers and civil servants who got married could stay at work as long as vacancies could not be filled by single women or men. Contracts given to married women were always to be temporary[57] and could be terminated at two months' notice. They were not in any case to run longer than until January 1950. According to Heringa-van Ruth, Posthumus-van der Goot and de Waal (1968:270), the Netherlands was in 1948 one of only four European countries (other three not identified) where married women did not have the right to choose for themselves whether or not to participate in the labor market. The obligation on married women to have a registration card (*arbeidskaart*), was (officially) lifted in October 1971 (Blok, 1978:100).

In 1955 an amendment was accepted by a majority of only one vote calling for a reassessment of the bans on employment for married women. However, even 11 years later in 1966, measures to reduce disincentives for mothers to participate in the labor market were not recommended "*gezien de huidige opvattingen omtrent de goede vervulling van de taak van de vrouw in het gezin*" (in view of current ideas concerning the proper fulfillment of the wife's role in the family) (SER advisory report 1966). After 1957, obligatory dismissal on marriage was abandoned with regard to women in tenured posts in government service, although dismissal was still allowed if women were thought to be 'redundant' and were not breadwinners. Gradually local government followed. In the private sector it had also been customary to dismiss women on marriage or pregnancy. This ground for dismissal (with the exception of married women with disabled husbands) was even explicitly confirmed in the 1953 Guidelines for the Government Employment Exchanges (*Arbeidsbureaus*) (Blok, 1978:130), but was officially abolished in 1976. The breadwinner criterion was lifted only in 1979, when EC directives had to be implemented (Wentholt, 1990:31).

To the best of my knowledge, no such strict bans on the labor of married women existed elsewhere for such a long time. Until 1900 female teachers in France were forbidden by law to be married, while French telephone operators at that time had to be single and between the ages of eighteen and twenty-five. No such formal prohibition existed in England, but in practice local authorities prevented teachers who married from continuing to teach. This practice was outlawed in 1944 (Tilly and Scott, 1987:184). In general the ban on married women in public employment in Great Britain was lifted in 1946.

The measures taken in Nazi Germany were also strict. In 1933, the National Socialists started a campaign to strengthen the ideology of the "true destiny of women" and the family. Measures were taken to

---

[57] "The employment of married female staff should be most strictly limited. Departures from the principle that it is in the general interest that the place of married women is primarily in the home can only be deemed justified where there are urgent reasons from the point of view of the needs of the service." (Governmental Explanatory Memorandum, 1947, quoted in Van Kessel, Kuperus and Pott-Buter, 1986).

discourage female employment: only work in their own households, in agricultural activities or in domestic services was consonant with women's natural destiny (Jurczik, 1977:61). "*Im übrigen soll jede Berufstätigkeit den Mannen überlassen bleiben". .... "Die ideale Familie ist die bauerliche. Dort .... herrscht eine "natürliche" Autorität des Mannes. .... Kinder zeugen und gebären ist ein nationale Pflicht.*" (Otherwise every occupational activity should be left to the men. .... The ideal family is that of the farmer. There ... male authority is natural .... nursing and delivering children is a national duty) (Weber-Kellermann, 1974:181, see also Jurczik, 1977:52). Married women were dismissed and labor contracts withheld from unmarried mothers (as being bad examples). The measures were successful in discouraging women from entering or remaining in the labor market. However, after the beginning of the expansion of the Third Reich in 1937 the special female ideology was no longer convenient and policies changed. All women able to do so had then to enter the labor market.

9.3.2 Early retirement and pension systems

All seven European countries have achieved a high standard of provision and show considerable similarity with regard to the overall objectives of pension policies in terms of population covered (ILO, 1987:53). Countries differ mainly in the choice of means, institutional pattern etc. Schemes date back to the end of the last century or the beginning of the present one, but changes and new departures occurred mainly after World War II.

The standard pensionable age has remained unchanged at 65 years of age for a very long period (ILO, 1987:55). In 1986, this was still the normal pensionable age for men, except in Denmark and France (with 67 and 60 years respectively). These two countries had in that year the same high and low age limit for women, while Belgium and the United Kingdom in 1986 had a female retirement age limit five years below that of men (ILO, 1987:58).

General provisions to make retirement flexible were in force in Belgium, Denmark, Germany and Sweden. In 1972 France introduced a provision for all those aged 60-64 who left the labor force voluntarily. Between 1976 and 1983 a series of measures enabled all French wage and salary earners, and most of the self-employed, to retire at the age of 60 on full pension, subject to contribution conditions (OECD, 1992:213).

The actual age of retirement is much lower in all seven countries, since special (particularly social security) provisions have become available to many groups of workers, notably the disabled, the unemployed etc[58]. Generally, "(p)olicy differences can clearly explain

[58] For the number of beneficiaries of selected early retirement schemes in the period 1970 - 1990, and a review of the main early retirement programs from the late 1970s onward in selected countries, including all seven considered in

some of the rise in retirement, and account for the diversity in international experiences." (OECD, 1992:218). There has, moreover been an interaction between public and private incentives. Firms have followed changes in public schemes and have restructured their occupational schemes to complement the public ones (OECD, 1992:222).

In the Netherlands and to a certain extent in Sweden, disability systems have been used to reduce the size of the workforce of older workers, especially unskilled and redundant workers. Collective bargaining agreements have also stimulated early withdrawal in these two countries. However, the low degree of disability entitling Dutch workers to relatively generous benefits lasting until the age of 65 is a feature specific to the Netherlands. In 1990 nearly 900 thousand persons - 600 thousand men and 300 thousand women - (338 thousand of them aged between 55 and 65 years) received a disability pension (*AAW/WAO*), compared with a total of 4.2 million men and 2.7 million women in the labor force (SVr, 1992:64). This contributed to the very low participation rates of the Dutch men and women over the age of 55 years (see also OECD, 1992:222-228).

9.3.3 Disincentives in Social Security and Taxes

In the countries other than Denmark and Sweden there was no general consensus in favor of encouraging the participation of married women in the labor force. For this reason no systematic consideration was given there to (dis)incentives in social security and tax systems until very recently, and no explicit measures were taken to remove the existing barriers. Financial barriers to the employment of married women may reflect cultural preferences as regards the behavior of married women as housewives and persons principally responsible for the care of children. Disincentives may be created by the unit of taxation or levy of social security premiums, the unit eligible for social security benefits or tax allowances, the income considered (labor or non-labor income), the progression etc.

Detailed consideration of the position of women in social security and tax laws in all seven countries lies beyond the scope of this work. Disincentives to labor force participation of married women created by joint taxation of the married couple are probably the easiest to compare, but complicated by modifications as tax deductions. Very complicated are disincentives created by social security systems. In broad terms, it can be said that the social security systems in the Netherlands and the United Kingdom have traditionally been based upon the premise that the family is the primary social unit, and that the woman's place is in the home. Therefore, in the Netherlands more than in the other six countries, the right of equal treatment in social security issues and the right to economic

---

this study, see OECD, Employment Outlook, 1992: tables 5.14 and 5.15.

independence seem to have been dominating issues of the women's movement in the 1970s and 1980s.

The Dutch social security system is heavily segmented and fragmented, largely based on insurance contributions paid by employers and employees, with a tripartite decision-making structure (representatives of employers' organizations, employees/unions and government). It is considered one of the most extensive in the world and contains many disincentives to labor force participation of women, particularly those with partners receiving social security benefits (and in general for men or women receiving benefits, because many of these benefits are means-tested). In 1992, the disincentives are still especially obvious at low income levels, because breadwinner supplements at the minimum level of benefits are substantial, producing a high marginal tariff (near or above 100 per cent) where the wife of a man receiving social security benefits wants to enter the labor market. The extremely low labor force participation rates of women married to men receiving minimum social benefits illustrate the poverty trap.

To the best of my knowledge, international comparisons in this field do not exist to any extent, although tables comparing the Social Security systems in its Member States are published by the EC. In Denmark, Sweden and Germany, the emphasis in the social security system has always been on stimulating or maintaining the labor market position. In the Netherlands, (family) income protection was (until very recently) given a higher priority than participation in the labor market (even by men). The differences in attitudes and ideologies not only influence the patchwork of social security regulations but are also discernible in the development of the systems of family and child allowances in the seven countries (see below).

Tax systems

A preferable tax system from the point of view of equality between male and female in labor force participation would encourage spouses to divide market work and household work equally between them. In principle two tax systems can be distinguished on the basis of the tax unit: a joint tax system with the household as tax unit or an individual system with the individual as tax unit. A purely individualized income tax system can only be applied if each person is free to dispose of her/his own earnings (for legal competence see next section). In none of the countries did married women enjoy full legal competence at the time when income taxes were introduced. Therefore, all countries started with a joint tax system for married couples.

The after-tax income is $Y_{at} = (1\text{-}t_j)\ (w_h h_h + w_w h_w)$, where t_j is the joint tax rate and $w_h h_h$ and $w_w h_w$ the earnings of husband and wife respectively (and assuming no tax deductions or other taxable income exists).

In an individual system the after-tax income of husband or wife is $Y_{ati} = (1\text{-}t_i)\ wh_i$, where i = husband or wife and t_i the individual tax rate.

With a proportional tax rate there is no difference between tax systems, whatever the income of husband or wife. With increasing marginal tax rates the outcome is only equal where husband and wife have the same earnings and $t_j = t_i$.

The advantage of the purely joint system is that no difference exists in the taxation of the money no matter who earn it (although in practice only the husband was liable for tax); allocation of certain earnings (or deductions) to one or other of the partners to avoid taxation is not possible. The married couple is assumed to be the consuming as well as the tax unit. In reality, husband and wife need not have the same access to the after-tax income or be able to decide how to spend it. Purely joint taxation is generally seen as an unfair system because a family with a particular income is taxed the same as an individual with the same taxable income. There are other disadvantages. One is the disincentive on entering the labor market. For that reason the system was hardly ever applied to children, only to married couples. If a housewife enters the labor market her income will be taxed at the marginal rate on the couple's joint income. To improve the net household income by increasing market hours, the wife's hours have to compete with the husband's overtime hours. If his (overtime) wage rate is higher than her (part-time) rate, the husband's overtime hours will pay more and the wife will be discouraged from performing market work, while her husband will be encouraged to work overtime. Also, if there are increasing marginal tax rates and joint taxation of income, the tax liability can only be assessed at the end of the year, usually creating large additions to the taxes withheld from wages during the year. These retrospective tax corrections usually show very clearly that the additional income earned by the wife is very low.

A splitting system is a joint system dividing the combined income of a household by all its members before taxation. It is usually applied to married couples only, in which case it is unfavorable to single persons (when they are taxed at the same tax rates) and favorable to high income earners with a non-earning partner. Applied in its purest form to a household consisting of two partners, the joint income of husband and wife is divided into two equal parts, each partner being taxed on half the total household income: $t_s\ (w_h h_h + w_w h_w)/2$. It is obvious that this system is favorable to households where partners have unequal wage rates and there are rising marginal tax rates and extremely favorable in the case of a husband with a high income and a non-earning wife.

In reality none of the systems described above actually exist, since specific exceptions or tax deductions are allowed under all systems. These specific rules complicate an international comparison, even at the level of division into one of the three tax systems as regards disincentives for married women. Separate tax rates for married and single persons, tax deductions for partners and/or children, subsidies dependent on taxable income etc. can also create incentives or disincentives for married women to participate in the labor market. Moreover, the general level of taxation is important because it influences the value of the (non-taxed) housewife's time. The development of the Dutch tax system illustrates this point.

A general income tax system was introduced by law in the Netherlands in 1892, and revised in 1914 (introducing a tax deduction for children, which was abolished in 1980). The joint tax system for husband and wife, with the husband being liable for tax, used the same tax rates for married men and unmarried persons. (Usually different wages were paid to married and unmarried men). In 1929 a lump sum was added to the taxable income of unmarried persons, depending on the municipality in which this person lived (NLG 100, 200 or 300). In 1941 the German occupation introduced the German tax system, a joint system with strong splitting elements, dividing taxable persons into three categories. Married couples were relatively better off than before, while single persons were taxed more heavily. Tax deductions for children existed, while child benefits (introduced for the first time in 1939) were taxed, a feature particularly characterizing the complicated tax system existing since 1947. In 1962 a tax deduction was introduced for assisting wives and employed (part-time) working women. The number of assisting wives registered, particularly among farmers, increased enormously in the next few years. The tax deduction for women in employment was increased in 1964, from a maximum of NGL 500 to 2000. In 1970, 1971 and 1972 these deductions were increased further. The German system was replaced in 1973 by the Swedish system (introduced there in 1971, see below). This in principle individualized system was introduced mainly because it was difficult in the joint system with progressive rates to apply a simple pre-tax on wages or salaries and couples often had to pay relatively large tax bills (sometimes years) afterwards. In the Netherlands it was certainly not the intention to stimulate labor force participation of married women (Snijders-Borst, 1983, Nota: Op weg[59]), in contrast to the position in Sweden where this was the main reason for introducing a similar system in 1971 (Gustafsson, 1992:63). To prevent stimulation of participation by married women, different basic deductions were introduced for husband and wife (and different ones for unmarried persons above or below the age of 35 years). So, the tax system discriminated not only by marital status and sex but also (in the case of unmarried persons) by age[60]. This system existed until 1984.

The following example illustrates the different treatment of husband and wife (and of unmarrried persons on either side of the age barrier). Suppose husband, wife and single persons have the same taxable income of NLG 40,000 DFL in 1982 (the structure did not change between 1973 and 1984). The basic tax deduction in that year for a

---

59 Although it was admitted that the existing system was not consonant with developments, that the dependence of the net income of the wife on her husband widely fluctuated and that the tax deductions were arbitrary.

60 Pleas, particularly by Hieke Snijders-Borst (1985), to introduce a system with equal tax credits (comparable with the system introduced in 1973 in Austria) were received with ridicule and scorn, but were in fact in 1993 suggested by the Minister of Finance as a possible future alternative.

married man was NLG 12,078; for a married woman it was NLG 2,421 and for a single person aged over 35 years NLG 9,423 and below that age NLG 7,010. The same tax rate structure was applied to each of these persons resulting, in an after-tax income of NLG 32,843 for the married man (marginal tarif 32.75 per cent, excluding social security premiums); NLG 29,028 for the married woman and NLG 30,863 or NLG 31,829 for the younger or older single person respectively (all three at the marginal rate of 40.75 per cent). In the same year a husband and wife each having a taxable annual income of NLG 20,000 had an after-tax income of NLG 18,654 for the husband (marginal rate 17 per cent) and NLG 16,153 for the wife (marginal rate 32.75 per cent), while a husband earning 80,000 had a marginal rate of 59.75 per cent in that year. (The same basic deductions can be used to illustrate that a married couple, where the husband earned less than his wife paid more taxes than a couple in the mirror-image situation). Had pure individualization been applied in the same year, married couples together would have been paying much more tax, particularly married couples with one single earner (Odink and Pott-Buter, 1982:292). To the majority of married wives (working part-time and earning less than their husbands) the direct effect of the 1973 change was slightly beneficial, in contrast to the substantial tax relief it represented for unmarried persons. Applying the old tax system to the 1975 earnings of married couples shows that differences are slightly in favor of dual-earner couples but that their earnings would have been drastically reduced if a purely individualized system had been applied (because married men earned much more than married women).

In 1984 and 1985 new tax systems were introduced, the sex discrimination and discrimination by marital status was abolished, but a dependency between husband and wife introduced which had never existed before. Dual-income couples were on average taxed higher. As a result, some married women working part-time reduced their market hours even further. In 1990 tax deductions for dependent partners changed and integration of general social security premiums and taxes was realized, while for labor and labor-related incomes the tax system for partners with earnings exceeding the basic tax threshold remained individualized. Progression was somewhat decreased; the top rate was reduced from 72 per cent to 60 per cent for the highest incomes, while average taxes did not change much, partly also because about 80 per cent of all tax payers are in the lowest 35 per cent bracket (not including the social security premiums for employees and wage earners). The basic allowance in 1991 was NLG 4,660. The single parent supplement was NLG 3,728.

In all seven countries taxation of married couples' earnings has changed several times since income tax systems were first introduced. Income tax systems usually started as joint systems with moderate progressive tax rates. The disappearance of simple joint tax systems and their gradual replacement by splitting or individualized tax systems reflects the fact that the husband is often no longer the main or single earner of labor income in the family. Moreover, tax systems increasingly try not to discriminate between married and non-married couples or between single and cohabiting people. High marginal tax rates for married women and low rates for single women, stimulate cohabitation and discourage marriage, while splitting systems work in opposite direction. In individualized systems tax allowances often have been granted for income dependent partners, while specific allocation schemes for tax deductions (mortgages, gifts, life insurance and health premiums) can be designed in the same way as for non-labor income such as interests and rents.

The Belgium system is in principle a joint tax system, although increasingly mixed with complex splitting and individualized elements. In 1988 and 1989 options were introduced for choice between a more or less individualized or a splitting system (with a ceiling at 270 thousand BEF and 288 thousand BEF in 1991) (Dumon, 1993:46). Before that time, tax allowances and deductions for earning a labor income were quite substantial.

In Denmark there is separate taxation of both labor income and wealth. Local taxes and tax deductions usually employ linear rates. The general income tax allowance can be transferred to the spouse. In 1991 the basic allowance for wage and salary earners is 3 per cent of gross wages and salaries up to a maximum of DKK 3,700. Each person is granted a personal allowance, which is converted to a wastable tax credit by the marginal tax rate in the first bracket of the income tax schedule. For a person between 18 and 67 years the tax credit in 1991 amounts to DKK 6,776 for general government income tax and DKK 7,182 for local government income tax and church tax.

The French tax system which has existed since 1945 is quite unique. It is a splitting system applied to the whole family, whereby the division factor is related to a family quotient (children counting for ½, adults for 1, disabled people for ½, etc.). There are rules to prevent over-compensation (Dumon, 1993:45).

The German system has for a long time resembled a splitting system, although the division factor was lower than 2 (about 1.8) before the introduction of the real splitting of spouses' incomes in 1958. This has remained controversial ever since, arguments against it being particularly that it ignores the number of children and rewards higher male incomes if the wife is not employed. In 1977 single-parent families were allowed a compensation (Höhn, 1990:82), while in 1986, 1988 and 1990 tax reforms were implemented broadening the tax base and decreasing progression. The option to be taxed individually (as a single person) is now available, but splitting is nearly always more favorable to couples. In 1991 a tax allowance of DM 3,024 per child was granted.

In the United Kingdom joint taxation existed in principle, with the option of subtracting the tax exemption of a single person in the case of labor earning of the wife, or being taxed indepedently for these earnings, the latter option being profitable in the case of relatively high earnings by the wife. In 1990/91 an individualized tax system was implemented. As in Denmark and the Netherlands, the general income tax allowance can be transferred to the spouse, but the United Kingdom is the only country were this is combined with a fixed tax allowance for having a spouse; in 1991 the basic allowance was GBP 3,295 and the married couples allowance GBP 1,720.

Income taxation was introduced in Sweden in 1902. As early as 1904 during the first parliament preceedings on the subject, it was argued that joint taxation was disruptive to marriage and encouraged 'sinful liaisons' by women participating in the labor market, and mention was made of the retrospective corrections which had to be made in the tax paid by dual-earner married couples (Gustafsson, 1992:63). However, only a deduction (*förvärvsavdraget*) was introduced for participating married women. In 1952 this was replaced by a system with separate scales for married and single people, which meant that the splitting system was applied to 90 per cent of couples (Gustafsson, 1992:63). The medium-term economic forecasts of 1959 and 1965 stating continuing shortages of labor led to the 1971 tax reform, as already mentioned above, an individualized system with a housewife's deduction for single earner families, the nominal value of which, however, was never increased in successive years (Gustafsson and Bruyn-Hundt, 1991:37). The marginal tax rate for a woman working half-time with a full-time employed husband, both with average blue-collar wages, fell from 55 per cent to 32.5 per cent between 1970 and 1971. Throughout the 1970s marginal tax rates rose steeply for full-time workers, but were reduced in 1982 (Sundström, 1991:180). In 1990 tax deductions were introduced for single parents, while the main purpose of the 1991 tax reform was to reduce marginal tax rates. The system is now individualized for all sources of income. In 1991 the basic allowance was SKR 12,500.

Income tax is a potential tool for subsidizing families (Gustafsson, 1991). Tax deductions for children existed in the income tax systems of all seven countries at some time during the twentieth century. Germany in 1933 was exceptional: families with five or more children were given complete tax exemption. Gradually child allowances (see also below) have been introduced, either means-tested (as, for example, in Denmark from 1971 to 1986) or as an addition to taxable income (as, for example, in the Netherlands from 1941 to 1980). Nowadays non-means-tested child allowances have been substituted for the general tax deductions for children everywhere except in Belgium and Germany (and via the *quotient familial* to a certain extent in France). No tax relief exists for dependent children in Denmark, the Netherlands, Sweden and the United Kingdom, with the exception that in the Netherlands as well as in Sweden the higher tax exemption for lone-parents can be considered as an additional tax relief for having children. Sometimes (additional) tax deductions exist for child care or for handicapped children (for example in Belgium and France).

Tax incentives for women in Germany, the Netherlands and Sweden have been analyzed by Gustafsson and Bruyn-Hundt, 1991. Wives in Dutch dual-earner couples contribute 30.2 per cent to family income before tax. In the 1988 Dutch tax system this was reduced to 27.4 per cent after tax and in the 1990 system to 29.5 per cent. Under the 1984 Swedish tax system the 30.2 per cent before tax would increase to 34.4 per cent after tax, but under the 1984 German tax system it would reduced to 25.9 per cent after tax. "Obviously other factors not explicitly treated in this analysis of the tax systems also contribute to explaining female labor force participation." (Gustafsson and Bruyn-Hundt, 1991:53). According to an OECD study (1990:167), tax influences on women working part-time are estimated to cause cross-country differences of up to 20 percentage points on overall rates of female labor force participation. These outcomes may not be fully accurate but they certainly are consistent with the idea that taxation *structure* has an effect. The results do not support the idea that high (marginal) tax *rates* reduce labor supply (OECD, 1990:169).

9.4 Suffrage, marriage laws, child care and family policies

9.4.1 Suffrage[61]

The 'natural' division of labor which had to some extent existed for centuries, with women in charge of domestic affairs and men earning the money, started to come under increasing criticism in the nineteenth century. It is a remarkable fact that the subordination of women was actually being more firmly embedded within the constitutional framework of the new liberal states at exactly the same period.

The continental countries, unlike Britain, had written constitutions (Hepple, 1986:17). Belgium's constitution of 1831 was the most liberal in Europe at that time. Sweden followed in 1839. The Dutch constitution dates from 1848, as does the French and that of the German Piedmont-Savoy, and the Danish from 1849. All these liberal states confined the right to vote to men with property, tax and/or educational qualifications. In Belgium, universal male suffrage was achieved in 1893 with plural voting for men with special qualifications. War widows were granted the right to vote in 1920. Female suffrage for local government elections followed in 1921, but universal female suffrage only in 1948. In France, universal male suffrage was granted in 1871. Local franchise for women was achieved in 1932, but universal female franchise only in 1944. In Britain, the Reform Act of 1867 extended the franchise to working men in the towns (doubling the electorate to about 2 million) and the 1884 Act to agricultural workers (increasing the electorate to 5 million). Nearly a quarter of the male population remained without the vote until 1918, when the principle of female suffrage was also accepted (although with restrictions on grounds of age and marital status). Universal female

61 Sources: mainly Hepple, 1986; for other sources see Appendix to chapter 9.

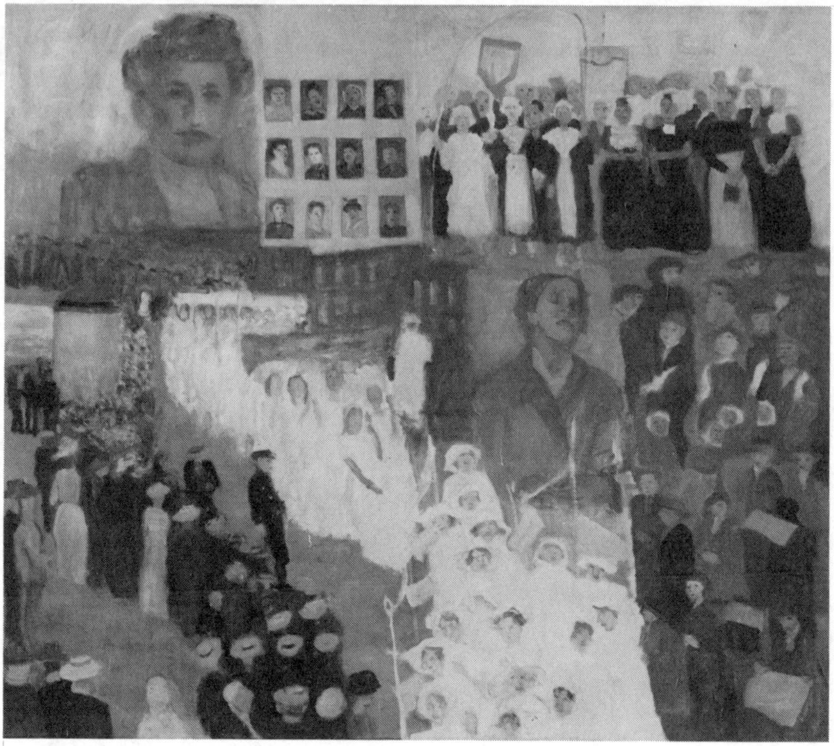

Clara de Jong (1928 - present)
Aletta Jacobs and her era. The struggle for suffrage, 1981
Amsterdams Historisch Museum

suffrage on equal terms was granted in 1928.

In the Netherlands, the reforms of 1887 and 1897 increased the (male) electorate from 2 to 14 per cent. Universal suffrage for men was implemented in the Constitution of 1917 and suffrage for women in 1919. In Denmark, the first bill for local suffrage had been put forward as early as 1886, but it took many years and many attempts before local electoral reform was implemented for men and women in 1908. General franchise was granted in 1915 and the first parliamentary election in which women could vote was in 1918. In Germany and Sweden, female franchise was given in 1919 and 1918 respectively. German female suffrage was abolished again in 1933, because: "*Die Deutschc Frau braucht sich in den wirklich guten Zeiten des deutschen Lebens nicht zu emanzipieren*" (German wives do not need emancipation in genuinely good periods in German life) (Hitler, 1933 quoted by Jurczik, 1977:62).
To summarize, in five out of the seven countries, women could vote for parliament immediately after World War I; German married women lost the vote again in 1933 and regained it at about the same time as it was being granted in the two remaining countries, Belgium and France, at the end of or shortly after World War II.

9.4.2 Marriage laws and legal competence

In some countries, unmarried women and widows were treated in many respects as the same as men in private law: they could enter into contracts of service, sue for wages due or for other breach of contract etc. The notable exception was related to succession in cases of intestacy (Creighton, 1979:15).

Except in Great Britain and Sweden, Napoleon had reversed the more liberal legal provisions of the previous era. His Civil Code of 1806, implemented in all the other five countries, placed severe restrictions on women and gave married women the status of minors in all civil and legal matters. Moreover, in France the liberal divorce legislation of 1792 (divorce by mutual consent) was suspended. After the defeat of Napoleon the new liberal Constitutions did nothing to change the position of women.

Married women in all countries "were subject to a series of incapabilities and disabilities which by the start of the nineteenth century had reduced them to a status little better than that of chattels to their husbands. To all intents and purposes they could not own or acquire property in their own right, and in the law of torts and of contract they were treated as mere appendages to their husbands. These disabilities gave rise to some doubts as to their capacity even to enter binding contracts of service without the consent of their husbands, and as to whether or not they had any rights to the fruits of their labour independently of their husbands." (Creighton, 1979:15).

All women, married or otherwise, were severely disadvantaged in relation to public law. In most countries it took some considerable time before married women won the right to dispose of their own incomes (around 1900[62]) and usually even longer before married women could sign labor contracts. In Belgium and the Netherlands the first right was limited to deposits drawn from a certain bank and was accompanied by a clause admonishing women to use the money for household necessities only. In Sweden, in the 1920 marriage act, women were granted legal rights to sign labor contracts and to dispose of their own labor earnings. Danish married women were the first to acquire full legal competence, in 1922. British and Swedish married women received the right in 1935 and 1939 respectively, while German, Dutch, Belgian and French married women achieved it in 1953, 1957, 1958 and 1965 respectively.

In Denmark, the draft Majority Act, giving unmarried women the right to control their own affairs, came before Parliament in 1857[63] (Dahlsgård, 1980:85). Moreover the Trade Act in the same year laid down that: "The making of millinery and of garments for persons of the female sex and for male children under ten years of age, the sewing of linen goods, bonnets, neckbands and the like, shall be regarded as trades open to women." (Dahlsgård, 1980:86).

9.4.3 The right to prevent motherhood

The subject of the right to prevent motherhood by means of contraception aroused passionate controversy in all seven countries, with strong resistance of a moral and religious character. In all seven countries, abortion had become a criminal offence by the end of the nineteenth century. Propaganda in favor of birth control was suppressed and in the early twentieth century legislation was introduced to prohibit the sale of contraceptives and the dissemination of knowledge concerning methods and means to prevent maternity.

The decline in the fertility rates in the 1930s gave rise in several countries to debates regarding the future development of society and of the population. In Sweden the issues involved were analyzed in a book called *The Population Crisis* by Alva and Gunnar Myrdal (1934). They suggested that the family needed to be strengthened to provide a framework in which both children and adults would be able to thrive.

---

62 British married women were the first, gaining in 1870 the right to dispose of their own earnings and in 1882 the right to sign labor contracts.

63 Which Hans Christian Andersen called the extraordinary year, because it saw so many changes: the abolition of the guild system, the introduction of freedom of trade etc. On the same day as the king signed the Majority Act, he also signed two other statutes of importance to women. The first made inheritance equally applicable to men and women and the second, the Trade Act, gave widows, deserted, separated and divorced wives and unmarried women over 25 years of age the right to carry on a business on the same terms as men (Dahlsgård, 1980:86). Widows could continue the business of their deceased husbands, but lost this right if they remarried.

Economic equality between families with and without children ought to be established through tax legislation, family allowances, the availability of child care, assistance for single mothers, promotion of sex education and similar measures. The Myrdals' ideas strongly influenced the ensuing legislative proposals for family policy not only in Sweden (Gustafsson, 1984) but also in Denmark (Dahlsgård, 1980:187,188).

Other countries, like Belgium, France, Germany and the Netherlands (although declining fertility was not a Dutch problem, see chapter 7), tightened up the rules for divorce, banned married women from the labor force or prevented women from studying. Moreover, all five countries - and particularly the first three - adopted policies of granting tax deductions and child allowances to large families.

The development in Sweden (followed by Denmark) in the 1930s was in remarkable contrast to that in the other five countries. In Sweden Alva Myrdal and other feminists managed to change the question of the right of married women to market work into the question of the right of women to participate in the labor market and to have a family and the debate shifted to how to subsidize families with children (Gustafsson, 1991).

9.4.4 Child Care, Child Allowances and Family Policies

In France, Germany and Sweden, family policies were strongly influenced by the demographic decline after World War I (see chapter 7). Despite the variations in attitudes and ideologies, the overall trends are fairly similar, with only the timing and argumentation differing.

Family policies can be defined[64] as the creation of conditions to facilitate the decision to opt for family life, children and home activities, as compared with other decisions. This encompasses assistance to young families, protection of the unborn, suitable housing and health programs etc. All seven countries have, explicitly or implicitly, a range of policies that affect families, particularly families with children. There seem to be four types of motivation: population policy (declining birth rates are seen as a threat to the nation); protection of (poor) children; concern to enable families to make choices, and the harnessing of family policy to goals concerned with sex roles and the labor market (ILO, 1987:31).

Historically, the different countries have each emphasized one or more of the objectives set out above. This section below offers a few remarks on child care, child allowances and some general aspects of family policy in the seven countries (for extensive discussion see reports of the Childcare Network and European Observatory of National Family Policies both of the Commission of the European Communities and

---

[64] This corresponds to the definition by the German government (see Höhn, 1990:80). The definition by the ILO (1987:30) is "practical measures which affect the family unit".

OECD, 1990). Other policies such as housing policies, policies concerned with low pay etc. are also of great importance to families but to consider all these areas would be to digress.

Child Care

In some countries child care services are an integral part of family policy. Child care services have many different facets depending on the age of the child, the function performed (educational, child minding), coverage (a few hours a week, every day), the type of organization (public or private) and the price. Each country has its own history and own range of types of child care services, and each country has a patchwork of services, with many different names, catering to the differing needs of children under a certain age (usually about 6 or 12 years). To discuss them all would be beyond the scope of this study. Suffice is to say that in all seven countries the supply of registered and publicly financed child care services for children of pre-school age has increased over the last three decades, while charity and religious-based child care services which were prevalent at the beginning of the twentieth century have disappeared.

In Belgium the government began in 1842 to grant funds for children aged 3 to 5 whose mothers performed market work outside the home, and after 1880 nursery schools were created and subsidized. As in the case of France, therefore, there is a long tradition of child care. In 1910 social and educational elements were introduced and in 1919 the National Committee for Child Welfare (*Nationaal Comiteit voor Kinderwelzijn NKW*) was established (Van Dongen, 1993:231). Since 1960 there was a strong increase in all kinds of child care. In 1988 budget cuts caused a drop in subsidies but fiscal deduction was introduced. This caused a shift from private to statecontrolled child minders (the child is being cared for in the child minder's home) and a decline in available places in day-care centres (from 8000 places in 1980, to 7800 places in 1989 and up again to 8000 places in 1991). The number of children aged from 3 months to 3 years in child care increased from 43 per cent in 1983 to 54 per cent in 1991, while the proportion of child care provided by grandparents declined from 54 to 48 per cent over the same period (Van Dongen, 1993:233). Together with France, Belgium stands out as a country with very high enrolment levels for very young children - 2 or 3 years - at pre-primary schools (OECD, 1990:129). The official child care sector in Belgium now falls into two main parts: the subsidized services and those services which are not subsidized but are under the control of the government. The subsidized sector consists of crèches and services for child minders. There are also private child minders and private centres. Family members and especially grandparents provide more than half of the regular care in Flanders (Sels and Dumon, 1990:11).

In Denmark municipality day-care centres (nurseries for children under 2 years and nursery schools for children aged 3 to 6) multiplied fivefold in the 1970s and 1980s and by 1990 for 55 per cent of all children places were available (Soren, 1990:43). According to Smith (1990), publicly provided child care was available for 6 per cent of all children in 1958 and 60 per cent in 1988. Charges vary greatly from one community to the next. In 1991 there were still waiting lists, so incentives were provided for the provision of private child care, particularly by companies (Dumon, 1993:88). Families with children where both parents or the single parent is employed face special problems if the child is ill. In Denmark many collective labor agreements allow the parent to stay at home on the first day of the child's sickness (a provision usually restricted to children under 12 years and to employees with at least one year's tenure) (Soren, 1990:46).

In France nursery schools were made part of the primary education system as early as 1881. By 1990 about 95 per cent of the children aged 3 to 5 were attending pre-primary schooling and 40 per cent of the 2-year-olds (Childcare network, 1990:19). In the 1970s and 1980s several institutional reforms were introduced to change the financing and organization of the existing systems of child care. Certified child minders supplement day-care centres, the latter covering 24 per cent of all children under 2 years of age (OECD, 1990:133). However, day-care by family members is the most popular type of care for young children.

The large degree of decentralization in Germany is also apparent in its child care facilities. They are often run by the churches and other non-profit agencies (Höhn, 1990:79). The number of registered child care places is limited (9 per cent of young children with parents involved in market work in 1986). The predominant form of publicly funded provision for children aged 3 to 6 is *Kindergarten*, in 1987 attended by 68 per cent of children in this age group (Childcare Network, 1990:15).

In the Netherlands religious charity nurseries existed as early as the seventeenth century. The nurseries existing since 1827 for very poor children - mainly financed by (religious) charity funds and supplemented by government subsidies since 1910 - gradually disappeared in the twentieth century.

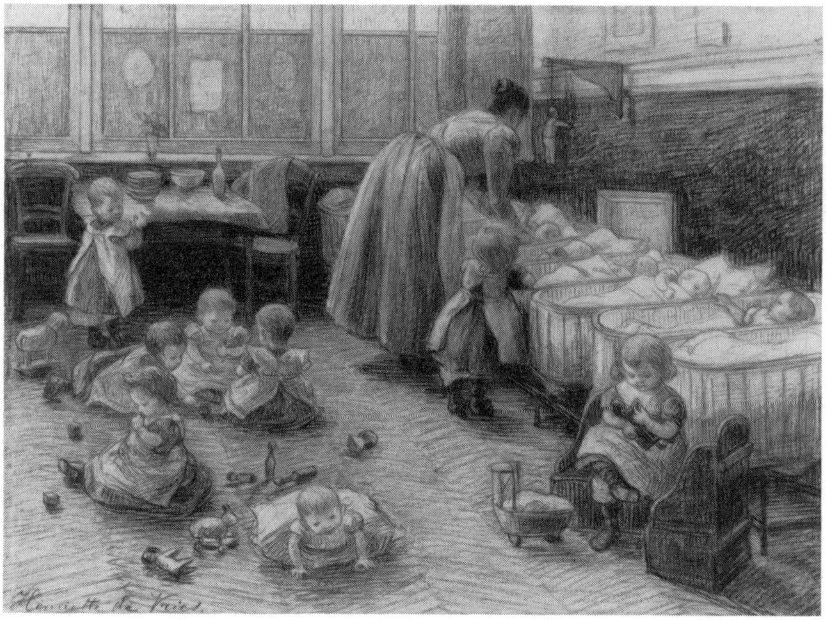

Henriëtte de Vries *(1886-1942)*
Day-care centre for poor children
(Femina Muller Kleine-Kinderen bewaarplaats), 1910
Historisch Topografische Atlas van het Gemeentearchief Amsterdam

The Femina Muller day-care centre in Amsterdam was opened in 1872 for children of poor parents with paid employment and has existed until 1937. It was named after the chairperson of the (private funded) Association to improve day-centres (Vereniging tot Verbetering der Kleine-Kinder Bewaarplaatsen) founded in 1869.

In the 1960s playgroup centres were introduced, a type of child care service for children aged 2 or 3 and for a few mornings or afternoons a week. They were and are publicly subsidized (on the ground of pedagocical motives) and employ professionally trained staff. They certainly were not introduced with the aim to provide child care for participating mothers (they did not exist at that time, see chapter 8). Child care useful for these mothers became available when private child minders projects were encouraged (from the end of the 1970s) and subsidized child care centres were established (for the first time in 1975). A new subsidy system was introduced in 1984, although in 1987 only 1 to 2 per cent of children under 4 years old could be placed in such subsidized child day-care centres. Since then the number has doubled and employers subsidized child care increased[65]. By contrast, the majority of children visit a playgroup. The Netherlands and England both stand out because for their large number of playgroup places in the registered child care sector. Playgroups provide two-thirds of all registered places in England and four-fifths in the Netherlands. Being of limited use for mothers participating in the labor market it is not surprizing that between 1985 and 1987, only 4 per cent of those mothers used professional child care in the Netherlands (De Graaf, 1989:7).

In Sweden day-care centres are the predominant form of registered child care. The community day-care system was introduced in 1974, and the ratio of places to children increased from about 15 per cent of all children aged 0 to 6 in 1975 to 47 per cent in 1987 (Gustafsson and Stafford, 1992) and 48 per cent in 1988 (Sundström, 1991:183).

In the United Kingdom health authorities were authorized in 1918 to set up and subsidize collective crèches for children up to the age of 4 (OECD, 1990:147). Day-care centres in 1988 covered about 10 per cent of all children aged 0 to 5, child minders day-care 26 per cent and playgroups 64 per cent (OECD, 1990:133). A new Children's Act was approved in 1989, covering many aspects including child care services. It improves the regulation of private child care for children up to the age of 8, and requires local authorities to review the whole range of child care services in their area every 3 years (Childcare Network, 1990:37).

The availability of places is a matter of concern in all seven countries. Alongside increasing government assistance for the use of child care, there is growing involvement by employers (sometimes stimulated by the government) and private arrangements supervised by government regulations and encouraged by tax deductions. A trend reducing demand is the introduction and extension of parental leave.

---

65 Again different sources give different figures. For recent reviews see: VNG, 1991 and Hooghiemstra and Niphuis-Nell, SCP, 1993.

Child Allowances[66]

Belgium and France have fairly identical histories in this field, both starting child allowances relatively early as compared with the other countries. France was the first country to introduce child allowances, as early as 1860, though only for sailors and calculated per child per day. Gradually more and more categories of workers became eligible and in 1918 the first child allowance fund was established, resulting in 1932 in the granting of child benefits for all first-born children. The system was extended over the next few years[67], until in 1939 the "*Code de la Famille*" replaced the allowance for the first child with special allowances for mothers working in their own households and without additional paid work. The Code contained special measures to protect families and introduced a maternity benefit and benefits for families with only one salary (*allocation de salaire unique*) (Pieters and Schell, 1990). As already mentioned, pro-natalist arguments played an important role, again after World War II leading to increases and extensions in 1946 and 1973 respectively.

In 1978 and 1980 France granted a kind of income-tested guaranteed family income to families with 3 or more children (ILO, 1987:39). Substantial changes followed in 1985, with a 'young child allowance' for children under 3 years of age (universal for the first 9 months - 5 months before the birth, the month of the birth and 3 months after the birth - and then income-tested), a single-parent allowance no longer wholly income-tested and a parental leave allowance, payable for up to two (since 1987 three) months to any parent who leaves employment to raise the third or subsequent child. A special education allowance is paid to parents with a handicapped child under 20 years of age (Commaille, 1990:72).

Developments in this field in Belgium started in 1915 with child allowances for miners, the establishment of a fund in 1921, extensions in 1928, 1930 and 1937 and the introduction of a maternity benefit in 1942. Increases and extensions occurred in 1944, 1957 and 1972. Besides pro-natalist arguments, social arguments also played a role, but the result was fairly similar to that in France. It was not until the seventies that single mothers became entitled to child allowances, since although the allowance was paid to the mother it was based on the employment of the father. In comparison with those in the other countries, child allowances and tax reductions for children are relatively high in Belgium (Sels and Dumon, 1990:10).

---

[66] The issue of the legally enforced allocation of parental resources in divorced families is disregarded here; for an overview of family law and child support to lone-parent families in OECD countries see Maclean, 1990.

[67] In 1938 a decree (*décret-loi)* made family allowances independent of salaries (Commaille, 1990:69).

Denmark, Germany, the Netherlands[68], Sweden and the United Kingdom did not introduce general child allowances systems until after World War II. Gradually these allowances were extended (see Appendix to chapter 9), replacing the tax deductions which had existed before and producing one system for all children. This change had been more or less accomplished by 1969 in Denmark, 1975 in Germany, 1977 in the United Kingdom, 1981 in the Netherlands and 1983 in Sweden. Arguments in favor of supplementing low wages by child allowances (that is, social arguments) were used in Germany, the Netherlands and the United Kingdom. Recently they have been increasingly replaced by arguments to the effect that society has a general responsibility for the future generation. In Denmark child allowances are now explicitly recognized as a right of the child itself[69] (Pieters and Schell, 1990:49), to which all children under 18 years of age have been entitled since 1987 (Soren, 1990:48).

Particularly in the Netherlands and the United Kingdom, the size of the allowances is too small to produce any unintended pro-natalist effect. (For a 1991 review see: Dumon, Commission of the European Communities, 1993).

Family Policies

In the Netherlands there is still today no explicit family policy and the word "family" (in Dutch *gezin* - nuclear family - or *familie* - including other relatives) does not occur in the name of any Dutch Ministry. This is a remarkable feature in a country which places such a high value on family life. However, a policy of non-intervention in family affairs and a reluctance to intrude into the privacy of the family have characterized the view of successive Dutch governments. An even more remarkable feature is the reluctance to act in population policy matters. The steady growth of the population, the high rate of fertility and the high density of the population ("to the point of overflowing")[70] have led to discussions on how to prevent overpopulation, while the government has since 1985 taken the position that society is capable of effecting demographic change without direct government intervention (Jonker, 1990:279). Even today, population and family policies have a low priority in the programs of all political parties, although these attitudes have been challenged, for example by Verwey-Jonker. This does not imply that policy matters relating to the family have remained completely unchanged in the last few years. There is a noticeable increase in interest in children, child care and the child's wellbeing, leading to special measures for single mothers with

---

68 The Netherlands introduced child allowances for third and subsequent children of employees in 1941.

69 I have often pleaded for a similar approach in the Netherlands (Pott-Buter, 1985, 1988, 1989, 1990).

70 The Queen in her annual speech opening the parliamentary year in 1979, also quoted by Jonker (1990:278).

young children and causing tension in the trend towards a more individualized social security system (Presvalou and de Hoog, 1993:34).

However, the general acceptance of the importance of the family is reflected indirectly in legislation already mentioned above, as in the social security system, and family policy is in fact more or less tacitly integrated into general welfare policies. For example, on the establishment of the Ministry of Welfare and Social Work it was argued[71] that one of its most important tasks would be to strengthen the framework in which people lived.

In contrast to the Netherlands, Belgium has played a pioneering role with respect to family policy (Sels and Dumon, 1990:5). More recently, since the constitutional change in 1980, each of the three language communities has pursued its own 'non-material family policy' but the national government has remained responsible for social security provision (including child allowances), taxation, law (abortion) etc. Family policy is more explicit in the Dutch-speaking area than elsewhere (Sels and Dumon, 1990:5). Family and population policy has been supported by all parties since the interbellum, but particularly by the catholic section of the population. Nearly all ministers with responsibility for family matters have come from one of the catholic parties (CVP or PSC). The history of family policy in Belgium can be broken down into three successive stages, in which first an economic enabling policy, then a non-material welfare policy and finally a mixed policy have been pursued (Sels and Dumon, 1990:9). In the first stage, family policy was in conflict with the emancipation of women. Over the last few years, attempts have been made to reconcile the economic and non-material policies along the lines pursued in the Scandinavian countries. Assessment of the various measures on harmonizing family and professional life is now in progress (Dumon, 1993:2). Family law is still awaiting legislative reform on divorce and children's rights have made major steps forward (Fierens and Meulders-Klein, 1993:3).

Denmark has been less concerned about population policy than Sweden. The concentration has been on family policy aiming "to lend support to parents in their function as parents... It is important to underline that ecclesiastical viewpoints have hardly influenced the Danish debate on family policy. The 'modern family' is so accepted that family policy has never been a hot political issue, ... The family is more an instrument and means than the end itself so far as family policy is concerned, in recognition of the importance of the family to the child, and the family's suitability as a basis for achievement of the main adult-life objectives. In that way there is a narrow link between family policy and child care policies and programs." (Soren, 1990:41). In 1992 legislation has been

---

[71] "In this context, one of the most important tasks of the social work system is to prepare itself to strengthen the framework in which people live. This means in the first place the family. A healthy family life prevents the occurrence of many needs." Proceedings of the Upper House 1952-1953, III 28000, chapter XIIIA, Social Work, Memorandum in Reply no. 2, p.1).

introduced to improve the legal status of children and to increase parent's influence in day-care institutions (Schultz Jorgensen and Pruzan, 1993:5).

French interest in family policies is confirmed in the Constitutions of 1946 and 1958 and also shows in the establishment of a High Council of the Family and Population under the authority of the President of the French Republic. A National Allowance Fund is responsible for direct financial assistance to families (Commaille, 1990:71). The French pro-natalist family policy was already clear, but measures to promote the birth of third and subsequent children (a neo-natalist policy) particularly characterize the year 1979/80 and the 1986 - 1988 period, while more recently consideration has been shifting to compatibility between family and market work (Comaille, 1990:74). The public facilities and services policies have the special feature of being a combination of incentives and measures on both a national and local level. They involve general aid to families (access to specialized services, counseling) and temporary facilities (different types of day-care for children) (Commaille, 1990:73). Four aspects may indicate possible new trends in French family policy: political transition (towards non-intervention and measures to reconcile family and professional life), internationalization, child-centred family reconstitution (bills on descent and succession) and the "*economisation*" of the home (with for example fiscal measures introduced in 1992 to stimulate the employment of paid staff for household tasks, child minding, assistance to elderly people in the home etc.) (Commaille, 1993:20).

In Germany, the Constitution of the Weimar Republic already contained elements of family policy. "It is the task of the state and the communes to maintain the purity and health of the family and to promote it socially. Families with children are entitled to equalizing support. Motherhood may claim the protection and support of the state" (quoted by Höhn, 1990:81). However, it was the Nazi government that launched an explicit population and family policy, including marriage loans, birth grants, a total ban on abortion, and measures restricted to the German 'Aryan' population (Höhn, 1990:86). The racist principles and catastrophic consequences of that government placed a stigma on population policy that has since overshadowed the more humane elements of population and family policy in Germany.

In 1983, Chancellor Kohl nevertheless announced a new family policy. The dual system of child allowances and considerable tax deductions for children was reintroduced. Fundamental judgments handed down by the Federal Constitutional Court in the summer of 1990 established that the subsistence level for children should be exempted from income tax. In 1991 the *Bundesministerium für Familie und Jugendfragen* (Ministry for Family and Youth Issues) (which has existed since 1961) was replaced by the *Bundesministerium für Familie und Senioren* (Ministry for Family and Senior Citizens). Moreover, the Taxation Amendment Act of 1992 improved child-related relief for families by raising child benefits for the first child and income tax allowances for all children (Wingen, 1993:7). In addition, an entirely new provision was introduced into the pension scheme: the *baby year*, granted to all women born after 1921 who have raised a child, when they reach the age of 65 (Höhn, 1990:84).

In Sweden, pro-natalist policies have been framed as social welfare policies and social welfare policies made acceptable to conservative politicians by their intended pro-natalist effects (Gustafsson, 1991). In the other countries, emphasis has been given to the provision of support and stimuli for larger families.

The United Kingdom, like the Netherlands, is a country without explicit population or family policies. In the 1930s concern about the declining birth rate was a powerful force behind the discussions on family allowances, leading eventually in 1944 to a Royal Commission on Population (Wicks and Chester, 1990:105). The post-war increase in births in 1946 and 1947 postponed the feared decline and therefore the policy initiatives. As in the Netherlands, family matters are considered to be private and the size of the British population (rather too large than too small) is not a matter of concern. Alva Myrdal observed that the strong impact of individualism in English social philosophy may to some extent be responsible for this (Myrdal, 1945, quoted by Wicks and Chester, 1990:106). According to the same authors, geography may be another factor. "For whatever reason, the birth rate, family size and population levels are not perceived in the UK as indicators of national potency" (Wicks and Chester, 1990:106).

9.5 Conclusions to chapter 9

The struggle for the right to education and the corresponding right to decent jobs during the second half of the nineteenth century was characteristic of the first feminist wave. The problem of poor middle class women with no means of subsistence created a large supply to fill the few jobs to which they had access. A spectacular achievement in this period was gaining admission to universities, but it was compulsory schooling that created the basis for education for all girls. The coincidence in the dates at which women were first admitted to universities is remarkable. In five of the seven countries women were admitted within a few years of each other, with the Netherlands being the first. Despite differences in admission to the various disciplines and before women and men were admitted on more or less the same terms, historical developments in all seven countries are similar. The same applies to the development of meaningful work in teaching, nursing and new occupations. The gradual nature of the introduction of compulsory schooling (again) does not suggest any remarkable differences between the seven countries. Generally speaking, the right to education was granted somewhat later to girls than to boys, particularly at the secondary and higher levels. More rigorous analytical work is needed to draw specific conclusions with regard to the impact on labor force participation of women.

Early legislation in all seven countries was aimed at prohibiting employment of young children in factories, mines and so on. The inclusion of women in the protected category was in general the next step. Despite powerful support based on public concern, noble motives and the desire to combat immorality, it is a remarkable feature that this legislation was implemented only in those sectors where women and children were working together and in direct competition with men. For this reason, the initial impact of this legislation on the position of women in the labor market was limited to women working in certain sectors of industry. The protective restrictions reduced women's remuneration, at the same time ensuring that women remained at a competitive disadvantage in the labor market, with the majority of women leaving the labor market on marriage or having to combine paid employment with unpaid work relating to family responsibilities.

The fear of women undercutting male wage rates and disturbing European Community Markets was (again) the main reason for the considerable legislative effort to ensure "equal pay for equal work". Again legislation was implemented in those sectors where women were in direct competition with men. This accorded well with the women's movement and its ideas of emancipation. In Denmark and Sweden, with a large influx of women into the public sector, the equal pay principles were extended to this sector at a relatively early stage.

The early restrictions left many of the main areas of women's employment were unprotected, notably shop and office work, nursing, domestic service, teaching, catering and agricultural labor. However, in all these segments (apart from domestic service and agricultural labor) women were subjected to marriage bars, in Germany, the Netherlands and the United Kingdom in particular. The fact that such restrictions existed, and usually survived until the second half of the twentieth century, gave rise to the common feature of virtually all women's employment: that it was unskilled, badly paid, and terminated either on marriage or on the birth of the first child. Even women engaged in relatively skilled and well-paid work were disadvantaged compared with their male counterparts in terms of conditions of employment and promotion prospects.

Generally speaking, suffrage like education was granted later to women than to men. Men received the vote relatively early in France, Germany and Great Britain and relatively late in Denmark, the Netherlands and Sweden. However, women in these last three countries received it shortly after the men and - as also in Germany - relatively early, while women in Belgium and France were denied suffrage until the end and shortly after World War II respectively.

Differences between private labor laws are disappearing and there has been an increasing convergence in the 1980s, due to international conventions and directives. The Netherlands was relatively early in introducing educational opportunities and labor laws, lagged somewhat behind with respect to family laws and far behind as regards the abolition of marriage and pregnancy bars (in 1979). It was also late in removing other disincentives preventing married women, and in particular mothers, from participating in the labor market.

Since the 1970s radical changes have taken place affecting the separate spheres of women and men. New labor laws have to prevent discrimination on grounds of sex, marital status, pregnancy or motherhood. Family laws have started to cease discrimination on grounds of sex. In most countries, the 1970s were marked by a tremendous upsurge in legislative activity concerning women's rights, in both the public and the private sphere.

All seven countries showed a gradual increase in maternity leave. France and Sweden introduced substantial maternity leaves relatively early but Sweden was the first (and for quite a long time the only) country to introduce parental leave. France and Belgium introduced child care services relatively early and are still countries with very high enrolment levels at pre-primary schools. Community day-care systems for children aged 0 to 7 are extensive in Sweden and Denmark. The Netherlands has less day-care places than the other 6 countries. In general the Netherlands and the United Kingdom are lagging behind in explicit family policies.

Apart from the fact that Denmark and Sweden had consistent policies to facilitate parenthood and paid market work fairly early, no specific pattern can be distinguished in terms of a permanent ranking of countries according to the timing of introduction of legislative measures. In general, although with time lags, policies run more or less parallel in all seven countries.

CHAPTER 10

FACTS, THEORIES AND FAIRY TALES

> *"Economists believe that what people do is more relevant than what they say."*
> *Victor R. Fuchs, 1983:14*

The previous chapters have shown that female labor force participation is affected by many factors such as age, marital status, fertility and population growth, the formation of human capital, cultural values and the demand for labor. Marriage, childbearing and women's primary responsibilities for raising children have strongly influenced, and still influence, their work and employment prospects. Section 10.1 summarizes the *Facts about female labor, family and fertility* already stated in chapters 2 to 9. The facts are divided into separate subsections for each of the different aspects, distinguishing the facts into those true of all seven countries and those where the Netherlands differs from the other six countries. Some facts contradict general popular beliefs, and these are therefore relegated to the status of *Fairy Tales* (section 10.7).

What theory is capable of explaining the trends signaled in female labor force participation, the international differences and the low Dutch female activity rates? Any such theory would need to encompass endogenous education, family formation (and dissolution), fertility, wages, standard of living and cultural values. However, no such theory seems to exist, either in economics or in sociology or in any other science. Nor is there any economic model of female behavior encompassing family decisions made over the life cycle under changing economic conditions. Indeed, it seems unlikely that any such theory will be constructed or that any single theory can ever explain differences in female labor force participation, family and fertility over time and between countries. Attempts to construct such a theory are doomed to fail, as probably are all single theories. By narrowing the focus onto a single one of the topics in the trio of female labor, family and fertility, however, it may be possible to explain some of the trends and differences by reference to existing theories.

Sections 10.2 to 10.5 discuss potential *Theoretical explanations*. For the reasons mentioned above, the purpose of these sections is not to construct a new theory but to confront the facts of section 10.1 with some of the existing theories and to indicate which theories correspond to the trends signaled, which theories can explain the differences and which explanations are myths and therefore belong among the *Fairy Tales*. Section 10.2 offers an introduction to economic theories. Section 10.3 gives a compendious review of standard microeconomic/neoclassical explanations of labor and family formation. Section 10.4 discusses theories of fertility and section 10.5 other labor theories. Section 10.6 of this chapter aims to combine the minor stitchwork of the subsections to produce a combined patchwork design providing a comprehensive explanation of all the main findings. Section 10.7 contains the *Fairy Tales*.

10.1 Facts about female labor, family and fertility

10.1.1 International facts about female labor

1 *The trends in female labor force participation rates in Belgium, Denmark, France, Germany, the Netherlands, Sweden and the United Kingdom have differed ever since national labor force statistics first became available.*

The long-term trend in Belgium was a declining one until 1947, after which it started to rise again, although the rates in 1990 are still lower than those between 1846 and 1866. Denmark has shown a persistent rising trend in female economic activity ever since 1855, with the exception of the 1950s and 1960s. France showed a marked increase in female labor force participation at the beginning of the century, reaching a peak in 1921. The levels declined thereafter until 1967. Despite the increase since then, the 1921 percentage has in 1990 still not been surpassed. Germany also reached a relatively high level of female economic activity at about the same time as France, in 1925, and this level was equalled in 1983. In the Netherlands, the rates declined slightly between 1849 and 1889 and gradually increased again between 1889 and 1947. A low female activity level was registered in 1960, but female labor force participation rates have been rising since then. For nearly a century, between about 1860 and 1940, female activity rates in Sweden and the United Kingdom remained roughly stable.

2 *It is only recently that the trend has been an upward one in all seven countries: since the 1940s in Belgium, Sweden and the United Kingdom, since the 1960s in Denmark, France and the Netherlands and since the 1970s in Germany.*

Common trends in female labor force participation rates are otherwise difficult to distinguish, although rates seem to have been relatively low in all seven countries at some points between 1860 and 1880 and again at some points between 1940 and 1960.

3 *Differences in female labor force participation rates between the countries are sometimes quite considerable and in general greater than those between different years in the same country.*

Differences in *male* labor force participation rates are much smaller both within and between countries. In most countries the initial decline in male activity rates has been compensated by the rise in female activity rates, producing a remarkably stable pattern in the total labor force participation rates. Denmark and Sweden are the only two countries where there has been a persistent rising trend in the *total* labor force participation rates ever since about 1855[1]. The total labor force participation rates in the other countries have increased only slightly since the 1960s and 1970s, while the difference between the rate in the first census and that in 1990 is less spectacular[2].

Some of these differences can be attributed to differences in market opportunities between countries and over time within the same country, and between and within certain groups of women. In most countries the rise of cottage industries in small towns and villages heralded the breakdown of the guild system and the start of industrialization: the transformation from mainly manual labor to mechanical methods of production, transportation and communication. This industrialization (particularly related to mining, steam engines and machine-building) started relatively late in Sweden, the Netherlands and Denmark, and relatively early in England and Belgium. This is reflected in the proportion of female workers in *industry*[3] and particularly in textile manufacturing from the mid-nineteenth century onward.

4 *In the second half of the nineteenth century, female activity rates in the industrial sector (particularly textiles) were low in Denmark, the Netherlands and Sweden and high in England and Belgium.*

The *industrial sector* showed a variable female labor pattern in each of the seven countries considered. The female labor force participation rates in this sector frequently rose initially but declined later.

5 *Trends in female labor force participation rates in the other sectors distinguished are fairly similar in all seven countries*[4].

Everywhere the role of *agriculture* in providing female market work suffered a long-term decline. In addition, the relative decline in the importance of *domestic service* for women was compensated by an increase in employment in *non-domestic services. Trade and transport* revealed a secular rising trend.

---

1 In Denmark, the increase from that date until 1990 has been 14 percentage points, and in Sweden 19 percentage points.

2 In Belgium and France it declined by 5 and 8 percentage points respectively, while in Germany, the Netherlands and the United Kingdom the rise respectively amounted to 6, 5 and 5 percentage points (see chapter 2).

3 The sectors distinguished are agriculture, industry, trade and transport, domestic service and non-domestic services (see chapter 4).

4 In general, the trends for men and for women parallel each other, though the participation rates for men as compared with those for women are relatively high in *industry*, while in the *service sector* the opposite is the case.

6 *The rise in non-domestic services varies from the fairly to the extremely spectacular.*

Except for the trade and transport sector, where the levels of female activity have been fairly similar in all seven countries, the levels of female activity differ tremendously. With respect to participation in agriculture, the data are not fully reliable due to differences in definition and particularly in the definition of unpaid family workers. The differences in industry are probably more reliable.

7 *Occupational segregation in all seven countries was and is fairly similar and appears to have persisted. It moves from the old sectors (agriculture, domestic service and the textile industry) to the new female sectors, with occupations like junior white collar/administrative work, sales and caring and teaching services emerging.*

As industry developed, the distinction between self-employed people, unpaid family workers, employers and permanent wage-earners became more marked. Unfortunately, lack of data makes it impossible to attribute differences in female labor force participation rates between the seven countries to differences in a three-fold classification by *status*[5]. Only since about 1910 has it been possible to compile such a classification, and then only a two-fold one (see chapter 5). In general, *unpaid family labor*[6] has been added to the group of *self-employed*[7]. By analogy with the industrial female labor force participation rates, a calculation was performed to discover how much these female categories of *employed* and *self-employed* contributed to the female labor force participation rate.

8 *Differences between countries are (as expected) much smaller within the* ***employed*** *category, but no common trend can be distinguished prior to World War II.*

In six of the seven countries female activity rates of the *employed* reached their lowest values in the first census after World War II, while in Denmark alone the lowest point was in 1940.

---

5 a) *Self-employed* (including *employers* and *workers on their own account*).
b) *Employed* (including wage earners and salaried employees).
c) *Unpaid family worker.*

6 Despite all inaccuracies in registration, unpaid family labor (if registered at all) diminishes in importance, especially after World War II.

7 For this reason, self-employed women form a heterogeneous group, often consisting not only of employers and women working on their own account but also of unpaid family workers such as assisting wives. In all countries, registration by status proves to have changed several times since the turn of the century.

9 *In all countries the trend of the* ***employed*** *women has been upward ever since World War II until the last survey in 1990.*

It is a remarkable feature that between these low-value censuses and 1970 progress was very slow in Denmark, Germany and the Netherlands (only a single percentage point increase in female labor force participation rate of the *employed*), and moderate in Belgium, France and the United Kingdom[8]. By contrast, it was spectacular in Sweden: 15 percentage points. Progress picked up very markedly, however, between 1970 and 1980 with a very spectacular Danish increase of 18 percentage points, followed by Germany, Sweden, Belgium and the Netherlands[9], while in France and the United Kingdom the increase amounted to a mere 2 percentage points.

10 *The* ***self-employed*** *category (including unpaid family workers) was relatively large in France in particular (24 per cent in 1906 and 1921) and relatively small in the Netherlands (the equivalent figures were 4 per cent in 1909 and only 2 per cent in 1920).*

Between Belgium, Denmark, Germany and Sweden, differences in this category are small prior to World War II. Where measured separately, the *unpaid family workers* category declined.

11 *Child labor and market labor by elderly people disappeared almost completely in all seven countries.*

Over the life cycle, all seven countries show similar trends in female labor force participation rates, but (again) actual levels of activity[10] differ tremendously.

12 *In general, female activity rates in youth (15 - 19 years) increased initially and then decreased again.*

There more than in any other age group, differences in definition prove how difficult international comparisons are. With full-time schooling in this age group increasing, labor force participation rates might be expected to decline. Surprisingly, however, rates actually increased, particularly in those countries where (full-time) students with small jobs are counted as being in the labor force, such as Denmark, Sweden and (recently) the Netherlands. *The same applies to the category of young people aged 20 - 24 years*: in Belgium and France participation in this age group has declined over the last decade due to more prolonged education, while in

---

[8] An increase of 5, 7 and 4 percentage points respectively.

[9] With respectively 13, 10, 8, and 6 percentage points (see chapter 5).

[10] In contrast to the definition of female activity rates mentioned above, female labor force participation rates within a particular age group are now defined in relation to the female population in that age group only, rather than to the total female population (see chapter 6).

the other countries an increase emerged because even very small part-time jobs contribute to a higher labor force participation rate.

13 *In all seven countries, female labor force participation rates were at first particularly low in adulthood (25 - 49 years), but the increase between 1900 and 1990 has been fairly spectacular in this age group* (despite a few minor deviations in the trend).

A similar spectacular increase is noticed in Denmark and Sweden in *middle age* (50 - 64 years). By contrast, the Netherlands did not show any increase in the latter age group until the 1980s, while Belgium, France, Germany and Great Britain again showed a decline over the same decade.

14 *In all seven countries there seems to have been a redistribution of market work from the younger and older age groups into the period of adulthood, a development shown even more drastically among men.*

The squeeze of female market activity into adulthood coincides with an increase in married women's labor market activity rates. This increase conceals the rising trends in part-time market work.

15 *At the beginning of this century, labor force participation rates of married women were relatively low in all seven countries, except in France. Prior to 1950, married women's labor force participation does not conform to any simple pattern.*

In most countries there was little or no increase in married women's labor force participation; in Germany and Sweden alone it was slow and evolutionary from the beginning of the twentieth century onward, while in Belgium, Denmark and France there was a decline until after World War II. In England as well as in France, just before World War I there actually seem to have been fewer married women employed than there had been fifty years before. The very high French labor force participation rates of married women were partly due to the high rates in agriculture and, up to World War II, to their participation in clothing textile industries. Therefore, the share of married women in the French total and female labor forces was always high, while in other countries the share was rapidly increasing after World War II. The 49 per cent share of married women in the French female labor force in 1954 was equalled in Sweden in 1965, where in 1950 it had still been only 30 per cent. In the other countries similar balances between married and unmarried women were reached even later.

16 *After 1960, in all seven countries labor force participation rates of married women increased.*

In all seven countries, participation rates of married women have been and still are closely related to family composition. Activity rates of married women belonging to more recent generations are everywhere higher than those of the older generations before the birth of the first child; thereafter the patterns differ between countries. In general, participation behavior of married women without children is converging in all seven countries, but the behavior of women with small children still differs. The latter fact may be due partly to differences in the period of maternal leave, during which women previously working full-time in the labor market are still registered as full-time employed, although they are actually at home.

17 *A remarkably high proportion of the recent rise in married women's labor force participation rates has been due to an increase in part-time work.*

In general, large shares of part-time work in a country coincide with high labor force participation rates. The Netherlands seems to be the exception to this rule, for men as well as for women with high shares of part-time employment coinciding with low labor force participation rates. Recalculating labor force participation rates in full-time equivalents (40 hours a week) as a percentage of the potential working time of the female population aged between 15 and 65 years shows that female labor force participation in the Netherlands is still lower than in any of the other six countries, with 26 per cent in 1987 (a percentage not much different from the 24 per cent level for the whole population in 1846). In terms of full-time equivalents Belgium and the Netherlands have no longer equal labor force participation rates, but female activity rates in Belgium are 11 per cent higher (37 per cent for the female population aged 15 - 64, about the same percentage as the level for the total female population in 1856). In Denmark the same calculation produces an activity rate of 49 per cent, in Germany 41 per cent and in France 38 per cent.

18 *In all seven countries the presence of children reduces the labor force participation rates of married women.*

This reduction is less in Denmark and Sweden, where there was a rapid increase in market work among mothers of pre-school children in the 1970s and 1980s. The most recent figures for Denmark and Sweden tend to indicate that mothers are increasing their working hours and fathers reducing theirs. However, many women in these countries are now registered statistically as being in the labor force while in reality they are still at home taking care of the children. The labor force participation rate of women with children under seven years of age was 86 per cent in Sweden in 1987, but their at-work rate was only 55 per cent (although still high compared with the other countries). Clearly there is still a marked division of labor in all seven countries, even in Denmark and Sweden.

10.1.2 Female labor: the Netherlands as compared with the other six countries

19 *Female labor force participation rates in the Netherlands were lower than those in the other six countries over nearly the whole period observed, except for 1947 (when Belgian rates were one per cent lower), and 1987 when they equalled those of Belgium, before overtaking them in 1990.*

Apart from Belgium for these few years, the difference with the other six countries was sometimes quite considerable (as much as 26 percentage points compared with France in about 1920).

20 *It seems likely that Dutch female labor force participation rates were lower than those of the surrounding countries from as early as the seventeenth century, although no national figures about labor force participation exist to prove this in the centuries before censuses took place.*

Probable reasons for these lower rates would have been the early labor division between activities in agriculture and industry (particularly cottage industries) and the (preferred) dominance of the bourgeois family (see also subsection 10.1.4).

21 *Women's shares in labor force participation in the Netherlands were always lower than those in the other six countries throughout the whole period observed.*

The advantage of using participation shares is that these figures are less sensitive to differences in definitions between countries. Because the difference with the other countries is now smaller, this may indicate that differences in definition play a role to the extent that such differences affect females and males alike. It also reflects the fact that male labor force participation rates have also been relatively low in the Netherlands, especially between 1910 and 1981.

22 *Dutch female activity rates in agriculture remained extremely low throughout the period*[11].

Only in Great Britain were the rates even lower (1 per cent between 1861 and 1891). In Great Britain, however, these low female activity rates in

---

[11] No more than 3 or 4 per cent between 1859 and 1947 and 1 per cent thereafter, but 10 per cent in 1849. In Belgium, female activity rates in agriculture reached a peak in 1880 with 19 per cent, rapidly declining to 3 per cent in 1910. The corresponding peak figures for Denmark are 12 per cent in 1860 and 1901; for France 17 per cent in 1920; for Germany 14 per cent in 1907 and 1933, and for Sweden 14 per cent in 1880 (see chapter 4).

agriculture were compensated by relatively high activity rates in *industry*[12], unlike the situation in the Netherlands[13].

23 *Since 1849, industry can be held responsible for reducing the overall female labor force participation rate in the Netherlands by at least 4 to 8 percentage points as compared with the average trend value of the other six countries, and agriculture for doing so by about 2 to 6 percentage points.*

In contrast, differences with the other six countries in female labor force participation rates in trade and transport have been very small, while in domestic service the Dutch rates were fairly high[14]. In non-domestic services differences have not been extreme. The overall conclusion with respect to the low rates of Dutch female labor force participation in the sectors distinguished is that they have been so low because of the relative lack of participation in both agriculture and industry over nearly the full century and a half examined in this study.

24 *Although low, Dutch female labor force participation rates of the* ***employed*** *over the period from around 1910 to 1990 were not the lowest.*

In 1930, Belgian female labor force participation rates were even lower (3 percentage points) and the Belgian 1961 rates equalled the Dutch 1960 rates (both 14 per cent). Around 1920, the Dutch rate of participation of the *employed* was 4 percentage points lower than the highest in the seven countries (Germany), while around 1930 it was 5 percentage points lower than in Denmark and 8 percentage points lower than in Great Britain.

25 *In general, the low Dutch female participation rates before World War II can be attributed almost entirely to the low participation rate of* ***self-employed*** *women (including unpaid family workers), while participation rates of Dutch* ***employed*** *women were relatively low during the first three decades following that war.*

26 *Differences over the life cycle show that Dutch female labor force participation rates were low (but not always the lowest) in all the age groups distinguished but that female labor force participation rates were particularly low in adulthood (25 - 49 years) and middle age (50 - 64 years).*

---

12 This rate was 14 per cent in 1851, declined to 9 per cent in 1931 and increased to 12 per cent by 1956, the post-World War II maximum value.

13 The rate of women in industry was only 2 per cent in 1889, increasing slightly to 4 per cent in 1930, a percentage equalled only by the 4 per cent post-World War II maximum reached in 1960.

14 Dutch rates were 8 per cent in 1849 and 1859, still low compared with the English 13 per cent in 1871 and the same figure in Denmark in 1930.

In *adulthood* the difference between the Netherlands and the countries with the next to lowest and with the highest activity rates was 5 and 36 percentage points in 1900, while in 1960 it was 13 and 35 and in 1970 11 and 42 percentage points. In *middle age* differences have been less spectacular, but in 1900 French rates were 20 percentage points higher, while in 1960 Swedish rates were 31 percentage points higher in this age group than in the Netherlands. Since 1950, however, Belgian rates in this age group have been the lowest of all seven countries (in 1990 as much as 61 percentage points lower than the Swedish rates, which were exceptionally high in that year at 74 per cent).

27 *Labor force participation rates of married women in the Netherlands were very low throughout the whole twentieth century until the 1970s.*

In 1960 the labor force participation rate for married women was still only 6 per cent, while the labor force participation rate of married female employees or wage earners was even lower at 4 per cent. Only about 0.6 per cent of the married women in the labor market (excluding assisting wives) were mothers of young children and they were often working in high educated professions. Gradually in the 1960s and 1970s, more and more married women remained in the labor force after marriage, although usually in part-time work. In the 1980s, more and more women delayed marriage and childbirth, while at the same time increasing numbers of mothers remained in the labor force, nearly always part-time. Of all women participating part-time in the Netherlands in 1988, one third had a job of less than 10 hours a week while 40 per cent worked over 10 but less than 20 hours a week. Therefore, measured in full-time equivalents, female labor force participation rates in the Netherlands are still the lowest of all seven countries.

10.1.3 International facts about the family

28 *The trends in the seven countries with regard to household size, new household forms, marriage rates and average ages on first marriage all point in the same direction.*

All countries have seen a decline in household size from an average of four to five members per household in 1900 to an average of only two to three in 1990. In those areas of Europe where multi-generation households existed (particularly in the relatively poor agricultural areas in France, Germany and Sweden), they have gradually disappeared over recent decades. Recently too, many non-traditional household forms have become increasingly prominent, especially cohabitation outside of legal marriage and one-person households. Marriage rates increased in the early part of this century, but declined again in the 1960s or 1970s. Average age on first marriage declined until the 1970s, when postponement of marriage and an increase in cohabitation reversed this trend. The Scandinavian countries have been the pacesetters in the development of many of the recent changes in family life.

Many of these changes have been attributed to the process of industrialization and connected with the idea that there was some previous period in which women participated fully in 'productive activities', while the transfer of work out of the home into factories assigned men as producers to the public sphere and women as housewives to the private sphere. It seems doubtful that there was ever such a period (see section 10.7).

For ideas concerning a *gradual* trend involving the rise of affective family relations in the nuclear family, based on mutual assistance between husband and wife and a common responsibility for the upbringing of children, particularly since the mid-nineteenth century, see also section 10.7.

10.1.4 Family trends in the Netherlands compared with the other six countries

29 *In Holland (the western part of the Dutch Republic), and in some other prosperous agricultural regions, cottage industries had already disappeared by 1670, separating industrial activities such as spinning and weaving from the agricultural activities carried on around the homestead. This separation stimulated the practical realization of the ideal of (married) women looking after their households and men earning the income to support them.*

The relatively high productivity of the agricultural sector since then may have prevented the industrialization of these areas. Only in the poorer agricultural areas in the south and east of the country, close to the Belgian and German borders, where this early separation had not happened, did textile industries develop in the nineteenth century to any extent.

30 *The ideal of domesticity, even for women without the 'natural' duties of wives and mothers, seems to have been fairly dominant in Holland at around the close of the seventeenth-century and most (married) women seem to have been excluded from performing market work, particularly women of the bourgeois middle classes.*

In addition to agriculture, however, there was a general acceptance of unpaid family labor in craft and trade and of female labor in domestic service (see also facts about female labor). This suggests that Dutch labor force participation rates of women may have been low in comparison with those in the surrounding countries long before census figures became available.

While the ethos of other seventeenth century states was built around the aura of a dynasty or the historic privileges of a city commune in the Netherlands it was the bourgeois family household. The early dominance of the cultural norms of the rich bourgeois middle classes seems to have contributed to a development that made the Netherlands unique in comparison to the surrounding countries.

31 *It seems likely that in the Dutch Republic, during the Dutch Golden Age (the seventeenth century), the familial behavior of the middle classes, centered around the nuclear family, was already the dominant (or preferred) form of household behavior, long before it spread to all European countries in the eighteenth and nineteenth centuries.*

This bourgeois family ideal, while bestowing a higher status on women working in their own households and establishing the domestic sphere as the central locus of quality considerations, was based on the same asymmetric gender roles that existed in the labor market. It seems likely that in general the well-being of all members of a household improved where men provided the financial resources and companionship and women were responsible for raising or maintaining the quality of life of the household. (Although, in contrast, the position of non-married women was weakened and the same division of labor laid the foundation for many of the present inequalities between men and women, see also theories discussed below.) The scarce evidence available suggests that the nuclear family has long been, and is still today, relatively important in the Netherlands and that this affective family model is likely already to have existed as far back as the seventeenth century. Paintings, poems, and other forms of cultural expression, as well as figures on household size - relatively small until the end of the nineteenth century - confirm these statements.

32 *Dutch women seem to have enjoyed more freedom than their counterparts elsewhere. During the Golden Age, Dutch women could make commercial contracts and notarized documents and had the formal qualifications needed for active commercial or business dealing.*

Widows, in particular, used these qualifications. The relative freedom of Dutch women may have been closely connected with the Calvinist doctrine of marriage, based on mutual assistance, and the relative prosperity of the Dutch Republic. The introduction of French administrative regulations, imposed in 1811 and remaining in force after the French defeat in 1813, meant for Dutch women the loss of certain rights. As a result, their socio-economic position became more heavily dominated than before by the position of fathers, brothers or husbands. However, the importance attributed to marriage and the nuclear (affective) family model remained.

33 *A remarkable feature, specific to the Netherlands, is that there was apparently a further gradual strengthening of the ideals of marriage, motherhood and family life during the nineteenth century as a result of pillarization or columnization: the existence*

throughout society of organizations of all kinds with similar goals but different denominational bases.

To guarantee its future, each (religious as well as non-religious) denomination (pillar) emphasized motherhood and child care (see also facts about fertility). This pillarization has only gradually broken down since the 1960s.

34 *Divorce rates have been relatively low, as have been births out of wedlock.*

The proportion of married women in the population, marriage rates and average age on first marriage have since 1850 all been fairly similar in the Netherlands to those in the other six countries. Figures for legal abortion are currently the lowest in the world. (Figures for countries without legal abortion, if they exist, cannot be compared.) The importance of the family in the Netherlands was confirmed in and strengthened by legislation (see below).

10.1.5 International facts about fertility

35 *The fertility trends between 1900 and 1990 showed a fairly similar pattern in all seven countries (except in France during World War I), but the levels of the total fertility rate differed tremendously.*

The overall trend is a long-term decline in fertility, interrupted only by the 'baby booms' directly after the two world wars. Since the 1970s, differences in the levels of total fertility rates have become smaller.

36 *France had relatively low rates at the beginning of this century, followed at some distance by Great Britain. In the 1920s the sharp decrease in fertility rates produced similarly low levels in Germany, Sweden and the United Kingdom, while in the 1930s Belgium, France and Denmark had equal and slightly higher levels. Between 1910 and 1972, Dutch fertility rates were markedly higher than those in the other six countries. French fertility rates were the highest of all seven countries from 1973 to 1988, since when, Sweden has taken the lead.*

Since these two countries were among the first to show the decline in fertility, this may indicate a reversal of the trend.

37 *Comparing the trends for female labor with those for fertility shows that marked decreases in fertility within a country precede increases in female labor force participation.*

However, fertility trends show a fairly similar pattern, labor force participation rates not.

10.1.6 Fertility in the Netherlands compared with the other six countries

38 *The most striking difference between the Netherlands and the other six countries is the very high total fertility rate sustained in this century until the 1970s.*

Again, as with female labor force participation rates, the Netherlands proved to be unique in this respect. Since the 1970s, however, Dutch fertility rates have been in between those of the other six countries.

39 *In 1990, the Netherlands still remained exceptional in the fact that the average age of the mother at the birth of the first child was higher here than anywhere else in the world.*

40 *The high total fertility rates in the Netherlands up to the 1970s produced a greater population increase here than elsewhere over the whole period.*

10.1.7 International trends in legislation

41 *The coincidence in the dates at which women were first admitted to universities is remarkable.*

In five of the seven countries, women were admitted within a few years of each other, with the Netherlands being the first. Developments in all seven countries are similar in terms of admission to the various disciplines and before women and men were admitted on more or less the same terms. The same applies to the development of meaningful work in teaching, nursing and new occupations in - for example - the telegraphic and telephone services. The gradual nature of the introduction of compulsory schooling (again) does not suggest any remarkable differences between the seven countries. Generally speaking, the right to education was granted somewhat later to girls than to boys, particularly at the secondary and higher levels.

42 *Early legislation in all seven countries was aimed at prohibiting employment of young children in factories, mines and so on. The inclusion of women in the protected category was in general the next step.*

Despite many noble motives, this legislation was implemented only in those sectors where women and children were working together and in direct competition with men. For this reason, the initial impact of this legislation on the position of women in the labor market was limited to women working in certain industrial sectors. The protective restrictions reduced women's remuneration, at the same time ensuring that women remained at a competitive disadvantage in the labor market, with the majority of women leaving the labor market on marriage or having to combine paid employment with unpaid work connected with family responsibilities.

43 *The fear of women undercutting male wage rates and disturbing European Community Markets was (again) the main reason for the considerable legislative effort to ensure "equal pay for equal work".*

This accorded well with the women's movement and its ideas of emancipation. In Denmark and Sweden, with a large influx of women into the public sector, the equal pay principles were introduced in this sector at a relatively early stage.

44 *The early restrictions applied only to limited segments of the labor market, whilst many of the main areas of women's employment remained unprotected or less restricted, notably shop and office work, nursing, domestic service, teaching, catering and agricultural labor. However, in all these segments (apart from domestic service and agriculture) women were subjected to marriage bars, in Germany, the Netherlands and the United Kingdom in particular.*

The fact that marriage bars and restrictions existed, and usually survived until the second half of the twentieth century, gave rise to the common feature of virtually all women's employment: that it was unskilled, badly paid, and terminated either on marriage or on the birth of the first child. Even women engaged in relatively skilled and well-paid work were disadvantaged compared with their male counterparts in terms of conditions of employment and promotion prospects.

45 *Generally speaking, suffrage - like education - was granted later to women than to men.*

Men received the vote relatively early in France, Germany and Great Britain and relatively late in Denmark, the Netherlands and Sweden. However, women in these last three countries received it shortly after the men and - as also in Germany - relatively early, while women in Belgium and France were denied suffrage until respectively the end and shortly after World War II.

46 *Differences between private labor laws are disappearing and there has been an increasing convergence in the 1980s, due to international conventions and directives.*

In the period immediately prior to the 1960s married women in most countries were given the same rights as single women and both were given many of the same rights as men. Since the 1970s radical changes have taken place affecting the separate spheres of women and men. New labor laws prevented discrimination on grounds of sex, marital status, pregnancy or motherhood. Family laws began to cease to discriminate on grounds of sex. In most countries, the 1970s were marked by a tremendous upsurge in legislative activity concerning women's rights, both in the public and in the private sphere.

47 *All seven countries showed a gradual increase in maternity leave.* France and Sweden introduced substantial maternity leaves relatively early but Sweden was the first (and for quite a long time the only) country to introduce parental leave. France and Belgium introduced child care services relatively early and are even today countries with very high enrolment levels of children at pre-primary schools. Community day-care systems for children aged 0 to 7 are extensive in Sweden and Denmark. The Netherlands has less day-care places than the other 6 countries. In general, the Netherlands and the United Kingdom are lagging behind in explicit child care and family policies.

48 *Apart from the presence in Denmark and Sweden of fairly early consistent policies to facilitate the combination of parenthood and paid market work, no specific pattern can be distinguished in terms of a permanent ranking of countries according to the timing of introduction of the legislative measures,*

In general, however, policies run parallel in all countries.

10.1.8 Legislation in the Netherlands compared with the other six countries

49 *The Netherlands was relatively early in introducing educational opportunities and labor laws.*

50 *The Netherlands lagged somewhat behind with respect to family laws and far behind as regards the abolition of marriage and pregnancy bars.*

Between 1904 and 1924 there were 10 legislative proposals attempting to forbid all employment to married women in the public service and factories. The first legal marriage bar was the 1904 Royal Decree to dismiss women on marriage in postal and telegraph services. In the 1930s measures were intensified. The last legal pregnancy bar was removed in 1979. Gradually other disincentives preventing married women, and in particular mothers, from participating in the labor market are removed as well.

10.2 Economic theories of labor: Women don't work?

10.2.1 Institutional, Keynesian and neoclassical theories

Early economic theories show little specific interest in labor markets, except for long-run aggregate labor supply and fertility (see section 10.6). Moreover, those three famous economists who did pay attention to labor markets (Adam Smith, 1776; Alfred Marshall, 1890; and John R. Hicks, 1932) hardly mentioned women (Pujol, 1992). In Adam Smith's *The Wealth of Nations* "(t)he connections between the sexual division of labour within the labour market and in society as a whole and the social division of labour are completely bypassed." (Pujol, 1992:17). "Women are as invisible in Smith's work as in the work of succeeding economists, with the exception of that of J.S. Mill. Their fundamental role in reproducing the nation's 'human capital' is taken for granted." (Pujol, 1992:21).

In general during the first half of the twentieth century, labor markets had a Cinderella status among the various areas of economics. Labor markets were seen as an area in which institutional factors played a dominant role; they did not demand specific intellectual challenges and it was thought that the analytical tools of (micro)economics could not be applied to them (see Addison and Siebert, 1979:1).

Only more recently, since World War II, have these ideas changed and has interest in labor markets accelerated. Since then, three categories of (economic) labor market theories can be distinguished: institutional, neoclassical/microeconomic and Keynesian, each displaying a certain degree of hostility towards the others (Hartog and Theeuwes, 1989) and each originally formulated without specific attention to sexual distinctions.

Institutionalists represented the dominant labor market approach prior to World War II. They study institutions, such as unions, social laws and other organizational aspects. Institutionalists' theories have been mainly descriptive without the application of mathematical tools. Not the individual but institutions and the behavior of groups form the analytical categories. The neoclassical approach neglects the detailed world of the institutionalists and is dominated by concepts such as choice, demand, supply, prices and income, concealing much of what institutionalists emphasize as special in the labor market. Its method of analysis can be characterized as "deductive in nature and aiming at the derivation of testable hypotheses and predictions out of a few fundamental assumptions" .... "full of confidence in the concept of equilibrium and without any analytical attention for all sorts of complications." (Hartog and Theeuwes (1990:317).

In Keynesian theory, the labor market is an aggregated market with homogeneous labor, where downward wage rigidity explains unemployment. "According to the institutionalists the individual characteristics of the specific situations are so dominating that the abstractions of the neoclassical thesis are too strong. According to the Keynesians, the tendency to equilibrium is a misconception and, in practice, the market mechanism can fundamentally fail." (Hartog and Theeuwes, 1990:317). Keynesians do not believe markets are working well and Adam Smith's invisible hand fails. (Although New Keynesians build macroeconomic theories about recessions and depressions and rigidities from new developments in microeconomics). Theories about dual and segmented labor markets also focus on rigidities in the economy. These theories illustrate that the different treatment of men and women is embedded in the economic structure and the outcome (wages, function levels) dependent on the economic power of the agents in the labor market.

In explaining individual labor market behavior, the neo-classical/microeconomic view emerged as the dominant theory. Its analytical power, simplicity, and charms, in addition to the fact that wages and prices were becoming less rigid, while institutional barriers were rapidly changing, contributed to its growing importance over recent decades. For this reason, this theory is treated in a separate section (10.3). Although the neoclassical/microeconomic analytical approach is based on theories already partly formulated in the previous century, in works such as Marshall's *Principles of Economics* (1890), the application to labor markets did not take off until the 1950s (Hartog and Theeuwes, 1990:313,314,315). The first neoclassical textbooks about labor markets appeared in the 1970s, the most well-known being Addison and Siebert (1979) and Hamermesh and Rees (1984). Almost from the beginning, empirical attention in this approach focused on (married) women. A special edition of the *Journal of Labor Economics* (founded in 1983) was completely dedicated to the proceedings of a 1983 conference on "Trends in Women's Work, Education, and Family Building" (Layard and Mincer, eds., 1985). In this edition, including a 12-country[15] comparison of female labor force trends, the main focus was on the growth in the labor force of married women in the years 1960-1980 (see next section for further details). The *Handbook of Labor Economics*, published in 1986, also pays special attention to women. It is clear then that neoclassical economics cannot be blamed for any lack of attention paid to female labor by economists in general (as it so often is, see e.g. Pujol, 1992; and also section 10.7).

10.2.2 Early contributions to Labor Economics

The late attention paid by neoclassical theorists to labor in general, and for female labor in particular, does not mean that no attention at all was paid by economists to female labor. In the Netherlands, the contents of

---

15 Australia, Britain, France, Germany, Israel, Italy, Japan, the Netherlands, Spain, Sweden, the United States and the U.S.S.R.

two Dutch academic journals, *De Economist* (founded in 1852) and *Economisch Statistische Berichten* (founded in 1915), clearly reflect the interest in female labor coinciding with the three feminist waves: comments on female education in the nineteenth century, on the protective legislation concerning female labor and suffrage in the early years of this century and the neoclassical take-off in the 1970s. The majority of the 'scientific' papers before the 1970s - with the exception of those written by Anna Polak (1847-1943) in *De Economist* - are comments characterized by descriptions full of preconceived ideas concerning women's supposed physical weakness and intellectual inferiority (see Gustafsson, Bruyn-Hundt and Pott-Buter, 1992:254). Elsewhere, Hélène Mercier (1839-1910), Marie Jungius, Marie Heinen, Clara Wichmann (1885-1922), Willemijn Hendrika Posthumus-van der Goot (1897-1989) and Elisabeth Caroline van Dorp[16] were, among others, publishing about female labor, the legal restrictions and the problem of the low female education.

In England, Barbara Bodichon (1859) was one of the first to emphasize the conditions characterizing women's employment such as its unskilled - and therefore badly paid - nature and rarely lack of training opportunities. John Stuart Mill's feminist ideas, influenced by Harriet Taylor whom he met in 1830 and married in 1851, led him to publish *The Subjection of Women* in which he condemns the legal subordination of women to men, while his *Principles* "is the first text in political economy which gives more than passing consideration to economic matters affecting women and which considers them as autonomous economic agents. Mill and Taylor insisted that women should have the same claim as men to property, to the ownership of their own earnings and to inheritance. ... They opposed the restrictions to women's work in the Factory Acts ... (and) identified as the real motive behind the Acts: ensuring women's continued availability as dependent servants in the home" (Pujol, 1992:24).

Between the 1860s and 1890, the economists showing interest in women's work and pay were Mary Paley and her husband Alfred Marshall. In *The Economics of Industry* (1881) "women's low wages are attributed to the 'habit' of women and of their employers 'of taking it for granted that the wages of women must be low' (Marshall and Paley, 1881:175). For the authors, general opinion rather than any observable deficiency in women's productivity was the determinant of women's wages. It is likely that such statements were from Mary Paley's pen as in

---

[16] Elisabeth van Dorp was in 1901 the first Dutch woman to graduate in law. She was editor of *De Economist* and in 1894 co-founder of the *Nederlandse Bond voor Vrouwenkiesrecht* (Dutch Alliance for Female Suffrage). In 1910 she wrote the yearly report for the Dutch Economists Society (*prae-advies voor de Vereeniging voor de Staathuishoudkunde en de Statistiek*) about paid market labor by married women and adviced that it should not be increased or encouraged because that would fail to give due recognition to the importance of the family. For a biography, see Fase (1988).

the first edition of his *Principles of Economics* (1890) Marshall opposes equal pay for women, seeing it as detrimental to a socially desirable sexual division of labour ... Sidney Webb seems to be the first male economist to give the question of equal pay some serious thought: in his 1891 empirical article 'Alleged Differences in Wages Paid to Women and Men for Similar Work'." (Pujol, 1992:53). Beatrice and Sidney Webb were among the few scholars studying labor conditions at the turn of the century, while the early twentieth century saw the publication of *Labor Problems: A Textbook* (1905) by Thomas Adams and Helen Summer (Blau and Ferber, 1992:3[17]).

Reasons often given for the paucity of interest in women's labor include (among others mentioned by Pujol, 1992) the general assumption that the majority of female work is not productive and the fact that economics is the most male-dominated of all sciences (Ferber and Teiman, 1981), and a science with the hegemonic control by one paradigm (considered anti-feminist): the neoclassical school. (See also section 10.7: Fairy Tales.)

10.3 Neoclassical economic theories

What do neoclassical theories explain with respect to labor markets and differences between countries? This section briefly reviews some current neoclassical economic theories, concentrating on those implications of the models which may contribute to the explanation of the facts.

The models are distinguished into various categories, although the demarcation line between the models is merely historical and each model has been extended and combined with the others. Within each category, models have been developed for single persons (or for households acting as single persons) as well as models concerning decisions by multi-person households.

In some cases, aside from the facts of section 10.1, I shall refer to relevant empirical work that has come to my attention. No systematic testing or treatment of the theories mentioned has been attempted, the empirical work quoted serves only as to illustrate the arguments.

---

17 In their brief review of women's early contributions to labor economics Blau and Ferber also mention Edith Abbott's *History of Women in Industry* of 1909, Elizabeth Brandeis' contribution to the *History of Labor in the United States* produced under the auspices of John R. Commons in 1935, Margaret Reid's *Economics of Household Production* of 1934 and the article by Paul Douglas and Erika Schoenberg "Studies in the Supply Curve of Labor" in *JPE 45,* 1937. More recently (1950) Joan Robinson was one of the most prominent economists to critically examine Marx's theory of the exploitation of labor. (Blau and Ferber, 1992:3,4).

This section will begin with a brief outline of the theoretical models underlying demand and supply curves, and then use elements of these models to interpret observed facts. The interpretation will be no more than crude and sketchy, as detailed work will be undertaken on another occasion and beyond the scope of this study.

10.3.1 The Neoclassical Theory of Demand and Supply in the Labor Market

The market for labor is an analytical construction intended to describe the process of pricing and allocation of buyers and sellers of labor. Supply and demand simultaneously determine price (wage) and quantity (labor force) in the labor market. Supply represents the behavior of sellers of labor, demand that of firms. In the simplest model, supply is measured in market hours at the individual level (but often in persons at the aggregate level), depending on real wages, non-labor income and preferences, while demand depends on real wages, technology and real prices of other factors of production. With - according to theory - demand not positively related with real wages and assuming supply to be not negatively related, the equilibrium values of the real wage and the labor force at a certain moment are established. The relative wage elasticities of demand and supply in these equilibrium points explain the direction of the changes in real wages and labor force.

Changes in preferences for market work shift the labor supply curve. For example, the weakening of the prejudice against mothers and wives participating in the labor market shifts it to the right. An increase in population - at given labor force participation rates - also shifts the supply curve to the right. Labor productivity increases shift the firm's demand curve to the right. The more inelastic labor supply is, the more important demand will be, while with relatively inelastic demand, supply will be more important in determining the outcome of the labor market.

Many attempts have been made to estimate the relative importance of demand and supply factors, with the demand-centered explanation receiving support in the work of sociologists (see Goldin, 1990:123, 124). It is often difficult to disentangle changes in supply from those in demand or to separate changes in constraints from those in choice. For example, a decrease in fertility may be considered a change in choice by one group and a change in constraints by another (e.g. because of advance in contraceptive technology). The increases in female labor force participation rates since the 1960s are often used to confirm the notion that feminist ideology contributed greatly to economic change. This can be interpreted to mean that the supply side of the labor market has been the dominant factor, via the inference that women must have changed their preferences for paid work. It could be viewed alternatively, as meaning that the demand side was altered by changed constraints on the employment of women, and changed attitudes among employers toward married women in the labor force, and that this caused the growth in female labor force participation. There is room for interactions between the two sides, in practice causing many problems for neoclassical empirical economists.

In spite of these difficulties, the supply and demand framework will be used to to interpret the developments observed. To start with, demand and supply models will be discussed in some greater detail.

10.3.2 Labor demand models

The demand for labor is a derived demand, depending on the goods and services produced by labor and other factors of production and the market value of these goods and services[18]. The crucial concept is marginal productivity. Profit maximizing firms equate labor's marginal productivity with the wage if they are in perfect competition. If they are monopsonists, they equate marginal wage cost to the marginal product value[19]. The labor demand curve is downward sloping in its own wage, at the level of an individual firm or industry. The demand can also be analyzed for an entire country and for heterogeneous labor (skilled/unskilled, male/female, disaggregated by occupation etc.). The elasticity of the demand for labor depends on: the elasticity of demand for the product, the proportion of labor costs in the total production costs, the substitution elasticity for labor by other production factors and the supply elasticities of productive services other than labor. A shift in any of these factors (i.e. in product market conditions, in technology or in supply conditions of other factors) shifts the demand curve for this particular type of labor. Cross elasticities may be positive or negative depending on relations of complementarity and substituability.

Estimates of the own-wage elasticity of the demand for labor, holding output constant - the substitution elasticity - for developed economies in the late twentieth century are probably in the range of - 0.15 to - 0.50 (Hamermesh, 1986:453). Because, at the level of the economy as a whole, scale effects are likely to be small, the overall demand is probably also inelastic, although less so, about - 0.75 (Ehrenberg and Smith, 1991:115). A brief review of aggregate labor demand studies in the Netherlands yields short to long-run demand elasticities between - 0.1 and - 0.3 (Theeuwes, 1988).

The lower the skill-levels in a group of workers, the higher the own-wage elasticities of demand will be, e.g. teenagers even between - 7.0 and - 9.0 (Hamermesh, 1986:464). This is in accordance with the expect-

---

18 See for an extensive treatment standard textbooks on labor economics, e.g. Addison and Siebert, 1979: chapter 2; Elliott, 1991: chapter 8; Ehrenberg and Smith, 1991: chapter 3.

19 Monopsonists may be countered by unions. The analysis of female wages and employment under the influence of male unions has barely begun (see e.g. Sap, 1993).

ation that a person with more options will have a more elastic demand (in absolute value). "Thus, skill per se ties employers to workers by making labor demand less sensitive to exogenous changes in wage rates." (Hamermesh, 1986:462). For the cross-wage elasticities, evidence is sketchier. Empirical results suggest that teenagers and female adults are substitutes *in production*, but whether they are gross substitutes in the labor market as well is uncertain and depends on the scale as well as the substitution effects. Evidence on the size and sign of these effects is generally lacking (Ehrenberg and Smith, 1991:117). Evidence on cross elasticities of male and female demand is also largely absent.

Important characteristics of labor demand are sectoral and sexual division, technical progress and geographic location. Over the whole period considered in this study, the nature of demand changed, e.g. the decrease in average annual working hours and rise of white collar work. Particularly since World War II, the net increase of women in the labor force has been absorbed partly by the industrial sector, but mainly by the service sector (see chapter 4). According to Reynolds (1979:67), a decisive factor is the differing movement of output per worker and the amount of labor needed to achieve a given volume of output has been shrinking much faster in industry and agriculture than in services. Activities for which demand is income-elastic and price-inelastic, such as education, have absorbed a steadily increasing proportion of the labor force. Service industries employ a high proportion of white collar workers, of women workers and of part-time workers.

A 'shift-share'[20] analysis, applied to Dutch women over the period 1947 to 1985 shows that the change in sector structure was unfavorable to women over the period up to 1975 but very favorable from 1975 to 1985 (Mol, van Ours, Theeuwes, 1988:21). A study conducted by Gustafsson and Löfström (1990) on time series data relating to the manufacturing industries over the period 1950 - 1985, concludes that structural changes in industry and business cycles had negative effects on female labor demand.

The number of demand studies is relatively small compared with supply studies. Problems of privacy make data on individual firms less ready available than household data. Some demand side theories concentrate on explaining differences between the economic positions and/or wages of men and women. Those include job competition theory and theories of discrimination within the labor market by employers or male workers. Discrimination theories involving the possibility of bias prior to the labor market, in the education system or in the family - treating boys differently from girls - belong to the supply side theories. In

[20] Women's average share in the labor force is $a = \Sigma\, a_i\, W_i$, where a_i = share of women in sector i and W_i = labor force share of sector i in the total labor force. The shift-share is: $a(t)-a(t-1)=\Sigma\, [\{(W_i(t)-W_i(t-1)\}a_i(t-1)+\{a_i(t)-a_i(t-1)\}W_i(t)]$, with the first term the sector structure effect and the second the participation effect. The analysis is applied to 6 sectors: agriculture, industry, trade, transport, commercial services and other services (including domestic service).

reality, demand and supply sides are interrelated. This interaction is relatively important in the crowding theory (women are crowded into certain sectors, hence the low wage), segmented labor markets (highlighting the importance of type of employment and function) and matching theories. All these theories offer explanations for the lower economic position of women in the labor market as compared with men and their lower wages (For reviews see Reynolds, 1978; Polachek and Siebert, 1993; Schippers, 1987). Because the emphasis here is on labor force participation and not on wages (although wages play an important role in the supply theories, see next section), these theories will not be further explored in this study.

10.3.3 Labor supply models

When interpreting changes over time, it must be remembered that almost all variables have changed which might have influenced female labor supply, including social and cultural gender norms, family relationships, dependencies within the family, technology improvements (e.g. with respect to the household, market, health and contraceptives) and legal constraints. Zimmermann (1985:63) mentions economic, political, social, demographic and medical factors influencing the labor supply of married women, while moreover *Gesellschaftliche Rahmenbedingungen* (cultural frameworks) are of importance. The published figures in chapter 2 are the result of all these changes. To distinguish between these influences, we have to be more specific. Therefore, in the majority of labor supply models, attention is paid to only a few variables explaining changes in and levels of female labor force participation, highlighting the importance of these specific variables and the direction of the changes.

The method of analysis employed in these labor supply models, based on rational behavior, provides the framework nowadays applied to nearly all aspects of human life[21] (see also next section). The analyses provide insight into the behavior of individuals, family organization and structure under different laws, circumstances, and cultures (Becker, 1991:17). The behavior is coordinated by implicit or explicit markets. In these models, the decisions individuals take throughout their lives can be most easily shown and understood through far-reaching simplifications, each emphasizing the aspects to be investigated and understood. Each model focuses on one or two of these aspects, in general neglecting the interaction with others.

The basic labor supply model (1), the extensions such as the Becker model and the Gronau model (2) and the Human Capital model (3) are reviewed in brief below. The implications for explaining the facts are discussed thereafter.

---

[21] The models are mainly headed by Gary Becker, and for which he received the Nobel Price in 1992.

1 The basic model of choice and the allocation of time

Labor supply models are based on the basic choice model of consumer theory, the foundation on which all extensions are built[22]. The simplest consumer choice model is that of a single, sex-neutral, person maximizing a utility function with market goods as arguments, subject to a budget constraint. Knowing the individual's preferences, her/his income and the prices of the market goods, the demand for goods and services by this individual can be explained. The theory is too vague about preferences to make predictions with regards to the effects of changes in exogenous variables. The preference structure can however be estimated from observed choices. Then, assuming stable preferences, predictions can be made about choices in new situations. The simple model is also used to explain the allocation of time[23].

In the simple neoclassical *labor supply model*, only market work can be performed and only market goods consumed. Time (T) is divided into leisure (t_l) and (paid) market labor (t_m). To simplify the demand for the goods and services distinguished can be aggregated into one category of *market or consumption goods* (C, with price p). The model focuses on leisure/market work and explains the allocation of leisure and market hours by an individual. Money income is no longer given as in the basic models of consumer's choice, but is determined by this allocation of time.

The choice problem is now formulated as maximizing a utility function with leisure and consumption goods as arguments $U = u(C, t_l)$, subject to a *full income* constraint. This full income is defined as the money income that an individual (or household) could attain if it used its time and physical capital at full capacity: $pC + wt_l = Y_0 + wT$ (where w is the wage rate and Y_0 is non-labor income). The optimal labor supply, under the condition that the ratio of the marginal utility of leisure to the marginal utility of total consumption (income) equals the real wage, is a function of the wage rate, non-labor income and the tastes of the individual.

A change in the wage rate not only appears in the role of a normal price effect, but also affects the full income. Hence, the income effect of an increase in the wage rate is positive on the demand both for goods and leisure (if both are normal goods), and of course negative on labor supply. The substitution effect is negative on leisure and positive on labor supply. As the wage rate increases, people may work more or less. This leaves the question whether the labor supply curve of market hours is *backward bending* or *forward rising*, over what wage ranges and for which groups.

---

22 This section assumes some knowledge of neoclassical/microeconomic consumer theory. The basic model is given in all microeconomic textbooks e.g. Gravelle and Rees, 1983. For mathematical representation and treatment of the extended models, references are given.

23 The scarcity of time was already mentioned by Gossen, the founding father of consumer theory, in 1854 (Heertje, 1992:288).

If leisure is a normal good, a rise in non-labor income leads unambigously to a decline in market hours. This effect (if measured at all) turns out to be very small (see also Killingsworth and Heckman, 1986:134). Supply curves also shift with changes in other exogenous variables, such as tax rates, social security provisions, presence of young children and measurable taste effects (e.g. between religious groups).

The general consensus in all seven countries seems to be that men show a *backward-bending supply curve* and women a *forward rising* one (mainly based on time series in the U.S). This backward-bending supply curve of men could be explained by the notion that on average the income effect is stronger than the substitution effect, so that an increase in the wage rate results in a decrease of hours of market work, as shown in time series. Despite the fact that the long-term decrease in male labor force participation rates is usually confirmed by empirical results for males in many countries (see below), there are potential objections to, or problems with, this conclusion[24] (Ehrenberg and Smith, 1991:199). The results of cross-section studies are even more ambiguous.

Long-run labor supply of men appears to be more elastic in the United States and less elastic in the Western European countries. Empirical results are ambiguous, but evidence for Germany and the United Kingdom suggests very steeply sloped, if not vertical, supply curves (Elliott, 1990:17). Theeuwes (1988:26) also concludes an inelastic labor supply for Dutch men, while Kooreman's results for men - with wives participating in the labor market - suggests a forward bending supply curve for men with relatively low wages and a backward bending supply curve for men with relatively high wages (Kooreman, 1986). Because labor force participation rates of adult men (aged 25 - 49) have hardly changed over the past century and a half - in 1990 still being over 90 per cent in all seven countries - an inelastic supply for this age group seems an inevitable conclusion.

The positively sloping supply curve usually found for women (see below), can only be explained by the dominance of the substitution effect over the income effect (although for recent doubts see Elliot, 1990:119, 120). As already mentioned, the bulk of supply analyses concentrate on labor force supply of married women (particularly the increases of the last two decades), while there has recently been some attention to the labor force supply of lone-mothers. Surprisingly little is known about labor supply of young girls, although young girls were in all countries a very substantial part of the female labor force up to about 20 years ago. An economic approach explicitly modelling the division of girls' time can

---

[24]. These authors doubt that for men the income effect is stronger than the substitution effect and mention the increasing availability of pensions and disability payments, the small decline in weekly working hours since World War II (may be due to a countervailing power from the demand side) and the influence of increased participation of married women on their husbands market hours independent of the male wage. See for a treatment of problems which arise for deriving meaningful behavorial parameters also Pencavel (1986).

reconcile apparently contradictory explanations (see below). It incorporates the fact (argued in the previous chapters) that women have seldom been able to take their labor force participation decisions independently of the family of which they were a part.

Up till now, the extensions of the simple model to multi-person households mainly concerned labor supply decisions by husband and wife or by cohabiting couples. Such labor decisions by wife and husband may or may not be based on a joint household utility function[25]. Where a household utility function is maximized subject to a joint budget constraint, the *labor supply of wife and husband* are determined simultaneously. Both depend on the couple's tastes for *commodities*, *leisure*, on *non-labor income* and on the *wages of wife and husband.*

If individual labor supply functions of both spouses are maximized, many different combinations may result. To determine a specific solution, behavioral postulates have to be introduced; for example, game theory outcomes - based on psychological advantages and gains due to economies of scale and specialization - such as a Patriarchal/dictator solution or a Nash solution (e.g. Manser and Brown, 1979; Ott, 1991, Kooreman, 1991). An attractive feature of these game theory models is their potential for shedding light on the decision process within households. However, as noted by Kooreman and Kapteyn (1990), if this potential is to be fully employed, direct information on the preferences of individual household members is needed in addition to information on observed behavior (Kooreman, 1991:3; Killingsworth and Heckman, 1986:134)). Such models may increase in importance, reflecting the increasing freedom of individual members to take decisions, in turn leading to an upsurge in negotiations and bargaining between these members. Alternatively - as a simpler approach - the market/household labor decision of a married woman may be constructed in a *secondary worker* model[26]. This implies that the labor force decision of the husband is determined independently of his wife. His optimal level of working hours and income depends only on his tastes and his own wage and wealth. His optimal income enters the

---

25 The validity of a joint utility function for husband and wife and/or other family members has been widely discussed. Samuelson (1956:9,10) asserted that the family will behave as an individual if an individual family member's utility is independent of the level of utility of any other member of the family, so that interdependency in utility and jointness in consumption is excluded. "But they are precisely the factors most responsible for the existence of the family as the predominant social institution in which individuals live." (Willis, 1979:29). Unfortunately the claim of caring and intrafamily transfers is not generally true, see also Killingsworth and Heckman, 1986:130,131).

26 In principal, this *male chauvinistic model* (Killingsworth, 1983) may be reversed into a *feminist or women's lib model* (see also Gustafsson, 1991) by substitution of male for female and the other way around. However, given the fact that married men in their prime ages always (if possible) worked full-time and married women not, such a reversed model will not contribute to the explanation of past trends.

budget constraint of his wife as *non-labor income*. Therefore, her optimal supply decision not only depends on her own tastes and own wage, but also on this non-labor income. Considering the findings of the previous chapters, this seems a more realistic model to explain historical changes than joint utility or separate utility models.
The model is supported by generally very low cross-effects from female wages on male labor supply.

The static model has also been converted into a time allocation model over the life cycle (first study by Ghez and Becker (1975)). In the life cycle context, with a life cycle constraint (full life cycle) when individuals expect wages to increase with age, there will be no income effect, only a positive substitution effect can be expected (see also Polachek and Siebert, 1993: 104; Ghez and Becker, 1975:12), explaining why (for men in particular) market hours increase with age.

The model also demonstrates the difference between permanent and transitory wage changes on labor supply. Transitory changes in income and wages can be expected to have more of an effect on hours worked than permanent changes, because people adjust their consumption to their permanent rather than their temporary income. Contrasting persons with permanently higher wages throughout their lives with persons with permanently lower wages, an income effect may be expected. However, a temporary wage increase will create mainly a substitution effect. "In good times, for example, wages will increase, and workers can be expected to work for longer hours while this lasts - to 'make hay while the sun shines'." (Polachek and Siebert, 1993:104). The existing link between market hours and earnings also has implications for consumption patterns. With leisure at a high price, people buy more ready-to-use products. "Thus at ages where wages are high, people work more, earn more and consume more." (Polachek and Siebert, 1993:106).

Many empirical studies suggest that female wage elasticities are large and men's small or negative (see also below). The standard interpretation 'explaining' why female (uncompensated) wage elasticities are higher compared with those of men is that the elasticity of demand for a good (leisure/non-market time) with respect to its price (wage) will be greater, the greater the availabity of alternatives to that good. This begs the question why women have more alternatives than men and why home production is primarily performed by women. Introducing alternative time uses, the explanatory power of the simple model increases, particularly with the extensions of Mincer, Becker and Gronau (see below: 2).

In general: the simple model should explain differences in labor force participation rates between men and women, or between women in different countries by different tastes and different wage levels. It does not explain why tastes and wage levels differ, nor can it predict which effect will dominate in which country[27].

2 The Becker model and the Gronau model

The analysis of the basic labor supply model would be appropriate wherever leisure time and hours of work in the market in fact constitute an exhaustive dichotomy (Mincer, 1962:43). Not even true for men, it is certainly not sufficient to analyze the labor force behavior of married women in terms of the demand for leisure: their demand for work at home must also be taken into account. "The latter is a demand for a productive service derived from the demand by the family for home goods and services." (Mincer, 1962:43). Income (equal to total family income) is assumed to have a positive effect on the demand for leisure, and hence a negative one on the hours of market work. With the income effect on the demand for home goods and services not likely to be negative, the effect of a family income increase (and stable prices) would be negative on supply only in the absence of substituability in the home production, which is obvious not the case. The degree of substituability is likely to have changed in the course of history and is likely at a given moment of time to differ depending on the content of home production. Substitutes for a mother's care of small children may be different from substitutes for food production. The strength of a wage effect is a matter of the degree of substitution between wage goods and home production (Mincer, 1962:46).

Mincer was the first to introduce home production[28] into the utility function, alongside leisure and market consumption goods. The extension of the simple model to a utility function with market goods (x_i) and more time uses (for example, time for home production) than leisure (t_{hi}) alone can be generalized as maximizing a utility function:

$U = u(x_1, x_2, \dots, x_n, t_{h1}, t_{h2}, \dots, t_{hm})$;

subject to the full income constraint $\sum p_i x_i + w \sum t_{hj} = Y_0 + wT$.

---

27 Other shortcomings of the models (for which they are often criticized) such as the assumed constant wage per hour, the neglect of institutional restrictions in the labor market (e.g. fixed hours of work, taxes, overtime, unemployment or disability insurances and rationing) can and have been integrated in the models. In addition, the models have been extended in many more ways.

28 This suggests a relatively late interest in the productive side of the household. However, Reid (1934) had already defined the concept of household production and mentioned the value of family labor, while Cairncross (1958), for example, mentioned the similarities between firms and households with respect to production. At the macroeconomic level, Kuznets (1941) argued that neglecting household production in the Gross National Product disturbs welfare comparisons (for a further discussion see Goldsmidt-Clermont, 1982 and Bruyn-Hundt, 1983, 1993).

Although the distinction is of value in interpreting female behavior, shortcomings of the model remained. One is that the utility function does not provide any insight into substitutionary and complementary relations between goods and time (Becker, 1991:25). A compensated increase in the wage rate could even increase time spent at most household/leisure activities. This is not the case in Becker's model (1965). The utility function in Becker's approach is separable in goods and time used to produce the same commodity; not the market goods itself but the *commodities* (Z_i) produced in the household with time t_{hi} and the market goods (x_i) entered the utility function (see also Becker, 1991:23ff)[29].

$$U = u\ (Z_1, Z_2, \ldots , Z_m), \text{ and } Z_i = f_i\ (x_i, t_{hi}; E_i), i = 1, \ldots ,m$$

where E_i represents household ability, human capital, social and physical climate, and other environmental variables. The shadow prices π_i of the commodities are equal to the minimum cost of production and the full income constraint is $\sum p_i x_i + w \sum t_{hi} = \sum \pi_i Z_i = Y_0 + wT$. The choices made in market and home activities depend on the wage rates of husband and wife, and on their household productivities. This implies that an increase in the wage rate necessarily decreases the output of time-intensive commodities relative to good-intensive commodities (Becker, 1991:25).

The main difference in interpretation of, for example, an observed decline in market working hours between the simple extended model and the Becker model is that the former stresses the growth in productivity in market work time and implies that of the resulting income and substitution effects the income effect is dominating, while the latter model explains the decline mainly on the grounds that time-intensive commodities have been luxuries (and income and substitution effects tend to offset each other). (See Becker, 1965:81). The model can be generalized to distinguish consumption at different ages (see subsection 3: investment in human capital).

A simple version of the time allocation model, assuming that the commodities are produced in the household according to a constant returns to scale Cobb-Douglas production function, can provide an explanation for the relatively large elasticity of married women's labor supply. "(S)o long as wives are 'better' at (having a higher output elasticity in) nonmarket production than husbands and earn wages no greater than those of (their) husbands, the *level* of labor supply will be lower but the *elasticity* of labor supply will be greater for wives than for husbands."... Identical conclusions can be reached with the simple model for analyses of *market* time "which means that from an empirical standpoint they are indistinguishable for all practical purposes" (Killingsworth and Heckman, 1986:138,139).

---

[29] Cigno (1991:39) prefers the more traditional usage of 'good' for something that yields direct utility (and which may not have a market) and 'commodity' as something that can be bought or sold in the market. Note that Becker (1991) is an enlarged edition of his 1981 Treatise of the Family, containing among other theories his 1965 theory.

Gronau (1977) simplified the theory by introducing a separate *household production function* in his *new home economics model*. The budget/household production constraint faced by, for example, the woman alone or the wife and husband together, is no longer linear[30]. The opportunity set combines household production with market opportunities. To construct the full opportunity set, the budget line is shifted upwards until it is tangent with the household production function. The more convex ('curved') the household production function is, the less substitutable market work will be for home work and the smaller the reduction in household working hours if wages increase. However, an increase in wages unambiguously reduces household working hours. For simplicity, Gronau assumes constant returns to scale and no joint production (or joint production and consumption: watching television while mending clothes, cooking as hobby or production)[31].

The model decomposes a wage effect into a production-substitution effect (depending on the substituability of market work for household work in the production of commodities), a consumption-substitution effect (between leisure and market hours) and an income effect. An increase in wages reduces household work, but the reduction will be smaller the less substitutable market work is for household work, such as the bearing, rearing and care of small children. An increase in non-labor income has no effect on the household work of employed men and women, but the household work of non-participating women declines (Bryant, 1990:136-140). This effect is expected to be more marked if the increase is transitory (Polacheck and Siebert, 1993:111). The model still cannot predict the net effect of a wage increase on market hours; again, this depends on the size of the substitution and income effects. However, the decrease in household work makes it more likely that an increase in market hours will result, in particular turning non-participating women into participants. The importance of the household production function is underlined by time use data (Juster and Stafford, 1991), indicating that specialization of tasks still exists (Polacheck and Siebert, 1993:111).

The model is basically a single person model again, implicitly assuming that the household production function applies to married women only, with non-labor income being equal to other household income, particularly the husband's earnings.

---

[30] The simplest household production model is describing Robinson Crusoe's situation, who is able to perform labor in household production, but not in market work (Bryant, 1990:122-125; Varian, 1987:502-515).

[31] In reality of course joint production exist. Another problem is the fact that in practice the distinction between consumption and production is unclear, causing many problems in the definition and measurement of time use (for discussions see: Hawrylyshyn, 1977; Bruyn-Hundt, Driehuis, Koot and Mossel, 1983; Begeer-van Tuinen, 1984; and Juster and Stafford, 1991).

The production function is sensitive to:
- education of the wife
- household technology
- investments in labor-saving equipment
- substitution possibilities

Changes in behavior can now be explained not only by changes in the shadow price of producing commodities (through changes in market prices and wages) and changes in full income and tastes, but also by shifts in the production function and by the demand for household production (family size).

3 Investment in human capital

The human capital theory was developed by Mincer (1958), Schultz (1960) and Becker (1964) (see also Becker, 1991:25). In this theory education is considered as an investment in human capital[32] in which time and current money can be traded for future pay (and no longer, as before, a consumptive activity). Greater education is associated with higher earnings and these earnings are viewed as a return on that investment[33]. Investments tend to decline with age. Individuals continue to a varying degree to invest in their human capital after the end of compulsory schooling through activities that involve a current cost in order to increase expected future earnings, such as on-the-job training. The prediction of the (basic) human capital schooling model is that individuals will base their schooling decisions on expected returns (Oosterbeek, 1992:13). In perfect capital markets, the present value of expenditures equals the present value of earnings and non-human assets. The optimal investment at any age is determined by the equality of marginal investment costs and marginal returns. Investments tend to decline with age, because fewer years then remain in which to receive returns, while investment costs tend to be lower at younger ages because the foregone value of time spent investing is cheaper then. The optimal stock of capital would rise at a diminishing rate, reach a peak and decline toward the end of life as depreciation exceeds gross investment (Becker, 1991:27).

The benefits and costs differ among individuals. In particular, children from poorer families are likely to spend less time in education and girls less than boys. The model emphasizes the view that if gender-specific role differentation in education begins in early childhood it will continue throughout adult life.

---

32 As with many concepts in neoclassical theory, the phrasing is not sympathetic (see also Fairy Tales, section 10.7).

33 References with strong empirical evidence are given by Oosterbeek, 1992: chapter 2.

The relationship between women's human capital accumulation and earnings has been examined in several studies (e.g. Hill and O'Neill, 1992; Mincer and Ofek, 1982; Mincer and Polachek, 1974, Polachek, 1975 etc.) and has been used to explain the lower level lower female wages compared with male. There is much criticism of the hypothesis that women by individual choice mainly tend to opt for female jobs, where the deterioration of skills is less, so leading to the greater tendency of women to be in low-skill jobs. This is also supposed to be the reason why women are concentrated in only a small number of occupations within each skill category. Differences in earnings between men and women which cannot be attributed to differences in human capital or other observable variables are labelled as wage discrimination. A weakness of the theory is that low female wages are cause and effect (through low investment activity) of the low female labor force participation rates. For this reason, the model gives an additional but still unsatisfactory explanation for female and male wages and for differences in female labor force participation rates. That different activity rates are based only on differences in human capital seems unlikely.

Other shortcomings are also signalled: in deciding whether or not to participate in formal education, the alternatives are easily recognized. In on-the-job-training, however, where nowadays the main differences between female and male education occur, there is usually no directly observable alternative (Hartog and Theeuwes, 1990:331). The same authors also discuss the shortcomings 'segmentationalists' see in this theory and the alternative screening or signalling theory.

4 Division of labor

The previous chapters have shown that the division of labor in the labor market was closely connected to the division of labor within households, with married women devoting most of their time to domestic activities and married men being engaged in market activities. The marriage contract protected women and children against abandonment.

Husband and wife both gain from a division of labor. The gain comes from increasing returns to investments in sector-specific human capital. "Specialization in the allocation of time and in the accumulation of human capital would be extensive in an efficient family even if all members were biologically identical" (Becker[34], 1991:30). Although Becker believes that biological differences are very important in explaining why women have traditionally done most of the child rearing, the main lesson from his analysis of an efficient division of labor is the

---

[34] Becker is nearly always misquoted here in as saying that he relies on biological differences to explain the division of labor and the fact that women are more productive at childbearing and rearing than men (See, for example, recently Van der Lippe, 1993).

gains to the family. Neither biology nor discrimination causes the traditional division of activities between men and women, he says, and in fact biological differences have probably even weakened the degree of specialization (Becker, 1991:4;30).

Misquotations or misunderstandings of Becker's theory are usually based on the following quotations, in which he argues that the sharp sexual division of labor is also partly due to intrinsic differences between the sexes and the fact that: "Women not only have a heavy biological commitment to the production and feeding of children, but they also are biologically committed to the care of children in more subtle ways. (..) Moreover, women have been willing to spend much time and energy caring for their children because they want their heavy biological investment in production to be worthwile. In addition, a mother can more readily feed and watch her older children while she produces additional children than while she engages in most other activities. This complementarity has been important because, until the last century, practically all women spent most of their prime adult lives with children." (Becker, 1991:38). Becker's analysis makes it clear that although women suffered from discrimination, no market discrimination or strong biological differences are needed to explain the division of labor or the large gap in earnings between men and women. Becker also argues that an efficient division of labor is perfectly consistent with the exploitation of women by husbands and fathers. The gain to men from exploitation tends to increase as the allocation of resources becomes more efficient. Thereby, exploitation is a separate issue from efficiency in the division of labor (Becker, 1991:4). An increase in divorce, longevity, and a decline in fertility and in the value of housework induce lesser degrees of specialization.

Ott (1992) stresses that specialization and the division of labor is undesirable. She applies a game theory model with a Nash solution. The threat points are determined as the points of utility each partner achieves if the marriage ends. If both partners agree to the traditional household division, their joint utility will be increased in the initial period. However, in the following period the negotation power of the woman will be reduced, lowering her threat point. The wife's power depends on her education, her own income, the presence of dependent children, etc. (See also, Gustafsson, 1993:9-12.)

10.3.4 Models of household formation and marriage

Coale (1971) noted that, although age patterns at first marriage and proportions ever married differ widely across populations, there is a remarkable similarity in these patterns once adjustments have been made for location, scale and the proportion ever experiencing the event. This demographic model has been widely applied and extended (see Montgomery and Trussell, 1986:215).

The simple economic models of marriage analyze the behavior of persons in a marriage market. The phrase 'marriage market' signifies that the mating of human individuals is highly systematic and structured (Becker, 1991:81). Participants prefer to marry if, and only if, their utility from marriage exceeds their utility from remaining single. The mating of likes or unlikes takes place when such pairings maximize aggregate commodity output over all marriages, regardless of whether the trait is financial (wage rates, property income), biological (height, race, age, physique), or psychological (aggressiveness, passiveness) (Becker, 1991:112, 113). An important factor in determining the potential gains from marriage is the existence of goods which satisfy two properties: they are difficult to obtain via market exchange and their production exhibits increasing returns to input of time (Montgomery and Trussell, 1986:239). Becker's model contrasts with models assuming a given ranking of potential mates which determines rather than is determined by the equilibrium sorting. These models are formulated in terms of optimal search strategies. Any marital offer valued above a threshold level (of the characteristics of the prospective spouse) is accepted, while offers below that level are spurned in favor of further search. These models then generate the distribution of age at marriage. Extensions which allow marriage offers to arrive with probabilities per period, uncertainty, intensive search and marital dissolution are considered in more advanced models (Montgomery and Trussell, 1986:235).

A central difficulty in applying search theory to marriage is the absence of a single observed variable, such as the wage rate in labor market search theories, which can fully characterize a prospective spouse (Montgomery and Trussell, 1986:237).

In addition to economic models explaining why a man and a woman might find it advantageous to marry, economic explanations are presented as to why they favor a public form of marriage contract (Cigno, 1991). The literature on marital dissolution follows the same lines as the formation models: search theories and bargaining models.

Given enhanced earning opportunities for women, greater financial hardship suffered by women with children after divorce, and reduced gains from marriage, these theories predict a decline in the popularity of marriage.

10.4 Theoretical highlights of fertility behavior

What determines the number of children born? Nearly every science has contributed to the factors involved in answering this question: biology, theology, psychology, sociology, demography etcera.
The first economic theory of population growth was formulated by early English economists, of whom Malthus (1798) is the most well-known.

Like so many other economic theories, it was formulated within an equilibrium context. The theory assumed that the supply of land is fixed. Population growth and diminishing returns to scale of food supply gradually increase the price of food. The inevitable food crisis stops the population growth. (Schultz, 1979:15). "When income falls because the growth in population exceeds the growth in subsistence goods, marriages are delayed, the frequency of coition within marriage is reduced, and fewer children survive to adulthood. The first two factors are "moral constraints" and the last produces "misery" (Malthus, 1933, bk.I, chap.II). Moral constraints would be the main check on excessive population growth if the demand for births had a high income elasticity, whereas misery would be the main check if the number of births were insensitive to income." (Becker, 1991:136)[35].

Advances in useful knowledge, embodied in human and non-human capital, have destroyed the general validity of the assumption of the fixed supply of land, while at the same time economic growth and fertility decline have coincided[36]. In more recent theories this assumption is replaced by the fixed supply of human time. This causes increases in the price of human time relative to the price of material factors and goods. (Schultz, 1979:15). Hence, more recent economic theories of fertility are founded on the scarcity of human time and as such can be used in a choice-theory framework. In these theories the decisions about the *demand and supply*[37] of children are taken by the potential parents or (to simplify) the potential mother[38]. Children are viewed as producer durables (producing a future income for their parents) and consumer durables (producing a stream of future utilities). Leibenstein was the first

---

35 Becker also mentions the Darwinian theory. Darwin, greatly influenced by Malthusian theory, states that by natural selection the population tends to become highly fertile, fertility being inherited from parents (Becker, 1991:136,137).

36 According to Siegers (1987:92), Doubleday, Spencer, Brownlee and Gini held physiological reasons responsible for this fertility decline and Dumont democratizing processes and increasing competition. It was not until the beginning of this century that Brentano and Mombert showed statistically that there is a negative relationship between welfare level and fertility (Siegers, 1987:92).

37 To non-economists the concepts used in these economic theories of fertility often look fairly strange: children are considered as (producer or consumer durable) commodities, of which mature persons are both demanders and suppliers. The *production of children* is supposed to take place within the family and involves time and money costs. The (often only) commonly assumed distinction between *children* and other *home produced* commodities is that children are more time intensive (see Becker, 1981, Willis, 1979, De Tray, 1979).

38 According to Fuchs (1989) the demand is higher from women than from men. The evidence he gives is very weak.

to develop an economic theory along these lines in 1957 (Siegers, 1987:93,94), and Becker, Schultz, etc. soon followed. Easterlin (1987:304) distinguishes two main lines of work explaining fertility behavior within an framework of economic theory, the "Chicago-Columbia" and the "Pennsylvania" models.

Chicago-Colombia models

The first line is based on the *New Home Economic theory*. Standard microeconomic theory of demand could not explain why fertility declines with income, unless children are inferior goods[39]. Marshall wrote: "a permanent increase of prosperity is quite as likely to lower as to raise the birth rate" (Marshall, 1972:439, quoted by Siegers, 1987:91). The incorporation of the household production theory and the theory of the allocation of time, led to a new theory of "the demand for children". Not the number of children is the *commodity* demanded and supplied, but a concept named *child services*, consisting of the *number/quantity* and *quality* of children. Supply is determined solely by biological factors. The theory explains a decline in fertility by a decline in the demand for child services. In its turn, the decrease in the demand for children is brought about by a strong increase in the relative price of children (ascribed mainly to the rise in the opportunity costs of the mother's time). This price effect is much stronger than the income effect due to the average increased levels of income. "I believe that the growth in the earning power of women during the last hundred years in developed countries is a major cause of both the large increase in labor force participation and the large decline in fertility." (Becker, 1991:140). Many economists have contributed to the development of this theory and of empirical evidence to support it, such as Becker (1960, etc.), Ben-Porath (1973), Cigno (1991), Lancaster (1971), Mincer (1963), Nerlove (1974), De Tray (1973), Willis (1973, 1979), T.W. Schultz (1974), and T.P. Schultz (1976, 1981). The number of children is negatively related to the value of married women's time, and is more often positively than negatively related to the wage rate or earnings of husbands (Becker, 1991:140).

---

39 In 1956 Fuchs presented a simple version of a relative-income hypothesis in order to explain why fertility was high in the 1950s and why he expected it to decline. According to Fuchs, the direction and rate of the change in income is far more important than the absolute level of income. When people are more prosperous in adulthood than they had expected to be, high fertility rates will result. "The failure of the 1970s to meet the rising tide of expectations undoubtedly contributed to the increase in the age of marriage and the low fertility rate in that decade." (Fuchs, 1983:22). If this were true, we should have expected a decline at the end of the 1980s; this was certainly not the case in Sweden.

Other factors mentioned by Becker adding to the explanation of the decline are that households prefer their own children and - to a certain extent - changes in sterility and knowledge of birth control methods[40]. Similar to the development in labor supply theories, there has been a gradual evolution of this theory with the successive incorporation of many factors influencing fertility.

Agnosticism about preferences is common among economists; however, the importance of altruism within families began to be recognized systematically by economists during the 1970s (Becker and Barro, 1988:3 and the two earlier studies by Barro and by Becker mentioned in that paper). Becker and Barro (1988) rely heavily on the assumption of altruism towards children to generate a dynamic analysis of fertility and population change. They show that fertility in an open economy depends positively on the world's long term interest rate. Fertility also depends negatively on the rate of technological progress and the growth rate of transfer payments in the economy. Uncertainty, marriage and the spacing of births are neglected.

Pennsylvania models

In Pennsylvania models, supply is constrained by behaviour that has the unintentional effect of limiting fertility. This second line of work accepts the importance of the demand factors mentioned above. Nevertheless, two other factors are also seen as important: i.e. the potential supply of children and the costs attached to deliberate fertility control, in particular the social cost of deviant behavior. The first additional factor depends on *fecundity* (the ability to conceive children). It is surprising how little is known about this factor, despite the tremendous progress in medical science and careful long-term records kept by demographers. The question arises whether the probability of a successful conception is dependent on maternal age, or not. Recent medical research seems to indicate that this probability first increases and decline after about the age of (nowadays) 32 years.

Rational absence of fertility control, i.e. *natural fertility behavior*, prevails if there is excess demand for children or if the disutility attached to fertility control exceeds the disutility of an excess number of children (Easterlin, 1989:304).

The demarcation between the two lines of work is not always clear and more and more economists stray across it. For example, Heckman and Willis (1975) and Michael and Willis (1975) also pay attention to the supply side, although doing so via uncertainty. Two more recent studies dealing with uncertainty are presented in Cigno and Ermisch (1989) and

---

[40] Becker (1960) gave an affirmative answer to the question whether major changes in average (natural) fertility had been caused by changes in sterility and knowledge of birth control methods. In 1981 he believed that the major changes had been caused primarily by other changes in the demand for children.

Barmby and Cigno (1990). Allowing for uncertainty does not alter the signs of the effects of personal characteristics on fertility behavior. The latter two studies also investigated factors influencing the timing of births. The birth of a child reduces the mother's earnings directly by reducing her labor force participation and indirectly by slowing down or decreasing her human capital for labor market work. Cigno and Ermisch (1989) show that women with more human capital at marriage or with higher earning husbands have their children sooner, while women with steeper career profiles (e.g. clerical in contrast with manual occupations) have their children later.

Most recent fertility models are closely related to that advanced by Willis (1979:28). This model abstracts from the sequential and stochastic nature of the family's economic and demographic life cycle. It also neglects several other characteristics, such as the parental obligations to the child[41]. Husband and wife, making all the family decisions, are assumed to have perfect and costless control over their fertility and perfect foresight concerning their lifetime plan. In reality, the only control they can excercise is the attempt to influence the monthly probability of conception and, given conception, the probability that a pregnancy will terminate in a live birth. Imperfect fertility control and child mortality and morbidity pose additional constraints on family fertility behavior and add further dimensions to family choice (Willis, 1979:27).

To explain the long-term decline in fertility rates, a combination of the two models, focussing on the two dimensions of the cost of children, seems attractive. Cost have increased through higher education and longer dependence of the child and the higher opportunity costs of the mother, as stressed in the Chicago model. The social cost of the choice of small families, or even no children, has decreased, as small rather than large families have become the norm, supporting the Pennsylvania approach.

Finally, it may be pointed out that recent work shows that economic models may indeed be useful in analyzing fertility behavior, particularly in influencing the timing of the first birth (Heckman and Walker, 1990; Heckman and Walker, 1990a; Groot and Pott-Buter, 1992).

---

[41] Willis (1979) mentions seven characteristics of fertility behavior making it difficult to analyse fertility within a choice-theoretic framework. 1) Most child bearing and child rearing activities are non market activities without any observed transaction costs. 2) Children acquire time and money costs. 3) The parental obligation to a child tends to be a long term one. 4) The wide variation of parental expenditures in time and money suggests that parent's obligation to children is not exogenously determined. 5) Fertility is motivated by consumption, saving or investment considerations. 6) Parents cannot exercise direct control over the number and timing of the children they will bear and rear to maternity. 7) The appropriate unit of analysis is difficult to define. Decisions concerning age at marriage, to have children, and the characteristics and preferences of the marital partners are closely intertwined. Moreover, as children mature they may have an independent effect on family decisions.

10.5 Non-economic labor theories

Many sciences have tried to explain the division of labor in the labor market. Some claim that from the beginning of anything worthy of being called 'society' men have always being dominated women and that this is reflected in the universally lower status of female activities (Lévi-Strauss, 1969). This sexual division of labor is built into all human societies due to physical differences between the two sexes. Others put even more stress on physique and aggression, portraying hunting as the primal activity and the driving force behind human evolution: the bonding of males in hunting (and warfare) is seen as the basis of universal male domination (Tiger and Fox, 1971, quoted by Bradley, 1989). Sociobiologists also see genetic and biological differences as the cause of the asymmetrical division of labor (Bradley, 1989:29). The same author quotes many others theorists (including Ortner, Rosaldo, Firestone, Ardener and De Beauvoir) who 'root femaleness in biology and maleness in the social domain', with (for Ortner and Rosaldo) a key factor being the symbolization of women as closer to nature and the identification of men with culture, which they see as nearly universal. Whatever men do then becomes the high-status activity. Others argue that the growth of competitive exchange between lineage groups led to men controlling the labor of women in order to procure surplus goods for exchange. Thus the growth of male dominance is inextricably involved with the development of class hierarchies.

These views of male dominance ignore anthropological and historical evidence of female power and are challenged by MacCormack and Strathern (1980), who stress the variability of the sexual division of labor, and the relativity of meanings attached to it and to other gender categorizing systems. They reject all attempts, whether by Marxists or cultural structuralists, to develop universal models of gender relations. Even to generalize is seen as dangerous.

Some Marxist accounts rest on the notion of a 'sudden break', that is, some moment in history when men actively seized power from women. This goes back to the ideas of Bachofen and Engels, who both suggested that the earliest societies were matriarchal, based on a 'mother-right' derived from women's reproductive power, which was later ousted by patriarchy (Bradley, 1989:31).

Sociological and feminist debates

As with neoclassical theories, sociologists interest in women's employment has expanded rapidly since the 1970s (Martin and Wallace, 1984:1). Sociology also has no one single theory which explains each and every aspect of social life.

In the Netherlands, Jeanne de Bruijn (1989) has described the developments in research on women's labor force participation from the end of the nineteenth century until 1988. In the first two decades of the century, the *Nationaal Bureau voor Vrouwenarbeid* (National Bureau for Women's Work) carried out a large number of empirical studies. Work was then considered an economic necessity for working class women. The empirical activities of the Bureau ceased after the 1920s, after which time the Bureau undertook only careers advice and job-guidance for women. The only problems of working girls deemed worthy of academic study were pedagogical ones: how to prepare girls to become good mothers.

At the turn of the century Steinmetz, who later became the doyen of Dutch sociology, developed a paradigm concerning the necessity of a difference between the sexes. Women were divided into 'real women' and 'traitors to their own sex'. He saw a need to protect the monogamous family and to protect 'femininity' by excluding women from paid work and by confining them to household duties. Only women unsuitable for marriage could learn a profession, so that their breed would become extinct. This paradigm became incorporated into the basics of sociology in the period between the two world wars. Right through until the end of the 1960s and the start of women's studies in the Netherlands in the 1970s these roots of the sociological discipline remained unchallenged (De Bruijn, 1989:436, 437).

The first sociological research on the issue of women's work started at the end of the 1950s. It concerned itself solely with the attitudes of married women, whether working outside their homes or not, related to factors such as age, educational level, number of children, income, etcera. Combining a job and household duties was labelled a personal conflict of roles for the woman herself. Household duties were not considered to be work (De Bruijn, 1989:435).

Feminism, in its debate with existing forms of sociological analysis, opened up new areas of investigation. In the Netherlands as elsewhere, the relations between men and women in terms of power became the central issue. Bradley (1989) reviews the existing (English) literature by focusing on a series of debates and disagreements within historical and sociological studies. The writer is most sympathetic to explanations based on the argument that an understanding of sexual divisions must embrace both work and home, production and reproduction. "Without doubt, patriarchy has been the key concept used in the feminist critique of other types of social, political and cultural theorising. Yet there is considerable disagreement over its meaning, except at the most general level, and some feminists have come to feel considerable doubt as to its usefulness as a concept. Much has been written on this topic, and the debates have been particularly well surveyed by Barrett (1980) and Walby (1986), who provide useful and full accounts of the various individual contributions." (Bradley, 1989:51). The debate about the relative power of capitalism and patriarchy as frameworks for explaining sexual divisions, and about the precise nature of the link between the two systems, has been going on since the early 1970s and volumes (literally) have been written on this topic[42]. To explain gender segregation in employment, sociologists have developed concepts drawn from economic theory, such as human capital. Walby describes the use of women's labor in the nineteenth and twentieth centuries in terms of a conflict between the desire of capitalists for cheap labor (pulling women into jobs) and the motivations of capitalists as men and, particularly, of male workers to keep women under patriarchal control within the family (pulling them back into the home). This is not just a matter of fear of female competition, as assumed in segmented labor market theory, but of a wish for a comfortable home with a full-time domestic worker catering to her husband's needs, allied to a desire that women should not challenge the authority of the male breadwinner by gaining full economic independence. This Walby argues, accounts for the ebbs and flows of women's labor market participation. Yeandle (1984) has distinguished similar conflicts between 'economic' and 'traditional' motives affecting the choices of families in the 1980s: families want the additional earnings of wives, but at the same time tend to adhere to the traditional view of the ideal family as male breadwinner with wife as full-time mother.

These views still focus too narrowly on market work and neglect the pre-market social conditioning role of the family. Although the family no longer directly assigns its members to specific jobs outside the home, it still has a crucial role in preparing young people for segregated work through processes of differential socialization (Oakley, 1981). Within the family, children develop ideas about proper behavior by girls and boys, women and men, and develop expectations about their own adult futures. This process is then carried on into schools and other educational establishments; research has shown that the expectations of teachers, parents and other pupils all tend to push boys and girls towards jobs considered suitable for their sex (Sharpe, 1976; Oakley, 1981; Wainwright, 1984).

Feminists have often criticized sociologists' use of the concept of socialization for the danger it holds of a too deterministic view of these influences in early life. The individual's exposure to social definitions and redefinitions of sex roles goes on all through adult life. Research by women who have studied in detail the relationships in particular factories or workplaces has revealed the crucial role of the work environment as a site for these processes. The key idea here is that of a 'gendered work environment' or 'work culture'. Bradley (1989) mentions several studies which have shown how in factories segregated workgroups of women and men develop their own highly specific and mutually exclusive cultures. Women's cultures centre on their home lives, on families and domesticity: conversation, rituals and symbols are concerned with homes, romance, marriage, children, clothes, food and the feminine lifestyle. Cakes and

---

[42] Bradley mentions as two of the key texts: Kuhn, A. and A. Wolpe (1978) *Feminism and Materialism* and Sargent, L. (1981) *Women in Revolution: The Unhapyy Marriage of Marxism and Feminism.*

recipes are exchanged, clothing catalogues circulated, advice on how to handle husbands and boyfriends passed on. By contrast, men's cultures are more work-centred, and also emphasize exaggerated versions of masculinity (sometimes symbolized by aggressive initiation rituals): talk features sport, heavy drinking, sexual bravado; anecdotes stress strength, audacity, resistance to authority and physical exploits of various kinds. The boss adopts the role of a patriarchal father, and in return for total obedience and commitment to him the women are allowed to develop their own gender-based rituals and activities. Women 'feminize' the office with photos and pot plants, developing their own homely patterns of social contact. In this way, patriarchal control is subtly maintained. By contrast, studies of women entering male-dominated professions show how women have to struggle to fit into male work environments and cultures, often finding themselves excluded from male friendship groups and social activities crucial in making contacts and furthering careers.

The importance of these gendered work cultures has not yet been sufficiently recognized. Reflecting and enhancing segregation, they serve to divide the work force and to set women and men apart as rivals, if not downright competitors. They help to preserve conventional views of proper masculine and feminine behaviour both inside and outside the world of work.

They 'domesticize' or 'masculinize' capitalist working conditions, making them more human and tolerable, but also ensuring that people are less likely to challenge them or to seek reform. They also perpetuate views of sexuality which portray men as aggressive and predatory, and women as seductive and flirtatious, so that sexual relations are conceived as a game or even a war, rather than a free merging of equals. As much as any other social institution, gendered work cultures maintain the idea that the sexes are inherently different; in so doing they ensure that men's and women's work experience does indeed remain different and jobs stay sex-typed (Bradley, 1989:70).

10.6 Interpreting broad historical trends in labor force participation

This book presents a large amount of data on women, men and work. The next step would be to confront data with theories, to find out what the data mean for the theories - as a test of their relevance - and what the theories mean for the data - as a framework for interpretation. This is a major undertaking, which will be addressed at a later date. What can be given here is broad-brush outline of major developments. Child labor has disappeared (below the age of 12 around 1930, below the age of 15 shortly after World War II). Labor force participation of girls first increased (until the 1950s or 1960s) and then decreased. For young men it steadily decreased. Labor force participation of married women first decreased at the end of the nineteenth or beginning of the twentieth century and then, especially after 1960, rapidly increased. Participation of the elderly, both female and male, decreased throughout.

To apply a standard neoclassical supply and demand framework to the broad picture observed, one might divide male labor into subgroups on the basis of age: young, adult and elderly. For the young the participation decision interacts with schooling decisions and for the elderly with retirement decisions. For females the same subdivision may be applied, but now marital status is also relevant. As a first approximation, young might be equated with single, adult with married and elderly with widowed, but this may be too crude.

In a smooth equilibrium model, wages would be determined at the intersection of the supply and demand curves. In a model with less flexible wages, unemployment may be an intermediary variable, with discouraged supply as a dampening variable for open unemployment. Shifts in demand and supply curves generate shifts in employment and in wages (and/or unemployment). Full application of such models is not feasible as data on wages and unemployment over the long run are not available. But some tentative analysis is certainly warranted.

10.6.1 Interpreting the historical developments for male participation

Labor supply of young males is reduced as schooling participation increases. The latter is probably caused more by easier access to funds for human capital investment (parental income, student grants) than by any increased pay-off on schooling.

A child's time can be divided into leisure, investment in human capital and productive time. Assuming that over the first 10 to 15 years parents are predominantly responsible for the allocation of the child's time, what influences the outcome? The poorer the family, the more difficult, it will be to raise the funds to finance investments in the human capital of children. Moreover, the principle of diminishing marginal utility of money will require higher marginal rates of return from investments, and these may be less obvious to parents who did not receive much schooling themselves. In addition, these private investments by the parents in their children will in general result in private returns to the children rather than directly to the parents themselves. It is likely therefore that in poor families, children will have to participate in productive activities as soon as possible. Legislation preventing children from performing industrial labor is seen as a constraint, particularly if wages for children in other sectors are lower. The same applies to compulsory schooling. Schooling reduces additional household income from children, but on the other hand the public financing of compulsory schooling reduces the cost for poor families. This explains the resistance by poor parents to child labor laws and compulsory schooling. It also explains why, despite increasing government subsidies and increasing incomes, children from poorer families receive less investment in human capital.

At the macroeconomic level, the reduction in labor supply of young males as a result of increased schooling might be expected to produce an increase in relative male youth wages, unless demand contracts at the same time or young males are perfect substitutes for other labor (e.g. experienced males, or certain categories of female labor). Increased supply of educated labor should depress wages for the more highly educated. Sketchy observations suggest that this has certainly been the case (wage differentials have been reduced across the boars), although this depressing effect has no doubt been countered by the increased demand for more highly educated labor emanating from technological developments.

Adult males are not very interesting in terms of participation behavior. Participation is rather inelastic, wages follow the increase in labor productivity and part of the gain is used to buy more leisure: the labor supply curve in hours is backward bending.

Earlier retirement for males is mostly due to rising incomes (i.e. a positive effect on leisure demand from increased own income, or income from children who support their aged parents), to a large extent presented as institutionalized pension and retirement schemes. The latter schemes have even been used as a policy instrument to reduce supply at times when there was a general excess of labor. Hence, to explain (or interpret) historical developments in male labor force participation reference is made to technological developments that have increased demand for educated labor and, by raising the general wage level, increased the demand for leisure (shorter working hours, earlier retirement) and made funds for human capital investments more generally available. There is no a priori need to invoke shifts in preferences other than those related to income level, i.e. with stable preferences, reservation wages may go up with income.

10.6.2 Interpreting the historical developments for female participation

This involves some features similar to those discussed in relation to male participation: retirement behavior can be interpreted as a strong income effect on the demand for leisure dominating the substitution effect, and reduced participation of young women as increased schooling due to cheaper and easier funding. However, the reduced participation of young women was preceded by a period of increased participation, as teenage girls no longer stayed at home but entered the labor market. Whether at home or in the labor market, they worked to a large extent in (unpaid or paid) domestic service, thus gaining experience for the most important activity during married life. Increased productivity in other jobs and the creation of new jobs pushed up wages and annihilated the demand for domestic service, except from the relatively rich.

Within the economic profession the explanation that commands the widest consensus is that higher wages have attracted more married women into the labor force (Fuchs, 1983:131; Mincer, 1985; Becker, 1991). To explain why there was no increase in married labor force participation during the first half of the twentieth century, demand side constraints are usually mentioned. Atkins and Hoggett (1984:18), for example, mention several reasons for the absence of any increase in Great Britain. The first reason is that increased work opportunities for women created mainly white-collar jobs, where a marriage bar operated; the second, that in 1922 married women were disqualified from drawing unemployment benefits, even if they had been in an occupation for which they were payable. The third reason was the number of single women who were forced to provide for themselves after World War I. Tilly and Scott (1987:197-200) attributed the decline of married women in Great Britain and France at the end of the nineteenth century partly to declining opportunities for married women, partly to the increase in men's real wages, partly to the decline in family size and partly to the prolonged residence of working children in the parental household, contributing to the household budget. In the Netherlands, the late industrialization and the large supply of male workers up to World War II may have ensured a low demand for married women in industry. However, demand for women in industry was also low in Denmark and Sweden. The sociological and feminist explanations concerning male authority over women's labor and cultural definitions of gender roles add to our understanding of the persistent sexual division. Although all factors mentioned in sections 10.3 to 10.4 may be of influence, none of these theories offer a satisfactory explanation of the trends of married women in all seven countries.

To interpret the developments for married women within an economic framework, one may conceive of a consumption-leisure model with 4 categories of goods: home care, personal child care time, leisure and consumption commodities. Child care time is a luxury good and so initially is home care. Rising wages of husbands increased the demand for child care time and home care and induced married women to stay at home as soon as they could afford to do so. Eventually, however, the demand for home care by the wife has lagged behind and lost its luxury character: improved household technology (and increased capital intensity which families could now afford), together with reduced family size have decreased the demand for home care. This decrease has been stronger than the increase associated with the increased income levels. A similar development can be distinguished for child care time, which is gradually losing its luxury character. So, the substitution effect eventually has come to dominate the income effect, and married women prefer more market work to combine with home care and child care time.

The relatively high employment of married women outside the home in nineteenth-century Europe can now be explained. The model is characterized by a continuity of traditional values, untouched by the behavioral changes which occur when economic circumstances change.

If current trends continue, the division of labor will in future be less and less linked to gender. Sex will be a declining predictor of income and labor activities. Men will specialize more in household work, and women more in market work. Both men and women will then able to enjoy the combination of caring for children and having paid market work.

10.6.3 Differences between the Netherlands and the other six countries

It is obvious that differences between the Netherlands and the other six countries are closely related to low labor force participation rates of married women, the dominance of bourgeois family ideals and high fertility rates[43]. The ideals of motherhood and family life, bestowing a higher status on married women working in their own households and not in the labor market were supported by all kinds of legislation, which at the same time acted as a constraint on every married woman who wanted to follow a deviant pattern. The division of labor in the households was reflected in the labor market by the low participation rates of women in the industrial sector (this not being a suitable preparation for motherhood).

The interpretation of lower participation rates of married women using the neoclassical theoretical models described above leaves the possibility of differences in preferences, female wages, non-labor income, prices of child care, home care or production technology. There is no evidence that production technology in the Netherlands differed from that in the other six countries[44]. Data about wages are not available, but there is no reason to expect much lower female wages in the Netherlands. Increases in non-labor income seem also the same as those in the other countries[45], although average levels of Gross National Income were relatively high at the beginning of the twentieth century. Shadow prices of child care or home care may have differed though. Net wages for married women used to be low because of the marriage bars and other disincentives in the tax and social security system. Own child care and own home care, being luxury goods, could be acquired relatively early by many families in the Netherlands due to the high level of National Income. This in turn created a tradition of strong preferences.

---

43 Differences due to registration and demographic composition are disregarded here.

44 Many authors believe that changes in household production have not been a major determinant of increases in married women's market hours (see Polacheck and Siebert, 1993:110).

45 For a more detailed review of increases in Gross National Product in the Netherlands compared with the other six countries and of other indicators suggesting different economic developments see: Pott-Buter and Reitsma (1993).

According to sociological theories, pre-market social conditioning of sex roles reinforces the existing patterns. Patriarchal power completes the picture. Strong market incentives and changes in political powers are necessary to change the dominant behavior.

The high preferences for own child care and own home care are reflected in substitution elasticities for married women in the Netherlands higher than those found in any of the other six countries. However, these are declining.

For this reason, without being able to quantify the effect of the other variables, a specifically high long-term preference for child care (and home care) may well be a strong candidate for explaining the Dutch peculiarities in female labor, family and fertility.

10.7 Fairy Tales

1 *Female labor force participation has increased continuously since industrialization.*

One of the most widespread common beliefs is that female labor force participation has increased continuously ever since industrialization. The facts have shown this is not the case, either for all women together or for married women in isolation. This also implies that the history of women's work cannot be understood as a gradual evolution from a traditional place at home to a modern position in paid employment outside the home.

2 *Industrialization gradually transferred tasks originally performed in the home and on the farm, such as spinning, weaving, candlemaking and brewing, to the factory. This made it increasingly difficult to combine motherhood with productive labor.*

This generally accepted idea about the effect of industrialization is sometimes even seen as *destroying domestic industry* and the *balance* between motherhood, domestic work and market labor, separating women from 'productive activities'. It seems doubtful whether these statements are true, either as regards timing or as regards the destruction or separation of productive activities.

The processes separating productive activities from the home and transferring them into factories and workshops seem to have started much earlier than the nineteenth century, at various times depending on the industrial structure of the country in question. On the other hand, this separation was limited. The division of labor between market work and household work was (and is) less strict in small shops, small handicraft workshops and on farms than in larger-scale industrial enterprises. The idea of the transfer of activities from the home to the market is refuted by the considerable number of women who continued to work as outworkers or homeworkers or who remained involved in family-based productive market labor. Even if industrialization did bring a transformation (of market labor into productive/consumptive labor at home) the evaluation of the outcome as 'better' or 'worse' is subjective and differs from, for example, views held in the early twentieth century. As was shown in the previous sections of this chapter, productive/consumptive labor in private households increased at least until the 1960s, with only the products changing, and if there has been a decline it is only a very recent one, due mainly to declining fertility.

3 *The transfer of work out of the home or farm into factories assigned men as producers to the public sphere and women as housewives to the private sphere.*

The view mentioned in fairy tale number 2, has also given rise to the idea of a previous period in which women were thought to have participated fully in 'productive activities', while the transfer of work out of the home or farm into factories assigned men as producers to the *public sphere* and women as housewives to the *private sphere*. The notion that capitalism and industrialization led to a sharp split between the private sphere of the home and the public sphere of work and politics has long been part of orthodox sociological thought. This overlooks the fact that the private sphere performs quite useful functions for the public sphere (at the same time contributing to its perpetuation). Fairy tale number 2 already brought into question the extent to which the separation of productive activities has in fact really occurred. In a more general way, the family remains linked to the world of work, performing some important functions for it, especially those of training. The strong tradition of children following their mothers and fathers into their particular field of work work gradually weakened. But in the nineteenth century, and among poorer families right up until World War II, it was still commonplace for parents to decide what work their children should take up (Bradley, 1989:42).

4 *The decline in productive activities of women at home led to the rise of feminism, to changes in the family, to a deterioration of the position of women, to channelling women into inferior work and to job segregation.*

With the decline being doubted, the causal effects have to be doubted too. Moreover, if separation of home and work were indeed the cause of the job segregation in particular (and therefore of low wages and low labor force participation) return of work into the home should be a way of breaking it down. However, "homeworkers are at the bottom of the pyramid in each occupation, in terms of pay, fringe benefits, promotion changes and status - and are mainly women. All this suggests that, whatever the original effect of the move out of the home, this is no longer the major cause of segregation." (Bradley, 1989:43). This argument is closely related to the following common belief.

5 *Women's economic position has improved considerable since labor force participation of women increased.*

Comparing women's position now with that in the past is a difficult matter if the criteria are not clear. Usually what is meant is that the position of married women or women in the prime of life has improved, because their economic independence is increased by having their own earnings. It may be doubted, whether women's position relative to men has in fact improved. Certainly, many women are still involved in the least protected types of employment. Part-time and temporary work generate atypical employment relationships, as do putting-out systems, outworking and sub-contracting. In contrast to the more visible character of temporary and part-time working, outworking has a lower profile in the labor market (although productive activities in the market can be combined with one's own home activities).

Outworking consists of work at home or outside the employer's or organizer's premises. It can take the form of piecework or a combination of piecework and fixed payments. Intrinsic to outwork is the dependent, subordinate and isolated position of the almost always female (married) worker, isolated from the sale or marketing of her output. It has the advantage of offering women the opportunity to become economically active, but places them in a vulnerable position. Of course, the same applies to domestic servants working part-time in private households. Domestic service and home working are two of the more constant features of the position of women in the labor market.

Like home workers, unpaid family workers (other than the assisting wife in some countries) are poorly protected by social or labor laws. This type of employment can, however, constitute a buffer against unemployment. Home-based types of employment reinforce traditional stereotypes of women as only occasional and marginal participants in the labor market. Moreover, all these types of work attract women into sectors in which they are already well represented, thus reinforcing the sex segregation of women in the labor market.

6 *The need for women to participate in the labor market in the second half of the nineteenth century was created by an excessive supply of women.*

The thesis is too general, however, and has at best a weak general support. Increased supply and participation concerned middle-class women. However, the middle classes were becoming poorer at that time and increased participation may well have been an income effect.

7 *Both World Wars have weakened social norms circumscribing the work of women.*

The break through in women's market labor due to each of the two World Wars was only temporary, except in France after World War I, where it was predominantly a demographic effect. While women may indeed have demonstrated their capacity to perform all sorts of tasks, including the heaviest and most responsible, previously done by men in Belgium,

France and Germany and the United Kingdom, the pre-war division of labor was quickly restored and even reinforced during the great depression. Neither war caused any sharp change in female labor force participation rates, certainly as compared with countries not involved in World War I. In all seven countries, female labor force participation rates were relatively low in the decade after World War II. The belief that men and women *naturally* occupy separate spheres within which they pursue quite different tasks was not shaken during either war: after all, men were not expected to take an equal share in domestic responsibilities.

8 *Changes in cultural patterns, linked to the women's rights movement, created employment opportunities for (married) women.*
The idea that married women entered the labor force because of a breakdown in social norms and the emergence of a feminist ideology has gained wide acceptance.

That the feminist movement changed public thinking may be true, but a strong feminist movement is not a dominating factor in the creation of an increase in female labor force participation. The relatively strong feminist movement in the Netherlands and its long tradition would contradict such a view, apparently having no influence on the fact that female labor force participation in the Netherlands continued to be much lower than in the other six countries. However, it may have improved the position of those women participating in the labor market.

9 *Legal developments and public policies such as laws concerning marriage, family, child care, labor force and equal pay, taxation and social security benefits have been responsible of the choices of groups of women with respect to labor force participation and fertility in the different countries.*
These laws and policies seem endogenous rather than exogenous and appear to follow rather than lead market developments. Tax treatment of participating married women improves after their participation in the labor market has started to increase. The same applies to the introduction and improvement of maternal and parental leave or child care facilities.
This implies extra effort of those women being the first to participate in the labor market and trying to change the constraints and political power balance.

10 *Married women have to participate in the labor market, as the cost of living is too high to allow them to stay at home.*
This is an idea particularly often applied to Sweden. This explanation cannot be correct because in earlier decades men's real wages were much lower, yet married women did not participate. "Needing money is a universal, a constant, and a first rule of method is that one cannot explain a variable by a constant." (Nathan Keyfitz, 1980, quoted by Fuchs, 1983:130). In all seven countries there has been a striking growth in money and real wages over the last 30 years. Yet there has been a huge upsurge in employment of married women.

11 *The emergence of the nuclear family is a recent development.*
This is not a correct statement. A *gradual* trend involving the rise of affective family relations in the nuclear family, based on mutual assistance between husband and wife and a common responsibility for the upbringing of children, was already discernible before the mid-nineteenth century, certainly in the Netherlands. The form may have varied and fluctuated, but familial behavioral relations seem fairly consistent and persistent.

12 *"The hierarchical division of labor within the family which assigned the husband the role of breadwinner and the wife the role of domestic manager and moral guardian emerged clearly only in the nineteenth century and was associated with the growth of the middle class and the diffusion of its values."* (Scott and Tilly, 1980:97).
Again this conclusion can be challenged for the Netherlands where the division can be identified at least as early as the seventeenth century.

13 *Fertility declined not until the introduction of the pill and the elimination of the legal bans on contraceptives.*
This is not correct as fertility showed a decline in all countries at least from the beginning of this century with only a minor long-term impact from the pill and from the elimination of bans.

14 *Microeconomic theory treats women's work as unproductive.*
That female work is considered unproductive, even when market work, is often illustrated by Adam Smith's statement that "The value of the menial servant, on the contrary adds to the value of nothing". However, this statement condemns both *female and male* servants as performing unproductive work. Smith's statement that he considered work in manufacturing to be productive was at least one step forward compared with the physiocrats who considered only agricultural labor productive. As described in chapter 4, agricultural work (like domestic service) was always an important form of female as well as male paid labor.

It is true that the focus of economic theory was for a long time confined to market-related phenomena, but the theory was not sexist or anti-feminist per se. There was, in theory and empirical measurement, a gradual recognition of work predominantly done by women, although the labor performed within households is still relatively unexplored. (As are female and male hobbies or do-it-yourself activities). Until recently the theory has treated the household as a 'black box'. However, the household was not the only 'black box' not studied by neoclassical economists, it is even more true of the firm.

15 *Microeconomic theory neglects women.*
One of the reasons put forward for the neglect of women in microeconic theory is that economics is the most male-dominated of all sciences (Ferber and Teiman, 1981; Pujol, 1992). The hegemonic control by one

paradigm, the neoclassical school (which is also accused of being antifeminist, see below), is another reason. John Stuart Mill is nearly always mentioned as the one remarkable early exception to "mainstream/-malestream" (Pujol, 1992) neoclassical economics.

The arguments completely ignore the fact that when male neoclassical economists became interested in labor market behavior, they almost immediately focused their attention on women and the activities they performed within the household (see sections 10.2 and 10.3).

16 *In the neoclassical theory, issues relevant to women are "not addressed, or, when they are, it is within a framework which redefines them in a blatantly antifeminist fashion"* (Pujol, 1992:2).

Certainly, the terminology conceived by the economists in Chicago is not always friendly to women and often sounds anti-feminist (creating in turn most of the myths or misunderstandings - as given in section 10.3). Equally, the theory's comparison of children with commodities (to be both demanded and supplied by households) fills those not familiar with the theory with an aversion. Equally thoughtless at first sight is the concept of human capital, which compares people with machines in which time and current money is invested in return for future pay. Even economists need time to realize that the notion of education as an investment in human capital is a powerful analytical tool and that only the *term* is not sympathetic (Oosterbeek, 1992: Preface). In the theory even *love* is analyzed as a commodity to be consumed and produced (but only within marriage!).

It is certainly true that the theory has not been innovative in focusing attention on women's role in society. However, this is not sufficient reason to reject it. A theory should be judged on its explanatory performance. Moreover, once attention did shift to women, the theory proved quite useful.

17 *Household work is unskilled work.*

This description is commonly used, but it neglects the fact that courses in household work take as many years as those preparing for semi-skilled technical trades and that many activities performed at home (like child care, cooking, education and nursing) require advanced training if performed in the market.

18 *Snowwhite can only be happy if she is kissed back to life by a stumbling prince.*

The fairy tale is wrong. Snowwhites no longer have to find a surrogate home and serve seven people of doubtful origin, nor do they have to eat free but poisonous apples forced upon them by jealous stepmothers. They can get a decent education, go out into the world, and kiss handsome princes if and when they choose.

BIBLIOGRAPHY

Statistics

Belgium

Statistique de la Belgique:

---- *Recensement Général*, 15 Octobre 1846, publié par le Ministre de l'Intérieur, Bruxelles, Th. Lesigne: Population, 1 vol. in 4°, 1849. Agriculture, 4 vol. in 4°, 1850. Industrie, 1 vol. in 4°, 1851.

---- *Recensement Général*, 31 Décembre 1856, publié par le Ministre de l'Intérieur, Bruxelles, Th. Lesigne: Population, 1861.

---- *Recensement Général*, 31 Décembre 1866, publié par le Ministre de l'Intérieur, Bruxelles: Population, 1870.

---- *Recensement Général de 1880*, publié par le Ministre de l'Agriculture, de l'Industrie et des Travaux Publics, Bruxelles: Agriculture, 1885.

---- *Recensement Général de 1895.* 1898-1903: publié par le Ministère de l'Agriculture, de l'Industrie et des Travaux Publics, Bruxelles: Agriculture, 5 vol. in 4° et un atlas. 1898-1901, publié par le Ministère de l'Intérieur et de l'Instruction Publique, Bruxelles: Population, 2 vol. in 4°, 1903.

---- *Recensement Général des industries et des métiers*, 31 octobre 1896, publié par le Ministère de l'Industrie et du Travail, Bruxelles, 1900-1903, 18 vol. in 4° et un atlas.

(Statistique de) Royaume de Belgique:

---- *Recensement Général*, 31 Décembre 1900. Population, 1903. Recensement de l'Industrie et du Commerce, Office du Travail, Bruxelles.

---- *Recensement Général*, 31 Décembre 1910. Population, tome V, 1916. Recensement de l'Industrie et du Commerce, Office du Travail, Bruxelles.

---- *Recensement Général*, 31 Décembre 1920. Population, tome I, publié par le Ministre de l'Intérieur et de l'Hygiène, Bruxelles.

---- *Recensement Général*, 31 Décembre 1921. Recensement de l'Industrie et du Commerce, Office du Travail, publié par le Ministre de l'Intérieur et de l'Hygiène, Bruxelles.

---- *Recensement Général*, 31 Décembre 1930. Population, tome I, publié par le Ministre de l'Intérieur, Bruxelles.

---- *Recensement économique et social*, 27 février 1937/Economische en sociale telling van 27 februari 1937. Ministèr de l'Intérieur/ Ministerie van binnelandse zaken, Bruxelles/Brussel.

---- *Recensement Général*, 31 Décembre 1947. Tome IV. Répartition de la population par degré d'instruction. Annexe III: Répartition de la population active totale d'après le sexe, l'état civil, l'état social et l'activité (groupe) dans laquelle la profession principale est excercée.

Annuaire Statistique de la Belgique, years 1870 to 1883 and 1885 to 1893. Le ministère de l'intérieur et de l'instruction publique.

Nationaal Instituut voor de Statistiek, Brussel:

1951 *Algemene Volks-, Nijverheids- en Handelstelling*, 31 December 1947, deel IV.

1953 Deel VIII.

---- *Algemene Volkstelling 31 december 1961.*

1975 *Volkstelling 31 december 1970.* Deel 8 - Beroepsbevolking. Koninkrijk België, Ministerie van Economische Zaken.

---- *Algemene Volkstelling 1 maart 1981.*

---- *Statistisch Jaarboek van België*, Ministerie van Economische Zaken:

1970 Boekdeel 90.

1976 Boekdeel 96.

1980 Boekdeel 100

1987 Boekdeel 107.

1992 Boekdeel 112.

1991 Kabinet van de staatssecretaris voor maatschappelijke emancipatie/Cabinet du secretaire d'état à l'émancipation social. *Vrouwen in de Belgische samenleving/Les femmes dans la Societé Belge*, Brussel/Bruxelles.

Denmark

Danmarks Statistik, Statens Statiske Bureau:

1883 Statistisk Tabelværk, *Folkemængden I Kongeriget Danmark, 1880*, Statiske Bureau, Kjøbenhavn.

1903 Statistisk Tabelværk, *Folketællingen I Kongeriget Danmark*, den 1. februar 1901. Statens Statiske Bureau, Bianco Lunos Bogtrykkeri, København.

1904 *Folketællingen I Kongeriget Danmark,* Bianco Lunos Bogtrykkeri. vol. 2, København, 1904.

1905 Statistisk Tabelværk, *Befolkningsforholdene I Danmark i det 19. århundrede*, Bianco Lunos Bogtrykkeri, København, 1905.

1914 Statistisk Tabelværk, *Folketællingen I Kongeriget Danmark* den 1. februar 1911. Bianco Lunos Bogtrykkeri. vol. 2, København.

1917 Statistisk Tabelværk, *Folketællingen I Kongeriget Danmark* den 1. februar 1921. Bianco Lunos Bogtrykkeri, København.

1920 Ehrvervs- og Indtægtsforholdene ved Folketællingen den 1. februar 1916.

1925 Statistisk Tabelværk, *Folketællingen I Kongeriget Danmark* den 1. februar 1921. Bianco Lunos Bogtrykkeri. vol. 2, København.

1935 *Folketællingen I Kongeriget Danmark* den 5. november 1930.

1949 Statistisk Tabelværk, *Folketællingen 1940.* Bind I and Bind II: Befolkningens fordeling efter erhverv. Bianco Lunos Bogtrykkeri, København.

1957 Ehrverv, fag og arbejdsstilling ved Folketællingen 1950. Bianco Lunos Bogtrykkeri, København.

1970 *Folke- og boligtællingen*, 27.- september 1965, København.

1974 *Folke- og boligtællingen*, 9. november 1970, C1, København.

1977 *Folke- og boligtællingen*, 9. november 1970, C3, København.

1989 -- *Statistik Årborg*, Statiske Bureau, København. Also: 1990, 1991 and 1992.

1992 Levevilkår i Danmark, Statistisk oversigt 1992.

Germany

Herausgegeben vom Kaiserlichen Statistichen Amt:

1880 -- *Statistisches Jahrbuch für das Deutsche Reich.* Jahrgänge 1880 bis 1909.

1884 Berufsstatistik des Deutsches Reichs nach der allgemeinen *Berufszählung vom 5. Juni 1882*. Teil 1: Berufsstatistik des Deutsches Reichs und der kleineren Verwaltungsbezirke und Band 4: A,B,C der Statistik des Deutschen Reichs. Berlin.

1888 *Die Völkszählung im Deutschen Reich* am 1 Dezember 1885. (Neue Folge Band 32 der Statistik des Deutschen Reichs). Berlin, 1888.

1892 *Die Völkszählung im Deutschen Reich* am 1 Dezember 1890. (Neue Folge Band 68 der Statistik des Deutschen Reichs). Herausgegeben vom Kaiserlichen Statistichen Amt. Berlin.

1909 *Berufszählung vom 14. Juni 1895* und *Berufszählung vom 12. Juni 1907.*

Herausgegeben vom Statistichen Reichsamt:

1924 -- *Statistisches Jahrbuch für das Deutsche Reich*. 1924/25, 1930, and 1938.

1928 *Völkszählung, Bevölkerung des Deutschen Reichs* nach den Ergebnissen der Völkszählung 1925. Berlin.

1941 *Volks-, Berufs- und Betriebszählung* vom 17. Mai 1939. Berlin.

Herausgegeben vom Statistischen Bundesamt:

1952 -- *Statistisches Jahrbuch*. 1952 to 1990, several years, Stuttgart (later) Wiesbaden.

1992 *Statistisches Jahrbuch 1991 für das vereinte Deutschland*, Wiesbaden, 1992.

France

Statistique de la France:

1859 *Résultats du Dénombrement de la population en 1856*. Imprimerie Administrative de veuve Berger-Levrault.

1864 *Résultats Généraux du Dénombrement de 1861*. Imprimerie Administrative de veuve Berger-Levrault.

1873 *Résultats Généraux du Dénombrement de 1872*. Imprimerie Nationale, Paris.

1904 *Résultats Statistiques du Recensement Général de la population*, 24 mars 1901, Imprimerie Nationale, Paris.

1908 *Résultats Statistiques du Recensement Général de la population*, 4 mars 1906, Imprimerie Nationale, Paris.

1913 *Résultats Statistiques du Recensement Général de la population*, 5 mars 1911, Imprimerie Nationale, Paris.

1925 *Résultats Statistiques du Recensement Général de la population*, 6 mars 1921, Imprimerie Nationale, Paris.

1928 *Résultats Statistiques du Recensement Général de la population*, 7 mars 1926, Imprimerie Nationale, Paris.

1933 *Résultats Statistiques du Recensement Général de la population*, 8 mars 1931, Imprimerie Nationale, Paris.

1942 *Résultats Statistiques du Recensement Général de la population*, 8 mars 1936, Imprimerie Nationale, Paris.

1949 *Recensement Général de la population*, 10 mars 1946, Imprimerie Nationale, et Presses Universitaire de France, Paris.

Institut national de la statistique et des études économiques (insee):

1960 *Recensement Général de la population* de mai 1954, Imprimerie Nationale, et Presses Universitaire de France, Paris.

1971 *Recensement Général de la population* de 1968 (résultats du sondage au 1/20), Imprimerie Nationale, Paris.

1972 *Recensement Général de la population* de 1968 (résultats des sondages au 1/20 et au 1/4), Imprimerie Nationale, Paris.

---- *Recensement Général de la population* de 1982 (résultats du sondage au 1/20), Imprimerie Nationale, Paris.
1990 *Annuaire Statistique de la France 1989*,
1991 *Annuaire Statistique de la France 1990.*
1992 *Annuaire Statistique de la France 1991.*

The Netherlands

Centraal Bureau voor de Statistiek:
---- *Uitkomsten der derde tienjarige volkstelling in het Koninkrijk der Nederlanden op den negentienden November 1849*, Ter Algemeene Landsdrukkerij, 's-Gravenhage, 1852-1853.
---- *Uitkomsten der vierde tienjarige volkstelling in het Koninkrijk der Nederlanden op den een en dertigsten December 1859*, Part 2, Van Weelden en Mingelen, 's-Gravenhage, 1864.
---- *Uitkomsten der vijfde tienjarige volkstelling in het Koninkrijk der Nederlanden op den een en dertigsten December 1869*, 's-Gravenhage.
---- *Uitkomsten der zesde tienjarige volkstelling in het Koninkrijk der Nederlanden op den een en dertigsten December 1879*, 's-Gravenhage.
---- *Uitkomsten der beroepstelling in het Koninkrijk der Nederlanden op den een en dertigsten December 1889*, 13 delen, Van Weelden en Mingelen, 's-Gravenhage, 1894-1895.
---- *Uitkomsten der beroepstelling in het Koninkrijk der Nederlanden op den een en dertigsten December 1899*, 13 delen, 's-Gravenhage, Belinfante. 1902.
---- *Inleiding tot de uitkomsten der achtste algemeene tienjaarlijksche volkstelling in het Koninkrijk der Nederlanden van een en dertig December 1889* en daaraan verbonden beroepstelling en woningstatistiek, 's-Gravenhage, Belinfante. 1904.
---- *Uitkomsten der beroepstelling in het Koninkrijk der Nederlanden gehouden op den een en dertigsten December 1909*, 3 Parts, 's-Gravenhage, Belinfante. 1912-1913.
---- *Inleiding tot de uitkomsten der negende algemeene tienjaarlijksche volkstelling* in het Koninkrijk der Nederlanden van een en dertig December 1889 met daaraan verbonden woning- en beroepstelling (1909), 's-Gravenhage, Belinfante. 1913.
---- *Uitkomsten beroepstelling 31 December 1920*, deel 3 (van de 3 delen), 's-Gravenhage, Belinfante. 1924.
---- *Volkstelling 31 December 1930*, deel VII en X (van de 10 delen), 's-Gravenhage, Algemeene Landsdrukkerij. 1932-1934.
---- *12de Volkstelling*, annex woningtelling 31 mei 1947, deel 2 (van de 6 delen), Utrecht, W. de Haan N.V. 1950-1952.
---- *13e Algemene volkstelling*, 31 mei 1960, deel 10 (van de 11 delen), Zeist, W. de Haan N.V. 1964 and Hilversum, W. de Haan N.V. 1965, 1966.
---- *14e Algemene Volkstelling*, 1971, see Berends and Boelmans-Kleinjan, 1979.
---- *Arbeidskrachtentellingen*, 1973, 1975, 1977, 1979, 1981, 1983, 1985.
---- *Enquête Beroepsbevolking*, 1987, 1988, 1989, 1990
1984 *Vijfentachtig jaren statistiek in tijdreeksen.*
1987 *De statistieken van het CBS, inhoud, samenhang en perspectieven, meerjarenprogramma 1987-1990.* Voorburg/Heerlen.
1989 *Negentig jaren statistiek in tijdreeksen.*

Sweden

Sveriges Officiella Statistik, Statistiska Centralbyrån, Stockholm:

1968 *Historisk statistik för Sverige*. Del 1. Befolkning. Andra upplagan 1720-1967.

1890 *Statistisk Tidskrift 1890.*

1901 *Statistisk Tidskrift 1900.*

1911 *Statistisk Tidskrift 1910.*

1917 *Folkräkningen den 31 December 1910.* II Folkmängdens fördelning efter kön, alder och civilstand. III Folkmängdens fördelning efter yrken.

1927 *Folkräkningen den 31 December 1920.* V Yrkesräkningen.

1937 *Folkräkningen den 31 December 1930.* VII (1937), VIII (1938) Folkmängden efter yrke, inkomst och förmögenhet.

1943 *Folkräkningen den 31 December 1940.* III Folkmängden efter yrke.

1955 *Folkräkningen den 31 December 1950.* VI Totale räkningen.

1964 *Folkräkningen den 1 November 1960.* IX Näringsgren, yrke, pendling, hushåll och utbildning i hela riket.

1977 *Folk- och bostadsräkningen 1970.* Del 13. Sysselsättning och utbildning. Definitioner, jämförbarhet och utveckling m m.

1985 *Folk- och bostadsräkningen 1980.* Del 9. Yrke.

1989 *Arbetsmarknaden i siffror.* Sysselsättning Arbetslöshet 1970-1988.

---- Statistik Årsbok för Sverige, 1951, 1972, 1989, 1990, 1991, 1992, Stockholm.

United Kingdom/ Great Britain, England and Wales

Her Majesty's Stationary Office, HMSO, London:

1901 *Census of England and Wales.* Vol. 1, General Report and Vol. 2, Summary Tables.

1911 *Census of England and Wales.* Vol. I, General Report and Vol X, Occupations and Industries.

1921 *Census of England and Wales.* General Tables.

1971 British Labour Statistics, *Historical Abstract 1886-1968.* Department of Employment and Productivity.

Central Statistical Office, *Annual Abstract of Statistics*, 1991, no 127; 1992, no. 128.

Other sources of labor force or population statistics

ILO, International Labour Office, Geneva:

1983 -- *Year Book of Labour Statistics*, annually 1983 to 1993. (Since 1980 separate statistics for women have been presented on a systematic basis.)

1936 *Employment of women and children.*

1938 *Statistics of the Gainfully Occupied Population.* Series of Leaque of Nations Publications II: Economic and Finacial, 1938, II.A.12.

1975 *Womanpower.*

1976 *International Recommandations on labour statistics.*

1985 *Women in economic activity: A global statistical survey (1950-2000).* Published jointly with the United Nations Research and Training Institute for the Advancement of Women (INSTRAW).

1986 *Women at Work, Young Women Workers Today.*

1987 *Women at Work, Equal Employment Opportunities: Trends and Perspectives.*

1989 *Women in the World of Work: Statistical analysis and projections to the year 2000.* (see also Nuss, 1989).
1991 *Statistical Sources and Methods*, volume 5: Total and Economically active Population, employment and unemployment (Population Censuses).

United Nations/Nations Unies, Statistical Office/Bureau de Statistique, New York:
1982 -- *Demographic Yearbook.* Several years. Latest 1989: New York, 1991.

OEEC, Organisation for European Economic Co-operation, Paris:
1954 *Labour Force Statistics.*
OECD, Organisation for Economic Co-operation and Development, Paris:
1971 *Labour Force Statistics* 1958-1969.
1973 *Labour Force Statistics* 1960-1971.
1975 *Labour Force Statistics* 1962-1973.
etc. annually to 1993, *Labour Force Statistics* 1971-1990.
OECD, Organisation for Economic Co-operation and Development, Paris:
1979 *Demographic Trends* 1950-1990.
1989 *Historical Statistics* 1960-1987.

Books and articles

Åberg, Alf, 1988. *Vår svenska historia.* femte upplagan (specialutgåva), De Truck AB, Lund.

Addison, John, J. and W. Stanley Siebert, 1979. *The market for labor: an analytical treatment.* Goodyear Publishing Company Inc., Santa Monica, Californa.

Addison, John, J. and W. Stanley Siebert, 1991. The Social Charter of the European Community: Evolution and Controversies. *Industrial and Labour Relations Review.* Vol. 44, No. 4 (July 1991), Cornell University: 597-625.

Aerts, Erik, and François Crouzet (eds.), 1990. Economic Effects of the French Revolutionary and Napoleonic Wars. Session B-1, *Proceedings of the Tenth International Economic History Congress*, August, Leuven University Press.

Almqvist, Carl Jonas Love, 1839. *Det går an*, translated in Dutch by Polet, Cora, 1982, *Waarom niet!* Meulenhoff Nederland, Amsterdam.

Amsden, Alice H. (ed.), 1980. *The Economics of Women and Work.* Penquin Books.

Amstel, R.J. van, 1986. *Zwangerschap, moederschap in combinatie met betaalde arbeid*, Ministerie van Sociale Zaken en werkgelegenheid.

Amstel, R.J. van, 1992. *Evaluatie van de nieuwe zwangerschaps- en bevallingsverlof voor vrouwen in loondienst.* Ministerie van Sociale Zaken en Werkgelegenheid.

Andersen, Otto, 1977. *The population of Denmark.* CICRED 1977.

Ariès, Ph. 1960/1973. *L'enfant et la vie familiale sous l'Ancien Régime*, Parijs. (first edition 1960).

Arons, Gary, 1979. Frauen und Wissenschaft. *Beitrage zur Berliner Sommeruniversität für Frauen.* Juli 1976. Courage Verlag Berlin.

Ashenfelter, Orley, 1979.
Comment in: Schultz, Theodore W. (ed.), 1979, *Economics of the Family, Marriage, Children and Human Capital*. University of Chicago Press, Chicago/London, 2nd Impression 1979: 117-119.

Ashenfelter, Orley and Richard Layard (eds), 1986.
Handbook of Labor Economics, North-Holland.

Atkins, Susan and Brenda Hoggett, 1984.
Women and the Law, Basil Blackwell, New York.

Baars, D., 1978.
Ontwikkeling van de mogelijkheden tot toekenning en export van de zgn. overgangsvoordelen-AOW in de nationale wetgeving en in de internationale coördinatieregelingen, in: *Europees Sociaal Verzekeringsrecht*, Kluwer: 135-170.

Badinter, Elisabeth, 1990.
De een is de ander, De relaties tussen mannen en vrouwen, translated by Rosalie Siblesz (*L'un est l'autre: des relations entre hommes et femmes*. Paris, Jacob, 1986). Uitgeverij Contact Amsterdam.

Bakels, H.L., 1987.
Kluwer Schets van het Nederlands arbeidsrecht, Kluwer, Deventer.

Bakker, Nelleke, 1982.
Een mooi beroep voor een meisje. Onderwijzeressen tijdens het Interbellum, in: *Derde Jaarboek voor vrouwengeschiedenis 1982*: 98-128.

Banks, Karin, 1991.
Equal pay and equal treatment for men and women in Community law, in: *Social Europe* 3/91, Commission of European Communities, Brussels.

Barmby, T. an A. Cigno, 1990.
A sequential Probability Model of Fertility patterns. *Journal of Population Economics*, 3.

Barrett, M., 1980.
Women's oppression today, Verso, London.

Becker, G. S., 1960.
An Economic Analysis of Fertility, in: *Demographic and Economic Change in Developed Countries*. Universities-National Bureau Conference Series 11. Princeton University Press, Princeton.

Becker, Gary, S., 1964/1975.
Human Capital. Columbia University Press, for the National Bureau of Economic Research, 1st ed. 1964, 2nd ed. 1975. New York.

Becker, Gary, S., 1965.
A theory of the allocation of time. *Economic Journal*, 75 (299), September: 493-517.

Becker, Gary, S., 1981/1991.
A Treatise on the Family. Harvard University Press, Cambridge. Enlarged edition, Harvard University Press, 1991.

Becker, Gary, S. and Robert J. Barro, 1988.
A Reformulation of the Economic Theory of Fertility. *Quarterly Journal of Economics* 103 (1): 1-25.

Becker, Gary, S., and H. Gregg Lewis, 1974/1979.
Interaction between Quantity and Quality of Children, in: Schultz, Theodore W. (ed.), 1979, *Economics of the Family, Marriage, Children and Human Capital*, University of Chicago Press, Chicago and London, 1974, 2nd Impression 1979: 81-90.

Beer, de, CBS, 1989.
Jaren tachtig: ombuiging of voortzetting van demographishe trends? *Maanstatistiek van de bevolking* 37, no12: 16-35.

Beets, G., 1989.
Kerkelijke Gezindte (Religion). *Maandstatistiek van de Bevolking*, oktober 1989: 32, 33.

Begeer, W. and H.K. van Tuinen, 1984.
De informele economie. *Preadviezen van de Vereniging voor de Staathuishoudkunde*, 1984, Stenfert Kroese, Leiden/Antwerpen. (Reprint in: Statistisch Magazine, 1985, 5, nr. 1: 5-16.)

Ben-Porath, Y., 1973.
Economic Analysis of fertility in Israël: Point and counterpoint. *Journal of Political Economy*, 81: S202-S233.

Berends, A.B. and A.C. Boelmans-Kleinjan, 1979.
Beroepsarbeid door vrouwen in Nederland. Monografieën volkstelling 1971, nr. 7, CBS and Siswo, Statsuitgeverij, 's-Gravenhage, 1979.

Bergmann, Barbara R., 1986.
The Economic Emergence of Women, Basic Books, United States: 372.

Bierens, H.J. and H.A. Pott-Buter 1990.
Specification of Household Engel Curves by nonparametric regression, *Econometric Review*, December: 125-184.

Blanpain, R., 1986.
Sixty years of Labour Law and Social Security in Germany, in: M. Rood (ed.) *Fifty years of Labour Law and Social Security*, 1986, Kluwer Law and Taxation Publishers, Deventer: 69-88.

Blanpain, R., 1991.
Europees Arbeidsrecht, Die Keure, Koninklijke Vermande: 265.

Blau, Francine D. and Ferber, Marianne A., 1986.
The economics of women, men, and work. Prentice-Hall, Englewood Cliffs, New Jersey.

Blau, Francine D. and Ferber, Marianne A., 1992.
Women's Contribution to Labor Economics: Part I. *Newletter Spring/Summer, American Economic Association*, Committee on the Status of Women in the Economic Profession (CSWEP): 2-6.

Blok, Els, 1978/1989.
Loonarbeid van vrouwen 1945-1955. SUN Nijmegen.
Reprinted in 1989: *Werkende Vrouwen in de jaren veertig en vijftig.* Van Gennep, Amsterdam.

Boekholt, P.T.F.M. and E.P. de Booy, 1987.
Geschiedenis van de school in Nederland: vanaf de Middeleeuwen tot aan de huidige tijd. Van Gorcum, Assen.

Borchorst, Anette and Birte Siim, 1984.
Kvinder i Velfærdsstaten, mellem moderskab og lonarbejde gennem 100 år, Aalbor Universiteitsforlag.

Bradley, Harriet, 1989.
Men's Work, Women's Work, A sociological History of the Sexual Division of Labour in Employment., Polity Press, Cambridge, UK.

Brandt, Gisela, Johanna Kootz and Gisela Steppke, 1973.
Zur Frauenfrage im Kapitalismus. Suhrkamp Verlag: 252.

Braudel, Fernand, 1979/1990.
Beschaving, economie en kapitalisme (15e-18e eeuw). Deel III: De tijd van de wereld (translated by Roland Fagel, Eef Gratama and Koen van Gulik, 1990. Original title: *Civilisation matérielle, Economie et Capitalism XVe-XVIIIe siècle. Tome 3: Le temps du monde.* Colin, Paris, 1979). Contact, Amsterdam.

Bridenthal, Renate and Claudia Koonz (eds), 1987.
Becoming visible. Women in European History. Boston, respectively: 139-164, and: 251-278.

Broeder, Corina den and André de Moor, 1992.
De kwaliteit van het onderwijs in Nederland. *Economisch Statistische Berichten*, 30-9-1992: 954-956.

Bronsema, Harry, 1986.
De Europese bevolking in cijfers, *Demos*, jrg 2, nr. 2.

Bronsema, Harry, 1990.
Over Bevolking. Een wegwijzer voor de praktijk. NIDI, Bohn Stafleu Van Loghum.

Brok-ten Broek, J., 1968.
De ontplooiing in de negentiende eeuw, in: Posthumus-van der Goot, Wilhelmina H. & Anna de Waal, eds. *Van Moeder op dochter*, Bruna & Zoon, Utrecht/Amsterdam, first edition 1948, third edition 1968: 13-92.

Brophy, Julia and Carol Smart, (eds), 1985.
Women in Law, Explorations in Law, Family and Sexuality. Routledge & Kegan Paul, London, Boston, Melbourne and Henley.

Brugmans, I.J., 1973.
De arbeidende klasse in Nederland in de 19e eeuw, 1813-1870. 9th edition. Het Spectrum. Utrecht/Antwerpen.

Bruijn, Jeanne de, 1989.
Vrouwenareid en arbeidssociologie in historisch en emancipatorisch perspectief, Sua, Amsterdam.

Bruyn-Hundt, Marga, 1983.
De waarde van onzichtbare arbeid gemeten. *Economisch Statistische Berichten*, 27-07-1983.

Bruyn-Hundt, Marga, 1988.
Vrouwen op de arbeidsmarkt: Nederlands situatie in de jaren tachtig en negentig. Spectrum, Utrecht.

Bruyn-Hundt, M., W.Driehuis, Y.M. Koot and L. Mossel, 1983.
Verschuivingen in de verhouding tussen betaalde en onbetaalde arbeid. Stichting voor Economisch Onderzoek, Amsterdam.

Buyst, Erik and Joel Mokyr, 1990.
Dutch Manufacturing and Trade during the French Period (1795-1814) in a Long Term Perspective, in: Aerts, Erik, and François Crouzet (eds), 1990, *Economic Effects of the French Revolutionary and Napoleonic Wars*. Session B-1, Proceedings of the Tenth International Economic History Congress, August 1990, Leuven University Press: 64-78.

Bryant, W. Keith, 1990.
The economic organization of the household. Cambridge University Press, US.

Cain, G. 1976.
The challenge of segmented labor market theories to orthodox theory: a survey. *Journal of Economic Literature* 14 nr.3: 827-885.

Cairncross, A.K., 1958.
Economic Schizophrenia. *Scottish Journal of Political Economy*. Vol. 5: 15-22.

Calvert, W.E., 1946.
Social Denmark, a survey of the Danish social legislation, edited by Socialt Tidsskrift, George Allen & Unwin Ltd., London; Thaning & Appels Forlag, København.

Cats, Jacob, 1712.
Alle de wercken I, II. Amsterdam.

Christensen, Jorgen Peter and Jorgen Estrup, 1979.
Strukturændringer På det Danske Arbejdsmarked I 1900-Tallet, in: J.P. Christensen et al (eds), Vækst og kriser i dansk økonomi i det 20. århundrede, r økonomisk Institut, Aarhus Universitet.

Centraal Bureau voor de Statistiek, CBS, 1982, 1988 and 1992.
Onderzoek Gezinsvorming (Dutch Fertility Survey), Den Haag.
1982: *Statistisch Magazine*, 5, nr. 1: 51-66. Sociale Maandstatistiek, 1986, 1987.

Centraal Bureau voor de Statistiek, CBS, 1988/9.
Gehanteerde begrippen (Used terms). *Maandstatistiek van de bevolking.* September 1988: 21

Centraal Bureau voor de Statistiek, CBS, 1990/5.
Population trends, *Maandstatistiek van de bevolking*, May 1990: 5.

Centraal Bureau voor de Statistiek, CBS, 1990/9. Demographics.
Maandstatistiek van de bevolking. September 1990:4.

Centraal Bureau voor de Statistiek, CBS, 1992/6.
Demographics. *Maandstatistiek van de bevolking*. Juni 1992.

Cigno, Alessandro, 1991.
Economics of the Family. Clarendon Press, Oxford.

Cigno, A. and J.F. Ermisch, 1989.
A micro-economic analysis of the timing of births. *European Economic Review* 33:737-760.

Clark, Alice, 1919/1982.
Working Life of Women in the Seventeenth Century. (Originally published in 1919). Routledge & Kegan Paul, London, Boston and Henley.

Clason, Christine E., 1982.
The Family in the Netherlands 1945-1980. Development in the Family in the light of social change. Reprint from: Changes in the Life Patterns of Families in Europe. Current Research Reports no. 30. Vienna Centre, International Social Science Council. European Coordination Centre for Research and Documentation in Social Sciences.

Coale, Ansley, 1971.
Age patterns of marriage. *Population Studies* 25, 2: 193-214.

Collier, 1966.
Collier's Encyclopedia; Halsey, William, D. editorial editor; Crowell Collier and Macmillan, Inc.

Commaille, J., 1990.
France, in: W. Dumon (ed.), 1990, *Family Policies in EEC-countries*, Office for Official Publications of the European Communities: 68-77.

Commaille, J., 1993.
France: Political Transition; in: W. Dumon, 1993. *National Family Policies in EC-Countries in 1991*. European Observatory on National Family Policies, Commission of the European Communities: 15-20.

Creighton, W.B., 1979.
Working Women and the Law, Mansell, University of Melbourne.

Dealemans, F, 1975.
Leiden in 1581. Een socio-demographisch onderzoek. A.A.G. Bijdragen, 19: 137-215.

Dahlsgård, Inga, 1980.
Women in Denmark yesterday and today. Det Danske Selskab.

Davidson, Caroline, 1986.
A Woman's Work is never done, A history of housework in the British Isles 1650-1950. Chatto & Windus, London.

De Pisan, Christine, 1404 and 1405, see Pisan.

De Raet, Lodewijk, 1914, see Raet.

De Tray, Dennis, N., 1973.
Child Quality and the Demand for Children. *Journal of Political Economy* 81 (2, part 2): S70-S95.

De Tray, Dennis N., 1979.
Child Quality and the Demand for Children, in: Schultz, Theodore W. (ed.), 1979, *Economics of the Family, Marriage, Children and Human Capital*, University of Chicago Press, Chicago/London. Second Impression 1979: 91-116.

Deursen, A. Th. van, 1978.
Het Kopergeld van de Gouden Eeuw, I. Het dagelijks brood. Van Gorcum Assen/Amsterdam.

Dijk, H. van and S.W. Verstegen, 1988.
Dienstverlening in Nederland en Duitsland, tussen eerste wereldoorlog en welvaaartsstaat (1920-1960). Swidoc, Noord-Hollandsche Uitgevers Maatschappij, Amsterdam.

Dixon, R., 1982.
Women in agriculture: Counting the labour force in developing countries. *Population and Development Review*. Vol. 8, No. 3: 5390566. New York.

Dongen, Walter van, 1993.
Nieuwe krijtlijnen voor Gezin, Markt en Maatschappij. Garant, Leuven-Apeldoorn.

Donzelot, J., 1977/1979.
La police des familles. Paris 1977. Trnslated in 1979: *The policing of families*. New York.

Douglas, Paul and Erika Schoenberg, 1937.
Studies in the Supply of Labor. *Journal of Political Economy* 45.

Drake, Charles D., 1981.
Labour Law, third edition, Sweet & Maxwell, London.

Dumon, W. (ed.), 1990.
Family Policies in EEC-countries, Office for Official Publications of the European Communities.

Dumon, W., 1993.
National Family Policies in EC-Countries in 1991. European Observatory on National Family Policies, Commission of the European Communities.

Duskin, Elizabeth, 1990.
Overview, in: *OECD*, 1990: 9-27.

Easterlin, Richard Ainley, 1980.
Birth and Fortune. The Impact of Numbers on Personal Welfare. Basic Books, New York.

Easterlin, Richard, Ainley, 1987.
Fertility, in: John Eatwee, Muray Milgate and Peter Newman (ed.) *The New Palgrave. A dictionary of Economics.* Macmillan Press Limited: 302-307.

EEG, Commissie der Europese Gemeenschappen, 1979.
Supplement nr 2, *Vrouwen van Europa*. Brussel.

EC, 1989, Commission of the European Communities.
Employment in Europe, Luxembourg.

EC, 1990, Commission of the European Communities.
Childcare in the European Communities 1985-1990, Brussels.

EC, 1992, Commission of the European Communities.
Employment in Europe, Luxembourg.

Eeckhout, Patricia van den and Peter Scholliers, 1990.
Geld in 't laatje, Arbeid en inkomen van Gentse arbeidersgezinnen circa 1900, in: *Arbeid in veelvoud, een huldeboek voor Jan Craeybeckx en Etienne Scholliers*: 192-213.

Ehrenberg, Ronald G. and Robert S. Smith, 1991.
Modern Labor Economics, 4th edition, HarperCollins Publishers, New York.

Elliot, Robert, F., 1991.
Labor Economics: A Comparative Text. McGraw-Hill Book Company.

E.N.W.S./R.E.E.F., 1992.
European Network for Women Studies/Réseau Européen d'Etues sur les Femmes, *Newsletter*, april 1992, nr. 6.

Erf, R.F. van der, 1989.
Buitenlandse migratie, CBS, *Maandstatistiek van de Bevolking*, oktober 1989: 18-19.

Ergas, Yasmine, 1990.
Child-care policies in comparitive perspective: an introductory discussion, in: *OECD*, 1990: 173-201.

Ermish, John, 1990.
Demographic aspects of the growing number of lone-parent families, in: *OECD*, 1990: 27-43.

Esveldt, Ingrid and Hanna van Solinge, 1992.
Huishoudens van ouderen: eigen haard blijft goud waard, in: *Demos*, 8, nr.7: 49-52.

Eupen, Th. A.G. van, 1985.
Kerk en gezin in Nederland, in: G.A. Kooy, 1985, *Gezinsgeschiedenis, vier eeuwen gezin in Nederland*, Van Gorcum, Assen: 7-30.

Fase, M.M.G., 1989.
Elisabeth Caroline van Dorp, in: *Biografisch Woordenboek van Nederland*, 1989.

Faessen, W.B.M., 1987.
Bevolking, Gezin en huishouden in Nederland sinds 1829. CBS, *Maandstatistiek van de bevolking*, januari 1987: 17-29.

Ferber, Marianne A. and Michelle L. Teiman, 1981.
The Oldest, the Most Established, the Most Quantitative of the Social Sciences - and the Most Dominated by Men: the Impact of Feminism on Economics. In: Dale Spender (ed.) *Men's Studies Modified, the Impact of Feminism on the Academic Disciplines*, Pergamon Press, New York: 125-139.

Fierens, J. and M. Th. Meulders-Klein, 1993.
Belgique - België: Declarations of intent before and after the elections; in: W. Dumon, 1993. *National Family Policies in EC-Countries in 1991*. European Observatory on National Family Policies, Commission of the European Communities: 1-3.

Flandrin, J.L., 1974/1979.
Familles. Parenté, maison, sexualité dans l'ancienne société, Paris. Translated in 1979: *Families in former times. Kinship, household and sexuality*. Cambridge.

Franz, Wolfgang, 1985.
An Economic Analysis of Female Work Participation, Education, and fertility: Theory and Emperical Evidence for the Federal Republic of Germany. *Journal of Labor Economics*. Vol. 3, Nr. 1, Part 2: S218-S234.

Frazer, Antonia, 1984/1985.
The Weaker Vessel. Woman's lot in seventeenth-century England. First publihed in 1984 by George Weldenfeld & Nicolson Limited. Paperback edition in 1985 by Methuen London Limited.

Fuchs, Victor, R., 1983.
How We Live, Harvard University Press.

Fuchs, Victor, R., 1989.
Women's Quest for Economic Equality, Harvard University Press.

Gamillscheg, F., 1986.
Sixty years of Labour Law and Social Security in Germany, in: M. Rood (ed.) *Fifty years of Labour Law and Social Security*, 1986, Kluwer Law and Taxation Publishers, Deventer: 69-88.

Garwinkel, Irwin and Patrick Wong, 1990.
Child support and public policy, in: *OECD*, 1990: 69-91.

Ghez, Gilbert R. and Gary S. Becker, 1975.
The Allocation of Time and Goods over the Life Cycle. Columbia University Press, for the National Bureau of Economic Research, New York.

Gibson, Wendy, 1989.
Women in Seventeenth-century France. Macmillan.

Goldschmidt-Clermont, Luisella, 1982.
Unpaid work in the household, International Labour Office, Geneva.

Goldin, Claudia, 1990.
Understanding the gender gap, An economic history of American Women, Oxford University Press, 1990, pp. 287.

Goode, W.J., 1963.
World Revolution and Family Patterns, Free Press, New York.

de Graaf, A., 1990.
The 'choice' for one child: voluntarily or unvoluntarily, CBS, *Maandstatistiek van de bevolking*, juni 1990: 12.

Gravelle, H. and R. Rees, 1983.
Microeconomics, Second impression, London and New York: Longman.

Grever, Maria & Annemiek van der Veen, editors, 1989.
Bij ons moeder en ons Jet: Brabantse vrouwen in de 19de en 20ste eeuw, Stichting Brabantse Regionale Geschiedbeoefening, 's-Hertogenbosch, De Walburg Pers, Zutphen, 1989, p. 168.

Gronau, R. 1977.
Leisure, Home Production of Time Revisited. *Journal of Political Economy*, vol. 85, no. 6.

Groot, Wim and Hettie A. Pott-Buter, 1992.
The timing of maternity in the Netherlands. *Journal of Population Economics* 5: 155-172.

Gustafsson, Siv, 1984.
Equal Opportunities in Sweden, in: Günther Schmid and Renate Weitzel (eds), 1984, *Sex Discrimination and Equal Opportunity*, Wissenschaftszentrum, West Berlin: 132-154.

Gustafsson, Siv and Roger Jacobsson, 1985.
Trends in female labor force participation in Sweden. *Journal of Labor Economics*, Vol. 3, no. 1, part 2: S256-S274.

Gustafsson, Siv and Åsa Löfström, 1990.
Policy changes and Women's Wages in Sweden, Research Memorandum 9006, University of Amsterdam.

Gustafsson, S.S., 1991.
Half the power, half the income and half the glory, the use of microeconomic theory in women's emancipation research. *De Economist* 139: 515-529.

Gustafsson, Siv, 1992.
Separate taxation and married women's labor supply. A comparison of West Germany and Sweden. *Journal of Population Economics* 5: 61-85.

Gustafsson, Siv, S. and M. Bruyn-Hundt, 1991.
Incentives for Women to Work: A Comparison between the Netherlands, Sweden and West-Germany, in: Backhaus, Jürgen, The Tax System and Female Emancipation, *Journal of Economic Studies*, vol. 18 No 5/6: 30-65.

Gustafsson, S.S., M. Bruyn-Hundt and H.A. Pott-Buter, 1992.
Emancipatie-economie, in: M.M.G. Fase and I. van der Zijpp (eds), *Samenleving en economie in de twinstigste eeuw*. Stenfert Kroese Uitgevers, Leiden/Antwerpen: 251-268.

Hagenaars, A.J.M. and S.R. Wundering-van Veen, 1990.
Soo gewonne soo verteert; economie van de huishoudelijke sector, Stenfort Kroese, Leiden/Antwerpen.

Hagenaars A.J.M. and R. de Zwart, 1987.
Betaalde en onbetaalde arbeid van de vijftienjarigen van nu. *Sociaal Maandblad Arbeid*, juni.

Haks, Donald, 1985.
Huwelijk en gezin in Holland in de 17de en 18de eeuw. Hes uitgevers, Utrecht.

Haks, Donald, 1988.
Continuïteit en verandering in het gezin van de vroeg-moderne tijd, in: Harry Peeters, Lène Dresen-Coenders and Ton Brandenbarg (eds), *Vijf eeuwen gezinsleven. Liefde, huwelijk en opvoeding in Nederland*, Nijmegen: 65-104.

Hall, Ray, 1986. 8:164
Household Trends within Western Europe 1970-1980, in: Allan Findlay and Paul White (eds) *West European Population Change*, Croom Helm, New Hampshire: 18-34.

Hamermesh, Daniel S., 1986.
The Demand for Labor in the Long Run, in: Orley Ashenfelter and Richard Layard, *Handbook of Labor Economics*, North-Holland.

Hamermesh, Daniel S. and A. Reesh, 1988.
Economics of work and pay. 4th edition, Harper and Row Publishers, New York.

Hartog, Joop and Jules Theeuwes, 1985.
The Emergence of the Working Wife in Holland, in: Richard Layard and Jacob Mincer (eds), *Journal of Labor Economics*. Trends in Women's Work, Education, and Family Building. Vol. 3, Nr. 1, January 1985 Supplement: S1-S235-255.

Hartog, Joop and Jules Theeuwes, 1990.
Post-war developments in Labor Economics, in: *Advanced Lectures in Quantitative Economics*. Acadamic Press Limited: 313-348.

Hawralyshyn, O., 1977.
Towards a definition of non-market activities. *Review of Income and Wealth*, Vol. 23: 79-96.

Hayghe, Howard V., 1990.
Family Members in the Work Force. *Monthly Labor Review*, March 1990, Volume 113, Number 3: 14-19.

Heather Bigg, Ada, 1894.
The Wife's Contribution to the Family Income. *Economic Journal* 4: 51-58.

Heckman, J.J. and J. Walker, 1990.
The third birth in Sweden, *Journal of Population Economics*: 235-275.305

Heckman, J.J. and J. Walker, 1990a.
The Relationship between Wages and Income and the Timing and Spacing of Births. Evidence from Swedish longitudinal data, *Econometrica*, Vol. 58, 6: 1411-1442.

Heckman, J.J. and R.J. Willis, 1975.
Estimation of a stochastic model of reproduction: an econometric approach, in: N.E. Terleckyj (ed.). *Household Production and consumption*. New York.

Heertje, A. 1992:291
Een impressie van zeventig jaar prijs- en welvaartstheorie, in: M.M.G. Fase and I. van der Zijpp (eds), *Samenleving en economie in de twinstigste eeuw*. Stenfert Kroese Uitgevers, Leiden/Antwerpen: 287-336.

Hen, P.E. de, 1985.
De industrialisatie van Nederland, in: F.L. van Holthoon, 1985, *De Nederlands Samenleving sinds 1815. Wording en Samenhang*. Assen: 3-18.

Hepple, B.A., 1986.
Fifty years of Labour Law and Social Security in Great Britain, in: M. Rood (ed.) *Fifty years of Labour Law and Social Security*, 1986, Kluwer Law and Taxation Publishers, Deventer: 101-120.
Hepple, Bob, 1986a.
Introduction in: Hepple, Bob and contributors, 1986.
The making of labour law in Europe: a comparative study of nine countries up to 1945, Mansell Publishing Limited, London: 1-26.
Heringa-van Ruth, E.A., W.H. Posthumus-van der Goot and Anna de Waal, 1968.
De laatste veertig jaar, in: Posthumus-van der Goot and Anna de Waal, 1968, *Van Moeder op dochter*, Buma en Zoon, Utrecht: 219-390.
Heywood, Colin, 1988.
Childhood in nineteenth-century France, Work Health and education among the 'classes populaires', Cambridge University Press.
Hill, M. Anne and June E. O'Neill, 1992.
Intercohort Change in Women's Labor Market Status, in: R.G. Ehrenberg (ed.), *Research in Labor Economics.*
Hilte, A.J.M., 1965.
De beroepsarbeid van gehuwde vrouwen in Nederland. *Maandschrift* CBS, december 1965, jrg. 60: 1323-1331.
Hicks, John R., 1932/1963.
Theory of Wages, 2nd edition in 1963, Macmillan, London.
Hoem, Jan, M., 1992.
Trends and Patterns in Swedish Divorce Risks 1971-1989: A case of Modern Demographic Analysis. *Stockholm Research Reports in Demography*, 64, pp.51.
Hofstee, E.W., 1954.
Regionale verscheidenheid in de regionale ontwikkeling van het aantal geboorten in Nederland in de tweede helft van de 19e eeuw, Academiedagen VII, KNAW, Amsterdam.
Höhn, C. 1990.
Country report Federal Republic of Germany, in Dumon, W. (ed.), 1990, *Family Policies in EEC-countries*, Office for Official Publications of the European Communities: 79-102.
Hooghiemstra, B.T.J. and M. Niphuis-Nell, 1993.
Sociale Atlas van de vrouw 2, Sociaal en Cultureel Planbureau, Den Haag.
Howell, Martha c., 1986.
Women, production and patriarchy in late medieval cities. Chicago.
van Hoorn, W.D., 1988.
Fertility: concentration and deconcentration, *Maandstatistiek van de bevolking*, CBS: 10.
Humanitas (International Correspondences), 1912.
Die Schutzgesetsgebung für Frauenarbeit in den verschiedenen Ländern/La Legislation du Travail des femmes dans les différents pays, Humanitas, La Haye.
ILO, International Labour Office, 1987.
Demographic development and social security, Report II, Fourth European Regional Conference Geneva September 1987, Geneva.
ILO, International Labour Office, 1991
Statistical Sources and Methods, Volume 5. Total and Economically Active Population, Employ,ment and Unemployment (Population Censuses), Geneva.
ILO, International Labour Office, 1992.
International Labour Conventions and Recommandations 1919-1991. Geneva.
INED, Institut national d'études démographiques, 1971.
Population, Numéro Spécial, (29), Juin 1971.

Jacobs, Aletta H., 1924/178.
Herinneringen. First edition in 1924 Van Holkema & Warendorf, Amsterdam. Sun Reprint 1978, Nijmegen.

Jaspers, A.PH.C.M. and L. Betten (ed.), 1988.
25 Years European Social Charter, Kluwer: 181.

de Jong, A. H., 1990.
Family formation and women with young children, *Maandstatistiek van de bevolking*, CBS, maart: 17-25.

Jonker, J.M.L., 1990.
The Netherlands, in: Dumon, W. (ed.), 1990, *Family Policies in EEC-countries*, Office for Official Publications of the European Communities: 277-289.

Jonung, Christina and Inga Persson, 1992.
Women and Market Work: the misleading tale of participation rates in international comparisons (working paper), Department of Economics, Lund University).

Juster, T. and F.P. Stafford, 1991.
The Allocation of Time: Empirical Findings, Behavioral Models and Problems of Measurement, *Journal of Economic Literature*, Vol. XXIX, no 2: 471-522.

Jurczik, Karin, 1977.
Frauenarbeit und Frauenrolle, Campus Verlag, Frankfurt/New York.

Kessel, Ellen van, Marga Kuperus & Hettie A. Pott-Buter, 1986.
Hoezo, gelijk belast?, Amazone/De Populier, Amsterdam.

Keilman, Nico, Anton Kuijsten & Ad Vossen (eds), 1988.
Modelling Household Formation and Dissolution, Clarendon Press, Oxford.

Kemp, A.A.M de, 1993.
Vijftigplussers weer aan het werk. *Economisch Statistische Berichten*, 10-02-1993: 124-128.

Killingsworth, Mark R., 1983.
Labor Supply, Cambridge University Press, Cambridge, England.

Killingsworth, Mark R. and James J. Heckman, 1986.
Female Labor Supply, A Survey, in: Orley Ashenfelter and Richard Layard (eds). *Handbook of Labor Economics*, North-Holland: 103-204.

Klein, Viola, 1961.
Women Workers, working hours and services. A survey in 21 countries. OECD.

Kloek, Els, 1990.
Wie hij zij, man of wijf, Vrouwengeschiedenis en de vroegmoderne tijd, Amsterdamse historische reeks, Verloren, Hilversum.

Knippenberg, Hans, 1986.
Deelname aan het lager onderwijs gedurende de 19e eeuw, dissertation University of Amsterdam, 18-04-1986.

Kok, J., 1992.
Ongehuwd samenwonen: toen en nu, *Demos*, 8, nr.7, p. 55, 56.

König, R., 1974.
Materialien zur Sociologie der Familie, Keulen.

Kooreman, Peter, 1986.
Essays on Microeconomic Analysis of Household behavior. Thesis, Wibro, Helmond.

Kooreman, Peter, 1991.
Empirical Models of Some Discrete Games with an Application to Household Labor Force Participation. Working Paper, Wageningen Agricultural University.

Kooreman, Peter and A. Kapteyn, 1990.
On the empirical Implementation of Some Game Theoretic Models of Household Labor Supply. *The Journal of Human Resources*. Vol. 25: 584-598.

Kooy, G.A., 1985.
Vier eeuwen ontwikkeling vanuit brede gezinssociologische optiek, in: G.A. Kooy (red.) *Gezinsgeschiedenis. Vier eeuwen gezin in Nederland*, Van Gorcum, Assen: 167-201.

Kronjee, G.J., 1989.
Gezin, levenscyclus en sociale verandering. *Beleid en Maatschappij*, no. 6: 322-331.

Kronjee, Gerrit Jacob, 1991.
Veranderingen in de levenscyclus, demografische veroudering en collectieve sociale uitgaven, ISOR, Utrecht.

Kronjee, G., 1992.
De dubbele werkelijkheid van het gezin. *Gezin, tijdschrift voor primaire leefvormen*. Vol. 4, Nr.3-4: 157-169.

Kuhn, A. and A. Wolpe, 1978.
Feminism and Materialism. Routledge and keegan Paul, London.

Kuysten, A.C. and S.Y. Voets, 1986.
Relatievorming: het perspectief van de kinderen, in: D.J. van der Kaa en R. Lesthaeghe (red.), *Bevolking: Groei en Krimp*, Van Loghum Slaterus, Deventer: 37-58.

Kuznets, S., 1941.
National Income and its Composition, 1919-1938, National Bureau of Economic Reasearch, New York.

Lamers, G., B. Sloot and O. Veldt, 1989.
Arbeidswetgeving in negen industriële landen. De vernieuwing van Nederlandse wetgeving in een nationaal perspectief. Ministerie van Sociale Zaken en Werkgelegenheid.

Lancaster, K.J., 1971.
Consumer demand. A new approach. New York.

Landau, Eve C., 1985.
The rights of working women in the European Communities, The European Perspectives Series, Brussels.

Laslett, Peter (ed.), 1972.
Household and Family in Past Time. Cambridge University Press, London.

Lawson, Sarah, 1985.
Christine de Pisan, *The Treasure of the City of Ladies or The Book of the Three Virtues*, Penquin Books Ltd, Harmodsworth, Middlesex, England.

League of Nations, 1919.
Report on the Employment of Women and Children and the Berne Conventions of 1906, Prepared by the organising committee for the International Labour Organisation Conference, Washington, 1919, Harrison & Sons, London.

Leibenstein, H., 1957.
Economic Backwardness and economic growth. Studies in the theory of economic development. New York.

Leibenstein, H., 1974.
An interpretation of the economic theory of fertility: promising path or blind alley? *Journal of Economic Literature* 12, 2: 457-479.

Lesthaeghe, R., 1991.
The second demographic transition in Western countries: an interpretation. IPD-Working paper, Vrije Universiteit Brussel.

Lévi-Strauss, C., 1969.
The Elementary Structure of Kinship. Beacon, Boston.
Leydesdorff, Selma, 1977.
Verborgen arbeid, vergeten arbeid, Van Gorcum Assen/Amsterdam.
Leydesdorff, Selma, 1990.
Nederlands feminisme, een speurtocht naar verklaringen, in: Bootsma, Henkjan and Ingrid van der Pluym-van Eijkeren, *Vrouwengeschiedenis*, Instituut voor Toegepast Historisch Onderzoek, Damon, Best: 11-21.
Lis and Soly, 1990
Living apart together: overheid en ondernemers in Brabant en Vlaanderen tijdens de tweede helft van de 18de eeuw, in: *Arbeid in veelvoud*, een huldeboek voor Jan Craeybeckx en Etienne Scholliers: 131-144.
Lieshout, Jannie van & Betty Rikken, 1989.
Geen lusten zonder lasten. Huwelijk, seksualiteit en geboorten op de Kempense zandgronden, 1850-1940, in: Grever, Maria & Annemiek van der Veen (eds), 1989, *Bij ons moeder en ons Jet: Brabantse vrouwen in de 19de en 20ste eeuw*. Stichting Brabantse Regionale Geschiedbeoefening, 's-Hertogenbosch, De Walburg Pers, Zutphen: 31-50.
Lippe, Tanja van der, 1993.
Arbeidsverdeling tussen mannen en vrouwen. Een interdisciplinaire studie naar betaald en huishoudelijk werk binnen huishoudens. Thesis, Utrecht.
Lloyd, Cynthia B, Emily S. Andrews & Curtis L. Gilroy (eds), 1979.
Women in the Labor Market. New York Colombia University Press.
Loeffen, G.M.J. 1984.
Boerinnen en tuindersvrouwen in Nederland. Landbouw Economisch Instituut. Den Haag.
Lowe, David and Jack Richards, 1988.
The city of lace. Nottingham.
MacCormack, C. and Strathern, M. (1980).
Nature, Culture and Gender. Cambridge University Press.
Macfarlane, A., 1978.
The origins of English Individualism. The family, property and social transition. Basil Blackwell, Oxford.
Maclean, Mavis, 1990.
Lone-parent families: family law and income transfers, *OECD*, 1990: 91-101.
Maddison, A., 1982.
Groeifasen van het kapitalisme. Utrecht/Antwerpen.
Malthus, Th. R., 1798/1970.
An essay on the principle of population. A. Flew (ed.), Harmondsworth.
Manser, Marilyn and Murray Brown, 1979.
Bargaining Analyses of Household Decisions, in: Lloyd, Cynthia B, Emily S. Andrews & Curtis L. Gilroy (eds), 1979, *Women in the Labor Market*, New York Colombia University Press: 3-27.
Marshall, Alfred, 1890/1936.
Principles of Economics. An introductory volume. Eighth edition, MacMillan and Co. Ltd. London.
Marshall, Alfred and Mary Paley Marshall, 1881.
The Economics of Industry, 2nd edition, Macmillan, London.
Martin, Roderick and Judith Wallace, 1984.
Working Women in Recession. Employment, Redundancy, and Unemployment. Oxford University Press, New York.
Matthaei, Julie A., 1982.
An Economic History of Women in America. Schocken Books, New York/ The Harvester Press, Brighton.

Meehan, Elizabeth M., 1985.
Women's Rights at Work, Campaigns and Policy in Britain and the United States, Macmillan, London.

Mehran, F., 1983.
Measurement of women's work, see Nuss, 1989.

Meijer-Wichmann, Clara, 1978.
De vrouw en de arbeid (articles written between 1912 and 1917), published after her death by her husband and reprinted in; *Vrouw en Maatschappij*, SUN reprint, Nijmegen.

Mendels, 1972 see Vanderpijpen, 1990.

Mertens, Noortje, Peter van der Meer, Joop Schippers and Jacques Siegers, 1992.
De arbeidsparticipatie van de gehuwde vrouw en de gezinsopbouw: gedragen Nederlandse vrouwen zich anders dan Vlaamse vrouwen? *Bevolking en gezin*, Brussel/Den Haag: 105-153.

Meulders, Daniële and Valerie van de Stricht, 1991.
Position of Women in the Labour Market in Belgium during the 1980s, paper EALE Conference, sept. 1991.

Michael, R.T. and R.J. Willis, 1975.
Contraception and fertility: household production under uncertainty, in: N.E. Terleckyj (ed.). *Household Production and consumption*. New York.

Mincer, J., 1958
Investment in human capital and personal income distribution, *Journal of Political Economy*, vol. 66.

Mincer, Jacob, 1962/1980.
Labor Force Participation of Married Women, Aspects of Labor Economics, A report of the National Bureau of Economic Research, Princeton, Princeton University Press: 62-73. Abridged version published in: Amsden, Alice H., 1980. *The Economics of Women and Work*. Penquin Books.

Mincer, Jacob, 1985.
Intercountry Comparisons of Labor Force Trends and of Related Developments: An Overview, in: Richard Layard and Jacob Mincer (eds), *Journal of Labor Economics*. Trends in Women's Work, Education, and Family Building. Vol. 3, Nr. 1, January 1985 Supplement: S1-S32.

Mincer, J. and H. Ofek, 1982.
Interrupted Work Careers: Depreciation and Restoration of Human Capital. *Journal of Human Resources* 17: 3-24.

Mincer, Jacob and S. Polachek, 1974.
Family Investments in Human Capital: Earnings of Women. *Journal of Political Economy* 82 (Supplement): S76-S108.

Ministerie van Sociale Zaken en Werkgelegenheid, 1990.
Kwartaalbericht Arbeidsmarkt, derde kwartaal, Den Haag.

Ministerie van Sociale Zaken en Werkgelegenheid, 1992.
Rapportage Arbeidsmarkt 1991, Den Haag.

Mill, John Stuart, 1861/1986.
The Subjection of Women, Promotheus Books.

Mol, P.W., J.C. van Ours and J.J. M. Theeuwes, 1988.
Honderd jaar gehuwde vrouwen op de arbeidsmarkt. Organisatie voor Strategisch Arbeidsmarktonderzoek (OSA) werkdocument nr. W 48.

Montgomery, Mark and James Trussell, 1986.
Models of Marital Status and Childbearing, in: Ashenfelther, O., and R. Layard (ed.) *Handbook of Labor Economics*, Volume I, Esevier Science Publishers: 205-268.

Moors, Hein, G. and Santo Koesoebjono, 1990.
Een baan en een gezin, situatie en beleid in enkele Europese landen. *Demos* 6, nr. 7:52-55

Mourik, A. van, Th.J. de Poel and J.J. Siegers, 1983.
Ontwikkelingen in de beroepssegregatie tussen mannen en vrouwen in de jaren zeventig. *Economisch Statistische Berichten* 68 :597-601.

Mourik, A. van and J.J. Siegers, 1988.
Ontwikkelingen in de beroepssegregatie tussen mannen en vrouwen 1971-1985. *Economisch Statistische Berichten* 73, p. 732-737.

Moy, Joyanna, 1988.
An Analysis of unemployment and other labor market indicators in 10 countries, *Monthly Labor Review*, April 1988: 39-50.

Murphy, M.J., 1983.
The life course of individuals in families: describing static and dynamic aspects of the contemporary family, in: The family: Proceedings of the British Society for Population Studies Conference, 1983, Office of Population Censuses and Surveys, Occasional Paper no. 31 (OPCS) London: 50-70.

Myrdal, Alva and Gunnar Myrdal, 1934.
Kris i befolkningsfrågan. Stockholm.

Myrdal, Alva, 1945.
Nation and Family. Kegan Paul, Trench, Tubner.

Nardinelli, Clark, 1990.
Child Labor and the Industrial Revolution, Indiana University Press, Bloomington and Indianapolis, pp. 194.

Nerlove, 1974.
Household and economy: toward a new theory of population and economic growth. *Journal of Political Economy*, 1974.

Nimwegen, Nico van and Hein Moors, 1990.
Leefvormen van Europese jongeren. *Demos*, jrg. 6, nr 8, p. 60-64.

Niphuis-Nell, Mary, 1987.
Demographic Developments and Government Policy in the Netherlands. Paper symposium: Women, Family, Work and Social Planning. Universiteit van Groningen, Sociologisch Instituut.

Neve J.H., and P.H. Renooy, 1988a.
Kinderarbeid in Nederland, Een verkennend onderzoek naar omvang en verschijningsvormen van kinder- en jeugdarbeid in Nederland. Ministerie van Sociale Zaken en Werkgelegenheid, oktober 1988.

Neve J.H., and P.H. Renooy, 1988b.
Kinder- en jeugdarbeid in Nederland, *Economisch Statistische Berichten*, 16-11-1988: 1076-1079, 1085.

Noordam, D.J., 1987.
Lust, last en plezier: vier eeuwen seksualiteit in Nederland, in: H.M. Dupuis, C. Naaktgeboren, D.J. Noordam, J. Spanjer, F.W. van der Waals. R. Kistemaker (red.). *Een kind onder het hart, verloskunde, volksgeloof, gezin, seksualiteit en moraal vroeger en nu.* Meulenhoff Informatief, Amsterdam; Amsterdam Historisch Museum: 127-170.

Noordegraaf, L., 1980.
Daglonen in Alkmaar 1500 - 1850. Historische Vereniging Holland, Apparaat voor de geschiedenis van Holland 9, 's-Gravenhage.

Noordegraaf, L., 1981.
Sociale verhoudingen en structuren in de Noordelijke Nederlanden 1770-1813; in: *Algemene Geschiedenis der Nederlanden*, No. 10: 361-383.

Noordegraaf, Leo, 1985.
Dearth, Famine and Social Policy in the Dutch Republic at the End of the Sixteenth Century; in: P. Clark (ed.). *The European crisis of the 1590's. Essays in Comparative History*, London.

Noordegraaf, Leo, 1990.
Overmoed uit onbehagen, positivisme en hermeneutiek in de economische en sociale geschiedenis. Verloren, Hilversum.

Noordegraaf, Leo, 1993.
Dutch Industry in the Golden Age, in: Karel Davids and Leo Noordegraaf (eds), 1993, *The Dutch Economy in the Goldon Age*, N.E.H.A.-Uitgaven, Amsterdam: 131-157.

Nota Op Weg, 1982.
Gelijke behandeling voor de loon- en inkomstenbelasting van de (werkende) gehuwde vrouw en haar man, en van deelgenoten aan vormen van samenleving en samenwonen. Tweede Kamer, zitting 1979-1980, 15835, nrs. 1-2.

Nuss, Shirley, 1989.
In collaboration with Ettori Denti and David Viry. *Women in the world of work, Statistical analysis and projections to the year 2000.* International Labour Office, Geneva.

Oakley, Ann, 1974/1990.
Housewife, first published by Allan Lane in 1974, reprinted by Penguin Books, 1990.

Oakley, Ann, 1981.
Subject Woman, Penguin Books, Harmondsworth.

Odink, J.G. and H.A. Pott-Buter, 1982.
Inkomensverdeling en de fiscale emancipatie van de gehuwde vrouw, *Maandschrift Economie*, Jrg. 46, p.276-297.

OECD, Organisation for Economic Co-operation and Development
Labour Force Statistics, see above.

OECD, Organisation for Economic Co-operation and Development, Paris.

1979 *Equal Opportunities for women.*
1980 *Women and Employment, Policies for Equal Opportunities.*
1984 *Employment Outlook*, September.
1985 *The Integration of women into the economy.*
1988 *Employment Outlook*, September.
1990 *Lone-parent families, The Economic Challenge, Social Policy Studies.*
1990 *Employment Outlook.*
1991 *Employment Outlook.*
1992a *Education at a Glance, OECD Indicators.*
1992b *Employment Outlook*, June.

Offen, Karen, Ruth Roach Pierson and Jane Rendall (editors), 1991.
Writing Women's History, International Perspectives, Macmillan, London.

Olsson, Lars, 1980.
Då barn var lönsamma. Om arbetsdelning, barnabete och teknologiska förändringar i några svenska industrier under 1800- och början av 1900-talet. Tidens förlag, Stockholm.

Onderzoek Gezinsvorming, 1982 and 1988, CBS.

Oosterbeek, Hessel, 1992.
Essays on human capital theory, Thesis, Amsterdam.

Ott, Notburga, 1991.
Fertility and division of work in the family: a game theoretic model of houshold decisions, working paper, Frankfurt.

Ott, Notburga, 1992.
Intrafamily Bargaining and Household Decisions, Springer Verlag, Berlin.

Paridon, C.W.A.M., 1990.
Arbeidsparticipatie in Nederland: plaatsbepaling in internationaal perspectief. Wetenschappelijke Raad voor het Regeringsbeleid, 's-Gravenhage.

Paridon, C.W.A.M., 1992.
Arbeidsparticipatie in Nederland: nog altijd laag! *Economisch Statistische Berichten*, 19-8-1992: 801-803.
Pencavel, John, 1986.
Labor Supply of men: A Survey, in: Orley Ashenfelter and Richard Layard (eds), *Handbook of Labor Economics*, North-Holland.
Peeters, Harry, 1988.
Vijf eeuwen gezin in West-Europa, in: Harry Peeters, Lène Dresen-Coenders and Ton Brandenbarg (eds), *Vijf eeuwen gezinsleven. Liefde, huwelijk en opvoeding in Nederland.* SUN, Nijmegen.
Pieters, D.C.H.M. and J.L.M. Schell, 1990.
Inleiding tot Het Sociale Zekerheidsrecht van de landen van de Europese Gemeenschap. Commissie Onderzoek Sociale Zekerheid. Den Haag, Zoetermeer.
Pigou, Arthur Cecil, 1920.
The Economics of Welfare. Macmillan, London.
Pinbeck, Ivy, 1930/1981.
Women workers and the industrial revolution 1750-1850. London 1930 (reprint 1981).
Pisan, Christine de, 1404.
Le livre de la cité des dames/The Book of the Cities of Ladies, translated by Tine Pontfoort, see also Pontfoort.
Pisan, Christine de, 1405.
Le livre des trois virtues/The Treasure of the City of Ladies, translated by Sarah Lawson, see also Lawson.
Phillips, Marian, 1922.
Frauen- und Kinderarbeit in der Textilindustrie. Verlag des Internationalen Gewerkschaftsbundes, Amsterdam.
Ploegmakers M.J.H. and L.Th. van Leeuwen, 1985.
Huishoudens in Nederland: twee decennia verandering - een statistische analyse over de periode 1960-1981. Den Haag, Ministerie van VROM.
Polachek, Solomon W. and W. Stanley Siebert, 1993.
The economics of earnings, Cambridge University Press.
Polak, Anna, 1909.
Beroepsklapper.
Polak, Anna, 1916.
Veranderende groepering van mannelijke en vrouwelijke arbeidskrachten. *De Economist*: 589-612.
Polak, Anna, 1919.
Nieuwe verschuiving van mannelijke en vrouwelijke arbeidskrachten. *De Economist*, Januari/Februari: 418-513.
Polak, Anna, 1921.
Geen afzonderlijke vrouwenarbeidsbescherming! *De Economist*: 377-399.
Polak, Anna, 1936.
Wijziging van het aantal mannelijke en vrouwelijke werkkrachten in de industrie. *De Economist*: 140-144.
Pontfoort, Tine, 1984.
Het boek van de stad der vrouwen, (translation of Christine de Pisan, 1405, *Le Livre de la Cité des Dames*), Sara, Amsterdam.
Poppel, F.W.A. van, 1981.
Demographische ontwikkelingen in Nederland, 1850-1950. Intern Rapport, Nederlands Interuniversitair Demographisch Instituut, Voorburg.

Poppel, Frans van, 1992.
Trouwen in Nederland. Een historisch-demografische studie van de 19e en voeg-20e eeuw. A.A.G. (Afdeling Agrarische Geschiedenis) Bijdragen 33. Wageningen.

Posthumus, N.W., 1908.
De geschiedenis van de Leische lakenindustrie. 3 delen. 's-Gravenhage 1908-1939.

Posthumus, N.W., 1914.
Bronnen tot de geschiedenis van de Leidse textielnijverheid, deel IV (van de 6 delen), 1611-1650, 's-Gravenhage 1910-1922.

Posthumus-van der Goot, Wilhelmina H., 1937.
Statistische Gegevens betreffende de Vrouw in Nederland, *Jaarboek I*, Internationaal Archief voor de Vrouwenbeweging, Leiden, 1937: 77-87.

Posthumus-van der Goot, Wilhelmina H., 1938.
Onderzoek naar den arbeid der gehuwde Vrouw in Nederland, *Jaarboek II*, Internationaal Archief voor de Vrouwenbeweging, Leiden, 1938: 135-87.

Posthumus-van der Goot, Wilhelmina H. and Anna de Waal (eds), 1948/1968. *Van Moeder op dochter*, Utrecht/Amsterdam, first edition 1948, third edition 1968, Bruna & Zoon.

Pott-Buter, H.A., 1985.
Emancipatiebeleid en de verzorging van kinderen. *Tijdschrift voor Huishoudkunde*, 6 (4) Wageningen: 97-98.

Pott-Buter, H.A., 1988.
Man, vrouw en gezin in de Sociale Zekerheid", in: A.L. den Broeder (red.) *Waardering van sociale zekerheid.* 's-Gravenhage, Vuga: 39-54.

Pott-Buter, H.A., 1989.
De spanning tussen financiële zelfstandigheid en de zorg voor kinderen", in: *1990 en de zelfstandigheid van vrouwen en mannen, moeders en vaders* Nederlandse Gezinsraad.

Pott-Buter, H.A., 1990.
Betaalde arbeid, economische zelfstandigheid van vrouwen en de afhankelijkheid van kinderen", in: J.J. Schippers (ed.) *Arbeidsmarkt en maatschappelijke ongelijkheid*, Wolters-Noordhoff, Groningen, 1990: 119-138.

Pott-Buter, Hettie, A., 1991
The economics of bringing up children in the Netherlands. *Women's Studies International Forum.* Vol. 14, No. 6: 599-606.

Pott-Buter, Hettie, 1991.
Kindvriendelijk emancipatiebeleid, in: Marie-Louise Tiesinga (red.), *Emancipatie in de jaren negentig*, Hameland Pers/Walburg Pers, Zutphen: 81-96.

Pott-Buter, H.A. en W.N.J. Groot, 1987.
Kosten van Kinderen. Nederlandse Gezinsraad, Den Haag, 1987.

Pott-Buter, H.A. en W.N.J. Groot, 1988.
Tegemoetkomingen in de kosten van kinderen. *Economisch Statistische Berichten*, jrg. 73, no. 3656: 471-475, 480.

Pott-Buter, H.A. en W.N.J. Groot, 1988.
Kosten van kinderen in Nederland: een literatuuroverzicht, *Maandschrift Economie*, jrg.52, no 3: 185-200.

Presvalou, C. and C. de Hoog, 1993.
Nederland: Increasing Interest in Children; in: W. Dumon, 1993. *National Family Policies in EC-Countries in 1991.* European Observatory on National Family Policies, Commission of the European Communities: 32-34.

Prodzynski, Isabelle, 1989.
Vrouwen in cijfers, supplement bij vrouwen van Europa. Commissie van de Europese Gemeenschappen.

Pujol, Michèle A., 1992.
Feminism and Anti-Feminism in Early Economic Thought. Edward Elgar Publishing Limited.

Quast, Jenneke, 1980.
Vrouwenarbeid omstreeks 1500 in enkele Nederlandse steden, *Jaarboek voor vrouwengeschiedenis*: 46-64.

Qvist, Gunnar, 1978.
Konsten att blifva en god flicka. Kvinnohistoriska uppsatser, LiberFörlaf Stockholm.

Raet, Lodewijk de, 1914.
Vlaanderen's Economische Ontwikkeling. D. de Vos-Van Kleef, Antwerpen.

Reid, M.G., 1934.
Economics of Household Production, Wiley, New York.

Renes, Gusta, 1991.
Working Women their Preferences and Constraints. Thesis.

Reynolds, L.G., 1979.
Labor Economics and Labor Relations, Prentice-hall

Richards, Janet Radcliffe, 1980.
The Sceptical Feminist. Pelican Books.

Riffault, Hélène and Jean-Francois Tchernia, 1987.
Non-salaried working women in Europe (based on the 1985 survey: *Faits et opinions*). Official Publications of the European Communities, Luxembourg.

Roberts, Elizabeth, 1988, reprinted in 1990.
Women's Work 1840-1940. Studies in Economic and Social History, Macmillan, London.

Samuelson, P.A., 1956.
Social Indifference Curves, *Quarterly Journal of Economics*, Vol. 10: 1-22.

Sanderson, Michael, 1991.
Education, Economic Change and Society in England 1780-1870. Macmillan Education Ltd.

Sap, Jolande, 1993.
Bargaining power and wages. A game theoretic model of gender differences in union wage bargaining. *Labour Economics*, Vol.1, 1: forthcoming.

Sargent, L., 1981.
Women in Revolution: The unhappy marriage of Marxism and Feminism. Pluto, London.

Schama, Simon, 1988.
The Embarrassment of Riches, An Interpretation of Dutch Culture in the Golden Age, Fontana Press.

Schellekens-Ligthart, 1961.
Buitenshuis werkende gehuwde vrouwen, huishoudelijke en financiële problemen. Rapport uitgebracht aan de Nederlandse Huishoudraad.

Schilstra, W.N., 1940, reprint 1976.
Vrouwenarbeid in landbouw en industrie in Nederland en in de tweede helft van de 19e eeuw. Amsterdam, Sun reprint Nijmegen.

Schmid Günther and Renate Weitzel, 1984.
Sex Discrimination and Equal Opportunity, The Labour Market and Employment Policy. WZB-Publications, Berlin.

Schmid, J., 1988.
Principles emerging from sociology for definitions and typologies of household structures, in: Keilman, Nico, Anton Kuijsten & Ad Vossen (ed.),

1988, *Modelling Household Formation and Dissolution*, Clarendon Press, Oxford: 13-23.

Schippers, J.J. 1987.
Beloningsverschillen tussen mannen en vrouwen: een economische analyse. Groningen, Wolters-Noordhoff.

Schulte-Kleemann, Suzanne (Hrsg.), 1990.
EG - Binnenmarkt - EuroPatriarchat oder Aufbruch der Frauen? Band 2, W. Gefken Druck und Verlags GmbH, Bremen.

Schultz, T.W., 1960.
The Formation of Human Capital by Education, *Journal of Political Economy.*

Schultz, T.P. 1969.
An Economic Model of Family Planning and Fertility, *Journal of Political Economy*, 77, nr. 2:153-180.

Schultz, T.P. 1976/1981.
Economics of Population. Addison-Wesley Co. Reading, Massachusets.

Schultz-Jorgensen, Per and V. Pruzan, 1993.
Danmark: Harmonizing Family and Work; in: W. Dumon, 1993. *National Family Policies in EC-Countries in 1991.* European Observatory on National Family Policies, Commission of the European Communities: 3-6.

Schwartz, Koos, 1988.
Trouw, 8 november 1988

Schwarz, K., 1988.
Household trends in Europe after World War II, in: Keilman, Nico, Anton Kuijsten & Ad Vossen (ed.), 1988, *Modelling Household Formation and Dissolution*, Clarendon Press, Oxford: 65-83.

Scott, Joan W. and Louise Tilly, 1980.
Women's Work and the Family in Nineteenth-Century Europe, in: Amsden, Alice H. (ed.), *The Economics of Women and Work.* Penquin Books: 91-124. (Reprint from: Compararative Studies in Society and History, vol. 17, no. 1, January 1975: 36-64).

Sels and Dumon, 1990
Great Britain, Family policy and population policy - the UK situation, in: Dumon, W. (ed.), 1990, *Family Policies in EEC-countries*, Office for Official Publications of the European Communities:-.

Ser, Sociaal Economische Raad, 1952.
Advies inzake het vraagstuk van gelijke beloning van mannen en vrouwen voor gelijkwaardige arbeid. 's-Gravenhage.

Sevenhuijsen, Selma L., 1987.
De orde van het vaderschap, Politieke debatten over ongehuwd moederschap, afstamming en het huwelijk in Nederland 1870- 1900, Stichting beheer IISG, Amsterdam.

Sharpe, S., 1976.
Just like a girl. Penguin Books, Harmondsworth.

Shorter, E., 1975.
The making of the modern family. Basic Books Inc. New York.

Siegers, J.J., 1985.
Arbeidsaanbod en kindertal. Een micro-economische analyse. Thesis Rijksuniversiteit Groningen, Enschede.

Silenstam, Per, 1970.
Arbetskraftsutbudets utveckling i Sverige 1870 - 1965. Industriens Utredningsinstitut, Almqvist & Wiksell, Stockholm.

Smith, Adam, 1776/1979.
The Wealth of Nations. Penquin Books Ltd., Harmondsworth.

Snijders-Borst, Hieke, 1983.
Belasting en leefeenheid. *Weekblad voor Fiscaal Recht*, 5578:191-207.

Snijders-Borst, Hieke, 1985.
Kortingsbedragen rechtvaardiger dan belastingvrije sommen. Open Forum, *Volkskrant*, 10 april 1985.

Soden, Kristine von, 1979.
Zur Geschichte des Frauenstudiums, in: Soden, Kristine von and Gaby Zipfel (Hrsg.) 1979, *70 Jahre Frauenstudium*. Frauen in der Wissenschaft, Pahl-Rugenstein Verlag.

Soren, J. 1990.
Danish Family Policy, in: Dumon, W. (ed.) *Family Policies in EEC-countries*. Publications of the European Communities: 33-59.

Sorrentino, Constance, 1990.
The changing family in international perspective. *Monthly Labor Review*, March 1990, Volume 113, Number 3: 41-58.

SoZaWe, Ministerie van Sociale Zaken en Werkgelegenheid, 1990.
Kwartaalbericht Arbeidsmarkt, Den Haag.

SVr, Sociale Verzekeringsraad, 1992.
Kroniek van de sociale verzekeringen. Wetgeving en volume-ontwikkelingen in historisch perspectief. Zoetermeer.

Sullerot, Evelyne, 1969.
Geschiedenis van de vrouwenarbeid, Paul Brand, Bussum.

Sundström, Marianne, 1991.
Sweden: supporting work, family, and gender equality. In: S.B. Kamerman and A.J. Kahn (eds), 1991, *Child Care, Parental Leave, and the Policy Innovations in Europe*. Auburn house, Westport.

Sundström, Marianne and Frank Stafford, 1992.
Female labor Force Participation, Fertility and Public Policy. *European Journal of Population*. Vol. 8: 199-215.

Stearns, P.N. and C.Z. Stearns, 1985.
Emotionology: clarifying the history of emotions and emotional standards. *American Historical Review* 90: 813-836.

Stone, Lawrence, 1977/ 1990.
The Family, Sex and Marriage in England 1500-1800. Abridged and revised edition 1979, reprint in 1990, Penguin, London.

Strachey Ray, 1938.
Chronological List of Leading Events in the Women's Movement in Great Britain, in: E.J. Brill, 1938, *Yearbook International Archives for the Women's Movement*, Leiden.

Tas, R.F.J., 1989.
Huwelijkssluiting en huwelijksontbinding, CBS, Maandstatistiek van de Bevolking, oktober: 20-22.

Theeuwes, J.J.M., 1988.
Arbeid en belastingen, in: *Preadviezen van de Koninklijke Vereniging voor de Staathuishoudkunde, Belastingheffing en Belastinghervorming*, Stenford Kroese, Leiden/Antwerpen: 11-143.

Thönnessen, Werner, 1959.
The Emancipation of Women, The Rise and Decline of the Women's Movement in German Social Democracy 1863-1933. Pluto Press.

Tiger, L. and R. Fox, 1971.
The Imperial Animal. Holt, Rinehart and Winston, New York.

Tilly, Louise A. & Joan W. Scott, 1987.
Women, Work & Family. Methuen & Co., Ltd. London. 274.

Tijdens, Kea, 1988.
Automatisering en vrouwenarbeid. Een studie over beroepssegregatie op de arbeidsmarkt, in de administratieve beroepen en in het bankwezen. Jan van Arkel, Utrecht.

Uitz, Erika, 1990.
Women in the Medieval Town. Barrie & Jenkins Ltd, London.

Varian, Hal R., 1987/1990.
Intermediate Microeconomics. A Modern Approach, 2nd ed. 1990, W.W. Norton & Compagny, New York, London.

Van der Erf, R.F. 1989, see Erf, R.F. van der.

Vanderpijpen, W., 1990.
De proto-industrialisatie in Vlaanderen: een grote regionale diversiteit, in: *Arbeid in veelvoud*, een huldeboek voor Jan Craeybeckx en Etienne Scholliers: 123-130.

Varinne-Fioux, Marguerite, 1969.
Enkele facetten van de promotie van de vrouw in België, Ministerie van Buitenlandse Zaken en Buitenlandse Handel, Teksten en documenten, nr. 254: 1-14.

Van Dijk, H. and S.W. Verstegen, 1988, see Dijk, H. van.

Van Nimwegen, Nico and Hein Moors, 1990, see Nimwegen, Nico van.

Van Mourik et al 1983 and 1988, see Mourik, van.

Verduin, J.A., 1985.
Het gezin in demografisch perspectief, in: G.A. Kooy (ed.) *Vier eeuwen gezin in Nederland*: 69-110.

Verduin, J.A., 1989.
150 Jaar samenspel van sociaal-economische en demographische ontwikkelingen, CBS, *Maandstatistiek van de bevolking* 10: 5-9.

Verhage, C.G., 1989.
Schets van de ontwikkeling van arbeidsstatistieken in Nederland, CBS, *Supplement Sociaal Economische Maandstatistiek* 6: 19-37.

Verhoef, R., 1989.
Geboorte, CBS, *Maandstatistiek van de Bevolking* 10: 14-15.

Versluys, Liliare, 1987.
Je rechten als vrouw. Epo, Berchem.

Verwey-Jonker, H., 1988.
Argumenten vóór een bevolkingspolitiek. *Socialisme en Democratie*, 45:298-300, 318.

Verwey-Jonker, H., 1985.
De man/vrouw relatie: een machtsbalans. In: G.A. Kooy (ed.) *Gezinsgeschiedenis. Vier eeuwen gezin in Nederland.* Van Gorcum, Assen: 69-110.

Vicinus, Martha, 1985.
Independent Women, work and community for single women, 1850-1920, Virago Press, London.

VNG, Vereniging van Nederlandse Gemeenten, 1991.
Kinderopvang in gemeenten: de stand van zaken per 31 december 1990. 's-Gravenhage.

Vries, Jan de, 1977.
An inquiry into behaviour of wages in the Dutch Republic and Southern Netherlands from 1580 to 1800, in: Aymard, Maurice, *Dutch capitalism and world capitalism:* 37-61.

Vrouwenlexicon, Groenewald-Froger, Maggy (eindredactie), 1989.
Scala, Het Spectrum, Utrecht.

Wainwright, H., 1984.
Women and the division of labour, in: Abrams, P. and R. Brown (eds), *UK Society: Work, Urbanism and Inequality*, Weidenfeld and Nicolson, London.

Walby, S., 1986.
Patriarchy at Work. Polity, Cambridge.

Walschots, J.J., 1985.
Bevolking en beroepsbevolking; enige voorlopige uitkomsten van de Arbeidskrachtentelling (AKT) 1983, Sociale Maandstatistiek, CBS.

Weber-Kellermann, Ingeborg, 1974.
Die deutsche Familie, Versuch einer Sozialgeschichte. Suhrkamp Verlag, Frankfurt am Main.

Weerdt, Denise de, 1980.
En de vrouwen? Vrouw, vrouwenbeweging en feminisme in België. Gent.

Wentholt, K., 1990.
Arbeid en zorg. Een verkenning vanuit het gelijkheidsbeginsel van de rechtspositie van werknemers met gezinsverantwoordlijkheid. Thesis publishers, Amsterdam.

Webster's, 1973.
Webster's New Collegiate Dictionary, G. Bell and Sons Ltd, G. and C. Merriam Co, London.

Wichmann, Clara, 1912 to 1917, see Meijer-Wichmann, 1978.

Wichmann, Clara, 1913.
Het vraagstuk van den bedrijfsarbeid der vrouw in Nederland.

Wicks, M. and R. Chester, 1990.
Great Britain, in: Dumon, W. (ed.), 1990, Family Policies in EEC-countries, *Publications of the European Communities*: 103-125.

Wilde, Inge de, 1982.
De bibliotheek van C.V. Gerritsen, de echtgenoot van Aletta Jacobs, *Jaarboek voor de Vrouwengeschiedenis*, SUN, Nijmegen: 245-255.

Williamson, Jeffrey G., 1990.
The Impact of the French Wars on Accumulation in Britain: Another Look, in: Aerts, Erik, and François Crouzet (eds.), 1990, *Economic Effects of the French Revolutionary and Napoleonic Wars*, Session B-1, Proceedings of the Tenth International Economic History Congress, Leuven University Press: 48-57.

Willis, Robert, J., 1973/1979.
Economic Theory of Fertility Behavior, in: Schultz, Theodore W. (ed.), 1979, *Economics of the Family, Marriage, Children and Human Capital*, The University of Chicago Press, Chicago/London, 2nd Impression 1979: 25-75. (First published as supplement to the *Journal of Political Economy*, March/April 1973: S14-S64).

Willms, Angelika, 1980.
Die Entwicklung der Frauenerwebstätigkeit im Deutschen Reich. Eine historisch-sociologische Studie. Institut für Arbeitsmarkt und Berufsforschung der Bundesanstalt für Arbeit, Nürnberg.

Wingen, M., 1993.
Deutschland: Continued Process of German Unification; in: W. Dumon, 1993. *National Family Policies in EC-Countries in 1991*. European Observatory on National Family Policies, Commission of the European Communities: 6-10.

Wistrand, Birgitta, 1981.
Swedish Women on the Move. Bohusläningens AB, Uddevalla.

Woude, van der, 1970.
Demografische ontwikkeling van de Noordelijke Nederlanden, 1500-1800, in: *Algemene geschiedenis der Nederlanden* V. Haarlem 1980: 102-168.

Yaukey, David, 1981.
Historic European Transitions: the Mathusian Component, *Demography: The Study of Human Population*: 188-194.

Yeandle, S., 1984.
Women's Working Lives. Tavistock, London.

Zanden, Jan Luiten van, 1985.
De economische ontwikkeling van de nederlandse landbouw in de negentiende eeuw, 1800-1914. Thesis, Wageningen.

Zanden, J.L. van, 1991a.
Den Zedenlijken en materiëlen toestand der arbeidende bevolking ten platten lande, Een reeks rapporten uit 1851. *Historia Agriculturae, 21.*

Zanden, Jan Luiten van, 1991b.
Arbeid tijdens het handelskapitalisme, Opkomst en neergang van de Hollandse economie 1350-1850. Octavo, Bergen.

Zanden, J.L. van & R.T. Griffiths, 1989.
Economische geschiedenis van Nederland in de 20e eeuw. Het Spectrum, Utrecht.

Zimmermann, Klaus, F., 1985.
Familienökonomie, Theoretische und empirische Untersuchungen zur Frauenerwerbstätigkeit und Geburtenentwicklung, Springer-Verlag, Berlin, Heidelberg.

Zuylen, Belle van/Isabella de Charrière.
Oeuvres complètes I Correspondence 1753-1766. Amsterdam 1979. *II Correspondence 1793-1794*. Amsterdam 1982.

Zwart, R. de and B.M.S. van Praag, 1990.
De arbeidstijden van middelbare scholieren. *Economisch Statistische Berichten* 75, nr.3747: 208-210.

FIGURES

TABLES

ILLUSTRATIONS

INDEX